AMAZON

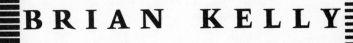

BRIAN KELLY

MARK LONDON

HARCOURT BRACE JOVANOVICH, Publishers

San Diego   New York   London

Requests for permission to make copies of any
part of the work should be mailed to: Permissions,
Harcourt Brace Jovanovich, Publishers, 757 Third Avenue,
New York, N.Y. 10017.

Library of Congress Cataloging in Publication Data
Kelly, Brian, 1954–
Amazon.
Includes index.
1. Amazon River Valley—Description and travel.
2. Kelly, Brian, 1954–   . 3. London, Mark.
I. London, Mark. II. Title.
F2546.K34   1983   918.1'10463   83–6164
ISBN 0–15–105463–0

Designed by Joy Chu
Endpaper map by Anita Karl and James Kemp

Printed in the United States of America
First edition
A B C D E

TO E AND B, AL AND JACK

Wild and wide are my borders, stern as
        death is my sway;
From my ruthless throne I have ruled
        alone for a million years and
        a day;
Hugging my mighty treasure, waiting
        for man to come . . .

Robert Service
The Law of the Yukon

And God blessed them; and God said
unto them: "Be fruitful and multiply,
and replenish the earth, and subdue it;
and have dominion over the fish of the
sea, and over the fowl of the air,
and over every living thing that
creepeth upon the earth."

Genesis 1:28

CONTENTS

 PREFACE

I went to the Amazon for the first time in order to make my life extraordinary. I wanted adventure; I yearned for intimacy with another world. Perhaps if I could see the Amazon my life would become less intimidating and more wonderful than if I stayed at home.

I was in law school then and aware that the Amazon was in South America, probably filled with wild animals and savage Indians and not much else. My expectations were drawn from Tarzan and *National Geographic.* I never had met anyone who had been there. But when the winter break came, I told my friends, "I'm going to the Amazon," and I went to the Amazon.

I did know that the Amazon flows through Peru, and I chose to go there because I spoke Spanish. I asked the concierge of the hotel in Lima how to get to the Amazon, and he told me, "By boat." In fact, few people in Lima knew more than he, and I grew frustrated seeking information about this promised land of mine. Had I taken my intentions more seriously I could have planned better, but for following a dream road maps seemed superfluous.

After four days, during which I sent scores of postcards to friends falsely announcing my arrival at the Amazon, I boarded a plane for Iquitos, a city of about 150,000 people on the Amazon River. When I arrived, I told the taxi driver at the airport, "Rio Amazonas."

As we drove toward the river I began not to celebrate but to despair. Jet planes had made my dream too accessible. What was I going to do once I saw the river? We passed a perfect replica of an American roadside Holiday Inn, and I asked the driver what it was.

"A hotel," he said.

A Holiday Inn in the Amazon jungle?

"It is air conditioned, and also it has a swimming pool," he said. "Would you like to stay there?"

I did want to stay there. I wanted to see the river, dive into clean sheets and go home. I was very lonely. I hadn't talked to anyone in days, and I was only minutes from my rendezvous with the destiny I had chosen in the silly way of students on their winter break.

We made it to the river, which looked dirty, slow-moving, not the stuff of dreams—just chocolate water with large tree trunks lining the opposite shore. I thought of the hours I had put in to pay for this trip, the bragging I had done about it, the disappointment I had set myself up for. I was at the Amazon. It was time to go home.

I sat on a bench across from the sagging and desolate Hotel de Turistas. A young boy in a yellow T-shirt asked me if I wanted to go to a camp about 60 miles downriver.

"Why?" I asked.

"To see the jungle."

"This is the jungle," I said, pointing to the far bank of the river.

"No," he said, "this is the city. The city is a *mierda*. The jungle is a *joya*." A jewel.

I wanted to believe him. He led me to an office where I paid out the last of my traveler's checks, and we set off in a launch from the river's edge.

His name was Lucio; he didn't talk much, and the scenery for the next four hours was monotonous—low jungle, hints of palm trees, a few thatched huts. It was hot; I was uncomfortable and hungry. My bad idea was getting worse.

Then came the magic, as if the Amazon herself rose up and slapped me for doubting her beauty and power. In the days that followed, my bravado and my insensitivity evaporated. The Amazon began to reveal her extraordinary life to me.

I saw a 15-year-old boy die from the bite of a fer de lance. He went into convulsions and expired on an uneven wood plank floor under a dried palm-leaf roof. I rode beside the river banks for a whole night in a dugout canoe with a flashlight in search of the frightened eyes of crocodiles. I went hunting with Indians who wore grass skirts and killed monkeys with blowguns and ate the testicles. I declined an hallucinogenic brew prepared from chewed roots and fermented for three days. I saw pink orchids dancing on brown limbs which shot out from black water. I saw orange birds, yellow birds, purple birds, parrots, macaws, toucans, and tapirs, deer and snakes. Trees of two hundred feet dwarfed me, and mosquitoes overwhelmed me.

I woke every morning with the first rays of the sun, irrepressibly eager to go out on the river and drift from one spectacle to another. I had no idea of the scientific names of the plants or animals I was seeing, nor of the customs or history of the Indians I met. A world apart from the one I had known was revealing itself to me, and I knew nothing about it—except one thing. My dream was worth having.

Recounting the trip to my friends at home was not easy. For many my tale was merely predictable; the Amazon was in a world they never wanted to know, and they were happy if I was happy.

Then there was Brian Kelly.

Brian and I had been newspaper reporters together before I became a lawyer, and we remained good friends. He pumped me for information about my trip and about the Amazon. He sensed a story there, but could not articulate what it was or why anyone would be interested in it. Yet a reporter, Brian felt, was nothing unless he could take an alien story and make it understandable to an average reader. We made a pact to find out about the Amazon, to find the story there.

For the next two years we read everything about the Amazon we could find, from *I Was a Headhunter* to "Quaternary Refugia in Tropical America: Evidence from Race Formation in Heliconius Butterflies." We interviewed political scientists, natural scientists, economists and businessmen. We learned the names of the purple and yellow birds and studied the history of the Indians of the Amazon. While Brian covered Chicago's city politics and I tried civil cases in the courtroom, nights and weekends were spent stuffing ourselves on whatever we could read about this faraway place. We looked at maps of the area like GIs eyeing pinups.

By the time we had learned what we could from a distance, we had convinced ourselves that the Amazon mattered, not only to us, but to our countrymen. The burning of the jungle was affecting weather patterns; our wheat belt might soon be in Canada. Brazil was considering mortgaging the mineral riches of the Amazon to pay off its enormous debt to American banks. As unexplored areas were exposed, men were literally stumbling upon rocks of gold. More Indian tribes were being discovered—and decimated. We read of a great migration into the jungle. Many millions of Americans might remember when their own forebears had such a spirit of renewal.

Brian put our musings into a memorandum to Jim Hoge, his editor at the Chicago *Sun-Times*, and suggested that a tremendous tension enveloped the Amazon. Would it remain jungle or become a desert? Would Brazil stay mired in the problems of the Third World or emerge as the next superpower? Does this earth still have a frontier in the American sense, a place as alluring as Horace Greeley portrayed our West or as Willie Loman believed Alaska to be?

Hoge liked the memo. We had found the story. By then I was fluent in Portuguese, the language of Brazil, and Hoge saw the logic of sending both of us to the Amazon.

I remember sitting on the runway in Miami, toasting our luck with champagne and telling Brian that a man was running after the plane yelling, "It was only a joke. Come back." But we outdistanced him and landed in Rio de Janeiro with an exuberance we may never feel again. We had harbored and fueled a passion for two years; we were about to play it out.

This book is about two trips to the Amazon, the first under the sponsorship of the *Sun-Times* and the second undertaken to complete the material for this book. Each journey was several months long; we have combined the two trips into one for the purpose of writing a continuous narrative. Every character in this book is a real person, and we have used actual names with the exception of Rafael Lesco who said so much in a trusting and unsuspecting way that we invented a name for him. Every quotation is one that was spoken. Nothing in this book is fiction, except the sequence in which we met people and an occasional moving of a conversation from one setting to another.

Nothing needs to be made up to convey the wonder of the Amazon. From that first day, the Amazon never stopped her enchantment. Each day became more interesting than yesterday. Each place added a new dimension to a fascinating and vibrant world, dizzy from its accelerating transition.

But what makes this the most special place of all are the people. The Amazon is the last great frontier in this world. As such, it is the stage for thousands of people who harbor dreams and passion, and suffer tragedies and disappointments.

For many the Amazon is the promised land, where past failures mean nothing, where men and women can measure themselves by what they achieve—how many hectares they clear, how well they adapt to a hostile environment, how much hope they can pass on to their children. The purity of their passion, their honesty with themselves and their devotion to their dream are not different from those qualities my grandfather had when he came to America, penniless and unable to speak English. The energy to create a better life than they had been born into need not be exaggerated with fiction.

The grandeur of the Amazon is its ability to accommodate any vision of any man or woman. Daniel Keith Ludwig spent $1.15 billion to create a tree plantation and develop the breadbasket of the 21st century on a tract of land larger than the state of Connecticut. Jose Maria da Silva found $6 million of gold in one day and kept his promise to build the greatest whorehouse the Amazon has ever seen. Kanhonk, chief of the Kayapo-Gorotire Indians, desperately wants peace to save his people from extinction, and Colonel Ary Santos, the toughest man in the Amazon, has vowed to see that he gets it. The Amazon is aflame with land wars between squatters and hired gunmen. They fight over miserable patches of land which, after back-breaking toil, will yield barely enough food for sustenance. But for the squatters it is their food, grown with their hands.

In our research we uncovered antecedents for all these dreams and the failures they became. We read about Henry Ford's attempt to establish the world's largest rubber tree plantation and its subsequent demise. Today's TransAmazon Highway still runs in the shadow of the Madeira-Mamore Railroad, an undertaking so disastrous that it is called the Road of the Devil. The farmers, escaping famine in Northeast Brazil, have forefathers who ran to the Amazon to prosper in the rubber boom and died of hunger when the market for Brazilian rubber collapsed. Every Indian chief who wants peace has learned that at the turn of the century there were three million Indians in Brazil and now there are 212,000.

Having read of these failures, we intended to call this book *Where Dreams Die*. But then we went to the Amazon, and we discovered what makes human beings the most fascinating of all the animals in this jungle—the ability to wonder and to believe that what we believe can be. The Amazon, because it is a frontier, reveals contrasts starkly—so much is black or white, good or bad, destructive or constructive. What ultimately happens to this land and why are questions only priests and scientists might attempt to answer. We have tried to paint a picture of what is happening now. For this moment in time the people of the Amazon are among the luckiest on earth—despite the disease, the violence, and the toil they still have hope. Their passions have not faded. Their dreams have not died.

AMAZONIA

At 5,000 feet, the forest below looks as if moths had feasted on a dark green carpet. Great chunks have been chewed, leaving splotches of brown and black. The land is scarred this way for a hundred miles. Occasionally a road appears. If it is new, it is rusty red, a long straight tear in the green. Old roads are gray-white, and along them at intervals on either side are notches of the same color, making the old roads look like cleaned fish spines.

At 500 feet the torn patches become three-dimensional. They are strewn with thin tree trunks, charred and lying about as if blown down by a fierce hot wind.

Viewed on the ground, these abstracts become real. The carpet is the tree canopy of the largest forest on earth. The white notches are the abandoned farms where dreams of dominating this land have died. The black patches are recently burned clearings where other dreams are just beginning.

This is the Amazon jungle. If anything can reduce the sprawling, baffling region to a simple description, it is this scene. The jungle looks this way in many places, the result of an immense struggle for control between man and nature. It is that struggle that we went to the jungle to try to understand.

We spent two years in preparation, reading old books and contemporary documents, drinking in a rich broth of facts so extreme they seemed legendary and legends so vivid they seemed real.

The Amazon is the largest single geographical feature of the South American continent. It is both a river and a giant river valley. What is usually referred to as the Amazon jungle is the tropical rain forest covering an area drained by the Amazon River and its hundreds of tributaries. Together, river and forest form Amazonia, what the world calls the Amazon.

The jungle is estimated to spread for 2.5 million square miles—about the size of the United States west of the Mississippi—and includes parts of eight countries: Brazil, Peru, Colombia, Ecuador, Bolivia, Venezuela, Surinam, and Guyana. The largest portions are in Brazil and Peru where, in both nations, the Amazons makes up about half the land area. If it were a country, the Amazon would be the ninth-largest in the world.

Authors of texts about the Amazon are awestruck when they write of this land of superlatives. The river itself starts in the Peruvian Andes and runs 4,007 miles along the Equator to the Atlantic Ocean. It is considered the second-longest in the world, after the Nile—unless you measure it the way the Brazilians do, in which case it is first by 50 miles; or the way the Ecuadorans do, with the source in their country, in which case it's shorter.

The river draws its initial strength from hundreds of small streams in the Andes, tumbling through steep gorges and eventually forming a mile-wide flow in northern Peru which grows to more than three for parts of its length in Brazil. As it crosses the Peruvian border, the Amazon runs into an enormous shallow bowl that makes up most of the center of South America. It is a remarkably flat basin that, if it were stripped of trees, might look a lot like the Great Plains of the United States or the Sahara of Africa. Through the middle of the bowl, the Amazon River cuts a deep trough that drops only 100 feet in its final 2,000-mile course to the Atlantic. The river's immense power comes from the many large tributaries that force their way into the channel, pushing an estimated 160 million tons of silt a year along the flood plain.

Hardly a reference is made to the river without pointing out an array of astonishing Guinness Book of Records type facts. The statistics are all remarkable and more or less true in magnitude, although seemingly equally reliable accounts can differ widely. It became apparent very early on to us that Amazon statistics were to be viewed with skepticism.

Among the facts that recur with some consistency are these: Each minute the Amazon River discharges 3.4 million gallons of water into the Atlantic, staining the sea brown with silt for 150 miles. The daily flow is 14 times the discharge of the Mississippi and enough to supply New York City with water for nine years. Called the Rio Mar, or River Sea, by Brazilians, the Amazon is several hundred feet deep at some points and often more than 7 miles wide, frequently flooding areas more than 100 miles across for months at a time. Oceangoing freighters call at the port of Iquitos, Peru, 2,300 miles upriver from the Atlantic. The Amazon basin is drained by 200 major tributaries, 17 of which are more than 1,000 miles long and ten of which discharge more water than the Mississippi. In all, the basin holds one-fifth of the fresh water in the world.

Geologically, the basin sits between two of the oldest rock formations on earth—the Guyana Shield to the north and the Brazilian Shield to the south. Prominent mountain ranges perhaps 600 million years ago, both have been worn down to rippled plateaus. The area between them may have been an ancient sea bottom which was drained during the Carboniferous Age, creating a series of rivers that flowed westward into the Pacific Ocean. But tens of millions of years ago, when the Andes began to push up, they bottled up the rivers and created another inland sea, the bottom of which is today estimated to contain close to a depth of two miles of sediment. Eventually the trapped water broke through the lowlands connecting the two shields near what is now the city of Obidos and cut its way to the Atlantic, grooving into the soft sediment with such force that in some places the river's main channel is more than 300 feet deep. As the lake drained, the thousands of tributaries that were forming in the watersheds, as well as all the runoff from the eastern slope of the Andes, sought that channel at the bottom of the basin. Over the intervening millions of years the shape of the basin and the rivers has remained the same, though the area has probably been extensively flooded and drained several times as the world's oceans rose and fell with ice ages. Even now when the basin, which is mere inches above sea level, suffers a particularly bad flood season, the region begins to resemble an inland sea.

Possibly because of the Andes' effect on the formation of rain clouds, the Amazon also became one of the wettest places in the world. There are variations between different parts of the basin and during different seasons, but the maximum rainfall, in the western Amazon, exceeds 150 inches a year; even in the central jungle, with its pronounced dry season, the total is usually well above 60 inches. The temperature averages 75 degrees Fahrenheit, though it is often above 90. Humidity stays at about 80 percent. The rainy season is divided in half with the forest north of the Equator getting heavy rain in April through August and the southern part from December to April. This variation keeps the Amazon River floods relatively in control, though the river tends to rise about 40 feet each year and crests in May or June.

This wet, stable climate has produced a huge variety of plant life. The vegetation that covers the basin is one-half of the remaining forest on earth. Those trees, according to some accounts, provide at least 15 percent of the world's new oxygen—although it is just as easy to find experts who say they provide none. The basin is, in variety of living things, the richest area on the globe. Perhaps one million of the world's estimated five million species of plants and animals live in the Amazon; many live nowhere else. Several hundred kinds of trees often can be found on a single acre of jungle. Scientists have cataloged 2,500 species of snakes, 2,000 of fish (by comparison, the Mississippi has 250), 1,500 of birds and 50,000 species of higher plants—about a fifth of the world's total. All accounts of this extraordinary place point out that little is known about most of the life, and scientists estimate that at least an equal number of species in all categories are yet to be discovered.

Until the last decade, one of the rarest species was man. For perhaps 12,000 years the land was occupied only by primitive tribes of hunter-gatherers who lived in small bands and roamed the vast forest, never developing a sophisticated culture or social structures. These tribes, which most likely migrated down from the Andes, may have numbered three or four million people when Europeans first came to the Amazon and made the lives of the Indians miserable, eventually reducing their number to 212,000 today.

By the early 1600s, French, Dutch, English and Portuguese had settled around the mouth of the Amazon, each group recruiting Indians to fight for them. When the Portuguese finally took control of the region in 1639, the Indians had been decimated by violence and disease. The whites, though, had no intention of colonizing, preferring to use the land for what could be exported to Europe. They reasoned that such a great, mysterious land must have many treasures.

Almost as soon as the first Westerners spotted the river, myths of what it contained were created and the lust to conquer it was spawned. "The recorded history of Amazonia is that of human greed," wrote Amazon scholar Georges Landau. "Whether it was the search for precious metals and stones or Indians to be enslaved or sheer territorial aggrandizement, Amazonia was prey to the feuds of distant warring kings."

The first European explorer to record seeing the river was one of Christopher Columbus' former captains, the Spaniard Vincente Yanez Pinon in February, 1500. He was drawn to the mouth of the river by the observation of fresh water several miles out in the Atlantic. He named the 200-mile wide estuary the Sweet Sea, having no idea that he'd found the outlet of a river. What he was looking for, as were most New World explorers, was El Dorado, the legendary city of gold that drove Old World marquises and lion-hearted adventurers berserk with desire. Dozens of expeditions around the edges of South America had come up empty and many explorers became convinced the magic land was somewhere in the jungle of the interior.

Yet in this desire to penetrate the jungle in search of wealth, the Europeans were not the first. A least a century earlier, kings of the advanced Inca civilization of the Peruvian Andes sent huge armies down the eastern slopes on jungle forays that routinely met with disaster. It was the Incas, perhaps out of spite after suffering defeat by the Spaniards, who heightened their conquerers' lust for El Dorado by telling them detailed though false stories of an empire filled with large and populous cities where the streets were paved with gold and the lakes bottomed with golden sand. The king of this empire was said to have servants who smeared him with oil every morning then covered him with gold dust. At night, he washed himself off in a pool that had become deeply sedimented with gold.

The Spaniards and the other Europeans swallowed the stories whole and sent platoons of soldiers into the jungle from all sides. One 19th-century historian with a gift for understatement summed up most of the expeditions in his account of a German venture from Venezuela in 1530: "The march by Ambrosio de Alfinger produced the usual story of perfidy and cruelty practiced upon the natives and of attack and misery experienced by the invaders. Alfinger died on the way back and, after two years, what was left of his followers found their way back to the coast."

After Francisco Pizarro overwhelmed the Incas of western Peru in 1532, he became convinced the gold and jeweled icons he was melting down were just tokens of what was to be found farther east. Several of his captains mounted armies and struck out over the Andes, invariably returning sick and starving or not returning at all. Francisco Pizarro's brother, Gonzalo, went in search of cinnamon trees, a valuable spice that Indian legend said grew abundantly in the forest. After his army slogged through mud for 70 days, they finally came upon the Land of Cinnamon. But there were no plantations as they had anticipated. The cinnamon trees were so spread out among the rest of the forest vegetation that it was impossible to harvest them. After he set his dogs on the local Indian tribe, he and his wretched band settled down for a Christmas dinner of boiled saddles and harnesses.

One of Gonzalo's lieutenants, the one-eyed Francisco Orellana, is credited with discovering the Amazon River itself. He left camp that Christmas day in 1542 with a small squad in search of food and was promptly swept down the Napo River 900 kilometers into the main channel of the Amazon. He was accompanied by Friar Gaspar de Carvajal, a Dominican priest who recorded the first fantastic account of travel in this jungle.

The routinely mythic character of Friar de Carvajal's and of almost all others' accounts is at once entertaining and frustrating to those who wish to learn about the Amazon. On the one hand, these recitations cement in the mind the emotional response this jungle brings out in people, the fantasies, the exaggerations, and not a few self-serving heroics. But as factual material, the accounts are not reliable. In the end, the many historical documents we read in preparation for our own travels seemed an impoverished attempt to encompass so wild and challenging a place.

Friar de Carvajal relates numerous encounters with wild Indians —who are summarily dispersed with crossbows and blunderbuses. The attacks become so commonplace as to be tedious. At one village, which would seem about halfway down the river, the Spaniards reported an attack by a fierce tribe commanded by female warriors. "These women were very white and tall and had their hair braided and wrapped around their heads," according to the friar, "and they were very muscular and wore skins to cover their shameful parts and with bows and arrows in their hands, they made as much war as ten men."

The Spanish retreated, convinced that they had stumbled on the land of the warrior women that the Europeans called Amazons after the Greek myth. The friar was somewhat skeptical because, as he noted, the women had not cut off their right breast, as the Greeks supposedly did, to keep it out of the way of a snapping bowstring. But his account was carried to the royal court in Spain and the river was named.

It was not remarkable for the Europeans to have expected some kind of great, exploitable civilization along this giant river. They knew their classical history and knew of the societies that had flourished along the Nile, the Tigris-Euphrates, the Ganges, the Indus and the Yellow rivers. That such an empire should not exist on the Amazon perplexed them. But more exasperating was the Europeans' inability to succeed at anything in the Amazon. The image of torn and hungry armies staggering out of the jungle was replaced by that of equally bedraggled and defeated colonists. For some reason, this land of plenty was not easily mastered, so the myths persisted and the desire to conquer the Amazon grew. As early as 1640, a crafty Jesuit named Cristobal Acuna made the case to the king of Spain that the indolent Portuguese should be driven out and Spain systematically should occupy the land he said was overflowing with wealth, particularly gold and silver.

The king, preoccupied elsewhere, showed little interest in the unruly Amazon. When Pedro Teixeira traveled 2,000 miles up the river in 1639 and claimed all the land east of Ecuador for Portugal, the Spanish crown did not protest. From then on, the Amazon was considered a separate colony from the large Portuguese agricultural settlements in the south which had already been named Brazil after the brazilwood tree, source of a coveted red dye. The journey from Belem to Rio de Janeiro was longer and more hazardous than the trip to Lisbon. The Amazon was not politically integrated with Brazil until independence from Portugal was achieved in 1822.

The first to discover any wealth were the naturalists who began arriving in the mid-1700s and reached a flood by the mid-1800s. But what they discovered was not marketable at the time. The Frenchman Charles Marie de la Condamine found latex, the milky sap of rubber trees that has a remarkably pliant quality, but not until 100 years later did Charles Goodyear figure out what to do with it. Condamine studied various Indian arrow poisons and quinine, soon the cure for malaria, and shipped a boatload of exotic plants back to Paris. He also did his part to perpetuate the Amazon myth. The otherwise-enlightened Frenchman claimed to have seen green stones —probably emeralds—that the local Indians said were given by the Amazon women to men who had provided them with children. The statement of a respected scientist like Condamine was not questioned, and had a predictable effect on the folks back home, launching new waves of fortune hunters.

Of all the early Amazon authors, only one, the Englishman Alfred Russel Wallace, was less than gushing in his notices. Upon arriving in 1848, Wallace expressed disappointment that the place had not lived up to its press clips. "The weather was not so hot, the people were not so peculiar, the vegetation was not so striking as the glowing picture I had conjured up in my imagination."

By the 20th century, tales of the Amazon had shifted from the exotic travelogs beloved by the Victorians to robust adventure stories.

Theodore Roosevelt wrote one of the first of this genre, an account that probably inseminated a whole generation of hair-raising tales by a succession of hearty, usually British, adventurer–explorers that have done much to create the modern vision of the Amazon.

Actually, Roosevelt's *Through the Brazilian Wilderness*, published in 1914, is one of the most tame and scholarly works of the genre. He was, of course, the personification of robustness, and sometimes could hardly keep from bursting with joy as he tramped through the forest, picking off game with his rifle left and right. And certainly he wouldn't have taken this trip if there hadn't been some danger involved. "South America," he wrote, "makes up for its lack, relatively, to Africa and India, of large man-eating carnivores by the extraordinary ferocity or bloodthirstiness of certain small creatures."

His description of one of those creatures, the piranha fish, is a model of exuberant writing. "They will rend and devour alive any wounded man or beast, for blood in the water excites them to madness. The razor-edged teeth are wedge-shaped like a shark's and the jaw muscles possess great power. The rabid furious snaps drive the teeth through flesh and bone. The head, with its short muzzle, staring malignant eyes and gaping, cruelly-armed jaws is the embodiment of evil ferocity. . . ."

Roosevelt continued on his journey, truly arduous by anyone's standards, telling of battles with vampire bats, ants that ate his T-shirt and gun case, termites that ate his pith helmet, clouds of mosquitoes and gnats, and of encounters with jaguars that he dropped at 70 yards with a single shot. He also proceeded to discover a river, which his Brazilian guides thoughtfully named after him. He ended by dubbing the land "the true last frontier" and made a plea for development that sounds as though it came from a speech by a modern Brazilian official: "Surely such a rich and fertile land cannot be permitted to remain idle, to lie as a tenantless wilderness, while there are such teeming swarms of human beings in the overcrowded, over-populated countries of the Old World."

As if Roosevelt's story were not enough to make anyone with red blood in his veins pack up and head for South America, there were more—and more lurid—tales to come. Dominating the literature of the Amazon from the 1920s to the 1950s, they all talked of the "green hell," the "green unknown" or the "green death." With titles like *The Lost World of the Amazon,* or *Wilderness of Fools,* all claimed to be true. The stories have many similarities. They start like Jorgen Bisch's *Across the River of Death*: "Tomorrow we set off into the Green Hell of the Mato Grosso territories, into which many have penetrated but from which so few have returned." All have the mandatory battle with a giant anaconda, which Bisch did as well as anyone. First he set the mood by recounting how an anaconda kills a man: "It knocks him unconscious by striking his head with its bony jaws." Then, having crushed all the man's bones to make him easier to swallow, the snake "spits out quantities of thick slime and saliva over the head before it starts on the actual meal." Of his own encounter with a 25-footer, Bisch reported: "The snake hissed. Its mouth opened. I could see rows of teeth. If it once gets those teeth into you, you will never come out of this struggle alive. Hold firm, hold firm, I whispered to myself. . . ."

Algot Lange, in his *In the Amazon Jungle,* displayed that same sense of anticipation—"I knew now that I was to face the awful master of the swamps, the great silent monster of the river"—but had a much more sensible solution. He pumped the beast full of 9mm Luger shells as "its great head rears above us, hissing in agony." The next day he measured it at 56 feet; alas, the extraordinary skin was lost in shipment to New York.

Indians, too, were confronted at every turn. In *I Was a Headhunter,* Lewis V. Cummings managed to run the gamut from warring with one tribe to eventually bedding one of its women. First he met the witch doctor, who beat him with a whip: "With sudden ferocity I wanted to fire bullets into that unemotional figure with the hot black eyes . . . to see the brief flame spurt from the muzzle as the swift bullet leaped on its way singing its song of havoc and death."

But later, in a jungle clearing, he came upon a lovely Indian maiden. "I arose and extended my arms, palms up, to her. She did the same. I took her hands in mine, and drew her, unresisting, down to the grassy earth. Beneath her left breast I could see her heart pounding.

" 'Daughter of the moon,' I said, 'I am but a stranger here who knows nothing but who is eager to know.'

"Her answer was low—and challenging."

Someone had to put his foot down and it was left to a serious

Dane, Hakon Mielche, who took the no-nonsense approach and called his book *The Amazon*. "What an appalling business it is writing a book about the Amazon!" he began. "There is nothing nice about that accursed river and all that can be said about its adventure, of going in peril of one's life, of superhuman exertions and glorious heroism, all that and much more has already been said. . . . And yet that is what people expect when they buy a book about 'the green hell.' You see how easily the hackneyed words trip off one's tongue!"

And so Mielche offered a solution. "I have written the truth about the Amazon, just as I jotted it down in my diary. And here it is with my apologies to all adventure loving souls." The apologies proved unnecessary, though, as even the disciplined Dane couldn't resist. No sooner was he in Belem, at the mouth of the Amazon, than he wrote: "To me it was the narrow opening in that green wall into which so many have gone and from which so few have returned."

Recent accounts of the Amazon are hard to come by, and infinitely more grim than the older self-proclaiming heroics. There is a sense of alarm in the newer writing, but not over some half-imagined encounter with a snake. Today's literature centers on the fear that man is destroying one of the greatest natural resources on earth. Little of the writing is between hard covers and none can be called popular. It is mostly papers produced by scientists from the fields of botany, ornithology, entomology—most of whom have departed from their specialties to decry the destruction of the jungle that has served as their vast laboratory. "Extinction and Conservation of Plant Species in Tropical America: A Phytogeographical Perspective," "The Development of the Amazon Rainforest: Priority Problems and the Formulation of Guidelines," "Endangered Plant Species in Habitats of Ecuador and Amazonian Peru." Not exactly the stuff of which movie rights are made, but a newly sober view of what has become, since the days of Victorian adventurers, the moth-eaten jungle that signals its distress to the skies.

These papers are serious attempts by respected people to try to understand what has been going on in an area they freely admit they know relatively little about—although this fraternity can certainly claim more knowledge of the Amazon than anyone else. What they have seen during their various expeditions in the jungle has disturbed them very much.

Warwick Kerr, a Brazilian scientist, predicted in the mid-1970s that if the clearing of the Brazilian forest continued at its present rate, it would be gone by the end of the century. Ghillean Prance, head of the New York Botanical Garden's Amazon project, says 25 percent is already gone. Scientists writing in the British journal *The Ecologist* say up to a third of the forest is gone and more than 20 million acres a year are being cleared. They conclude that events in the Amazon "could prove one of the most profligate misuses of natural resources in history."

As an aerial view of the jungle bespeaks changes of enormous magnitude, two of our earliest interviews focused for us the opposing views that are clashing in that jungle arena.

One interview was with Robert Goodland, an aptly named ecologist and one of the first scientists to raise the alarm on behalf of the forest. When we met him, he was working in a small office on the fourth floor of one of the many annexes of the World Bank, the giant international lending institution that is designed to promote development in the poor parts of the world.

Goodland, a gaunt, nervous Canadian, has a special interest in the Amazon, where the bank is investing nearly a half billion dollars in various projects. In 1975, when he was at the New York Botanical Garden, he wrote a book with botanist Howard Irwin called *Amazon Jungle: Green Hell to Red Desert?* In it, the two suggested a whole range of what they called "dire prognostications" if too much of the jungle were cut. They emphasized what may be the fatal irony of the Amazon: despite the apparent lushness of tropical forest, when you cut it down, it does not readily grow back. The fertile soil of the jungle floor is extremely thin—sometimes only an inch deep—despite the huge trees it supports. When those trees are cut that soil quickly erodes, baring a layer of clay which bakes in the sun to a brick-hard surface incapable of sustaining much life. The Amazon, half the remaining forest on earth, is an extremely fragile place.

"You can think of it as a desert covered with trees," Goodland explained to us. "What's happening down there now is a giant experiment and I'm afraid one can't tell with certainty what will actually be the result. But it is an experiment I would rather not see conducted on such a grand scale."

What Goodland thought could happen was, among other things, a drastic change in Brazil's climate prompted by a serious disruption in rainfall patterns. That disruption could extend to world weather patterns because, as he pointed out, "the Amazon is so big, it is like another ocean. Who knows what will happen if you tamper with something like that?"

One place to look, he suggested, might be the northeastern horn of Brazil where once-thick coastal forests were cut down by 19th-century settlers. That area is now a parched land that becomes a crusted, useless desert during the increasingly harsh droughts that have cycled through the area for the past several decades.

Then, too, there is the unknown effect that fooling with the Amazon might have on the earth's atmosphere. Goodland and the specialists we consulted are not sure what it means to cut and burn such a large forest, but they have some ideas. They feel it can only accelerate the "greenhouse effect," the gradual increase of carbon dioxide in the atmosphere that scientists believe already is changing the world's climate by heating the temperate zones. Burning the forest releases large amounts of carbon dioxide while it removes the plant life that would otherwise reabsorb the gas.

"What that means," said Goodland, "is that if the increase is severe enough, you could find a drying trend in the Midwest—the grain belt." What frustrates him is that by the time the change is noticed—in a decade or so—it will probably be too late to do anything.

"These are the more extreme problems, the kind of end-of-the-world stories that give people a scare, but there's nothing they can do about it. What I think is really the most alarming is the living things we're losing by cutting the forest. The Amazon is one of the great biological laboratories on earth. It is the last important tropical rain forest that you could say is relatively untouched by man—when you compare it with some of those ravaged forests in South Asia and Africa. So little is known about the Amazon; things are being destroyed before they are discovered—trees, birds, insects. There are plant species which may produce the next miracle crop or the cure for cancer, if they're discovered."

He sat back, fatigued by the lecture, or perhaps by what he sensed was the futility of it. He fidgeted with a pencil and stared out the window. "I'm not sure how you make people understand that."

Then, almost as an afterthought, Goodland mentioned the Indians. "Have you considered them? I guess people don't pay any attention to this any more either, but you know when you destroy that forest, you destroy the habitat of thousands of human beings who have lived there for thousands of years. They know how to survive in the forest, how to use the forest. They have discovered contraceptives, drugs, poisons that could all be of use to us. We only know how to destroy the forest, and to destroy them.

"What's happening to them is really rather inhumane. And for what?"

Paulo Yakota, a Brazilian official who is responsible for finding land for tens of millions of his countrymen, gave us an answer to that question—not on behalf of the jungle, but on behalf of the people who are cutting it down. The response he offered us seemed to say that the Amazon is one of the last safety valves for a country—and a continent—in danger of devouring itself.

Yakota is in charge of land settlement in Brazil, the nation with the fifth-largest land area on earth, and he is one of the country's most influential planners. Most of Brazil's more than 120 million people are crowded in slums along the Atlantic or fruitlessly tilling soil in the northeastern part of the country. Only recently have the leaders in Brasilia, the space-age capital city, begun to ponder what would happen if many of those people with no land could go to the Amazon, a vast land with few people. The TransAmazon Highway system was built a decade ago with this scheme in mind, and whenever anyone rides it to a new life on new land, he is entering Yakota's domain.

"We will develop the Amazon because we have to develop the Amazon." There was nothing apologetic about Yakota's tone. "We have no oil, but we have land with valuable wood, rich minerals and farmland for millions of people. How can we leave it alone? The environmentalists say don't touch it, but that is impossible."

What Brazil also has, Yakota admitted with no attempt at disguise, are economic problems on a scale unmatched in most of the world. Brazil has all the curses of the Third World—poverty, illiteracy, a soaring birth rate, inflation and a heavy foreign bank debt—and befitting its size, each is of colossal magnitude. The problems have made the leaders of this country wonder how they are to survive in the next century. One of the solutions they have settled on is the Amazon, just as the United States turned to the West in the late 19th century.

"This is our Oregon in 1870," Yakota said, pointing to a map of the sprawling Amazon that cuts through the fat part of the South American continent from the Atlantic Ocean almost to the Pacific.

Brazil long has looked at that area as both a treasure and a burden and has never been quite sure what to do with it. The jungle has resisted all plans to exploit it. But Yakota, an economics professor from the city, insisted to us that the odds are changing and the jungle will succumb. It has to.

Although we early realized that the lines of the clash are thus clearly drawn, the Amazon's reputation for mystery, if not malevolence, seemed to us well deserved. During the years of preparing for our trip, no person or document we consulted claimed to know much about the place—astonishing in an age when *National Geographic* can tell you as much about the bottom of the seas as you know about your hometown and when social trends are as carefully monitored as the weather. In particular, no one knew the chemistry of the clash itself, what happens to the jungle as it comes up against the people, or what happens to the people as they come up against the jungle. Scientists can't say what happens when people kill off the sterculia trees that the sap-feeding pygmy marmoset lives on, unless they can say what purpose the sap-feeding pygmy marmoset serves. But there didn't seem to be a purpose for the mandioca root until settlers found the Amazon tribes eating it. Today much of the world would starve to death without it: manioc has become one of the most important food crops on earth.

Those who did know something were, perhaps necessarily, narrow in their interests. Here is this vast, complicated, continent-size region apparently undergoing drastic change after years of isolation. It is change that has ecological, political, economic and social implications; yet our research turned up no one who had tried to cut across the lines of specialty, to understand how the pygmy marmoset relates to the Brazilian national debt—or rainfall in our Midwest.

This is not the first time the forest has been invaded, though it appears to be the first attempt that is enduring. Is the intuition of the conquistadores proving correct 400 years later? And if so, what does it mean to clear a million square miles of forest? And what of the legacy of failure that has claimed untold lives and frustrated the most spectacular dreams; is this latest conquest just the scene-setter for an even greater tragedy?

We had to take in the whole arena, as many parts of the jungle as we could get to, as many of the people who live and work there or consider its destiny, as we could speak with. This quest of ours was not to be a scientist's field trip, nor an adventure story, but a picture, a whole impression built up of many lines of inquiry, conversations with people, scenes that we could see with our own eyes. We were neither in man's nor nature's corner, but planted squarely in the middle: their meeting ground in the Amazon.

We planned to start in the south of Brazil, where the money and the leaders are, and then wind our way through the southern jungle, eventually getting to the mouth of the Amazon River as it empties into the Atlantic Ocean. From there we planned to go as far up as we could, however we could. When we bought our plane tickets, we booked the return from Lima, Peru, clear on the other side of the continent.

Even though we put on a stern front of journalistic inquiry, neither of us was immune to the romance that had trapped so many others. Despite the preparation, we liked to think that we were just picking up and heading for the Amazon. We knew before we started that some serious questions might be unanswerable; a team of 40 would have problems. It was asking the questions that counted.

We had something of a sense of apprehension, but it was muted. If all was unknown, what was there to be afraid of? On the other hand, some visions we couldn't shake. We had also seen "Creature from the Black Lagoon." And didn't it seem reasonable that some portion of even the wildest stories might have been true? Ultimately that was to prove the biggest challenge: to separate the myth from the reality.

"You're going to the Amazon? That's great!" said one of Kelly's colleagues, a man of no small reputation, shortly before the trip. "Isn't that where they've got all those big topless broads?"

It was time to find out.

SAO PAULO
AND RIO

Brazil's size quickly became apparent when the Pan Am pilot announced, about four hours out of Miami, that we had crossed into the country. It would be another four hours before we got to Sao Paulo, Brazil's largest city, but by no means its southernmost.

Entering the country over the Amazon jungle was as close to the rain forest as we would get for a while. Sao Paulo was an imperative first stop. Nothing of consequence happens in Brazil that does not involve Sao Paulo, we had been advised—and that includes the Amazon.

"The Amazon," one Brazilian expert said in Washington before we left, "is like a colony of Sao Paulo. It is as though the Paulistas

are trying to conquer an adjacent nation and bring back its treasures." Sao Paulo has the one thing that forces all Brazil to listen to it
—money. Much of the country's wealth is concentrated there and so
are the offices of most of the businessmen who see the Amazon as
their next investment.

Congonhas Airport is a microcosm of the bustle of Sao Paulo.
Once the pride of Brazil, it now more closely resembles one of those
urban shopping centers haphazardly stuffed into a crowded residential
and industrial neighborhood, a vast expanse of parking lot ridicu-
lously out of place. In the past 15 years the city has stumbled over
itself in its rush to grow, and the neighborhood, once on the outskirts
of Sao Paulo, has surged right to the white lines at the beginning of
the landing strip. The airport is now so hemmed in it cannot expand
to accommodate more or larger planes. It is, the Brazilians say, a very
dangerous place where split-second timing is required of pilots lining
up to take off or land the steady stream of commercial jets and
luxurious corporate aircraft. The alternative is the roomy international airport 60 miles from Sao Paulo but many of *its* patrons take
flights to Congonhas to reach the city.

Sao Paulo is not the postcard picture one has in mind for sultry,
tropical South America. Just the drive in from screeching Congonhas
made that clear. The city has 10 million residents who live in one of
the densest urban sprawls in the world. The highway from the airport
is a dirty eight-lane track that runs through endless miles of towering
office buildings and apartment houses. There is nothing deliciously
languid about the city. It moves with the pace of New York; it has the
masses of Tokyo and the gray, industrial grit of Gary, Indiana. It is a
city that, no matter where it is photographed from, looks the same;
no recognizable center, no distinctive architecture—just a forest of
30-story buildings.

But take Sao Paulo out of Brazil and you are left with a Third
World country without a prayer. The city and surrounding state account for 70 percent of the country's gross national product, which
is no small statement. Brazil's economy is the eighth-largest in the
world, and its gross national product is nearly $300 billion. Coffee
and sugar cane, the goods the world traditionally associates with
Brazil, have been overtaken by an auto industry that produces two
million vehicles a year; an arms industry that is now the world's sixth-

largest; companies that manufacture shoes, textiles, machinery and
computers for export; the world's second-largest shipbuilding industry and a diverse farming sector that is second only to the U.S. in
soybeans and is pushing hard in citrus fruits, corn and wheat. Sao
Paulo is a competitor, not a colony, of the industrial powers of the
West.

Much of this expansion came during the so-called Brazilian
Miracle of the 1970s when the economy grew at 8 to 10 percent a
year. The growth, however, was not without cost and Brazil has been
plagued with an inflation rate that has hovered around 100 percent
for more than five years. The country is also cause for sleepless nights
by bankers in the United States and Europe who have made loans to
Brazil of about $85 billion, the highest foreign debt of any country in
the world.

The ride from Congonhas also gave us glimpses of the greatest
burden Brazil suffers: too many people in the wrong places. The
shacks and shanty towns surround Sao Paulo in concentric circles—
called the rings of misery—of millions of people living below the
poverty level, trying to earn, beg or steal a living with virtually no
hope of aid from a government that feels it has a long way to go
before it can consider social welfare programs. And most of those
people are young; each year three million Brazilians enter the job
market. They come to the cities because, bad as life is there, it is
better than in the desolate rural areas where many were born. It is
expected that the population of Sao Paulo—as well as of Rio de
Janeiro with five million people—will double by the end of the century. Brazil's economy must grow rapidly if the country is to keep
from eating itself alive.

"For all its potential, Brazil has to come up with an ace in the
hole," Riordan Roett, one of America's leading scholars on Brazil,
had told us in Washington. "They have to have some kind of
bonanza that's going to push them over the top. A lot of them are
starting to think that's what the Amazon will be."

Joao Carlos Meirelles thinks that. He is a combination Horace
Greeley/John Jacob Astor figure of the Amazon, its most ardent pro-
moter and a businessman with a heavy investment in its future.

Brazilian experts in the United States had told us he was the man to see if we wanted to know what the makers of the Brazilian Miracle have in mind for the Amazon. Environmentalists referred to him in unflattering terms, suggesting that if he had his way, the Amazon would become the Sun Belt of the world, criss-crossed with towns, farms and industrial parks.

Meirelles' office is on the Brazilian Wall Street. At the foot is the imposing ribbed granite face of the Bank of Brazil, the mother figure for all Brazilian businessmen. Scurrying around her great stone aprons the morning of our appointment were ranks of dark-suited commuters en route from train stations to the office. They seemed mostly conservative Brooks Brothers types—pinstripes with narrow lapels and shiny black shoes. Lining the way up a slight incline is a succession of glass-and-steel towers housing the other big Brazilian banks as well as an array of United States and European concerns. The buildings reminded us of those occasional newspaper stories of high-rise fires—the ones with photos of crazed people leaping through plate glass 20 stories above the street.

Meirelles did not appear with the horn and tail the environmentalists had ascribed to him. He arrived punctually at nine, dressed in a dark, vested suit with thin stripes, watch chain at his waist, walking stick with sterling silver head in hand. His suit pants sported a button fly, the kind favored by old-line English tailors. Meirelles was slight and stern with large dark eyes balanced between thick brows and a full mustache, which he twisted with just a touch of wax at the ends.

After a *cafezinho*, the shot of sweet coffee that is a Brazilian ritual repeated several times during any meeting, Meirelles got down to business. As the long-time president of the Association of Impresarios of the Amazon, he is the spokesman for more than 300 well-heeled investors from the south of Brazil, including many of the largest corporations and wealthiest individuals in the country. Membership in the trade and lobby group includes the Brazilian subsidiaries of Volkswagen, Xerox, Nixdorf Computer as well as Brazil's largest private bank, Bradesco, and insurance companies, construction firms, sugar refiners and coffee growers. It is a Who's Who of Brazilian business, and each Wednesday afternoon, their representatives sit around a conference table in Meirelles' office to decide what to do with their share of the Amazon.

"You should meet these people," Meirelles said in his British-accented English. "They are not bad people doing the things which they are falsely accused of."

Meirelles is astute enough to realize that his group is seen by some as the vandals of the Amazon and he headed off tough questions by taking the offensive. "It is the Europeans who are so concerned with our jungle, the European magazines and newspapers that write about trees being cut and stir up the ecologists. They have time to worry about it and they cause a problem for us. There was no ecology movement when you were developing your country, but now everyone worries about us."

"They are ignorant, though," he said as he rose and walked to a cabinet. An engineer by training, Meirelles returned with a thick sheaf of maps which he spread on the table.

"There is not one Amazon. There are hundreds," he said, riffling the maps. "Those who criticize us say we are tearing down the jungle and turning it into a desert, but which jungle are they talking about? This? This?" His index finger danced over the maps in front of him—soil maps, temperature maps, rainfall maps—all indicating, he said, that the jungle was not a "monolith" but a series of diverse zones, some of which you can farm, and some of which you can't; some of which you can mine, and some of which you can't. The problem, he admitted, is that no one knows with precision which areas will work for a given purpose. A lot of guesswork is involved, Meirelles conceded.

"We think we can use about one-third of the Amazon for now and the rest should be left untouched for parks and Indian reservations and such things. We don't have the technology to do more now." That one-third would be about 1.5 million square kilometers, he explained, doubling Brazil's existing farmland and giving it more than any nation on earth.

We said we had heard that one-third was already cleared. Meirelles snorted.

"That jungle is so big, I don't think one percent is gone. But more will come down; it has to. We do not have the time to stop and study it. I'm telling you, it's impossible to stop the occupation of the Amazon. Even if we, the businessmen, stood by with our hands folded, the poor people would keep moving in. It is our role to make the occupation rational."

That last idea consumes Meirelles' energies. He is a supporter of private colonization projects and manages a company that is investing in a giant one. The idea is to buy a large tract of jungle, put in infrastructure—roads, electricity, water, a town—then sell off parcels to families from the south, making a profit on the land sale. It is a type of Levittown, but a few hundred miles away from the next closest shopping center. That is what Meirelles was calling rational occupation of the jungle.

His own project, called Juruena, is in the south central Amazon where most of the land is already owned by private colonization companies. He predicted to us that in 10 to 15 years, the area will have three cities and ten villages with a half million people.

"We are building a new country," he said, thumping his fist on a map.

Meirelles hopes that one day he can move his family to Juruena. His son, Joao Jr., a student at Brazil's top graduate business school, is working on plans to establish a university in the area. His daughter, Pia, is studying architecture and urban planning "to build the new cities of the Amazon."

"We are building the future and we are proud, not defensive, about what we are doing," said Meirelles.

Pride proved to be endemic among Sao Paulo's wealthy business-men. The picture in the silver frame on Jeremias Lunardelli's desk was of an elderly couple dressed in the severe black uniform of the Old World immigrant. The same kind of picture hangs in many houses in the United States: grandma and grandpa, the tough and optimistic forebears who made their way in steerage to the New World and scratched out a beachhead for the now successful clan. In the case of the Lunardellis, that success has been extraordinary. The senior Lunardelli, who came from the north of Italy in 1890, became the coffee king of Brazil. He started picking beans on someone else's plantation and eventually built an empire. The family now controls thousands of acres of coffee trees, producing the little bean that for decades was the staple of Brazil's economy. In addition to mammoth land holdings, the empire eventually included huge coffee roasting and processing plants, and Jeremias was in charge of one. About 12 years ago, he decided that his fate was his grandfather's—working the land, not managing an industrial plant.

"The coffee business was changing rapidly. It had become very risky, with all the price changes and now the frosts here. I said it's time we went back to what we know, working the land."

Lunardelli spoke as he slalomed his four-door luxury Opel through noontime traffic. "I think maybe we'll eat at my club. It's nearby and the steak is very good. They also have great oysters." He was fashionably dressed, a smooth young executive who could move easily in American or European business circles. Jerry, as his friends call him, perfected his English for the long negotiations that resulted in the sale of the coffee plant to Coca Cola.

"After we sold out, I began to think about some property my father had bought in the Amazon." "Some property," in this case, was more than a million acres that his father purchased after his plane crashed there, allowing him sufficient time to study the jungle. "In school we were taught that the Amazon was this terribly deep jungle that was uninhabitable. But the first time I visited I saw right away that it wasn't so, that it could be worked."

Lunardelli, with other family members, runs several cattle ranches that were cut from the jungle in a part of the eastern Amazon known as the Araguaia Valley. He spends one week a month there, flying up in his own plane. "That will one day be the richest part of Brazil," he said as he sliced through a thick filet and examined a chunk on his fork. "We are not making a profit now, but we soon will."

Asked about the effect this kind of development was having on the jungle, Lunardelli shrugged. "Now that there is a scarcity of capital, the pace of deforestation is slowing. But the place is so big, there'll be plenty left over."

The father of this grandiose attitude, we discovered, is Herminio Ometto, whom we met in his sugar factory on the northwest side of Sao Paulo. The building was in an industrial zone of brick-walled factories interspersed with clumps of wooden shacks. The view was like one of Upton Sinclair's descriptions in *The Jungle* of turn-of-the-century Chicago: "Half a dozen chimneys, tall as the tallest of buildings, touching the very sky—half a dozen columns of smoke, thick, oily and black as night. It might have come from the center of the world, this smoke, where the fires of the ages still smolder." But the packs of gaunt, dirty children who roamed the streets and slept in doorways suggested to us that perhaps Charles Dickens would have been the more appropriate chronicler.

The centerpiece of the neighborhood was the Union Sugar Company, the largest sugar refinery in Brazil, owned by Ometto, one of the richest men in Brazil. Meirelles had spoken of him with respect bordering on hero worship. "Ometto went into the Amazon before there were roads, before there were government incentives and tax breaks, before anyone thought it could be something besides a wild jungle," he had said in his solemn fashion. "All he had was his courage."

And his money. Ometto's grandfather took the same voyage as the Lunardellis; coming from Italy in the 1890s and landing penniless in Brazil, he planted nothing that didn't come up roses. The family built a small alcohol distillery on their sugar fields, and ultimately they became the largest refiner of sugar and distiller of alcohol in Brazil. The family group now forms the seventh-largest company in Brazil.

Yet Ometto was not the dashing figure we had expected. We were anticipating a Gary Cooper and instead found a character who looked like an aging Mafia don from *The Godfather*. His large head was set upon a burly body, draped in a tan silk suit. The executive offices seemed stark and small, a series of cubicles made of temporary partitions like an unimportant agency in a large bureaucracy. Ometto sat behind a desk in a room that held his own chair, two others and nothing more. He was silent for long minutes, his fingers steepled in front of his face.

"Why are you here?" Ometto asked finally. His eyes, distant behind thick lenses, rotated slowly from one to the other of us and back as we offered an answer: we had come to talk about the Amazon. For a long time only the eyes moved, then the heavy lids came down and we feared he had fallen asleep.

In a moment, he stood up. "Come in here."

Ometto led the way to a conference room dominated at one end by a five-foot-high wall safe. As he turned, a broad smile came across his face and he gestured for his visitors to sit. "Will you have a cafezinho?"

An aide scurried in and placed a pad and sharp yellow pencil in front of his boss, who had obviously undergone a drastic shift in mood.

"People ask me for many things. I wasn't sure why you were here," he said in a gravelly voice. "But if it's the Amazon, I am happy to sit and talk."

We told him of his reputation as a sort of discoverer of the Amazon, the man who opened it to the rest of Brazil. Ometto pondered, drawing meaningless squiggles on the pad, then nodded, indicating that he agreed. "It was the greatest thing I have done in my life. It was something a government should do, not a man."

What Ometto did in 1961 was to clear a 100,000-acre cattle ranch out of virgin jungle. He arrived on horseback and, in the ensuing years, hacked 400 miles of roads, moved two Indian tribes, built an airstrip and a small town, planted grass where it had never grown and trucked in thousands of head of cattle—hoping it would all work. It was his success, not apparent until the late 1960s, that prompted the first onslaught of development in the Araguaia Valley and that, we had been told, left the area an endless, treeless pasture.

"Now it's easy. The roads are in, there are cities nearby and we know how to do it. But back then it took courage. It took idealism to know that you could do something no one else had ever done."

When it became clear that, pioneering exploits aside, they had stumbled on a way to make money, the family sold the ranch to an Italian conglomerate in the 1970s. With his share of the proceeds Ometto bought his own 250,000-acre spread on the expanding frontier line to the west. He still visited there once a month, though now via his own Lear jet, to oversee the cattle, crops and swimming pool.

What concerned Ometto most about the Amazon is the government. His face contorted in a terrible sneer of disdain whenever he mentioned "politicians" or "bureaucrats." When we spoke to him, Brazil was preparing for its first elections since the 1964 military coup and, though Ometto apparently did not oppose the idea of democracy, some of its by-products seemed, by the expression on his face, to be upsetting his stomach.

"They are becoming concerned with a sense of majority rather than a sense of reality. The Amazon has become an issue and people who have never seen it are telling us what to do with it. Their concern is for the environment or the landless or the Indian, but not for making a resource for the whole world.

"Order and progress," he said, stressing the words that appear on the national flag. "You cannot stop the progress, but the government is inept and there is no order. The squatters are running wild and the jungle is being turned into a desert. The businessmen will not destroy it because it is not in our interest to do so. But thousands of small farmers, maybe."

He spoke in abrupt bursts, then regrouped his thoughts. As he talked he continued to doodle, and when a page was filled with scribbles, he folded it, tore it into little pieces and left it on the corner of the table from where it was whisked away by his vigilant aide.

"You know, I still believe greatly in her," he said referring to the Amazon with endearment. "She is wild and unknown. Look at your billionaire Mr. Daniel Ludwig and his great experiment. He is a great man and we should all thank him. But you must learn that in the Amazon, there's always something you cannot control. Things which you never expect which are sure to happen. That is why anything you do there is a gamble and that is why Mr. Ludwig lost."

But hadn't he taken the same bet and won?

"It is all right for you to say that," said Ometto, with transparent modesty. "But I won't."

Silvana Carreiro Carneiro is also a jungle addict, but we would never have guessed it. She is a woman who exudes class. About 45, slim, blue-eyed, she dresses with the thrown-together elegance of the truly wealthy. This is a woman who vacations in Acapulco and Las Vegas; adores New York theater, roulette and horses (her office is across from the Sao Paulo racetrack and we noticed binoculars on the window sill); displays in her bookshelf a worn leather-bound set of Nobel Prize-winning authors and runs the largest carpet manufacturing company in Brazil. Yet she wants to sell her Sao Paulo mansion and live in a small ranch house on an Amazon farm. "My mother thinks I'm crazy, but I can't stay away," the elegant blonde told us as she toyed with the heart-shaped diamond at her neck. "When I get my two girls married off, I'm going to live there for good." Her fellow Amazon landholders sometimes call her the Empress of the Amazon; she is the only woman who manages substantial property there.

"I grew up on farms. My family always had them. That's where I'm happy, out there with nothing," said Silvana, who, in typical Brazilian fashion, goes by a single name. Hard to believe that when she first decided to open the farm, she spent a month sleeping in a hammock swinging under a thatched roof. At night she would cook for the work party that was clearing trees. "I remember the first time I sent them vegetables, they sent a message back saying, 'We are not cattle. We do not eat this,'" she said. "Now they all have vegetable gardens."

At night they would play the guitar and sing, then she would take a few belts of the barely refined cane liquor called *cachaca* and fall asleep. Silvana built one of the most productive farms in the Amazon with cattle, sugar cane, rice and corn. "You cannot tell me this land will not grow things. It will grow anything. It will feed the world," she said, showing us pictures of purple sugar cane that towered above her husband—her second—on her 700,000-acre farm.

She was excited and the words came out in a rush. "The crime is that the land is idle, that so much of it is not producing. There is so much for us to do. This is the future."

"What's stopping you?"

"The ecologists and the priests. The ecologists shout about a lot of things but they just shout."

The priests, though, do more than shout, Silvana told us. One of the best known, Dom Pedro Casaldaliga, is from Sao Felix, the town closest to her ranch. He calls her the Blonde Devil, and the ranchers have responded by branding him the Red Bishop. He has earned their ire by the simple but explosive device of telling farmers in the region that just because ranchers claim the land that doesn't mean they have rights to it. The farmers, the Red Bishop says, may have legal or at least moral rights to the land, and they don't have to move.

"I represent progress and that's why he opposes me," an angry Blonde Devil said. "I have let some of them stay on my land and work as tenant farmers. They are happy and he cannot stir them up against me. I think that instead of the church telling me to give up my land, it should give up some of its own. My land is producing and feeding people."

When the door to the plane opened at the Rio de Janeiro airport, it was like seeing the white light on the road to Damascus. After the grit and gloomy monotones of Sao Paulo, Rio seemed to us another country. A brilliant, warm sun reflected from every shiny object, forcing us to squint to see surrounding sharp mountains jutting into an almost artificially blue sky. The ride to the hotel is alongside Guanabara Bay, wide and busy with freighters and tankers. To the right is an expanse of palm-studded park and behind that a solid wall of terraced apartment houses. The highway tunnels through one of the almost vertical mountain peaks and emerges on the Atlantic Ocean, at one end of the three-mile crescent of white sand called Copacabana Beach.

Rio *is* the postcard picture of Brazil, the sight everyone has seen. Magnificent Sugarloaf Mountain, rising from the sea like an obelisk; the huge statue of Christ the Savior, standing atop Corcovado Mountain with his arms outstretched—the dominant sight from anywhere in town. Both linger in the mind of the tourist brochure reader and dramatically serve as monuments to the beauty of this city.

We watched the soft green water surge in, a backdrop for the brown bodies jogging on the mosaic sidewalk or leaping at a volleyball net. It was early summer in Rio—winter in Chicago and Washington—and it became immediately apparent that those Girl from Ipanema photos that some newspapers delight in taunting their frozen readers with are not staged. The quantity of nubile women in the skimpiest of two-piece bathing suits astounded us, all the more so considering it was a Wednesday morning. And this was not to ignore the nearly naked men, almost feline in their preening and stretching as they stalked the beach.

If Sao Paulo is New York, then Rio is Los Angeles. This is the laid-back life-style of Brazil; the city of carnival and samba and bossa nova. It is a city so physically beautiful it defies one to put in a day's work.

As we walked along the beach near our hotel we could see, far up the side streets, curious, colorful splotches on the steep hillsides a mile or so from the ocean. They seemed to hang suspended over the tall, white apartment buildings, the same kind of terrain as Pacific Palisades in California where such heights are prime real estate.

We went closer, to the foot of the hills. Zigzagging up the steep slope we could see shacks, making a crowded pattern of wood sides and crimped metal roofs. Dozens of children—boys in grimy soccer shorts, girls in soiled pinafores—stood and stared. Down the center of the dirt street ran a rivulet of slimy green.

Later in the week it rained heavily. The papers carried stories about how 75 people were killed when their shacks washed down the sides of hills in different parts of Rio. We were told it happened all the time.

Rio is 200 miles north of Sao Paulo and in many respects is the other main part of the engine that drives this country. Once among the world's most elegant and lively political capitals, all its government and diplomatic business has now moved far inland to Brasilia. But much of the intellectual and cultural life has remained. We had come to Rio to find the thinkers, the other side of the neat package of inevitabilities the business tycoons had offered us. We were looking for dissenters—not an easy thing in a country that until a few years ago made dissidents disappear like magic.

One who had endured was Orlando Valverde, a bent old man with a flowing mane of white hair, who was the burr under the saddle of ambitious developers of the Amazon. His apartment smelled of old, unwashed dogs. A big English setter flopped around the worn furniture, perhaps the culprit but more likely only part of the problem. Once an elegant apartment house, a block from the beach in the old section of Copacabana, the building had lost its luster as the money of Rio moved farther south along the ocean front to Ipanema, Leblon and Barra da Tijuca. Most of the old residents have stayed, many of them retired military men like Valverde, a former naval officer. Trained as a map maker and geographer at the University of Wisconsin in the 1940s, Valverde was part environmentalist, part social liberal and part nationalist. When Kelly mentioned that he worked for the Chicago *Sun-Times*, Valverde laughed and clapped his hands.

"Ha-haa. That was the only paper we would read on campus. It was the one that supported Roosevelt and opposed that terrible, terrible conservative old Chicago *Tribune*." He spoke colloquial English in a nasal voice, punctuated with a whined exclamation. His laughs started low and ended on a high note.

Valverde headed the Commission in Defense of the Amazon, a loosely organized group of former military men, professionals and some politicians that had managed to stir up a surprising amount of support for their cause of keeping the giant Brazilian and foreign corporations out of the Amazon. They had brought together a diverse coalition that had taken one of the strongest stands against any government policy since the 1964 military coup. As the generals cautiously moved Brazil toward democratic elections and loosened the reins on the press and political debate, Valverde's group tried to make the Amazon one of the first national political issues.

"I had the advantage in the early days that as a former military man—as a member of the ruling class—they would let me speak. They thought no one would pay attention," he added with a mischievous leer.

What got Valverde started was a 1967 proposal by the Hudson Institute, the New York think tank, to dam the Amazon River to create a gigantic source of hydroelectric power and form a great lake in the center of South America to promote transportation and trade. The idea was bitterly denounced in Brazil as a subterfuge for establishing an American submarine base and a safe zone to which dangerous members of the Black Panther party could be shipped. Valverde's nationalism boiled to the surface as he called the plan a means for foreign governments to take over the Amazon. The idea struck a centuries-old fear of such a takeover in the Brazilians, and the Hudson study was roundly decried before anyone had really considered its merits. To this day it is the first example most Brazilians cite when they talk of the danger of letting multinational corporations into the Amazon.

A second incident galvanized Valverde and his supporters when the government in 1978 proposed to lease to private companies the timber rights to vast sections of the jungle.

"The government needed money because the oil bills were getting so high. They thought they would just mortgage parts of the jungle, let the companies come in and take all the trees or all the good trees and leave a forest of junk. Ha-haaa. But we fooled them. Yeeees. We taught them that the people are not stupid."

The government shelved the plan after a series of large protests throughout the country.

"So is the problem solved?"

"No, not at all. There are still many companies in the Amazon taking what they want. They are all cynical liars. But they are very clever; Meirelles is very good, he tells everyone it is for the good of Brazil what he does. Ahhh, but it is for his good. To me, it is all a kind of robbery. But they are rich and that is what counts."

Then he began to laugh to himself, a different laugh, sniffling out of his nose in short bursts. Cynicism and frailty marked his face, his mirth a bitter tribute to the skill of his adversaries and the system they operate in. He seemed to feel he could only hold them off for so long.

Valverde claimed that none of the Amazon development had helped anyone who lived there. "The rubber helped the U.S. tire companies, the manganese helped the U.S. steel companies. And we don't know anything about the secret projects like Mr. Ludwig's Jari or the bauxite mines that the Canadians have at Trombetas. They are cutting forest in the north that even the government does not know about."

He explained how the cutting was done. In the early days, only about a decade ago, it was men with axes who came in to clear land. A hectare (2.47 acres) could be cleared by eight men in six days. Then chainsaws came and one man could cut a hectare in two days. Now a thick anchor chain was dragged between two bulldozers, clearing 40 hectares in a day.

"I will tell you what I also know," he said, cocking one eye in a conspiratorial glower. "Some use Agent Orange to defoliate the trees. In the west I saw it; the killed trees stand naked, but with no signs of fire. With this, one man can clear 100 hectares in a day. And it also does a good job of getting out the Indians and the small farmers and the rubber gatherers."

We asked, as we were to ask over and over again throughout our travels, "How much is cleared?"

"They won't tell you exactly," he said, the "they" apparently meaning the government. "If they were to release the latest survey, it would be a national scandal. But we believe it is something more than 10 million hectares. We have seen some of the satellite studies. That is what you must find: in Brasilia, there is a man who does that, studies the satellite pictures."

Ten million hectares is 24.7 million acres or an area a little smaller than Indiana, a little larger than Maine. It is not one-third of the jungle, but clearing it is no small accomplishment, either.

Valverde shuffled to the door in his slippers to let us out. The apartment had grown dark and he had not switched on any lights.

"Well, good luck to you," he said. And he laughed again as we walked down the stairs, the sniffling laugh that told us he didn't give us or anyone much chance.

There was something besides the trees that we needed to learn about in Rio: the Indians, the subject of Robert Goodland's last musing to us before we started our journey, and the cause of his final shrugged "And for what?" Unfortunately the Friends of the Indians were going out of business when we arrived. It was hard to believe they couldn't keep up the rent on the shabby little suite of offices they occupied in a bad part of Rio, but Joao Pacheco, the president, said contributions were no longer coming in.

An intense, slight man who talked with compact but constant hand and arm gestures, Pacheco was an anthropologist at the National Museum. He started the Friends of the Indians in 1978 to fight the proposed Indian Emancipation Act. The law might have sounded like a good idea but, as Pacheco explained, it was a sure ticket to the check-out line for the 200,000 or so Amazonian Indians.

In Brazil, which has probably treated its Indians no worse than any other country in the world, the indigenous people are considered wards of the state, minors who have limited rights, but are guaranteed protection by the government. The emancipation bill would have freed them from second-class status—and left them prey to every con man, hustler and unscrupulous businessman with designs on their land. It was a meaty issue and provoked a cry of "foul" among many Brazilians and the international groups that watch such things. The bill was tabled.

Then a funny thing happened. The Indians, who have lots of other problems worthy of attention, slipped from the agenda of concerned citizens. There had been national outrage at their treatment before, notably the few times particularly horrible atrocities—machine-gunning them, bombing their villages from planes, poisoning their food—were revealed in the press. But Pacheco told us that the more insidious atrocities—the steady encroachment of their land and epidemics of white men's diseases that devastate them—go unreported and ignored. It was hard to get people to pay attention all the time. So while the press into the jungle is swelling, the concern for the original human inhabitants of that jungle is shrinking. Even as we were talking the Friends of the Indians were packing up.

Not that the office was ever much. It had the look of the typical activist warren anywhere: stacks of posters and pamphlets, a few diligent women in fatigue jackets hunched over typewriters, a picture of Che Guevara on the wall. Only the longbow and war club hanging above Che gave it away, those and the receptionist in jeans, army boots and cutoff army shirt who wore wooden dowels sticking through his ears and who approached London as we were leaving.

"You're from America, right?"

Yes.

"You know Marlon Brando, right?"

No.

"How about Jane Fonda? We want her to help us. You know her," he insisted, taking a firm grip on London's upper arm.

We left the Friends of the Indians strangely pleased to have been the victims of culture shock. Perhaps the experience might prove a valuable lesson, an antidote to the legend of the Amazon which, in its latest reincarnation, was bearing down on us.

The Amazon, we were finding, had become a public spectacle. Encouraged partly by the government and partly by romanticism, the national newspapers we read ran frequent articles about the invasion of the *mata* or *floresta,* as the jungle is called in Portuguese. Huge industrial projects such as the hydroelectric dam at Tucurui were often subjects of glowing accounts in the glossy magazines. Gold miners who had made big finds in the Amazon mines were portrayed as national heroes and the violent life on the frontier was darkly hinted at in profiles of various new boom towns. But always, we noticed, there was a sense of promise, of accomplishment. We began to glimpse that the Amazon is an idea the Brazilians need, a romantic vision of a world of simple values and unlimited opportunity. The government casts much of what is happening there as symbolic of the Brazilian Dream—Brazil, unlike other Latin American nations, is destined for greatness. The idea is one that has long been held fundamental as Brazilians settle down to discuss their national psyche, something like the idea of Manifest Destiny promoted in the United States in the early 19th century. Many Brazilian journalists are apparently infected with the notion and their stories sometimes read like Chamber of Commerce press releases.

A member of one of Brazil's leading business families tried to put the Amazon mystique into perspective for us one day during an off-the-record lunch—a cautious habit, he explained to us, that he had not gotten over from the days a few years back when any public statements could cause problems with the government. His company, he said, had considered investing some of its substantial assets in the Amazon, but decided that despite what the boosters were saying, it was too much of a risk. He was apologetic about the decision, as if business concerns had forced him to go against the national welfare. Or, at the very least, that the masculine, adventurous course was to plunge into the Amazon and that he was abdicating a certain amount of manhood by going the other way—into the electronics business, as it happened.

"I said before that the Amazon is to us what Alaska is to you," he continued, halving a grilled prawn the size of a lobster. He meant that the Amazon is the unknown frontier, open, unregulated space which holds untold riches—not the least of which is the suggestion of a better life. The mere idea of its existence, simply the fact that it is there, he argued, is as comforting to the Brazilian spirit as is their last frontier, Alaska, to Americans.

"But I would make one qualification," he added. "America may need the idea of Alaska, but it does not need the wealth it contains. I don't think the future of your country depends on what you do with Alaska. That is not the case with Brazil and the Amazon."

Later, we were invited to a dinner party given by an equally prominent family. When we squinted from the edge of the long veranda, we could just make out the neighborhood where the Friends of the Indians were closing up shop far down the hill, a dim mess of light before the bright bulbs of downtown. The house we were in was on the highest inhabited point in Rio. Only God, in the form of the spread-armed Christ, was higher, glowing orange and standing watch over the city below.

But for all the exotic view, we were nowhere. Rio, we realized, is almost as far south of the Amazon as Miami is north and dining with the equivalent of Brazilian nobility was farther removed from the jungle than we had been in Washington and Chicago. To the people at the party, the Amazon was theoretical, a fairy tale that may have some relevance to their future in an abstract sense. In reality, they knew it only as magazine photos.

"I really should know about it," said one woman. "It seems fascinating, but it's so far away. It's like another country."

"Oh, don't write about the Amazon," another dinner companion implored. "You'll just make everyone in America think we're a bunch of savages. You know every time I go to the States, I think people half expect me to unpack a grass skirt."

"I know what you mean," said the hostess. "My friends in Europe think we have snakes crawling through the house."

She paused, then giggled. "But I just remembered, last week I did find a snake in the basement. One of the gardeners killed it. He said it was one of those *jararacas*. They're supposed to be very deadly."

"I wonder if they have them in the Amazon," someone said.

BRASILIA

Brasilia, at night, is deceptive. What is supposed to be the thriving capital of a booming nation is practically a ghost town. Its highways are lit by humming orange potassium street lights, inaudible in most cities where they are drowned out by the sounds of life. Lights flicker on and off in the clusters of indistinct glass office towers as cleaning workers prepare for the next morning's onslaught. Various floodlit monuments and statues provide the appropriate civic deities for a capital, but no one is out noticing. There are no evening strollers on the city's few sidewalks; no movie marquees; no restaurants with canopies fronting on the roads; not even traffic lights to force people to pause to observe the desolation.

We found some life around the grounds of the Hotel Nacional, although it was fleeting. An irregular procession of young women moved along the sidewalk, hips and shoulders swaying to their internal rhythms. They wore tight satiny pants in shiny royal blue, red or blaring yellow with knit tube tops and heavy makeup: the look of Las Vegas hookers—tawdry but not sloppy. Occasionally a car would pull to the curb and one would get in.

"Nice, huh?"

The cab driver laughed at us.

"Yes, nice. If you like boys. They're mostly boys. In this city the boys are more beautiful than the girls. One must be careful."

Brasilia, 550 miles and a painless jet flight northeast of Rio, was to be our last stop before the jungle. Unfortunately, we knew it would be a long one. We had been forewarned that to accomplish anything in the jungle—to visit the Indians, the gold mines and the great industrial projects—we were going to need approval from one ministry or another. Here all the people with an interest in the Amazon had a piece of the bureaucracy to call their own. We would have to pay a call on almost all if we were to piece together the many parts of this government that plan and carry out policy.

We were quite uncertain, however, about who exactly called the shots for the Amazon. Most of our questions to that effect in the United States, Sao Paulo and Rio had drawn vague responses. Certainly it was not the Brazilian Congress, which was merely a figurehead at the time. The best conclusion we could come up with was that the President had substantial powers and some select members of his cabinet participated in the process, but looming over them all was the final approval of the National Security Council, a collection of military leaders. Despite Brazil's promises of democratic reform, the country was still run largely by a military junta. We had already been warned we would have no access to security council members; we would have to piece together their thinking from some of the officials around them.

The city itself hinted at the schism between planning and practicality that we were to find endemic throughout our tour of Brasilia. "We build our cities to reflect our society," a priest told us on the first day of our stay. Father David Regan, who works with the National Council of Catholic Bishops and thus the de facto opposition party, was trying to explain Brasilia by day. "I don't think the architects intended it, but the two dominant buildings in Brasilia are not the Congress towers but the large banks in the center of town."

Indeed, the hulking black glass shapes of the Bank of Brazil and the Central Bank seemed much more the center of the city to the newcomer than the intended focal point—the thin, white matching pair of 25-story congressional office buildings, which sit alongside the Presidential Palace and Supreme Tribunal. But on closer inspection, the dual row of identical eight-story ministry buildings that relentlessly lead up to the triangle of powers is anything but insignificant. The repeating glass boxes seem to be the apotheosis of bureaucratic architecture, an endless line of sameness suggesting the permanent government is well entrenched even if the people are not.

Built by Socialists with the idea of setting a blueprint for an egalitarian society, Brasilia has become the perfect setting for a government of technocrats and retired colonels. It is neat and disciplined; one imagines platoons of troops must snipe cigarette butts from the manicured lawns at dawn. It is mechanistic; all right angles and sterile open spaces revealing the red clay foundation of the city. It is corporate; the intended worker housing allows for minute but steady increments of luxury to physically assert progress up the ladder of authority.

Actually, social engineering was only a secondary goal for Brasilia. The capital city had been on the national agenda since 1823 when a postscript to the Constitution of the new empire referred to the goal of establishing a capital "in the center of Brazil, among the springs at the joint source of the Paraguay and the Amazon." The goal was rearticulated in the Constitution of the new republic in 1891 and numerous false starts occurred over the next 60 years. Always the leaders of Brazil realized the need to open up the interior—as the United States was doing at the same period—but they never could muster the support, the resources or the national desire. Rio was too seductive to leave, Sao Paulo too prosperous.

In 1955 Juscelino Kubitschek was elected President of Brazil, and he was determined to be the midwife for this oft-aborted project. Kubitschek, an enormously popular president who instilled in the country a sense of destiny much as John Kennedy later did for the United States, planned Brasilia as the nation's man-on-the-moon project. To direct it he chose Oscar Niemeyer, already Latin America's most able disciple of Le Corbusier, father of the concept of the totally planned, mechanistic city.

What Niemeyer and Lucio Costa, the city planner, created looks, on a map, like an airplane. The fuselage has the triangle of powers—President, Congress, Supreme Court—up where the cockpit would be. First class is the dual row of boxes housing the ministries. A business and commercial district is in the center of the plane. The wings are residential blocks, composed of low apartment houses, schools, and stores that form communities, all designated numerically, as in "I live at L-43, B-4N." Running through the wings and fuselage are broad highways that meet in intricate webs of cloverleafs making traffic signals unnecessary. Sidewalks are rare.

The construction of Brasilia was a remarkable accomplishment, a tribute to the Brazilians' ability to visualize and carry out grand schemes. Yet planning-book marvels aside, the city has an unreal feeling about it. From a distance it looks like a cover painting for a volume of science fiction, sitting as it does on the high, treeless *planalto*, much too close to the oversize cumulus clouds dominating the blue sky. After seeing Brasilia for the first time, the Russian astronaut Yuri Gagarin exclaimed, "I hadn't expected to reach Mars so soon." The closer one gets, the odder it seems. This is not a city for people, an assessment even its creator has reluctantly acknowledged. "It had seemed," Niemeyer said, "during the initial solidarity that the children of Brasilia would grow without complexes, but instead it has become the most discriminating city in Brazil."

David Regan, the priest, said it better. "We have plenty of fountains here, but go 20 miles outside the city and you'll find people without water to make coffee."

This was the context in which we were going to have to try to understand the plan for the Amazon. Here in this social experiment gone wrong are all the parts for the country's next social experiment, the Amazon. In Brasilia the rich and powerful, driven by greed, paternalism or, perhaps, a sense of justice, look out of their glass boxes and contemplate a horizon of first the poor and then of limitless forest. But what is it they study? Is the forest to be exploited by the greedy? or opened up to the poor? And what does it mean for the nature there? How much is already gone and how fast is the rest going? Brasilia, still a few hundred miles south of the edge of the forest, is the beachhead from which Brazilians hope to invade and penetrate the impenetrable jungle. Before we could see that jungle, we had to penetrate the plans of the generals and economics professors.

Our initial encounters with "the government" proved disarming. We lunched with Ana Cabral, a young foreign ministry officer who was to arrange some interviews for us with a number of ministers. As if dispatched by Central Casting, she immediately set about to confirm our worst fears about the jungle.

"I envy you going to the Amazon," she said during the chow mein course. "Everyone should see the jungle now, because in a few years it will be gone." She said it with offhand candor, as though there was little question.

"Do you really believe that?" we asked.

"Oh, yes. Absolutely."

"How much is gone now?"

"Very much. I don't know the numbers. There are some people at the forest institute who could tell you. There is a man named Carlos Marx. They say he knows." Valverde also had mentioned this man who "studies satellite pictures" but Carlos Marx had to wait. The bureaucracy was opening its arms to us, which meant several days of being on call for hastily scheduled interviews. The very first fell through, but we learned more than we expected.

On a table in the outer office of the Minister of Mines and Energy we came across a blueprint for development, in the form of a glossy pamphlet. The Minister's assistant with whom we had an appointment stood us up, but the brochure spoke volumes. It was intended for foreign companies looking for new investments and spelled out how far the Brazilians would be willing to go in terms of tax breaks and loans to attract business to the Amazon. It began:

Until quite recently, Amazonia was called a poor region. It offers today a new image and possibilities which attract, in a competitive race, groups of businessmen and business representatives from all over the country and the world at large. Things are changing fast. Amazonia is no longer that legendary region reflected in the often superficial and inaccurate accounts of bygone explorers mythically reminiscing on its rivers, flora and fauna. Surveys and research studies carried out throughout the region have amply demonstrated that this is one of the few areas in the world still open to economic development, with natural resources of enormous proportions, such as iron ore deposits, cassiterite [tin] and bauxite [aluminum], manganese and other ferrous and nonferrous minerals. The true potential of the region's natural resources has become known through careful mapping using radar and basic research. Improvements in the means of transport and communication has put an end to the almost complete isolation of the area, encouraging spontaneous as well as planned occupation.

The brochure spoke of the incentives the government was willing to offer if companies would invest in the Amazon, including low-interest loans and big tax write-offs on profits earned elsewhere in the country as well as ten years of no taxes at all on profits generated in the Amazon. Any machinery brought from abroad would be charged greatly reduced import duties if it went to the Amazon region. The brochure seemed a clear invitation to unlimited exploitation.

As we spent more tedious days trudging from office to office in the capital, the story got a bit more complicated. Brazil's government was slowly opening up, the plaster of 16 years of military rule beginning to crumble. Censorship officially had ended, and bureaucratic controls were gradually being lifted. But while many officials practically gushed at the opportunity to talk to a journalist, a prerogative denied them for years, other officials continued to guard their information closely.

It became clear that even among the powerful policy makers there was no unity about what to do with the Amazon—except the conclusion that it cannot be left alone. The most objective officials bristled at the suggestion of foreign environmentalists that most of the Amazon should be preserved for further study. "Impossible," said one top Foreign Ministry official with a shrug. "It is half of our country. Do you honestly think we could leave it alone as some nature park for the rest of the world?" Others were more blunt, inviting the environmentalists to pay them to let the land remain fallow.

The Brazilian leaders tacitly agreed with the contention of the environmentalists that no one really knows much about the Amazon.

The Brazilian method of discovery, however, seemed to us to be one of trial and error. "We will make mistakes," said Paulo Yakota, the land colonization minister, "but there is enough land and enough time to make them—just as you had in the United States."

There was at least a rhetorical concern expressed for the environment—perhaps reflecting the fact that it is becoming a political issue. Yet how much of the nation's scientific resources are being directed toward the Amazon is debatable. After one session with the head of the National Research Council, several of his staffers stayed around to describe how little was actually being done on questions such as the effects of deforestation. They compared the Brazilian effort to the U.S. trying to conduct its space program with a handful of scientists and without computers.

Many of the discussions centered on the need for a comprehensive policy for dealing with the forest. Such a document had been drafted by a high-level government commission, and when we were there it had been sitting on the desk of President Joao Figueiredo awaiting action for more than a year. It had become a controversial report, though the public had as yet no idea what was in it. Nonetheless, environmentalists were calling it the last best hope for the jungle; development-minded businessmen said it would tie their hands.

Mauro Reis, a former college professor who heads the national forest service, is one informed land policy expert with whom we spoke. He had helped draft the report and described how it sets aside great national forests, Indian reserves and preserves for scientific study as well as some regions for development.

This was an astounding step for Brazil, he said, because there had never been any kind of policy to deal with the question of the trees in the Amazon. The draft had been worked up by a group of government officials and academics put together the year before in the wake of those demonstrations protesting the government plan to allow multinational timber companies unrestricted logging rights— the same plan that had galvanized Valverde. The committee responded with some firm guidelines on how development should take place. The policy draft talked of the need to preserve much of the Amazon and the danger of unrestricted development—the first time these issues had been raised on the government level. Distinct boundaries were drawn marking areas that could be logged, and those that could be used for agriculture. Existing Indian reserves were greatly expanded and a system of national parks set up. Reis admitted that many of the areas were marked off with a broad brush since there is little research to suggest accurately which areas are best suited for farming, for example. He said he expected the policy would go to Congress in a few weeks and would certainly be the subject of a great national debate.

That same day we sat with Paulo Yakota, widely regarded as a man with close ties to the inner circle of generals and planners who made the policy decisions for the country. When we asked about Reis's contention, his face crumpled into a tight-lipped sneer. "Do you want to know what will happen to the forest policy?" he said as he picked up a bound report from his desk. "This," and he dropped the report into his wastebasket. "It was done by radical environmentalists who do not know about the real world. The people who drew up that policy talk about the trees as the most important asset. I say the people are the most important."

A protégé of the powerful head of the Planning Ministry, Antonio Delfim Neto, Yakota is seen as a key figure in the future of the Amazon. An economics professor from Sao Paulo, he is in charge of all government colonization in the Amazon; conservationists hate him, claiming his settlement programs are causing uncontrolled destruction; the Catholic Church says his land reforms do too little for too few; the Agriculture Ministry loves him because of the huge increase in crops in the areas in which he has directed settlement and the Sao Paulo businessmen praise him for lobbying to keep the Amazon an open frontier.

"Our knowledge of the frontier is very small. I think it is dangerous to take this partial knowledge and use it for the whole forest. If we don't know, how can we make generalizations? I think it is dangerous to establish such a great quantity of constraints, especially when the discussion of the Amazon is not rational but emotional."

But Mario David Andreazza, the Minister of the Interior, spoke of another factor besides macroeconomics and demographics—his grandchildren. We hadn't expected this concern for future generations of a man whom ecologists once considered Public Enemy No. 1, the chief violator of the Amazon. It was Andreazza who, as Minister of Transportation in the early 1970s, directed the construction of the TransAmazon Highway, the 4,000-kilometer road that slashes the jungle from the Atlantic Ocean to the border near Peru and opened up huge areas to settlers.

Originally the highway was to be a funnel to drain the people-bloated Northeast cities into the people-starved Amazon basin. Construction of the highway included towns for the settlers who, the government hoped, would spread back from the road, clearing all the trees for their farms and cattle ranches. This was to serve the dual function of winning large amounts of jungle and easing the discontent of the Northeast. The road was the key; all development would spring from it.

The road was also a mighty probe into the body of the jungle; the first time anyone had tried to get under the seamless green skin of the treetops away from the rivers to look at what was underneath, where almost no one ever went. The TransAmazon Highway was the first incision and the result was the opening of the "new Amazon," the latest discovery by man of a million-year-old marvel. There was too much at stake to wait, so, once the decision was made, plans were laid within a matter of weeks to push through the jungle. Andreazza was put in charge. Money was no object; the road would move in a straight line across the continent and the settlers would follow. Never mind that no one knew what the terrain was like until they were on top of it and discovered that maybe the road should have gone elsewhere, or what crops the soil would grow, or what happened when you cleared the trees away or what you did when you cut through a tribal hunting ground, or how farmers unsuccessful in a dry harsh climate were going to be any more successful in a wet harsh climate. Those were not the concerns. The object was to get the highway built, and Andreazza succeeded. But now Andreazza had become a born-again minister who publicly reversed his development-at-any-cost philosophy and claimed he was trying to inject rationality into the push westward.

Andreazza is no inconsequential force. A former colonel, he has been in ministerial offices since the 1964 coup, longer than anyone else in Brasilia. He has built a substantial private power base for himself—as well as, some say, an enormous personal fortune—

through the large number of jobs his position enables him to bestow. When we met him, he comported himself like the highest-class Chicago ward boss, though with his tanned face, his wavy silver hair and fine-cut silk suit, he looked like a million bucks on Miami Beach.

Just getting through the veil of Andreazza's staff was an undertaking. A press secretary ushered us through a series of offices and reception rooms, where we met along the way an array of secretaries, press agents, body guards, official photographers and administrative assistants. Most reappeared at a long conference table, poised with reports, charts and slides. Yet Andreazza damped their eager faces with a wave of his hand. This was a subject he would speak about without props.

"In 20 years the Amazon will be the most important region of the country. The roads will be paved, the mineral riches will be developed and the colonization projects will bring millions into the area. People are always naturally afraid of these great projects, but where would we be without them?" Beaming with a sort of paternal pride, Andreazza described how when he first went to Altamira, one of the new cities on the TransAmazon Highway, it had one jeep and 5,000 residents. "Now there are 50,000 residents and 4,000 vehicles."

It was the highway, he said, that taught the Brazilians some things about the jungle. The maps made by aerial radar surveys and the geological expeditions that went along with the road provided volumes of new data as did the simple process of knocking down trees and moving dirt around. Among the things learned was that the jungle is not flat—meaning its rivers can generate hydroelectric power —and that it contains mineral deposits. "Every day that passes, we find new riches, new opportunities."

Andreazza said the initial plans for the highway came from that persistent Brazilian fear that if they did not occupy the Amazon, somebody else, meaning some foreign power, would. *Ocupar Para Nao Entregar* (Occupy So As Not To Surrender), has been the motto of military leaders and politicians who endorse this justification for development. "The world does not understand this. International organizations talked of this as land that does not belong to anyone, but it is our land."

After the initial all-out push requiring hundreds of millions of dollars to build the highway, truck the settlers in, and raze the jungle for cattle ranches, Andreazza said he had a change of heart. "I thought, my grandchildren must live with what I do now. What we develop must be compatible with the ecosystem. We will permit the commercial exploitation of wood, but it must be accompanied by reforestation; what you take out you must put back in."

The giant cattle ranches, he claimed, were a "serious mistake," and he would approve no new large ranching projects in the forest. He also said he now considered the Indians "part of the forest and moving them is the same as killing them." Relocation of tribes in the way of roads had been a frequent phenomenon in Andreazza's administration. He is making sure, he said, that the "question of the Indians has priority over economic problems. We have an obligation to protect them."

But then Andreazza added that these were the ideals, and no more than that. He, who held absolute control of nearly every government initiative in the jungle, no longer can significantly alter the course of its development; the move to exploit it has acquired a momentum of its own.

"The Amazon is 500 million hectares, and it is impossible to know what happens in all parts. It is a world without end,"—he laughed and corrected himself—"a green world without end."

With the initial bout of interviews over, we had time to look for Carlos Marx. Marx is a well-kept secret in Brasilia. He is the man with the pictures, the man the national forest service has brought in to interpret U.S. satellite surveys of the Amazon and estimate how much is gone.

That had become our obsession: getting hold of some reliable figure of how much of the Amazon is gone. It is not the only important question, but it seemed a necessary starting point. Any discussion of the problem had to hinge on this number. We put the question to all the officials we interviewed—those in charge of trees, roads, soil and minerals—and got jokes, shrugs, excuses and an occasional guess, but no answers. Marx, though, was supposed to be the man who knew and thus we were somewhat surprised when, after we located his office and called for an appointment, he said simply, "Sure, come right over."

Like many scientists, Marx is not a man to push himself into public view, yet he seemed genuinely gleeful to see a couple of reporters. The plat books and charts that fill his office have lots of answers but no one outside the government had asked the questions. Marx, a wiry, energetic college professor with a goatee and a nervous manner, admitted his estimates were rough, but they were much better than guesses.

"I suppose you want to know the big number. Well it's not as big as you think. I would say that two percent of the Amazon in Brazil has been cleared," he said, spreading out a collection of photos provided by Landsat, the United States surveillance satellite that can pick out a cow in a field from 100 miles above the globe.

Two percent seemed like nothing, hardly justification for the international furor over the issue. Thirty percent is the figure commonly and blithely tossed about by even the most respected scientists. Two percent was just a little higher than the numbers used in response to international critics by Brazilian officials who say, "See? We're not doing anything wrong, so why don't you leave us alone?"

We thought Marx was finished. He wasn't. "However—" he began again, letting the word drift off as he rummaged through more piles. Marx was teasingly playing up the suspense for his captive audience. Minutes went by. "However, there are some other things to consider."

Marx explained that the two percent figure refers to all the 500 million hectares legally designated as "Amazon" by the Brazilian government. But much of that area is not forest. Some is natural grassland and some the marshy flood plains along the major rivers. About 280 million hectares are considered forest, so the 10 million hectares that have been destroyed really represent 3.6 percent of the trees.

Still, not exactly cataclysmic. Marx nodded. There were two other factors, he said. The satellite has a hard time distinguishing natural forest from the poor secondary growth that struggles up after the original cover is stripped.

"I can assure you that it does not all immediately turn to desert. There is something there, even if it may not be of much use to anyone." Marx conceded that because of this, the estimates may be higher, "but not much higher."

It was the second factor which troubled him: "The rate. That is what you must pay attention to. We first surveyed in 1975. Then again in 1978. We found a 100 percent increase in the rate of destruction. That slowed a little in our 1980 survey, but not by much."

He walked to a wall map with brightly colored splotches. "These are the endangered areas." He hit them with a pointer like the professor he was: the highway through Rondonia; the highway from Cuiaba north to Santarem; a huge chunk in the south of the state of Para; the swath south of the Amazon River along the TransAmazon Highway; the road from Brasilia to Belem and the area around Manaus, the city in the center of the jungle.

"Here the forest is falling very fast. Ten percent of Para is gone; the same in Rondonia. This is where we see what can happen. And it can happen very fast. But at the same time, you see the heart of the Amazon"—he pointed to the western region that runs to the Peruvian border—"is untouched."

Marx studied the endangered areas more closely. He opened a wide black plat book filled with pages of blue-and-white maps that looked like engineers' drawings. He smiled.

"What we have here are the details of every property in the south of Para. We know where their boundaries are and how much they have cut." The names were familiar. Volkswagen, Lunardelli, Bradesco. On some of the pages, the light areas representing deforestation were almost continuous; neat squares marching across the sheet.

"I think maybe this is a little dangerous," he said with an impish grin. The black book represents hard data and a basis for comparison as well as a list of names; the debate has never involved this kind of information before. He is, this small professor, a powerful man, though he didn't seem to realize it. In a country where truly valuable information is tightly controlled, his data will increasingly be crucial to anyone trying to make or influence policy.

Marx held up the book with both hands, like a trophy. "I don't know what these maps will do for my job, but let's publish them and see."

The man with the most knowledge about the problem sobered suddenly. He referred to INCRA, Yakota's colonization agency, as "the agency of deforestation," and he worried that his own "third-rate department" of forestry is powerless to change anyone's mind.

But he has faith. "We have this," he said, patting the book. "We have the pictures."

The gaps in the foliage on Marx's maps are inhabited by the settlers, ranchers and lumbermen already encouraged there by the government's incentives. But hidden in the smallest clearings are a less visible—and, from the forest's perspective, less destructive—people. Dotted in tiny villages across the Amazon are the people viewed as part native animal, part human being and whom no one knows what to do with—the Indians.

The Indians are Ivan Zanoni's problem: what to do with them when some want to do away with them, some want to fight to save them and most just don't care.

Zanoni is one of the top officials of FUNAI, the national Indian agency charged with protecting the rights of the nation's 200,000 or so Indians, most of whom are in the Amazon. It is the contention of the agency's legion of critics—mostly foreigners—that FUNAI's real function is not to protect but to exterminate the tribes who stand in the way of Brazilian development.

The image of the Brazilian government tolerating, even encouraging, the extinction of native tribes comes primarily from a 1968 government report charging the Indian Protection Service, FUNAI's predecessor, with corruption, torture, murder and slave trading. The report told a miserable tale of official betrayal of defenseless people. The reaction, in Brazil and around the world, was explosive. As a result, 134 employees of the service were charged with crimes and the agency was disbanded and replaced by FUNAI. The image, however, wouldn't dissolve. There were accusations in the 1970s of mismanagement and corruption as the agency became a dispenser of sinecures to retired military men. Agency presidents changed often. The critics still charge that while methods may have changed over the years, the effect remains the same: whatever the motivation, Indians are fast disappearing. From the Indians' perspective, FUNAI, like the Indian Protection Service before it, is consistently malevolent.

Zanoni's manner and appearance did little to dispel this image. Overly polite with us, he kept a humorless, open-mouthed smile in place beneath a bushy mustache, so that it was hard to read sincerity in his face. An air force officer who was trained in Texas, he speaks flawless, educated English. He once taught sociology and prefers the title professor to colonel. It had been widely reported that during the crackdown on the left in the late 1960s, he had been a government "interrogator."

"What can I do for you?" Zanoni said. We wanted permission to visit an Indian tribe. Zanoni, still smiling his joyless smile, quickly acceded to our request to visit the tribe of our choice.

"Just like that?"

"Just like that." The smile widened as if he would attempt to swallow us. He laughed when we reminded him that many anthropologists were kept waiting for months before receiving similar permission.

"Yes, the anthropologists," he said. "They are not the only ones who are important. The press is important." We were beginning to realize that public relations had arrived in Brasilia though it was still nascent enough to allow the official government spokesman, Octavio Bonfim, to claim that the Indians were an "insignificant problem overcovered by the press" and that it was simply a question of "an inferior culture meeting a superior one with predictable results."

Zanoni was more discreet. "We do not have the responsibility for all the Indians who have died since the Portuguese came here. Our responsibility is the living and our mistakes will be judged from here to the future." For him, the question of what to do with the Indians is resolved; only the logistics of accomplishing it remain. "We hope that, naturally, we can bring the Indian into Brazilian society."

The integration concept puts FUNAI staff to work with tribes, teaching them language and cultural skills for the day the leading edge of the frontier arrives at their villages. It is, many anthropologists claim, the surest way to destroy them.

"We call it integricide," Paulo Suess, head of the Catholic Church's admittedly radical commission to protect the Indians, said later. "By integrating the Indian people you often kill them, or at least their culture. FUNAI is the instrument of a society that does not respect the Indian people's right to live."

Zanoni did not strike us as a thoughtless man. In one respect, this hard-line colonel agrees with the Marxist priest. Both feel it is

Brazilian society as a whole that has been immune from caring about this anachronistic obstacle in their path to greatness.

"The Indian issue is a national issue, not just a FUNAI issue," said Zanoni. "We have to make the nation conscious. That was one of the mistakes the United States Bureau of Indian Affairs made; they worked only on the Indians, not on American society."

Perhaps that was why Zanoni gave us immediate permission to visit a tribe. Yet as we left with the small pile of official forms to fill out, we couldn't help but feel this man's plan for the Indians was as inscrutable as his smile.

We met our first Indian not in the depths of the forest, as we had pictured, but in Brasilia.

The first time we saw Mario Juruna, a chief of the Xavante tribe and the most famous Indian in Brazil, he left us laughing. We were in a Sao Paulo hotel, idly flipping channels on the color TV. A commercial came on, filling the screen with a man's broad, flat face. He had a wide nose, big round holes in his ear lobes and a cap of shiny black hair that looked as if it had been cut under a bowl. He was holding a bottle and spoke haltingly. We immediately recognized him as Juruna. There had been stories and photographs in several Sao Paulo papers about how the Amazon chieftain was planning to run for Congress. The liberal dailies portrayed him as an important symbol of the Indians and a spokesman for their rights. He had emerged from a village only a few years ago. Now he was selling a health tonic.

It could be said that Mario Juruna had taken to integration pretty well. He is, of the Amazon Indians, probably the most integrated in the country and has achieved something most Brazilians, whatever their heritage, can only dream about: superstardom. The Indian chief from the Mato Grosso, who did not see a white man until he was 17, has become a major media figure, popping up in interviews, ads and celebrity columns with remarkable regularity. He is part of the grist that keeps a gossip-hungry audience titillated, joining in one weeks' worth of newspapers and magazines the ranks of popular singers and starlets as well as Raul "Doca" Street, the playboy dubbed the "macho murderer" for shooting his unfaithful girlfriend model in the face; Hosmany Ramos, the plastic surgeon accused of being a jewel thief, and Jorge Barbudo, the Robin Hood of the Rio slums who administers vigilante justice to criminals.

Juruna to us was becoming a curious symbol of the jungle and its inhabitants. We saw him as an appropriately absurd figure, at once laughable and tragic; primeval man in the 20th century. He was a darling of the fashionable liberals who invited him to their dinner parties in a gesture of red-man radical chic; the politicians saw him as a marionette who could mouth their rhetoric and draw a crowd. Yet, we thought, the puppet had to have a life of his own.

We talked about Juruna a lot, and so we were stunned when, coming into the lobby of the Hotel Nacional in Brasilia, we saw him standing in the center of the room. The lobby of the Nacional was, as usual, a crossroads of commerce: a delegation from one of the black African nations where Brazil is trying to promote trade; a few Iraqis perhaps there to discuss the railroad and highway system Brazilian contractors are building for them on the other side of the world; a former prime minister of Japan in town on behalf of one of the dozens of Japanese firms with a major financial presence in the country.

In the middle of it all was Chief Juruna, alone and apparently waiting for someone. He wore a gray shirt and wide brown tie that came about halfway down his swelling middle—a government official had once told him he had to wear a tie and Juruna responded by requiring all government men who came to his village to wear head-dresses. From his shoulder hung a cassette tape recorder and a small airline bag with an STP Oil Treatment sticker on it. He had explained in a recent Brazilian magazine interview that he kept the tape recorder with him at all times to "record the lies of the white man."

Only at first glance did he look clownish, a country rube on Fifth Avenue. His hard brown eyes were set in a formidable stare. He stood with his thick arms folded, taking in the business around him. Everyone kept his distance; so did we, still in the nervous first stages of dealing with FUNAI.

Eventually we arranged an appointment through Juruna's promoters at the Democratic Labor Party. Lionel Brizola, the party leader and a candidate for governor of Rio, appeared first. He was obviously sensitive to the idea of Juruna being a party tool and said he thought it was an alliance that could benefit both sides. "Chief Juruna fits in with our party philosophy. We are the party of those outside the system—the blacks, the poor and Indians. Of all those minorities, the Chief is the most widely known symbol in Brazil. We think he will get the most votes of any congressman from Rio."

Brizola offered only one caution—the Chief sometimes has a short attention span and gets tired. "Gentlemen, this is Chief Juruna," he said, then left the room.

Juruna shook our hands, then sat down at the table and folded his own.

The first thing we noticed was his hair. The bowl look was gone, replaced by a spiky crew cut that made him seem bulkier. He had no neck, and his face, dominated by a thick nose, appeared so wide that it almost met his rounded shoulders. He wore a plaid shirt, tan jeans and, on his orange-brown arm, a large watch.

Juruna said he is in his early 40s—he didn't know the years exactly—and comes from a Xavante tribe in the northwest corner of Mato Grosso state. His tribe lives on the west bank of the Rio das Mortes, the River of the Dead.

"It was called that because any white man who crossed would die," he said, alluding to the well-known fierceness of the Xavante warriors decades ago.

But Juruna is not a fierce man. Although he comes from a long line of warrior chiefs, he decided at an early age that "I would war with my mouth." His adversary would be the white man.

He thinks the first white man he saw was in 1958. He had been taught whites were his enemy—the tribe's oral history had many tales of their shooting Indians. "I heard the stories. But I had no idea what they were talking about. I never believed they existed until one day I saw a man on a horse. I didn't get too close. I just watched."

There would be many more opportunities. Xavante land became the first of the big Amazon cattle ranches. In fact, Juruna was one of those Herminio Ometto, the Godfather of the Amazon we had met in Sao Paulo, meant in his offhand remark about having to move a few Indian tribes.

"Suia-Micu," Juruna snorted when we mentioned the name of Ometto's ranch. "That is Indian land."

It was that and other forced exoduses, eventually reducing the

Xavante nation from 30,000 to 4,500, that made Juruna realize the tribes would have to find new ways to deal with whites. He learned his Portuguese—his most potent weapon—from missionaries and cowboys. He speaks a rough version of it but occasionally crafted a sentence that was so correct we wondered if it was lifted from a script.

"I wanted to learn Portuguese so I could say to the white man, 'Stop.'"

Juruna got his soapbox in 1980 when he was invited to speak at an international Indian forum in Rotterdam, the Netherlands. FUNAI refused to let him go but Juruna, with the help of some anthropologists, did a remarkable thing: he challenged the government and won. In a widely covered case, the Supreme Court eventually ruled in his favor and he was issued a passport. The event was rare in a country where for almost two decades, nobody—and especially not a second-class citizen—beat the government. He began to spend more time in Brasilia and Rio.

But Chief Juruna would say little about what his life was like and brushed off personal questions. "I am not important. What I do is important." Then he yawned wide and long, called for a glass of water and, when it came, shot it down his throat in a single gulp.

Juruna had a speech to make and he wanted to be sure he got it all in.

"FUNAI is of the white man and it will not defend me. I have to defend myself and all the Indians. The Indian has more rights than the white man. We are the true Brazilians. We have suffered. We have been expelled. We have been hungry. Now we have nothing they can take away."

He pounded the table in a mechanical gesture that seemed rehearsed.

"What is most important is that our land be marked so the white settlers cannot come in and take it. I want the Indians to have farm equipment and plows. They must have medical help and they must have schools. That is what I will do.

"And I will end FUNAI."

He stopped, as if a switch had been turned off. He yawned again, this time audibly. Kelly had removed his eyeglasses and Juruna picked them up. He put them on, mugging. He listlessly answered some more questions, then took London's glasses and put them over

the other pair. Everyone laughed. And kept laughing, though it became uncomfortable as he continued the childish charade for too
many minutes.

The Chief, it seemed, could be difficult at times. On one of his
first trips to Brasilia, he made the cab driver circle the block until the
meter registered a fee large enough for his stature as a chief. When he
arrived at the modest Labor Party headquarters in a Rio residential
neighborhood, he pointed to a nearby mansion and told his new
allies, "That is a house fit for a chief. That is where I should stay."

He yawned again and it seemed the interview was ended. We
asked him casually if he liked Rio. Juruna put the glasses down and
said something he had not rehearsed.

"The white man is crazy. In the forest, he kills the hunting. He
kills the fishing. He kills the forest. White man is horrible. Every day
I learn much. His cities are worse than anything the Indians have.
The Indians do not have crime, pollution, liars. People who exploit
each other. Deceive each other." He pounded the table with each
sentence, this time moving his body behind his arm. "We have beautiful forest and the water is clear. We live with the forest. Not like
Rio."

Big city life has certainly taken its toll on the Chief. He is
overweight and the FUNAI people said he has a heart problem. He
admitted he has no friends and finds it hard to go back to his village.

As we were leaving, Juruna smiled and asked us each for a
dollar, a souvenir, he said. It is Indian custom to give a chief gifts.
He scowled fiercely as a party photographer took a snapshot of him
sitting with us. Then Mario Juruna turned and slowly walked upstairs
to the small room he stayed in.

One of the party faithful was busy at his typewriter. "So long for
now, Chief," he said, without glancing up.

B R-3 6 4

By the time we set out from Brasilia the vision of the Amazon as a lazy tropical paradise had left our minds. London's first impressions of poisonous snakes and Indians with blowguns hunting monkeys now seemed imagined; the Amazon even had fire hydrants, an executive of the national utilities company had told us.

We chose to begin in Cuiaba, the capital of the State of Mato Grosso. Known as the gateway city to the Amazon, Cuiaba has served as the link between the settled south and the unexplored north for almost a century. Brazil's horizon once ended here. Only recently has the government and the rest of the country stopped believing that beyond the horizon is an untamable forest which swallows up all who enter. News has begun to flow back through Cuiaba to the displaced tenant farmers in the south, the urban slum dwellers around Sao Paulo and the drought-stricken peons to the northeast that this land can sustain life. They flock through here in droves now, funneling thickly into the bus station, waiting to trail out again along the roads to the jungle.

We went to the cavernous precast-concrete bus station in Cuiaba to capture sights and sounds of lives in transition. It was our first visit into the field. Still shy and tentative, we didn't talk to anyone, just walked around and eavesdropped. The station was in a frenzy. It looked as if many of the people had been there for days, sleeping contorted among an array of fraying suitcases, cardboard boxes and plastic-wrapped parcels—the baggage of a people in flight. Many of the women were pregnant, and many more were burdened with wailing infants. Men congregated in bunches and we heard them mention towns like Ouro Preto and Ariquemes, which are being settled according to INCRA's plan. We heard them talk of *indios* with the same curious tone we had—what were Indians like, what did they want? We heard talk of *violencia* but not of what caused it.

Our impressions were inexact, of course. We were as nervous as these travelers, for Cuiaba was our watershed, too. Yet we knew we were going on, and so did they. Most of the men wore new straw cowboy hats. The talk of fears, problems, and danger seemed just talk: they would not be stopped. All the men had to do was look over their shoulders to see their families and belongings, all on the floor of the Cuiaba bus station. Their decisions had been made. They were living a great dream. No doubt, there had come a time when they, like Huck Finn, had said to themselves, "I reckon I got to light out for the territory ahead of the rest."

Our clumsiness in delving into these lives was best shown by our choice of companionship. The first person we spent time with on the frontier was not a settler, not a dreamer, and anything but a booster of the Amazon: Oldemar Oliveira, the corned beef king of Cuiaba.

Oliveira took us on a tour of the town in his tidy white Volkswagen.

"I'm from the civilized part of Brazil, not this jungle," he boasted. "It's horrible here. These people have been isolated from the rest of Brazil for 250 years. We don't even speak the same language. I can't understand them." He was speaking English affectedly, pronouncing the word "cawn't."

"Look at that," he said, pointing to a road crew. "You know what they are doing? They are paving over the river. Do you know why? They are doing it because so many people drive into it. These people do not know how to drive. They know nothing. They are not civilized."

Oliveira came to Cuiaba because the new slaughterhouse there offered him four times what he made in Sao Paulo. For 22 years he had worked for an English meat-packing company, most recently as head of its corned beef department. Corned beef is very important to the new plant because, due to poor inspection standards, Europe and the U.S. will not buy Brazilian meat on the bone. But the slaughterhouse is financed with government loans that require that some of its products be exported, and corned beef is the solution.

The combination of his previous employer and his importance to the present operation gave Oliveira a decidedly colonial bearing. When he talked of teaching his skills to the locals, it was as if he was proudly shouldering the white man's burden. "Sometimes I feel more English than Brazilian. I take tea instead of this disgusting coffee."

And no colonial administrator could have looked more the part than the thin and nervous Oliveira with his dark hair neatly parted and pomaded; thick, clipped mustache; sunglasses; plaid bermudas and dark socks. He was loath to sweat and quick with a handkerchief to wipe his brow or rub his hands.

His slaughterhouse, owned by a large packing company from the south, was one of the first industrial enterprises in the Amazon. It services the giant cattle ranches that spread out to the north and west. If Cuiaba is the beginning of the road for the people, it is the end of the road for the cattle. Business and government types had spoken of this slaughterhouse as a showpiece; Oliveira thought it a joke.

As he put on white coat, hard hat and bloodstained boots to give us a tour, he began a litany of complaints: supplies were too distant, skilled labor too scarce. The ramp to the killing room, he continued as we approached the first step from cow to corned beef, was too long. The cows had too much time to panic.

Inside was a little vision of hell. The executioner was using a sledgehammer. "He's supposed to be using a pneumatic hammer, but we're missing a part and it's going to take a long while to get it out here," Oldemar said, shaking his head. "It's actually illegal to do it this way."

Taken up by one leg to a conveyor, the cows had their throats slit in one motion. Carcasses of bleeding animals swung, one after another, from a chain that moved through a huge white-tiled room. Dozens of figures in white coats and helmets ran among them with flashing knives.

"We employ 1,500 people here—it is the biggest factory in Cuiaba. But even though the minimum wage is lower, we spend more on labor because we need two Cuiabans to do what one Paulista does." Oliveira attributed that to the social history of the area. "It goes way back. There were only two classes out here. Those with the enormous farms who were very rich and the poor who were content to fish."

As Oliveira took us from room to room of the model plant, the cows gradually were transformed into a collection of parts: guts dropped down a hole to the sausage and tallow departments; skin to the tannery; washed and scraped carcasses to the chilling room; finally an assortment of meat to the corned beef cannery.

"This is my department. You can see how clean it is," Oliveira said, allowing himself a thin smile under the mustache.

Not far from Oliveira's slaughterhouse runs the road called BR-364. It is one of the two main highways linking Cuiaba to the heart of the Amazon; the other being the Cuiaba-Santarem Highway, shooting straight north for 1,500 unpaved miles until it runs out at the Amazon River.

BR-364 connects Sao Paulo to Porto Velho, a distance of 2,500 miles. From Sao Paulo to Cuiaba the road is smoothly paved, and the journey long yet manageable. From Cuiaba to Porto Velho the road is not paved, and it takes three days to drive in the dry season of May to November. When it rains, the trip can take 40 days. People die on buses stuck in mud and rot in their seats before they can be buried in the next town. Yet, for many of the travelers in the bus station in

Cuiaba this is the road to the promised land. We followed their route to Ji Parana, the outpost for thousands of settlers who come up BR-364 from Cuiaba and scatter like pigeons into the surrounding jungle.

Set on BR-364 in the state of Rondonia, Ji Parana has burst from a small town of 9,000 settlers in 1970 to 122,000 inhabitants, according to the 1980 census. The town seemed really no more than a blown-up version of the chaos of the Cuiaba bus station. Sewers, water, electricity, roads, schools, hospitals can't come as fast as the immigrants. And so the streets are rambling bogs, the air stinks of fetid meat, and the infant mortality rate is an incredible 40 percent.

Commerce has the feel of an Arabian bazaar; merchants use every available space along wood-plank sidewalks to hawk axes, chain saws, rifles and even TV sets. The TV salesmen have to be particularly skilled, because there is no reception yet in Ji Parana. Tinny loudspeakers blare barely recognizable American tunes, bringing Motown to boomtown, and police stalk along, their pistol belts slung low, the holster ready for a quick draw. Order is maintained only by a sort of fundamental good nature on the part of the settlers who are convinced there is enough to go around for everyone.

The newspapers we read while we were there, however, let on that the prevailing amity could not conquer all. A hired gunman had confessed to killing a lawyer over a land dispute, though he had not revealed who had hired him. The government was very concerned with an outbreak of rabid dogs. An expedition to contact a previously hidden Indian tribe, the Uru-Eu-Wau-Wau, had turned back because all its members were stricken with malaria. Several doctors were advertising their prowess at curing venereal disease while half a dozen lawyers announced that they were available for defense of criminal charges.

A map would show that Ji Parana is at last the jungle. But we couldn't see it and the people here seemed uninterested in its whereabouts. The jungle has been put down and beaten as far as these hearty settlers were concerned. Only malaria mosquitoes and an occasional Indian village in the wrong place are reminders that the town and farms around were once tropical forest as remote and lush as anywhere in the world.

We moved on from Ji Parana in a jeep to visit the farms and

farmers along BR-364. Our guide was an employee of Paulo Yakota's INCRA—Carlos Fontenele, who joined the land agency because he believed in land reform and thought that Rondonia could be the stage for his ideals. Because Rondonia was not yet a state, the federal government owned all the land and had an opportunity to develop settlement policies designed to accommodate a large number of settlers. But Fontenele thought the government had blown its chance.

"We had an opportunity to do everything right, to give the right amount of land to people who deserved it. But they came too fast." He said that the year he joined the land agency, INCRA had sold, for a nominal fee, 20,000 titles to mostly 50-hectare plots. The same year, 90,000 people with no titles came to settle. All the carefully planned towns were overwhelmed; Ji Parana was a striking example. In 1977 the Brazilian government decided the flood of immigrants was getting out of control and to dissuade them it began to circulate rumors of hardships and disease in the jungle. We had overheard such horrendous stories in the bus station in Cuiaba. But the migration never paused.

The plans for an egalitarian settlement policy of everyone owning a small plot were upset by swarms of land-hungry settlers. Some carved out settlements before government surveyors even mapped out the areas, and the government allowed the people to stay on their new land. Some farmers grew homesick and sold their land to others who accumulated larger and larger plots. And, Fontenele said, there was talk of corruption and land accumulation by improper means.

We asked him if he was disillusioned. "A little," he confessed. "But what has happened has happened because of the hunger and desire of the people. Not by the dictatorship of the government."

Fontenele told us we would not be disappointed if it was the spirit of a *renascimento*, a rebirth, we were looking for. "You will find it in these people. And courage. Above all you will find courage."

He took us to a shack alongside an artery of BR-364, and we waded through mud to the open entrance.

The simple-minded grin on Antonio Pinheiro's face best explained to us the crazy relentless optimism that has seized this part of the world. His wide, gap-toothed smile spread across a sallow face which should have been incapable of boasting happiness. Pinheiro had just left the hospital after his third malaria attack of the year. His wife was eight months pregnant with their fifth child. Crops on his land 40 kilometers away were unattended because neither he nor his wife was well enough to travel. The family was living in this tiny dark shed surrounded by mud and Pinheiro was picking up a little money doing odd jobs on someone else's farm. Yet he saw no reason to be gloomy.

"I came here hungry, and now I have land worth 50,000 cruzeiros [about $4,000]," he said in a slow, high-pitched voice. "I came to look for a better life. It is hard here, but it is better."

We wanted to take a picture of the ragged family, but the mother protested. "They're so dirty. They look like Indians. Wait."

She wiped the children's faces and dressed the two boys in red shorts and T-shirts, the two girls in party dresses that had been washed many times.

"Now they look like my children," she said. Indeed, as they stood in front of the tilting bamboo shack, they did. Beneath thin smiles they wore their mother's look of apprehension, as if they were about to swim for the first time. Only the father's smile was untroubled.

Alfonso Andrade was one of the men Pinheiro pointed to in justification of his smile. Andrade had made it. He was shooting pool in his general store and asked the two of us when we wandered in early the next morning if we cared to join him for a friendly wager. The burly Andrade and his skinny friend with a long dark face and gray beard looked seedy enough to be good pool players, but appearances were deceiving. We couldn't seem to lose. The stakes were shots of cachaca—at 9 in the morning.

While we played and drank, farmers came in to pick up supplies. Sometimes they paid in money, sometimes they promised to deliver a hen or a pig. Andrade's wife conducted this commerce.

As Andrade lined up his wayward shots, he talked about his life. He seemed flattered that anyone was interested, and gleefully unhesitant to express his views. "There is no better place in Brazil for opportunity. What I've done in four years here, I couldn't do in a lifetime somewhere else."

Andrade had acquired 100 hectares from the government and 100 hectares from a friend who had sold his land to Andrade rather than sell it back to the government as the law required. He had 360 head of cattle, and grew rice, corn and coffee. "And last month I bought a tractor."

He took us to see his domain. We walked behind the store to his home—a series of rooms set on a concrete floor. In the living room was a picture of Christ the Redeemer proclaiming "God Bless This House." On the opposite wall was a calendar with a kneeling blonde in black lace panties about to pull up her T-shirt.

Andrade called his family. They came, one after another after another. Finally there were nine, accompanied by a large black hound. Andrade's wife was 12 years old when she married him; she had given birth to eight children and had just turned 30. She raised the children and ran the general store in which we had shot pool.

We walked out back with Andrade to a fenced yard which held pigs, chickens, a pet deer and an outhouse. Beyond the fence were humped white cows, grazing in thick grass that came up to their bellies. Western style, we draped our arms over the top rung of the fence, put our feet on the bottom board and talked, staring out into the distance.

"I had 75 hectares in Sao Paulo and grew cotton. When the price of cotton was cut in half, the bank took my land. My brother-in-law was here and I came to see. I liked it. I sold my Volkswagen and bought this land right then. I went back to pick up my family."

When the family arrived, he continued, they stood and looked at a solid wall of forest—their new home. Nobody cried. Eventually Andrade, with his wife and young sons, cleared the trees with machetes and axes. He first planted beans and rice then used that income to start a cattle herd, an accomplishment that makes him something of an important man here.

We asked the inevitable, self-evident question: had it been hard work? Andrade turned and half-grimaced, half-smiled, baring two gold teeth.

"Yes, it was, but it was—how do you say?—obligatory. I had a chance to do this before in Sao Paulo and I lost it. I will not lose it again."

At least if Andrade loses this chance, it won't be his fault. For all his brimming confidence, Andrade does not share the simple faith of the grinning Pinheiro.

"If we come back in five years," we asked, "will we find 2,000 hectares covered with cattle?"

"Could be. Or could be desert," said the suddenly remote settler. "Only God knows."

With Fontenele we barnstormed along the muddy cratered road, stopping to meet settlers and listen to abridged life stories. Wherever we went families would huddle in dark humid rooms and, as the men talked, the women prepared coffee and the children stared at us. We were beginning to develop a rhythm in our search and an understanding of who these people are and what they want.

Like these settlers', our journey was counterpoised against the rigors of BR-364. At 2 o'clock one afternoon, after an unusually heavy downpour, we set out on the 110-kilometer jeep ride from the town of Ouro Preto, where we left Fontenele, to Ariquemes along BR-364. Without lights, signs, shoulders or pavement, BR-364 is little more than a well-traveled path through the jungle, or what was once jungle. Alternating rain and sun have turned the clay surface to a brick-hard texture rutted in a series of valleys by the constant procession of heavy trucks. The trucks with their wide wheel bases have a better time stepping over the bumps; riding in a jeep felt like going through a trash compacter. After heavy rains, low spots wallow in axle-deep mud. Since so much time is spent waiting to cross through these giant mud holes, the least stretch of firm road, no matter how corrugated, is an excuse to put the accelerator to the floor.

About a half hour along, our black jeep came up behind a long line of buses and trucks. Our driver shut off the engine and blankly stared ahead, strumming his fingers along the steering wheel.

"What's this?" we asked.

"Something is stuck ahead and we must wait."

"How long?"

"Maybe one hour, maybe two. Only God knows."

We left the jeep to take a look. With our first steps we sank into the ground, steadying only when the mud had gone above our ankles. The driver laughed. We slogged past trucks, our arms extended like tightrope walkers. Mud, thick and reddish brown like coagulated blood, clung to our shoes until it formed gooey ten-pound cakes. London fell to his knees. Truck drivers howled.

The diesel engines idled with a monotonous click-click-click-click. The air smelled like an expressway tollbooth. We came to the edge of a deep pit that had been gouged in the road, an inch at a time, by passing traffic. Rain and the ceaseless vehicles had turned the bottom to smooth, glistening muck that had seized a bus and swallowed the back half. With the tortured whine of the bus's transmission and the low growl of waiting trucks, the scene resembled those museum paintings of prehistoric dinosaurs struggling in tar pits.

Ten or so men were trying to push the bus out, but it was going nowhere, just spraying them with mud. One young boy was scooping mud from in front of the front tire; if the bus did manage to dislodge itself it would roll ahead and crush him.

One of the men told us the bus had been in the hole for four hours. Soon, he predicted, the professional courtesy the truck drivers were showing would fade and they would plow out a new route around the mudhole, leaving the bus mired. Taking that as a clue, we scouted a path along the high bank, between trees and crops. We returned to tell our driver of the new route.

"No," he said. "We will wait."

"But that bus has been there for four hours," we protested incredulously.

"I have no hurry," said the driver as he continued strumming to the silent song in his head.

Soon, though, it began to rain again, very hard. The driver inexplicably changed his mind and took off down the path we had recommended. The rain hit the windshield with force and pounded an endless beat on the canvas top. We never went more than half an hour without running into a line of stuck vehicles. Each time, we diligently went to inspect the trouble and find a path around it. There was always a coffee klatsch atmosphere around the bogs as waiting drivers talked and watched, and the muddy children of neighboring farmers tried to interest them in their fathers' tractor and chains for $5 a tow. Always the buses were the hardest to move, and passengers, evicted to lighten the load, got miserably wet and shivered as they stood.

The jeep had no springs, or so it seemed, and after chafing with

a thousand bumps, London's back began to bleed. We had no idea
how much farther it was to Ariquemes. Neither did the driver; there
were no landmarks here. All that was visible was the few square
meters illuminated by the headlights.

Suddenly the headlights went off.

"Shit," the driver mumbled.

"What now?" said London, who was leaning forward, head between his knees to keep his ailing back free of the seat.

"The battery went dead."

The driver told us to push while he tried to restart the engine.
Shoving at a black jeep on a dark road on a rainy night, we could see
the headlights of a big truck approaching us and thought about its
driver, swilling cachaca and doing 60 on the first stretch of firm road
he'd seen in hours. We winced as the truck blew by. The driver
tinkered with the engine and finally the jeep started.

At 4 in the morning, 14 hours after we had set out, we arrived in
Ariquemes. It was a trip that would take less than 2 hours in the dry
season. At least we had arrived; we figured that not one of the large
trucks and buses we had passed would get to its destination for some
days yet.

To the settlers who stream into the jungle from BR-364, the road
is at once a lifeline and a noose around their neck. It is the road that
brought Gilberto Wensing to Ariquemes when he was a boy of 14,
and it is the road that connects him now with the commerce of
the south. But some years it has also been the road, clogged with
mud, that forced him to watch a bumper crop of rice sit and rot
because there was no way to move it.

"I miss the roads of Parana very much. During the rains, many
things are missing from the markets, things that must be brought
from Sao Paulo. And everything is always very expensive."

Wensing, a tall serious man, lean and hard with the dark hair,
pale skin and square face that advertise his German heritage, moved
to Ariquemes with his parents and brother in 1972 from a small farm
in the state of Parana. "At first we had to sell bananas from the trees,
then the trees themselves, to live. But now we get everything from the
land: milk, cheese, meat, rice. In Parana, we worked hard for a little;
here we work hard for a lot," he said, standing on the porch of the

neat sawn-wood house he shares with his married brother's family. A gentle rain splashed on the wide palm leaves. The cool air and bright tropical flowers made it seem a small paradise.

However idyllic the surroundings, Wensing made it clear he is not content to be a subsistence farmer. He has dreams of a large cattle ranch and to accomplish that he needs access to markets. "If they pave the road, we will have it."

It was a sentiment we heard all along BR-364. Paving the road was seen as the end to all problems. It would greatly raise land values and cause an even greater surge in immigration. Wensing told us paving the road would even make it easier for him to meet marriage-able young women, since it would bring more out and make the trip to town quicker.

The government has long had plans to pave BR-364 and es-timates it will cost $600 million. Much of the financing is to come from the World Bank, but the deal was held up when anthropologists discovered that the paving plan called for a new section of road straight through the hunting grounds of the Nambiquara Indians. After a tug-of-war with the Brazilian government, the bank succeeded in having the plan revised to sidestep the Indians. A $320 million loan was approved at the end of 1981.

But Wensing expressed deep skepticism. "They have been saying they would start every March since I've been here. Only God knows if they mean it this time."

In spite of the mired road and chaotic immigration, INCRA can point to impressive examples of its settlement dream-come-true. Jose Alves Gomes is such a showpiece. Having arrived in the early migra-tions, Gomes managed to accumulate 250 hectares, which he has planted with cacao, rubber and coffee. Not bad for a man who was, five years earlier, a street vendor in Belo Horizonte, the capital of Minas Gerais state. He is not a modest man, either: the entrance to his property bears the sign "Fazenda Alves." "When I plant a seed and watch it grow, I get excited," he told us as he lovingly gave a tour of his cacao trees, occasionally picking one of the large orange fruits and caressing the grooved skin. "Everything I plant comes out well."

Gomes is INCRA's model farmer, not only because of his re-markable success at agriculture, but because of his vision for the future of Rondonia. He had just finished a cacao bean warehouse to store and dry both his own considerable production of the beans that chocolate is made from and his neighbors' crops. While many still thirst for land, Gomes is developing an agro-industry which he sees as the real promise of this region.

"There is no reason for this area to ship all we grow to Sao Paulo. We should have a chocolate factory here and a mill to refine beans. That is the future." Gomes' vision seemed to grow firmly from his urban roots. "What we don't have here is comfort. I miss good roads and I miss air conditioners.

"You come back in five years and you will see a swimming pool, television, electricity and streets." He laughed at the picture he was painting, a hard, mirthful laugh that said he knew he'd get what he wanted.

On our return from Fazenda Alves to Ariquemes we picked up a young farmer who was carrying supplies in a cloth sack. We told him where we had been and his eyes widened. He dreams about the likes of Jose Alves Gomes. He confided that he married his wife because it gave him more points under the system by which the government evaluates prospective purchasers of land. He said he thought he loved her, but he loved land more. He was 22 years old, though he looked over the hill with his weathered hat and toothless grin. He and his wife were living in a one-room shack on someone else's land, where he worked for $5 a day. We talked to him as we sat on the cool dirt floor. There were no lights, and the only running water was that which leaked through the roof. The shack was uncomfortably dank, and the moisture held on to bad odors. His baby played in a cardboard box. But he, who had been waiting six years for a plot of land, said that he would be happy one day to own a house just like the one he was renting.

BR-364 is not the first route by which people have penetrated this edge of the rain forest. The first road was a railroad started a century before BR-364. People called it the Road of the Devil and said that a half million men died building it. When the survivors finished, no one had any use for it. The costliest and perhaps most senseless failure in the Amazon, the railroad is a monument to man's unquestioning faith in his ability to prevail.

"They say there is a skull resting on every tie," said Silas Shockness in the Caribbean-accented English he had learned from his father. "I do believe that, yes I do." With 1,630 ties for each of the 366 kilometers, that would be almost 600,000 skulls. Less naive historians have said the actual number is probably between 5,000 and 10,000, although no accurate record exists.

The railroad is properly called the Madeira-Mamore, Mad Maria for short. It was started in 1872 and, after a number of interruptions, finished in 1912. Cut through dense, swampy jungle from Bolivia to the Madeira River, a major tributary of the Amazon, it was meant to transport rubber—something it rarely did. Now it is a ruin.

We met Silas Shockness working in the old terminal building at the end of the line in Porto Velho, which is also the end of BR-364. He was painting a hand cart made by the American Locomotive Company of Schenectady, New York. The Brazilian government hopes to revive the road as a tourist attraction and Shockness, who had once worked maintaining it, is the only employee.

The railyard is a tidy, fenced-in area with a ticket booth, clapboard office and wooden waiting room that could have been taken from some quaint Connecticut suburb. The terminal once held 24 locomotives, but they have all disappeared. In fact, the only living reminder we saw of the early days were the pigeons, a flock of fat gray ones that sat burbling on the roof of the administration building.

"The Italian workmen brought them when they come. I guess the Italians don't do so well here, but their pigeons sure like it," said Shockness, in his father's lilting accents. His father had come from Grenada in 1914 to work on "the great American railroad in the jungle." Silas, a tall, muscular black man with a gentle manner and a lot of time on his hands, became a solderer for the road in 1945, just as the World War II rubber boom ended and the road began its final eclipse. He has not missed a day's work in 35 years, despite so many attacks of malaria he can't count them.

Not all of Silas' predecessors were as hardy; thousands succumbed as the disease swept through the early worker camps here, along with yellow fever and an array of odd diseases that epidemiologists never got a chance to record. The toll was scores of Irish, German, Turkish, Chinese, Greek and Italian workers. Only a handful of lives were lost to the snakes and jaguars that the builders had feared before they arrived.

The railroad defied construction. And logic. The idea was to give Bolivia, one of two landlocked countries in South America, access to the sea. Yet once the connection was made to Porto Velho, goods still had to travel 2,000 kilometers via the Madeira and Amazon rivers to get to the Atlantic Ocean. There was no BR-364.

In 1867, as part of a friendship treaty, Brazil and Bolivia agreed to build the railroad, which had actually been suggested 15 years earlier as part of an influential report by U.S. Navy Lieutenant William Lewis Herndon. But by 1874 two British companies had tried and failed to make a start; all their workers, mostly Irishmen, had died on the job. Four years later an American firm, P. T. & Collins, volunteered that Yankee technology was what was needed here. They managed to lay six kilometers of track which they inaugurated on July 4, 1879, just before an epidemic forced them to abandon the project. In 1883 Brazil decided to do its own study, but 16 months later the team returned less three engineers and 19 laborers; that same year another commission was sent out, but that one did not return at all.

The project languished until 1903 when, with Bolivia desperate because the price of rubber was soaring, Brazil agreed to finish the railroad as partial compensation for its annexation of the territory of Acre in the western Amazon. Brazil contracted the American firm of May, Jekyll & Randolph, one of the Panama Canal construction companies, in 1907. They came down with a United Nations of workers, many of whom had worked on the canal and were used to the harsh tropical climate. The company also had the good sense to refurbish and staff the hospital called Candelaria, transforming it into probably the best facility in all Brazil. A roadbed was cleared and track laid with relative swiftness—though it was hampered by the necessity of bringing all supplies, including railroad ties, all the way from the United States. The road was finally inaugurated in 1912. Ironically, that was the year the price of South American rubber peaked. In 1913 it began an accelerating decline and the costly railroad became less important every month. In 1931 it was nationalized and in 1972 the Brazilians closed it for good, ripping up some of the track to build a road along the same route—a project they never completed.

With the exception of Shockness and a few others, the local

people seemed blissfully ignorant of the railroad. We went to search for the graveyard—said to cover acres—by setting out along the roadbed. We passed a muddy slum that had sprung up on the edge of Porto Velho—no one there had ever heard of the railroad. As the houses became more sparse, the roadbed was more clear, a worn path through higher and higher jungle that since the railroad's demise had been used to haul bananas or nuts into town. The jungle now grew around us. It became immense, tall white trees standing as sentinels a few yards back from the roadbed, hundred-foot-long lianas looping down into the riotous underbrush. Tossed at intervals into that underbrush were long rusty rails. Then, farther along, the round, corroded hulk of a locomotive was choked with the vines and trees that grew around and through it. "Baldwin Locomotive Works, Philadelphia," could just be made out on the plating. Beyond that wreck was another and another: a dinosaurs' graveyard.

A toothless man doubled under a heavy sack walked by. We asked if he knew where the cemetery was. He said yes. He was the first person who knew anything about it.

He took us along the road for a while, then turned into what seemed solid forest. With his machete he cut a path up a long, slow hill. Mosquitoes and gnats swarmed around us with fury as we walked. Sweat rolled in long rivulets down our spines.

At the top was a clearing, right where the cemetery was supposed to be. But the old man seemed puzzled. He wandered around, poking at short bushy trees with his machete. The trees were planted in something approximating regular rows.

"I have not been here for a long time," said the old man. "Someone has turned up the cemetery and planted it."

We searched among the vegetation, finding occasional pieces of stone with sharp edges that indicated tombstones. Finally we found one intact stone with a slanted face and the faint impression of an inscription. Near it was a cross made of two pieces of iron pipe and the date 1/11/19 scratched on it.

"When I was a boy, the whole field was like that," the man said. "There are just too many people who want land now. Not even the dead can rest in peace."

SINOP

We were heading east, toward the town of Sinop—a trip that by road might take two weeks, but by plane was four hours. The flight was back over some of the same ground we had covered by road. Beneath us, BR-364 was a pathetic brown ribbon; when the angle was right the morning sun glinted off the numerous large puddles speckling its length. Caravans of miniature trucks and buses sat facing these mudholes in silence, the curses of their occupants only imaginable from 500 feet in the sky. We had quickly converted to the belief that the bush pilot and his Cessna were the saviors of the Amazon traveler.

Our particular messiah was the unfortunately named Maria Teresa Conte, a southerner of about 30 with a squeaky voice, curly

red hair and a ruddy face from a Hals painting. He preferred to be
called by his *nom de guerre*, Helio, from the Greek sun god Helios,
who rode a four-horse chariot through the sky. Perhaps to compensate further, he talked exclusively about whores.

The subject did not seem unduly to faze Father Thomas O'Connor who was riding in the back seat, dressed for November in Dublin
in a black suit and overcoat and carrying a black leather bookbag.
Father O'Connor, an Irishman of the missionary Order of St. Camil-
lus, complained about it being a "trifle stuffy" in the cabin but made
no attempt to remove any of his clothing. He was preoccupied looking out the window.

"Where's the blessed forest?" he wanted to know. And indeed
there was little to see. The cumulative effect of the struggling settlers
along BR-364 was a checkerboard of destruction that spread out in
either direction to the horizon. It made Carlos Marx' calculation that
10 percent of Rondonia had been cleared seem understated and his
prediction that 50 percent would soon be gone seem a certainty. Over
vast stretches it was hard to believe there ever had been a jungle, that
this land had been anything but natural farmland—until we noticed
how the black squares where the forest had recently been burned
were cut from the surrounding border of green with a precision that
does not occur in nature. There is a law in Brazil that only 50 percent
of the jungle from any one piece of property can be cleared, with the
rest remaining as a preserve. We concluded that the law is not obeyed
here. In fact, it is easily circumvented, because a farmer can sell his
50 percent preserve to someone else who can preserve 50 percent of
that and then sell his preserve and so on.

"You wouldn't have thought it could be done," said the priest,
his nose pressed to the side window.

Up front, Helio, unmoved by a sight he had seen many times,
paused in his monologue about the previous night's exploits and
asked the passengers to make sure their seat belts were fastened.
Almost immediately the small twin-engine plane was enveloped in a
cocoon of gray cotton. Rain drove into the windshield and the craft
began a series of roller-coaster bounds that dropped it 200 feet in a
few seconds. "No problem," Helio shouted with the casualness of an
urban cowboy who'd just dropped a quarter into a mechanical bull.
He was a good pilot, that was clear, but still the storm was a problem.

His hands quickly adjusted controls, some delicately and others definitely, and his feet on the rudder pedals busily clomped up and down as if he were riding an exercise bicycle.

Father O'Connor was deep red and his cheeks puffed out from the effort of trying to right his stomach. But true to his word, after a steady climb Helio brought the plane above the storm. We could see it now, behind us and to the right: a thick head of dark gray cloud with a thinner shaft of rain streaking down to the forest below, like some fabulous mushroom. In the distance were more of the same shapes, each an individual storm, all isolated and sweeping back and forth across the trees. The surface below was now treetops and nothing else. The patches of farmland were gone and only the endless, nubby green expanse remained. It went on forever; almost an hour of flight time—more than 100 miles—without interruption. It was at once tedious in its sameness and terrifying in its immensity. There was silence in the cabin. However remarkable were the accomplishments of the pioneers who cut this forest, its mere existence seemed all the more awesome.

The area is called the Mato Grosso, great forest. Only occasional rivers break the landscape, some light brown, others black and all but invisible. One of the largest is the Rio Roosevelt, once called the River of Doubt but renamed for the Rough Rider after his epic 1913 expedition when he first charted the river's course. It was there that Roosevelt wrote: "Every now and then someone says that 'the last frontier' is to be found in Canada or Africa, and that it has almost vanished. On a far larger scale, this frontier is to be found in Brazil and decades will pass before it vanishes."

Only a few years ago, not far from the Rio Roosevelt, a Brazilian radar survey team discovered a 400-mile-long river that had never even been hinted at. The Mato Grosso's reputation for remoteness was won originally when another explorer who put a premium on heartiness, the Englishman Colonel P. H. Fawcett, disappeared there with his son in 1925. The tragedy, one of the most publicized in Amazon history, sparked many column inches of stories about murderous Indian tribes and man-eating swamps and firmly stamped the Amazon as a place of savage mystery for a generation of travel writers.

Helio interrupted our reverie with a cheerful observation. "Notice how there's no place to land. I mean if we had an emergency. No fields. Nothing." He said he had heard stories of pilots who had belly-flopped their planes on the thick canopy, only to die when search parties were unable to find them. "Those trees just swallow you right up."

Sinop is one of the towns Joao Carlos Meirelles of the Association of Impresarios of the Amazon hopes will be the prototype for the future of the Amazon. It is the dream of one man, Eneo Pepino, who had pioneered farm colonies in the state of Parana, next to Sao Paulo, a half century before. Those early farm colonies had since become mechanized and were bought up by giant agro-industrial firms. Labor-intensive coffee farms were replanted with mechanically harvested soybeans. Small farmers couldn't compete because they didn't have the capital for this type of agriculture. Some of them managed to get service jobs in the employ of the corporate landowners; others packed up and motored onto BR-364, and some came to Pepino's latest dream, Sinop.

Pepino purchased almost 1.5 million acres 50 miles north of where the natural grassland ended and the jungle began, and sold it off in chunks to southerners, many of them descendants of his original farm colony property owners. Twenty-five thousand came to Sinop in the first five years. The town itself is like many of the colonies that dot the northern half of Mato Grosso—a rudimentary village occupied by hard-working, lower-middle-class farm families—with one exception. It is built around an unusual crop and a bold experiment. Along with rice, beans, coffee, pepper and other crops, the farmers of Sinop are encouraged to plant manioc, a starchy tuber that grows under the ground and looks like an ungainly potato. Called cassava in other parts of the world, it is used for tapioca in the United States; here, in Africa and in Southeast Asia it is one of the most important sources of food for the poor.

Pepino's dream is to grow manioc not for food but for energy. In the late 1970s, he invested $33 million—most of it government money—in a distillery that turns the root into alcohol through a process similar to that used for sugar cane. Already the incongruous mass of pipes and tanks in the jungle turns 850 tons of manioc into 150,000 liters of alcohol a day—the equivalent of 2,000 barrels of oil. He soon hopes to double production, if he can get enough manioc.

"This is a natural jungle crop. Indians have been growing it for centuries," explained Macao Tadano, a former congressman who works as an executive for the company. "We have found that elsewhere you may get 12 to 15 tons a hectare, but here we have gotten up to 75 tons."

As Tadano explained it to us, manioc seems a miracle crop. It can be harvested almost year round, unlike sugar cane, and does not need constant attention. The skin is 15 percent protein and can be used for animal feed. Cross-breeding has enabled Sinop's researchers to come up with some varieties that grow giant roots. We toured an experimental field with 55 strains of manioc. Tadano, obviously enthralled with their cultivation, dug up one of the small bushes and revealed a thick mass of roots that weighed 40 kilos, almost ten times the normal size. We couldn't quite match Tadano's enthusiasm, having never seen a normal manioc root to compare with this supposed behemoth. But for 25,000 people, what goes on here is more than important. It is everything.

For those lower-middle-class farmers who gave up their homes in the south to seek a future in Sinop, the manioc offers a sense of security. It is a year-round cash crop and the market—Pepino's distillery—is right next door. They traveled by the same road to Cuiaba as other migrants, but there where the roads become dirt they turned north instead of continuing west along BR-364. Those who went to Sinop felt their future more assured, because Pepino, a larger-than-life figure in the uniquely Brazilian colonization industry, is behind them.

But even to our inexpert eyes, there was a risk which Pepino, for all his talent, could not eliminate. The land around Sinop is jungle, but not nearly as lush as that in Rondonia. The soil is brick red, unlike the darker loamier earth to the west. Trees seemed to us to be scruffier, a lighter green with a crowded tangle of undergrowth beneath them; not at all the wet, broad-leaved plants and fat trunks topped with heavy crowns we had seen along BR-364. Sinop's soil is, according to agronomists, more typical jungle soil and as such it will not long support manioc or any other single crop. One analyst at the World Bank lauded Pepino's energy, but added, "If enthusiasm could conquer a jungle the Amazon would have been felled a long time ago.

"I'm not convinced Pepino has solved the fundamental problem," he told us. "Manioc is the ultimate slash-and-burn crop, which the Indians have lived on for years. They cut a patch of jungle, burn the trees to get the nutrient-rich ash in the soil, then plant the manioc. The soil will be good for three to five years. After that the Indians move to a new patch and repeat the process."

The oldest fields of manioc were only about four years old when we visited Sinop. If the soil there proves as fragile as many predict, the 25,000 settlers are in for a very hard future. Tadano admitted this was a concern of the company, but said experiments with crop rotation and new varieties would solve the problem. To most of the settlers, the question had never occurred, or they had put it out of mind.

The manioc farmers around the clapboard town of Sinop told us we must visit "the South African." They spoke with awe of his accomplishments. "My farm is just starting," they would say, "but you must see what the South African has done."

We were told he lived about 20 miles south of town. After a bruising ride on the dusty washboard surface of the Cuiaba–Santarem Highway, we came to a turnoff marked by the beginning of a neatly sawn rail fence. The fence ended in a high, square gate that announced "Fazenda Santa Silesia." The gate was shut with a heavy chain and lock.

The sun was setting and in the distance a man walked along the fence toward us, stooped behind a handcart, wearing a crumpled straw hat, shorts and cheap rubber sandals which flapped against his heels. His right arm swung stiffly at his side.

When he arrived at the gate, we could see he was different from the other settlers. Despite the caked dirt and ragged costume, a superior manner emerged as he asked what we wanted. Then we noticed the blue eyes under a grimy brow. In Portuguese, London asked if we could talk to him. The man thought a moment, then in precise but unmistakably accented English, he said yes, as long as we swore not to use his name. We could call him Karlheinz.

The name was not South African and neither was he. "Of course not. I am German. I went to South Africa after the war and I let the people here think I was born there if they want to."

We waited for him on the patio of the neat, whitewashed cottage where he lives with his wife, Lisle, as he showered and changed. A different man came out to talk. The stooped peasant was transformed into a barrel-chested Teutonic executive, thinning blond hair slicked back and face scrubbed to a ruddy pink. He shook hands crosswise, with his left hand. The right, he said curtly, had been useless since the war.

He was happy to talk about his work here, he said. "My history is not important."

His explanation for his success while his neighbors struggled was simple: he was a better farmer. "Some of them are hard workers, but they do not know what must be done. You have to treat this land carefully."

For Karlheinz that meant crops must be rotated every few years to keep down disease and pests as well as to renew the soil. "There is no doubt the soil is poor. But after working it, you can make this a paradise. Look at the climate. There is no frost, lots of rain and lots of sun. The land is flat enough to mechanize. That is what I can't wait for—when I can bring tractors in. Tractors don't talk back." Still, Karlheinz's optimism may be premature. The frailty of the jungle soil lies in the subsoil, under a thin nutrient layer, and the subsoil has been leached poor by relentless rains for thousands of years. His rotating techniques may have been ideal in South Africa, but this is a tropical land.

Karlheinz stayed away from manioc because he felt that it was no more than a slash-and-burn crop. He explained that he was experimenting with coffee and rice and rotating various strains, hoping they would replenish the soil. The fields around his house were deep green from the delicate grasslike rice plants. Soon, he said, he would have cattle.

"One of the problems with coffee is you need a lot of labor, and that is hard to find around here. Some of the people are very lazy. They say, 'Why does Senhor Carlos have such a big house? He's stupid. He just has to clean it.' Ha! How can I understand that? I not only have a big house, I have a lawn. And every Sunday out here in this jungle I get out and mow it."

In addition to his manicured lawn, we noticed rows of fruit trees and arbors of tropical flowers in the enclosed compound. His wife brought us a tray of tart lemonade made from the fruit of one of those trees.

They came to Sinop in 1975. Karlheinz said he was then an executive in South Africa for Siemens, the big West German electrical company. "Some of my family had been in Brazil for 50 years. I had bought this land some years ago and one day I read a story in the London *Times* about this TransAmazon Highway. I thought I better get to my land before someone else does."

Land, he said, had always been the most important thing to him. He grew up on a farm in Silesia, which was then in Germany but later became part of Poland. "We lost it all during the war." He did some farming in South Africa but feared the political situation.

Brazil seemed a better place. "Here I could start from scratch and no one would bother me. Here you don't have a past, only a future," he said. "A man can still make something if he works. There aren't many places left like that."

The big attraction in Sinop that night was a girls' *handbol* game, a sport transplanted from the south that is a combination of basketball and indoor soccer in which the object is to throw a 16-inch softball into a goal. The Sinop team is the best in all the colonies and many of the proud residents had come to the company-built gymnasium to watch. It had all the fanfare of a heated rivalry in the middle-class suburbs of America and none of the homespun hospitality we associated with frontier activities such as square dancing and taffy pulling. Pep bands blared and crowds of teenage boys and girls lounged in the parking lot, smoking and eyeing each other warily. Vigilant moms and dads were in the stands and a chorus of nonplaying females shrieked in uniform pitch at the delight or horror of every play. The goalie, a tall blonde who looked as if she had been recruited from a California beach, turned away shot after shot, sliding on her knees, kicking or batting the ball away to the beat of the band and the hearts of a hundred high school boys.

The scene was so familiar—even the gym's scent of sweat and disinfectant was the stuff of American high school basketball—as to be routinely boring. Until we realized where we were. Nowhere. The other team, from one of the neighboring towns, had traveled nine hours by bus through freshly cut jungle to get here. To order a new handbol from Sao Paulo, with express service, takes ten days—if the road hasn't washed out.

Tadano, the Sinop executive, said the scene at the handbol game was typical. "There is much community spirit here. There is an equality and a sense that everyone is making a better life." It is a feeling the company wants to reinforce. The alternative, an awareness of solitude, could be bad for business.

At dinner, in Sinop's sole restaurant, we ate *feijoada*, the Brazilian national dish that consists of whatever tidbits of meat are available, mixed with black beans and cooked all day until the sauce is rich and flavorful. Helio was whispering to the fat, giggling wife of a visiting government official. The subminister, who was obviously enjoying the Sinop company's hospitality, seemed not to care where his wife meandered. Father O'Connor had left earlier in the evening with the observation that some of the settlers did not seem to live so well. He had consulted the missionaries he had come here to visit and they told him of people with failing farms, deep in debt to the company and of brutal treatment of *posseiros*, who claim land by virtue of their work without title, deed or payment. "I don't know if some of these devils haven't traded one miserable life for another," O'Connor said to us as he headed out.

Tadano was made uncomfortable by the cleric's comment, but he didn't respond.

Suddenly the conversation in the crowded restaurant receded to a murmur. A group of six ragged people walked in. They looked straight ahead as they made for a large table, but almost every other eye in the place was canted to the side, observing their progress. They wore dirty and ill-fitting, tattered clothes. Their skin was almost black, much darker than most of the Sinop residents. The men wore their hair in tangled braids, like the dreadlocks of Jamaican rastafarians.

"Posseiros," someone at the table whispered. Squatters.

"They must have sold some crops," said another. "So they spend it on a night out."

Everyone stared. After a long time, a waiter went over to the squatters' table and the din of comfortable life in the company-town restaurant in the middle of nowhere resumed.

CAMPO ALEGRE

We exchanged Helio and his Cessna for a 15-seat Bandeirante, a rugged Brazilian-made plane named for the original pioneers of the country who went out from Sao Paulo to establish settlements in the south and center of Brazil. The craft has been the workhorse of the fleets of the two commercial airlines of the Amazon. Fuel efficient, they also have an impressive steadiness even when landing on unkempt plains that have become runways only because they are close to small towns. We were on the milk run that begins in Brasilia and makes seven stops on the way to Belem, at the mouth of the Amazon, taking up nearly an entire day. It was to be one of the last flights on this route for the Bandeirante, because it had done its job too well:

the frontier was so busy the airline had purchased a 60-seat Fokker to accommodate the flow. Our destination was the same place which the Godfather of the Amazon, Herminio Ometto, had come to in 1961 by boat before slashing his way through the jungle with his machete.

The area is called the Araguaia Valley, and it is to Brazil a place of promise and unrest. The valley is a soufflé of posseiros, Indians, gold prospectors and large corporations that own expansive ranches, with a sprinkling of some of the most activist bishops in the Catholic Church. The valley is a jungle without trees, where animals still kill animals, although in this case men are the murderers and the victims. When the trees are gone all the Amazon will be like the Araguaia Valley, we were told.

There were instances during this journey when a divine research assistant put evidence so close to us and made it so alive that it simplified what we feared would be a labyrinthine search for the social, cultural and economic conflicts in the region. Santa Theresina Airport, on the Bandeirante schedule, was one of those manifestations. It was as if we were treated to a show with an all-star cast of the key players among warring interests of the Araguaia Valley. A glum, destitute Indian with war paint under his eyes and a bottle of cachaca under his arm sat on a bench; the tribe of loneliness, sorrow, and confusion seemed to surround him. Pacing behind him was a loud-mouthed real estate salesman boasting to a companion about a deal he was putting together; because the land was in the vicinity the odds were good he was selling property that once belonged to this Indian's ancestors, who were Brazilians before there were Portuguese in Brazil. A wealthy Sao Paulo businessman spoke with a local rancher about the price of transporting live cattle to the south and the timetable for the completion of the slaughterhouse at Campo Alegre. Two gray-frocked priests—one, we later learned, was a cardinal—mused about the weather, remarking that they had forgotten how hot it was in the Amazon.

If what we had been told was true, nowhere else in the Araguaia Valley would these nine people mingle in peace and respect, at least for each other's space. Each was lost in his own world, and for this brief moment the worlds didn't clash. But it was a peace that was not going to last.

The centerpiece of the Araguaia Valley cow country is Campo Alegre, which means Happy Field. It sounds like a summer camp which, to some, it is. If BR-364 and Sinop are where the immigrant underclasses are striving for a piece of prosperity, Campo Alegre, a town of 5,000 that did not exist two years before our arrival, is where the middle class is making its stand. The advertised significance of the place is that it is an attempt to bring integrated industry to the cattle region via a soon-to-open slaughterhouse, much larger and more modern than the one in Cuiaba, that is owned by all the neighboring ranches. Permanent settlement of workers and service employees is the intended social benefit of the project.

What this plan has brought so far is the typical sprawling Amazon shanty town of worker housing and an enclave of managers who seem desperate to establish the first beachhead of the good life. The Shell station had just opened when we arrived and telephone service was scheduled to start in three months.

Yet, there had been other changes which were unintended, and ominous. Here, on the southeastern edge of the greatest rain forest on earth, it had not rained for 150 days. Finally, just before our visit, the first sprinkles came, but most of them were over the forest. The rolling pastures that have been cut from that forest remained largely untouched. It was worse than the year before when the dry spell lasted more than 100 days.

Robert Milne, who was raising 15,000 head of cattle on one of the corporate ranches in the valley, hadn't paid much attention to the drought until the week before when the cattle were killed. Now he was spooked.

"We kept having these dry storms," he told us as we sat on the porch of his ranch house. "You know, where the sky gets all dark and the thunder and lightning keeps building up in the distance? But then nothing happens. The storm keeps up like that for hours and you're just dying for it to rain, to do something, but it doesn't."

The night the cattle died, clouds rolling with sound and fury had sputtered out only a few miserly drops of water. The next morning Milne found in one of the north pastures a huddle of 24 dead steers, fried by the lightning, their tongues and eyes bulging out.

"It looked like a bomb had gone off in the middle. I've ranched all over the world and I've never seen anything like this. One, two dead maybe, but never such a group."

It got Milne to thinking. "We're definitely changing something. In the five years I'm here it has gotten drier every year. Maybe it's because of the pasture we're clearing. I just don't know."

No one does. Milne's reaction was actually more thoughtful than most in cattle country. Most of the ranchers we talked to would say something like "Now that you mention it, it does seem to be getting drier." But there were no statistics, only impressions.

The upper end of the Araguaia Valley is another of the danger zones on Carlos Marx's wall map. Starting to the south where Herminio Ometto in 1961 began to slash an opening into the jungle and moving north in a band about 100 miles wide along the river, the trees have been scraped away and grass planted. Some of the expanses are so great—like that at Volkswagen's Cristalino Ranch—that one can drive for hours over rolling prairie that once was forest.

There is a theory, advanced by a prominent Brazilian climatologist named Eneas Salati, that such vast clearing will cause an eventual and dramatic change in the rainfall patterns here. Salati has shown that half of the water that falls as rain over the Amazon originates in the trees; the rest is drawn up from the ocean in the normal process of evaporation. If you cut the trees, Salati reasons, you cut the rainfall by half. Carrying his proposition further, drier weather could result in more trees dying off and a greater decrease in rainfall, a viciously tightening spiral that could alter a very large part of the earth's surface.

Salati's study of rainfall and the theory he has proposed hadn't reached the reading list of Robert Milne or probably the rest of the 100 or so managers who run these farms in the Araguaia Valley for their absentee corporate owners. They only acknowledged to us that something strange was happening—a rain forest without rain and increasingly destructive floods when the rains finally came. That man was perhaps the cause was not on their minds.

Milne, a Scotsman with a calloused handshake and a soft burr, runs the Santa Fe Ranch for the owners of Brazil's largest Caterpillar Tractor dealership. The bosses give him the free hand he demands and he puts to good use the tropical ranching techniques he learned in

Jamaica and Guyana. Santa Fe is considered the best-run ranch in the valley. Milne wouldn't deny it as he sat on the porch of the main house digesting lunch.

"I can only apologize for the flies. Damn buggers. I swore I'd never live in a place with flies, but these kind of snuck up on us. This is the first year we've had them."

The flies looked like common black houseflies, not particularly exotic but for their numbers. Milne's neck muscles tightened as one lit on his receding hairline. He suggested a tour of the ranch to escape and ushered us into a dented Chevy pickup.

"This is the last field we cleared," he said as we came to a wide black gash that sloped away and to the right before rising again to meet the tree line. The gash was almost 100 acres and had taken less than five hours to clear and a morning to burn. All that remained was a twisted mosaic of charred tree limbs. Milne explained that the trees were taken down by dragging a 40-ton anchor chain between two Caterpillar D-8 bulldozers. Because their roots are so shallow, even the majestic 120-foot tall trees are easily toppled by the powerful machines. Occasionally one would require individual attention.

"We used to leave the big trunks standing," he said. "Out of respect, I guess. But it made it too tough to work the field. Now, everything goes." Milne said that by using this technique he can clear about 25 acres an hour.

Then the fun starts. After the field is allowed to dry, all the farmworkers—"Even my wife"—come out one morning with torches. Piles of tinder are ignited all along the perimeter of the field and all the wood quickly catches fire in an incredible torrent of heat.

"It's an amazing sight," Milne reminisced. "The flames whip through in no time with this frightening noise. And when they reach the center, if the fire's big enough, you get a small thunderstorm. A big boom and the fire sucks the moisture out of the air and there you're standing with rain coming down all around you. For the workers, that's the best part of the job. I think it makes them feel a little like the Almighty."

When the field cools, the workers go through and plant grass seed, hearty varieties called Colonial or Green Panic, that sprout tall thick blades. The grass comes up fine after the first burning, Milne said, but gets progressively more anemic as the years go by to the point that now, five years after the first fields were seeded, he has started to use fertilizer. "We're just experimenting, but some of the other ranches are very heavily using it. I think it will be the death of this place. The cost is staggering."

Milne was not particularly optimistic about the land he manages. He seemed to have a great deal more reverence for the jungle, which he claimed would endure, and his rationale was economic. "What you have to realize," he said as he poked his way through the charred remains, "is that no one is really making any money here. And if it weren't for the government and their giveaway programs everybody would be in deep trouble."

The land around Campo Alegre is corporate cattle country because of a program of government incentives that lets profitable companies use part of their tax money to invest in the Amazon. It is too good a deal to turn down, so hundreds of companies have snapped up hunks of jungle and started ranches. The choice is either pay taxes to the government on profitable corporate operations in the south or use the same money to buy ranch land in the Amazon. Back in Brasilia, Interior Minister Andreazza had assured us that incentives are being phased out, at least the subsidized land acquisition part of the program. Milne, for one, would not regret it. "Nobody's really making any money here," Milne repeated. "It's just a way to keep from paying taxes and hope that something big happens here. I'm one of those who thinks it isn't going to happen."

Milne also insisted that not only would big ranches fail without government support, the corporations wouldn't be here at all if it weren't for the government incentives—incentives that he said are often decided on the basis of well-placed gifts to bureaucrats. "Those who bribe the most get the most. That's the God's honest truth. Nothing is done honestly, on merit. The whole program is corrupt."

Milne was like many of the expatriates working in the Amazon in his criticism of the bureaucrats in Brasilia. "I've never seen people who like to make such big plans and then not carry them out."

But he also has a fondness for Brazil. "Let's face it, now. Brazil is still a man's country. A lot of the old values still hold and the challenge is still here. You go back to England or the States and the bloody women are running everything. Isn't that so?"

Man's country or no, Milne thinks that the greatest force at play in these fields is nature. "This won't be a desert. The bloody jungle creeps back too fast. I can't keep it back. In the end, the jungle will take it all back and we'll be gone. In the end, the jungle will win."

Wilson Lemos, a super-rich industrialist from the south of Brazil, seemed to lack Milne's respect for the inexorability of the forest. The coarse old capitalist who, we were told, drank a quart of whiskey a day and still ran an empire of utilities and manufacturing companies, had set himself up for his own private *mano a mano* with the jungle. His 300,000-acre cattle ranch ran right to the edge of the Araguaia River where, on a high bank overlooking a stretch of white sand beaches, we gazed at the magnificent house he had built, a weekend retreat estimated to have cost half a million dollars. It was surrounded by a swimming pool, lawn and gardens of carefully tended jungle flowers—an incongruous but idyllic setting, perched on the bluff where the cool breezes quickly made us forget this was a jungle.

There was only one problem: The bluff kept washing away.

The house was on a 40-foot-high bank, but the Araguaia in its furious flood season sometimes rises higher than that. As Wilson Lemos had higher levees built around his property, the river just surged that much more. The annual flood is a remarkable transformation, the calm, coffee-colored water churning into a tumbling maelstrom filled with rafts of uprooted trees and entire floating islands ripped from the shore. When the river behaves this way—usually every March—it often alters its course, carving new channels and silting over old ones, uncovering new islands and gouging hunks from the banks. The local woodsmen anticipated that this radical surgery would soon be performed on Wilson Lemos' beautiful but absurd creation.

"One day the river will come and cut through that point," said one of the ranch workers, gesturing toward the promontory from the beach far below. "Then the house will float down the river with all the other debris."

Like others who spoke of Lemos' house, his tone was mischievous but not malevolent; a schoolboy waiting for a prank to spring. Everyone admired the house, by far the nicest most had seen. But they admire the river more.

We traveled farther west through the Araguaia Valley, past fields marked by endless lines of wire fence interspersed with tangled jungle that forms high walls alongside the dirt road. We were headed for the ranch owned by Volkswagen, the German automobile company whose subsidiary produces most of the cars in Brazil. In the Amazon, the hump-backed Beetle—extinct in the U.S.—remains the prevalent means of transport. It does a fine job negotiating the treacherous rutted roads and stands up to an incredible amount of pounding. The popularity of these cars throughout South America is what enabled Volkswagen to start one of the largest cattle ranches in the Araguaia Valley. But Volkswagen is known, not for the size of the ranch, but for the size of the fire that was allegedly started to create it. Some press reports in the late 1970s said that a million acres were torched at once, creating a conflagration that could be seen for hundreds of miles. Visions of the jungle going up in smoke touched off a great environmentalist outcry around the world. No scriptwriter could have invented a better arsonist for the world's greatest jungle than the world's greatest car manufacturer.

But the stories weren't true. "We did have some pretty big fires," explained Ralph Wehrle, the 30-year-old veterinarian who runs the ranch's breeding program. "But nothing like those crazy reports. Hell, we only have 32,000 hectares of pasture and it's taken us almost eight years to get that."

Volkswagen's ranch, which is run directly by the parent company in Germany, is the most ambitious in the valley in terms of technology and size. There already are 32,000 head of cattle—one per hectare—with plans to expand to 110,000 on 60,000 hectares.

Volkswagen's hybrid grass experiments and breeding programs are well known throughout the valley. Robert Milne had told us the other ranchers were eager to learn what "they've cooked up" for a type of grass that could be planted repeatedly without robbing the soil of all its nutrients. Wehrle, however, was more interested in cattle. He explained that he was trying to breed an animal with the endurance to heat, disease and insects of the hump-back zebu, whose Valiumlike demeanor is perfectly suited to this lethargy-inducing climate. The problem with the zebu, whose bloodline traces back to India, is the taste and toughness of its meat; it was originally bred as a milk and draft animal. The cross-breeding project was in its early stages when we were there and already some of the tough Brazilian cowboys were grimacing as they were taught the messy process of artificially inseminating the snorting bovines.

"A lot of them thought they'd be riding off into the sunset, not sticking their arm up some cow's ass," said Wehrle as he donned a plastic glove and loaded up a long syringe with bull sperm. Two cowboys coaxed a penned-in cow along a series of gates to a holding stock where Wehrle impregnated her.

Over lunch of canned sardines and rice, Wehrle told us he would be leaving the ranch soon. "To go to Harvard Business School, if they'll take me." He smiled, predicting correctly that we were surprised to find this aspiration on a ranch in the Amazon.

"Don't forget," he said. "I'm from the south, not from this jungle—" he paused—"or what's left of it."

Wehrle admitted that in the five years at Cristalino Ranch he had a tremendous opportunity to practice what he had learned in veterinarian school. "But it's gotten frustrating the last two years," he added. He was referring to the loss reported by the car operations in the south. "If they don't show a profit, they don't pay taxes," he explained. "And if they don't have to pay taxes they don't have an incentive to invest any money here."

The plan is that one day the Volkswagen cows and those that graze other ranches will be herded through jungle-turned-pasture to the most modern slaughterhouse in South America, a ranchers' cooperative that is to be Campo Alegre's pride. The engineers' accolades for the construction project notwithstanding, our tour of the Atlas Slaughterhouse proved to us that the innards of a factory under construction in the jungle looks the same as the innards of a factory under construction anywhere else; already we were becoming jaded. The slaughterhouse has cost $10 million to build—mostly government money—and it is the most modern slaughterhouse design in Brazil. When completed and at peak operation, 1,200 head of cattle a day are to be marched in and butchered, then trucked to population centers in the region and down south.

"This is so well built, you could bomb it and it would keep running," said one of the engineers, inadvertently pointing out one excess of using someone else's money.

The Atlas Slaughterhouse plans to employ at least 600 people and the hope is that it will spawn subsidiary industries, such as one man's dream to open a tannery and another's to manufacture gloves. But the slaughterhouse's main significance is to the cattlemen who will no longer have to ship live animals all the way to Sao Paulo and can become more competitive with ranchers from other regions of the country.

Mario Thompson, one of the supervisors of the slaughterhouse and a former manager of the Volkswagen fazenda, said that the idea of the Amazon serving as a meat supply for the settled south was becoming anachronistic. "Demand will be right here," he said pointing to a coffee table with American cattle magazines spread out on it. He had just returned from a two-week visit to the King Ranch in Texas, which he said was "centuries ahead of the Amazon." He warned us that his English, which he called "inadequate," was even worse after the trip because he had been practicing a Texas drawl.

At 38 years of age Thompson seemed unsure if he had reached the point of being a philosopher. He apologized for preaching to us, but he said he had "strong thoughts to get out." He predicted that the notion of the Amazon being the land of opportunity would catch on. "I don't know why the boys—no, the men and women—of 22, 24 or 26 years, they do not move to Carajas or Tucurui." Carajas is the rich mining district 300 miles north of Campo Alegre where the government says it will spend $60 billion by the turn of the century for development; Tucurui is to be the world's fourth-largest dam, scheduled to open in late 1983 at a cost of $3 billion. "They're all going to have to eat," he said referring to the people who build and service these projects. "And the cattle coming through this slaughter-house can feed them. The opportunities are unbelievable. Sometimes you must abdicate the comforts of civilization to achieve something worthy."

Thompson practiced what he preached. He was one of the founders of the Volkswagen fazenda in 1973, sleeping in the bush and eating off the land or from supplies dropped from planes. Now he was building up his own ranch on 10,000 acres; already he had 135 head of cattle and planned to double that in a year. On weekends he would leave the Atlas construction site and drive a jeep down a narrow jungle path to a banana-leaf thatched roof covering his hammock. The rainy season meant having to walk the last ten miles. He and a local woodsman cut and burned jungle and planted pasture. "Some day I will be making money from it," he said. "I just hope I am here when that happens." He used that expression often in the two hours we talked with him. Because it was so ominous-sounding —did he have a terminal illness or was this utopia going to be a long time coming?—we didn't ask him what he meant. Perhaps he, too, wondered about the dry weather, the cost of fertilizer, the reliability of government support.

We asked Thompson if he wasn't being pious and self-defensive about living out in the jungle, glorifying something that really was pretty tough.

"No, no," he insisted. "My father was a wealthy man, a big farmer and even the Minister of Agriculture. I don't have to do this.

"My brother thinks like you, that I am crazy. He is vice president of the stock market and he has 12 telephones. No, I don't need one telephone. Here you can see what you are doing; you have participation."

There was a rejuvenating quality about Thompson which touched us deeply, because in many ways he was like us—about our age, educated, familiar with material comforts. But none of our friends at home were Mario Thompson, and this may be a difference between our countries in these times. Thompson had been able to say shove it and take his money and his body somewhere to "see" what he was doing. We were beginning to detect a simplicity in all the people we met, from the dirt-poor farmer who loved his land more than his wife to Joao Carlos Meirelles who, whether or not we agreed with him, had a vision to build his version of a better world.

The Amazon is to be their arena of achievement, and there is no way to overstate the importance of this in a macho society, which Brazil is. V. S. Naipaul, in his *Return of Eva Peron*, points out the significance of wearing a visible key chain in Argentina, a society wracked by machismo, as a not too subtle boast of property which that man controls. Even the lowly bus driver wears two keys on his belt loop. The keyless of Brazil look to the Amazon; ambitions to be somebody still have that stage to play on. And the Brazilian people, macho though they may be, also have an enormous sense of pride, not to be confused with mere male arrogance. To be somebody, not to beat somebody. Maybe it has to do with the fact that the Portuguese don't kill the bull in their corridas. The military coup in 1964 was nonviolent, as was the coup in Portugal a decade later. These are not violent people, although there is a meanness in them, as shown in the political crackdown in the late 1960s and early 1970s and in the stories of the treatment of squatters in the Amazon we were to hear more frequently the deeper we penetrated into the forest.

But Mario Thompson was not talking of these matters, only of himself and a small part of a country with a national recognition that it has been blessed with a bountiful land and cursed with a multitude of problems. The Amazon still is a place for the Mario Thompsons who want plain hardship without social problems. Many would argue it's escapist of him, because thousands still are malnourished. But he can counter with a strongly held belief that he is doing his share to feed them.

The rest of Campo Alegre struck us as a parody of this ideal, because to the players—Pio, Ronaldo, Guido—the Amazon is ex-urban Brazil, a colony of the middle class, where they go to become big men. To these people the Amazon is not so much a land to be conquered as a land to be settled and "civilized" as India was to be before the British gave up. But the imperial power of southern Brazil has an advantage the British never enjoyed. The Amazon Indians have been penned in and kept out of the Brazilianization of the Amazon. There are no people to conquer. Only a land to settle. Whoever comes first can own the supermarket, the Shell station, even the third-rate pizzeria we went to. Or, more likely, they can be employees, with no stake in the Amazon; on this frontier where a man can be his own man, most of these others of Campo Alegre whom we met still belong to someone else. To them, the Amazon isn't a land of opportunity because their dreams are too big, but a haven because their dreams are too small to compete in the cities and suburbs where their values were founded. We had dinner with Pio Pedroso, who is in charge of personnel for the slaughterhouse, and his sister and brother-in-law who had driven up to visit him for a week.

"It must have been a rough drive," we said. The brother-in-law shook his head as he searched for the olive in his martini. "No, we took turns driving." The only rugged stretch was the 200 kilometers of unpaved road from the Belem–Brasilia Highway to Campo Alegre. It was no more than a drive in the country. All you had to do, he said, was make sure you had enough gasoline to make it from the highway to Campo Alegre.

Pio was eavesdropping and nodding. He wanted us to recognize the ordinariness of what they had wrought, as if transplanting cars, martinis and pizza were a heroic feat. We had played soccer in the afternoon with the young men who held middle-level jobs in the slaughterhouse organization. "These are the men who conquered your West," Pio boasted to us after the game when we were cooling off with beers by the swimming pool of the hacienda-style Hotel Atlas. "Perhaps Westchester," we had thought to ourselves as we watched the young men wander from the pool to shoot billiards on a factory-new table and digest dubbed Westerns on videocassettes.

Sitting on orange plastic chairs at a Formica table in the brand-new pizzeria that night, Pio ordered one pizza with tuna fish and one with olives and anchovies. And more martinis.

Rani came by. He was a native of the jungle town of Conceicao da Araguaia. He ordered lemon soda and vodka. Rani's presence delighted the brother-in-law, who whispered to us, "Watch him. Watch him," with the anticipation of a father whose son is about to give his first piano recital.

Unremarkably, Rani told us that he was a bush pilot who transported gold miners to isolated areas of the jungle. As he drank more and more lemon soda and vodka (the brother-in-law kept shouting, "Just vodka, Rani") the pilot began to speak English. First single words, then half sentences, then sentences with inflection. But we realized that what he was saying was what we had just said. A human echo. "What's that?" we asked pointing to a chair. "What's that?" he answered. Then he started remembering—chair, table and so on. He was absorbing everything down to the "you knows."

"Play for them, Rani," the brother-in-law insisted.

Rani smiled and looked around the base of his chair. Making motions of opening a case and lifting an instrument out of it, he announced, "Ray Miller. 'Moonlight Serenade.'" He played it on his trumpet, although he didn't have a trumpet. As Rani could mimic the English language he could play back renditions of songs he had heard, right down to elaborate fingerings—"Strangers in the Night." "Raindrops Keep Falling on My Head." "There's a Hush All Over the World." The quality of his performance varied, and he apologized for some tinniness, explaining that he had listened to a bad record. Lips tightly pursed, eyes closed, his fist banged into his chin as the vodka diminished his dexterity but sharpened his mental ear.

The brother-in-law howled. He hit us in the ribs. "You see. You see." He demanded, "*Outro*" from Rani, treating him as a rare house pet, his own tamed savage.

But there was just so much invisible trumpet playing we could take, and we were gladdened by Pio's announcement that it was time "to go to the disco." He slapped both palms on the table, stood up, walked up to Rani and kissed him on the cheek. "My friend," he wanted us to know.

The brother-in-law agreed. "Oh, yes. Rani, friend." So much so that he said he would stay there with the pilot and drink.

Pio took us back to the Hotel Atlas where he organized a caravan including Ronaldo and Guido to drive 30 miles through the dark jungle night to the inauguration of Dona Claudia's disco. We picked up Pio's 21-year-old mistress in one of the shanties on the edge of town and set off into blackness. The silhouetted landscape, lighted by a hazy quarter moon, could have been New England. We could see fences and grassy fields, an occasional cow, low hills in the background. From time to time headlights would reflect off the eyes of an animal. Usually it was a capybara, a 350-pound relative of the rat.

The disco was in Berreira, the first new business to open there in recent memory. Hard by the Araguaia River, Berreira is just a dirty little main street with a few dozen pink, green and blue pastel one-story buildings. No matter the color, however, we saw that every wall in town had a brown ring, like soap scum on a bathtub, that ran about six feet high. The marks were from the floods of the previous several springs, the worst in more than 50 years, washing ten miles inland and dissolving the mud and bamboo houses of many residents. After that most people moved farther inland, right to the edge of the flood-water's reach, and founded Nova Berreira, a collection of thatched shacks. The successful businesses—the supermarket, the gas station—moved out of the old town into Campo Alegre. In the center of the old town we saw walls for an octagonal church that would have been by far the most impressive building had it been finished. A gray horse grazed in the moonlight on the grass that already covered the floor.

Guido had told us not to expect much at Dona Claudia's. "I remember Berreira when Berreira was Berreira," said Guido, a sentence nearly as difficult to say as to imagine. "I'm afraid all the good times have been washed away."

Dona Claudia was hoping happier recollections would lure the fun back into the town the river kept drowning. For that one night in a steamy, cement-block room adorned with Christmas lights it seemed she had beaten back that inexorable force. There was a friskiness in town, like a college mixer; the sophomoric question of "who will score" was in the air.

The goodness and camaraderie which Pio demanded we recognize were obvious. Everyone seemed to be sacrificing his good time to make sure our beer bottles were filled and our ears alive with stories of whom we were watching on the dance floor.

"You like her?" Guido asked. London was looking at a young girl in a jaguar bathing suit top and turquoise and white check pedal pushers.

"Not really," he admitted.

"That's good," Guido said, "because Celina wants to fuck you."

Celina, a nurse whom we had met the previous night, had asked us, "Do you know what love is?" Kelly quoted Shakespeare ("Ah me! how sweet is love itself possessed,/When but love's shadows are so rich in joy?") which London translated, and it was clear Celina thought we were on the right track. She had sat close next to London in the car, but that was unavoidable because we had been squeezed in so tight.

"How do you know?" London asked.

"Everybody knows."

London looked at Pio, and Pio winked. He was pouring dark rum from a bottle he kept in a Chivas Regal box. Probably he wanted everyone to think that he was pouring the original contents of the box, because Chivas Regal costs over a hundred dollars in the Amazon; there really is no finer status symbol.

The music was *carimbo*, like a fast reggae native to Northeastern Brazil. It was a droning sound, never ending; either the band was playing the world's longest song or a medley without recognizable breaks. Besides the jaguar, there were many other adolescent girls in bathing suit tops and mismatched shorts or pants. Some men who were undoubtedly real cowboys swaggered to the music as the girls gave their all in dancing. The men were scrubbed, and their jeans were stiff. The air smacked of sweat and was cut by high-pitched giggles and quick movements.

We drank large bottles of beer, quickly. They warmed rapidly in the steaming inside of Dona Claudia's, and it was vital to replenish the fluids that we were losing just by sitting there observing. It was too sticky for much body contact, but for some it was their only chance for the week—Ronaldo's 14-year-old girlfriend, for example. She saw the self-styled playboy, 24 years her senior, only once a week, and it seemed any space between them was time spent apart. Her adoration of him was such that his dark features might have been edible the way she licked and sucked his ear lobes, cheeks and lips. Ronaldo dispassionately accepted the affection and talked to others at the table with no more recognition of what was going on than if he were sitting alone.

Guido came back to London and told him it was "arranged."

"What is?"

"Celina. She wants to fuck you. And don't worry, I had her last night. She's clean." It was about the best thing he could say about her. He did add that she did it *violentamente* as if he could dispense with her fine qualities in a 30-second advertisement.

At midnight the town's electricity shut off, and Dona Claudia warned everyone not to stray far. "We have to get gasoline for the generator," she explained.

We walked outside and bought a skewer of meat charred over a small pot of coals. Across the street was a worn pool table in candlelight and more cold beer. Everyone was milling about in darkness waiting for the generator to start.

"*Ja!*" someone announced, and we could see the Christmas lights inside Dona Claudia's flicker on. But when we returned the band wasn't playing. An unshaven small man was holding a microphone in one hand and a plate of food in another.

"Three hundred cruzeiros. How much do I hear for this hen? Three hundred cruzeiros."

Someone yelled, "Six hundred." About $10.

He whined into the microphone, "Six hundred cruzeiros. Six hundred cruzeiros. Do I hear seven hundred cruzeiros to keep the breast of this hen from this man's lips?"

"700 cruzeiros."

Whining again. "700 cruzeiros. Keep its smell from his nose."

Pio shouted, "1,000 cruzeiros" and shot under the table to avoid being caught as the high bidder.

"1,000 cruzeiros to stroke the thigh of this hen. Do I hear 1,200 cruzeiros? 1,200 cruzeiros."

This was the original game of chicken, a form of capturing someone in a foolish bid or proving machismo by outbidding others. The meal alone, a broiled scrawny bird with rice, wasn't worth even the opening price, which then was bid up at least ten times. No one really enjoyed the meal, just the process of buying it or avoiding its purchase. Why? Dona Claudia smiled and whispered to Kelly, "*Entusiasmo.*"

The music had started up again, sometimes blasting forth on a surge of electricity from the generator and other times muffled by a brown-out. But the band tried hard to compete on equal terms with the auctioneer.

Pio emerged from under the table to tell London the Celina issue had to be resolved. London told him that he thought it bad form to come into a town, sleep with what appeared to be the only eligible woman, and leave. "That is not right," he said. Pio said he understood, but he warned London the others, including Celina, would not be as compassionate.

He was right. What would have been a noble gesture where we had been raised was treated as an insult. Celina ignored London. He saw her take a pill, and asked her why. "To get crazy," she responded coolly. Guido and Ronaldo averted their eyes from London, and when he tried to explain his position, they said, "Sim, sim" and walked away. This made Ronaldo's adoring girl very angry, and she gave London a dirty look.

The extraordinary aspect of the night was how ordinary it really was. Pio was right; the remarkable conquest of the jungle had not come from daring deeds or adventures but from stringing up wires to generators and plugging in record players and Betamaxes. We were made uncomfortable by this, and our lack of wonder at what the others considered exemplary clearly bothered them. What does it take to impress these Americans?, they must have thought.

What meant something to us was the simplicity we had detected before. People who wake up in the morning to plant their food or protect their families don't need discos to find meaning in life. We found the settlers' search for their own unknown potential—Mario Thompson's life story and the others we had heard along BR-364— more moving and impressive than this replanting and Xeroxing of egoism and self-indulgence in the name of civilization. Pio Pedroso said to us, "These are good people," and he was right. They are friendly, fun-loving, curious and hard-working. But they have no new plans.

ARAGUAIA RIVER

A snake came at us like a periscope slicing through the morning mist, its head cocked forward at a right angle to the dull black shaft that rose from the surface of the river. Only when it drew closer could we see the S-shaped undulations of the rest of the body, cresting the water and propelling the head toward the boat.

"*Jararaca*," the old pilot Eladio said. "Very deadly."

As he circled the low, narrow outboard around the snake, Eladio told London to take his pictures quickly since it would soon scare and swim away. It didn't. The black snake circled on itself, always keeping its head aimed at the center of the boat where we sat. The eyes were shiny dots in the dark head; the mouth a barely visible ridge, somehow more terrifying closed, in anticipation, than if the fangs had been out.

"Not too close," the pilot cautioned himself. He turned the prow down river and the mist rising in the early morning sun soon covered the snake.

The jararaca was the only animal we saw for the first part of that trip down the Araguaia River. When we left the beach at Barreira, where women were beating clothes on boards and their daughters mimicked them with dolls' dresses, we headed straight for the deep, swift channel in the middle of the river.

There was, in that part of the Amazon basin, less wildlife than we expected; then gradually, as we headed north, more than we imagined possible. The Araguaia River, one of a dozen major tributaries of the Amazon River, starts in the highlands west of Brasilia and makes a relatively straight course for more than 1,000 miles along the borders of Mato Grosso and Para until, just below the city of Maraba, it meets the Tocantins, whose name it assumes for the rest of its descent to the vast muddy plain that is the estuary of the Amazon. The Araguaia is like all the other rivers in the Amazon system in that it is unique; no two have exactly the same kind of water or nourish the same wildlife, though scientists are at a loss to explain why. Where the Araguaia passes over the old sandy soils of the Brazilian Shield at its source, it is called a blue-water river, clear and infertile. It becomes brown with silt and teems with life as it gets closer to the Amazon where it picks up the organic matter necessary to nourish life. The Amazon itself, which churns up vast quantities of silt from its inception in the Andes, is called a white-water river, though the color is more of a milky brown. Many that flow down from the tangled rain forest to the north—such as the Rio Negro— have a black cast, looking almost like oil on the surface, and are extremely pure and sterile.

This much and more we had learned from our months in libraries and from interviews with some of the leading experts on the Amazon. For the past few days we had been angling through some of the remaining stands of forest in the Araguaia Valley. We were tempted; we were fascinated. In this arena of conflict between man and nature, we had listened to many people. It was time for a hearing with the wilderness. But for all our research, we remained city people untrained in science and unaccustomed to sorting out the sounds and sights of nature. As we set out along the river through untouched jungle, we were as unnerved by our limitations as we were awed with the forest itself.

For the price of gasoline and a few dollars for his pocket, Eladio said he would take us the 125 miles down this river to Conceicao. Mario Thompson told us that Eladio was among the most experienced of the rivermen, a necessary asset when traveling in a small boat on the seemingly placid but unpredictable Araguaia. "For anyone who has not been on that river in a week, it is a new river," Thompson explained. "The channels, the banks and the sandbars are all new. They will be new to Eladio, but he reads them very well."

And throughout the day-long trip, Eladio was a picture of studiousness, sitting in the stern, twisted a little to the side to let his arm rest lightly on the handle of the ancient outboard engine. His eyes—one clear, one cloudy and drooping a bit—ceaselessly roamed the surface, shaded by a turned-down cloth hat. He had the classic build of the riverman: short, bandy legs with bulging calf muscles; thick shoulders that sloped to his neck, and a hard, round gut protruding from his open shirt, suggesting a man who does heavy work and eats a great quantity of beans for dinner. He had nothing to smile about and did not for the entire trip, even after he gulped a mouthful from London's flask.

Curious to use this natural pathway to penetrate deeper into the forest, we asked the pilot to venture up one of the networks of narrow streams that feed the Araguaia. We asked him to shut off the engine so we could drift in silence. With a frown that forced his droopy eye lower, he did. For slow minutes there was nothing but the occasional echoing cries of unseen birds deep in the tree line. We recalled that comment of Wallace, the English naturalist, who at first thought the Amazon "not so peculiar." The trees looming up from the sodden banks did not look so strange; the small green leaves and twisted branches could as easily have come from the Ohio Valley. A chirping bird was a chirping bird. Where was the exotica?

The boat, guided in the slow current by Eladio's paddle, drifted with the water softly lapping the sides. Sun made its way through the tree cover in long, bright shafts. It was warm, but not really hot yet, and the water felt soothingly cool.

Then suddenly the surface seemed to boil and explode just ahead of where Kelly had been dangling his fingers in the stream; a dark brown shape surfaced and pushed back down again with a large slurp. It was a *piraiba*, the Amazon catfish that grows to 300 pounds and more, a result of its indiscriminate diet which, Eladio believed, includes small children. Then, in succession, a flying fish popped from the water and vaulted over the bow of the boat; two long-limbed herons rose from a camouflaged perch on a nearby tree and flew off. A small caiman, close relative of the alligator, stirred from a rock ledge and flopped into the water.

This is what that other English explorer, Henry Bates, must have witnessed when he wrote "the stillness and gloom of the place became almost painful" until "sometimes, in the midst of the stillness, a sudden yell or scream will startle one." The jungle is populated by animals that have learned that disguise and deception are the only way to keep from becoming one of those screams. The whole place tries to cloak itself in a sort of green-flannel anonymity that provides an eerie but unsatisfying experience to the untrained observer floating through this flooded world. The life is there, but it is hard to see.

Once we were reminded that there were creatures all around us, the placid scene became a little more ominous. We knew it needn't have been. Despite its evil image, the jungle is a place of few large predators and only a handful of animals and insects harmful to something as large as a man. And almost anything that could be considered remotely dangerous hunts at night.

From where we sat, we were aware of the four levels at which animals in the tropical rain forest live: in the trees, on the ground, under the ground and in the water. Relatively few spend their time on the ground. Tapirs, deer, wild pigs and capybara can sometimes be spotted foraging among the trees along with a variety of small rodents. The sole enemy the larger mammals face—other than man—is the jaguar, the largest cat in the Americas and the only fierce predator in the Amazon. Smaller mammals are prey to several kinds of hawks and an enormous assortment of snakes, including the anaconda, which is capable of eating a fair-sized pig.

Above us, in the air and mostly in the tree canopy, was where the greatest activity was taking place. Mammals who spend most of their lives there include monkeys, sloths, bats and opossums, along with snakes, toads, spiders and every other kind of insect imaginable —flying and crawling—from beetles and cockroaches to wasps, flies, gnats and grasshoppers. There are thousands of species of birds, many similar to North American varieties though an equal number are unique to the tropics such as parrots, macaws, toucans and cocks of the rock. We could sometimes hear monkeys hooting or screeching from a distance or the solitary cry of a bird; up in the trees we usually saw only the butterflies, brilliant in blues and yellows, though we knew there were sloths and other beasts as well.

Beneath the ground, or under the matted leaf cover, was vibrant activity but on too small a scale to make itself evident to two journalists peering into the darkness on either side. Highways of thousands of leaf-cutter or other ants were transporting bits of food to their underground colonies. Billions of termites, the lowest level of forest scavengers, were boring away, chewing through decaying plant matter, speeding up the process of returning the nutrients to the forest system.

The last layer is under the surface of the murky water where the world's greatest collection of fish resides, fish that because of the flooding are as much a part of the forest as any of the other animals. Most are contained in two groups: the catfish, of which there are more species in the Amazon than anywhere else, and what are called the characins, a broad class of fish structurally similar to each other though varying greatly in appearance. The latter group, which includes everything from the famous home aquarium dweller called the tetra to the carnivorous piranha, is one example of how animals and plants in the Amazon have evolved into such subtly diverse forms in an effort to keep from competing with each other for food. The waters also hold many eels, including the dangerous electric eel; manatees or sea cows; turtles; caimans and a number of ocean fish such as stingrays, dolphins, herring and smaller sharks. But which species might inhabit that particular stretch of the Araguaia—and whether it was ever possible to glimpse them in that opaque brown water—we were too ignorant to guess.

Although it was the early part of the rainy season, streams had already swelled to cover much of what had been forest floor. The tall trees and tangled underbrush grew up out of the dark, still water.

This was the *varzea*, the flooded forest that stretches back from many Amazon waterways. Farther in from the major rivers, on higher ground is the *terra firme* forest, less choked with trees than the varzea and appearing somewhat orderly, even hospitable. Here in the lowlands life is more uncertain. Even the giant trees with roots that looked like the buttresses of Gothic cathedrals often fall when the floods come. The floor was littered with them, already mingled in a mass of vines and fungus.

The giant scale of everything overwhelmed: vines many times the diameter of our arms; fallen trees so long they disappeared into the distance, covered by growth. And way above, dimly perceived through the gloom, was the bottom of a canopy of leaves and branches that might be 50 feet thick. At some points the stream was completely covered by it, enclosed like a tunnel. When a downpour strikes the canopy, we had been told, the rain does not hit the forest floor until ten minutes later. No sunlight at all reaches the ground. For what seemed like minutes at a time, the only sound was Eladio dipping the paddle into the stream. We could hear the drops hit the water when he lifted it out. We spoke to each other in whispers, for no reason but that this solemn scene demanded it.

We were beginning to perceive one of the oddities of the Amazon: there is not too much of any one thing in the jungle—no flocks, herds, coveys or groves. It is, for the most part, a solitary place where the fight for survival is so intense that the clever rather than the strong survive. There is just enough of everything to go around, but an abundance for no one—a realization that occurred to many of the early explorers before they sat down to boil their last pair of shoes; the leafy green land they assumed would be full of game often provided little. That is why, anthropologists speculate, the Indian tribes are so small and nomadic and probably why a sophisticated civilization has never taken hold here as it has in virtually every other great river basin in the world. And that is why it is so hard to log the Amazon, because there may be three valuable mahogany trees on an acre of land—separated by 100 other varieties.

We left Eladio with the boat beached on a white sand strip and walked into what appeared an unflooded section of forest. Once we picked through the few yards of underbrush at the edge, we were inside what seemed like a room, cool, shaded and roofed. A thousand plant varieties surrounded us, and we were trying to pay attention. But we found the environment overawing, an advertisement to discourage anyone from hoping to study botany casually. Fat trees, thin trees, white trunks, twisted ones; no two leaves on the floor looked the same. Some trees grew on top of each other, or out of each other. All the larger trunks had something else growing on them: a vine, a weed, a fungus. Some of the palms were distinguishable and occasionally we would see a round, brown Brazil nut case on the ground, a tip that something in the vicinity might be a Brazil nut tree. If only we had known even our houseplants well, we might have felt a flash of familiarity. Many hothouse plants—orchids and bromeliads among them—grow rampant here. Here and there were individual orange or red flowers—never bunches—twisting up from among some roots or clinging to the crotch of a tree, absurd bits of color in a world of brown and every shade of green. This great confusion is what makes up the tropical rain forest, the most complicated, delicately balanced ecosystem on earth and one whose evolution still puzzles scientists.

One fact that seems clear—and accounts for some of the conglomeration—is that things that become too abundant usually suffer for it. A less-than-subtle example is what man has done to those animals that were conspicuous. In a less dramatic way, the same point applies for the natural order.

Caimans and alligators were once so numerous that early explorers reported islands that seemed to be made of them. The animals' prolificacy has been punished over the last decades with a hunt that has driven them near extinction. In 1950 Brazil exported five million alligator hides; it is now difficult in many areas to find even a small member of the species. Turtles too were once prominent, but as the American explorer William Lewis Herndon observed as early as 1850, birds, fish and particularly Indian tribes feasted freely on their tiny offspring as well as basketfuls of eggs. "Prolific as they are," he wrote in his journal, "I think the turtle is even now diminishing in number on the Amazon." Their scarcity is now confirmed by the fact that the river people consider turtle meat an aphrodisiac, an unwelcome nod of reverence to rare animals the world over.

What has survived are species of trees with individual specimens growing so far from each other that a disease epidemic does not have a chance to start; butterflies that are patterned to mimic their bad-tasting relatives and cause hungry birds to shy away; flowers that root on tree branches a hundred feet in the air and in the light of the sun. We looked particularly for, but did not find, one tree that has taken this survival strategy to the extreme. The strangler fig begins its life as a seed dropped by a bird in the high cranny of a tree. If the seed germinates, the fig tree grows slowly at first, sending out roots that take in what water and nutrients they can from the surface of the host tree. But the fig continues to send long roots down the host, and when they reach the ground, the fig takes over. The stronger fig roots actually crush the bark of the host tree, killing its limbs and eventually enveloping it in a basket of roots surmounted by its own broad crown. This kind of adaptability—and the diversity which allows for minute shades of adaptation—are what makes for survival in the jungle. Bates discovered an incredible 8,000 new species in his decade of wanderings more than 100 years ago, yet even in this age when the earth is so well combed by science, biologists say it is possible to duplicate the Englishman's feat.

And each species is often uniquely tied to another. One relationship that almost sounded like a children's fairy tale had been described to us by Ghillean Prance, the expert on Amazon botany—how the giant Brazil nut tree relies for reproduction on a specific high-flying bee and a rat. The bee pollinates the flowers in the crown and the rodent later disperses the seeds that fall to the ground, insuring that they will not all be consumed by seed-eating insects and that they will be moved beyond competition from the mother tree. When the forest is flooded, seed-eating fish apparently perform the dispersal function. Then there are trees whose flowers have intricate chambers that can be entered only by a certain species of tiny wasp, which then carries the pollen to fertilize new seeds. Other trees stagger the seasons at which their fruit develops so that the particular kind of bird that disperses their berries is less likely to overlook an individual tree as it harvests its year-round supply of food. Another tree provides a hollow-branch home for tiny, fierce ants who in turn drive away insect predators.

Observing such extraordinary adaptations, Wallace and Bates formulated a theory of evolution identical to, though less developed than, the survival-of-the-fittest concept being studied at the time by Charles Darwin. Faced with such diversity it was hard for Wallace and Bates to accept the creationist theory of life; even God could not keep such an inventory. Wallace later did his own paper on evolution, which was used and praised by Darwin, and Bates made much of his work available to Darwin.

Farther down this same Araguaia, closer to Belem, Wallace and Bates first began to compile examples of the singular animals that have fascinated the world since. Even among modern naturalists, the two, along with another Englishman, Richard Spruce, are credited with the most complete studies on the Amazon ever done. Their names are invoked by Amazon scholars with the reverence baseball fans hold for Babe Ruth.

Befitting this unfathomable jungle, Wallace and Bates were unlikely adventurers. Before they arrived in Belem in 1848, Wallace, then 25, had been hoping to become a surveyor in England and Bates at 23 was an apprentice sock manufacturer. Neither had scientific credentials and neither had much money. They planned to collect specimens of plants and animals and sell them to British museums and botanical gardens for a few pence each. Fortunately, they had picked the right place to set up a high-volume business.

The two soon moved upriver, Wallace to the Rio Negro where over the next four years he pursued his theories of evolution before moving on to the East Indies, and Bates to the upper Amazon where he spent 11 years and apparently took to native life quite well. Bates' *The Naturalist on the River Amazon* has become a sort of *Huckleberry Finn* for budding biologists, recounting with boyish charm the almost absentminded wanderings of its author.

Bates must have been an odd sight to the Indians, dressed, according to his own drawings, in an assortment of unmatched plaids and wearing thick spectacles, his attire festooned with specimen bags and pins, a shotgun over his shoulder. Yet he could have been no more bizarre than some of the sights he saw and duly reported back to the folks in London. He described the fabled umbrella bird as "a species which resembles in size, color and appearance our common crow, but is decorated with a crest of long, curved, hairy feathers having long bare quills, which, when raised spread themselves out in the form of a fringed sunshade over the head." He reported one performance by the bird which, while it must gladden the heart of any bird watcher, gives some indication of why it is hard for the nonnaturalist to appreciate the subtleties of the Amazon: "It drew itself up on its perch, spread widely that umbrella-formed crest, dilated and waved its glossy breast lappet, and then, in giving vent to its loud piping note, bowed its head slowly forwards."

The sounds of the jungle often perplexed Bates, the proof that something was going on that he could not observe. Many sounds he found impossible to account for, a "clang" or a "piercing cry" followed by "silence which tends to heighten the unpleasant impression they make on the mind." The natives had an explanation for it, he wrote. They called it the "Curupira, the wild man or spirit of the forest, which produces all noises they are unable to explain." Part of Bates' difficulty identifying noises—and the Indians' and ours for that matter—is that their source is in the canopy. We were plodding the jungle floor, and that's not where the action is.

Towering above us was this riot of life, not within arm's reach or even just beyond, but in the tree canopy, a sort of continuous roof as much as 100 feet above the ground. The canopy is the real main floor of the jungle where thousands of species of animals and plants battle for sunlight and survival. Biologist Donald Perry, one of the few scientists to spend extensive time living in the tree canopy, described the tree limbs up there as resembling "overcrowded lifeboats, their upper surfaces choked with plants clinging to the edge." He also found all manner of monkeys, snakes, insects and even earthworms that live out their lives in the aerial domain. Why so little is known about this region is also made clear by Perry's account of free-climbing a 100-foot strand of nylon rope attached to a branch. "Hanging 80 feet up in the virtual empty space above the lower vegetation and below the tops of the highest trees can be an unnerving experience," he wrote. "I force myself not to look down, but even looking up is unsettling" as fears of how weak those lifeboat limbs are begin to buzz in his head.

We were much more comfortably a part of the lower vegetation and thoughts of ascending to the canopy refused to stir in either of us. In some places, where the forest floor was clear, the canopy sat like a great black umbrella over our heads. Things were constantly dropping from it—usually just branches—but the clattering always caused a start. It was hard to gauge distance and direction of noises. We were tantalized to know what was going on up there, but a 100-foot hike up a rope is something to be left to experts.

As we absorbed what we were able to observe, we became con-vinced that something we had thought we noticed over the past few days was true. Much of the forest in the Araguaia Valley was defi-nitely less lush than what we had seen in Rondonia or even Sinop. It was messy. The trees had a cheap, fragile appearance here, as though they had been put up by a shoddy builder. The green wasn't green enough and the undergrowth lacked exotic broad-leaved plants. There were large trees—perhaps kapok, mahogany, jacaranda, Brazil nut—but they seemed thinly spread and never gave the sense of majesty and power we had felt when standing in a tiny patch some farmer had cleared in Rondonia and surveying the walls around us. It was easy to see how someone could bulldoze down a few dozen acres a day of this. And why not? The scene fell short of a national treasure like the Redwood Forest. The soil here was not supposed to be as good as Rondonia's—it was more typical Amazonian soil—and what we saw bore that out.

But that, say the critics of development, is when the problems start. Take down the trees over the average Amazon patch and the whole system collapses, leaving nothing of value to anyone. The soil is the key, the God-given constant that all jungle life has been forced to adapt to. Some scientists theorize that in parts of the Amazon even hard-to-dissolve metals and organic matter have been leached out, leaving a worthless acid layer of subsoil. Where rivers have cut down to that layer, they pick up some of the acid material and are stained a black hue, such as those sterile waters in the northwestern part of the basin. It is, according to Harald Sioli, a West German scientist who has studied Amazon rivers, nature's warning that the soil is worn out and that few life-sustaining elements remain.

Plant life exists despite this soil, not because of it. The jungle is dense because it thrives on itself, constantly recycling a limited amount of nutrients. The soil covering the jungle floor is thin, in some cases only a few inches of organic matter over the thick layer of infertile clay. Though the experts admit they do not totally under-stand the process, they theorize a system where plants take in nutrients by absorbing them from dead matter on the forest floor or in the tree canopy. Minute hairs on the roots and vines that web the jungle in effect suck nutrients out of decaying matter, much of which never reaches the forest floor. It is not unusual to see a fallen tree trapped in a net of vines that extend down from a dozen neighboring trees. Those vines are feeding. What looks like nature's equivalent of a ten-car pile-up is really a delicately balanced system with the dead constantly replenishing the living and the same pool of nutrients perpetually recycling.

Cut those trees down and burn them, the theory goes, and you will transfer many of the nutrients to the soil in the form of ash. But when you harvest crops or let cattle eat grass, you are taking nutrients out of the system and letting more than 100 inches of rain a year leach them out of the soil. Since there wasn't much to go around in the first place, after a few seasons nothing will grow.

It was getting late and our destination, Conceicao de Araguaia, was far away. The indispensable Bates had the sentiment that gave us comfort in leaving. "I was obliged to conclude at last," he wrote after a year on the upper Amazon, "that the contemplation of nature alone is not sufficient to fill the human heart and mind."

We walked out into the harsh sunlight and back over the white sand beach where the boat waited. The contrast was disorienting. From primal gloom we had emerged to a strip of sun, blue sky, sand and water befitting a resort. In fact, Eladio told us that in the dry season—when the beaches are wider and the fish more accessible in the narrower river—Conceicao is something of a resort, though he didn't know where the vacationers come from.

"They come to fish," he said gravely as he worked to start the engine. "They stay at the Tropical Hotel. Very nice."

The white sand banks followed us downriver, appearing at intervals among the flooded sections where gnarled tree roots came right to the water's edge. For long stretches the river was a half-mile wide and straight. Ahead it blended with the sky and gave the impression of dropping off the edge of the world. Somewhere in that direction was the Amazon River, the main artery of this veined land we had been trudging through for weeks.

Sometimes the river would seem to end in a road block, a solid bank with trees leaning menacingly over the water right in front of us. This was where the river broke up into a mysterious maze of channels, at which point Eladio would earn the very modest sum he had requested by deftly picking his way through. He never slowed down, though. Between the speed of the river and the outboard we were doing nearly 20 miles an hour. His squinting eyes watched the ripples and swells for sandbars and rocks which might occur even in the middle of what seemed a deep channel. At several points there were actual rapids and Eladio had to fight the swift currents which threatened to turn the boat around while he shot a course among the rocks.

In clearer stretches the problem was debris. Small limbs stuck up, sometimes belying 50-foot logs just beneath the surface. Whole trees were jammed into the river bottom, their crowns sticking absurdly through the surface. We motored past floating islands— complete with banks, underbrush and tall trees—that had apparently broken from shore and were flowing downstream. The world, it seemed, was in a headlong rush to get to wherever it was we were going.

The procession was dramatized by flying fish which popped out of the water every few minutes. One bounced off Eladio's chest and ricocheted back into the water, provoking the only emotional response—a curse—we saw out of him all day. Fish of all kinds are so plentiful in the Araguaia that most people don't use bait; just a shiny lure and hook will soon produce a basketful of tucunare, a sort of river trout that makes a nice broiled supper. From time to time something big would crest the surface, catfish probably or dolphin or pirarucu, a primitive-looking scaly beast which resembles a North American muskie but often grows to nine feet in length. At narrow passages, water snakes would sometimes slither out toward the boat, only to dart away when the wake splashed them.

For much of the middle part of the journey we saw no boats and no people. A random, washed-out fisherman's hut in a small clearing on the shore was the only sign of humanity. Then we saw one fisherman paddling his heavy dugout with a spade-shaped blade, two others on the bank casting a tangle of lines. All the dozen or so fishermen whose paths we crossed were close to the shore.

"It's shadier there," Eladio explained. "No one travels in the middle of the river during the day." We weren't sure where that left us or just how Eladio saw himself fitting into his declaration. Conversation was not an easy thing with him. A lot of the rivermen seemed put off by the "invasion" of foreigners, even though most of the invaders are from Sao Paulo. We were more foreign still with our strange language and odd requests to float through the forest and wander into the jungle. His suspicion was understandable.

"A popular local saying has it that 'the suspicious *caboclo* hangs up his hammock then sleeps under it,' " wrote Charles Wagley in his book *Amazon Town* about life in one river community. The stereotype, said Wagley, is that the *caboclo* is a wary fellow and makes others wary of him. The *caboclo*—Eladio was one—is usually considered to be a person of mixed Portuguese and Indian blood, the combination dating back to marriages or illicit liaisons hundreds of years ago. In the 1600s the Portuguese crown promoted a policy of intermarriage between Europeans and natives in an effort to increase the population in the Amazon—and thus their tenuous hold on that territory. Soldiers and other male colonists were given inducements such as free land, tax exemptions and even political posts to marry native women. Their descendants still display the high cheekbones, tightly drawn eyes and relatively hairless bodies that are characteristic of the American Indian.

Caboclo also refers to a man of the forest or river who lives according to the traditional ways of hunting and fishing. For many years it was considered a derogatory term, though many of the caboclos we met seemed proud of it. They consider themselves distinct from the light-skinned newcomers, not because of their color and facial features, but for their skill in nature. The newcomers need a caboclo to show them how to lash a hut together from vines, to hunt, fish and find their way through the forest. We needed Eladio to pick his way down the maze of islands on the Araguaia—and so would any of the conquerers of the Amazon we had met in Campo Alegre.

Wagley noted that even after centuries, only certain parts of European culture had taken hold in the Amazon. Speech, government institutions and the church are all from the Old World, but unlike North America, the techniques of food gathering to this day are those originally learned from the Indians. It is, as the advocates of the Indian way like to say, a life in harmony with the jungle. Things are not planted in groves or extensive fields but gathered from the jungle in a nomadic—others would say inefficient—manner. The few crops that are planted, such as manioc, are grown by the ancient slash-and-burn method: a patch of jungle is cut and burned and crops planted for several seasons until they come up poorly, then another patch is cleared, with the family often moving to follow the land. Almost all the farming is done on the less fertile high ground and little on the considerably more fertile flood plain which has proved too difficult to cultivate. The caboclos who don't farm work in a kind of feudal bondage for the small companies that trade in lumber, rubber, palm oil, jute and a handful of other traditional Amazon goods. Just as in the days of the rubber barons, many of the caboclos are tied by their debts to the company store or the trading post, a form of bondage that has endured in this region where a man must still rely on importers for his staple goods.

It is, for most of the caboclos, a meager, uncertain life, largely untouched by the immigration and development around them. Some, like Eladio, get occasional ferrying jobs from the ranchers. Others pick up a few weeks' work at one of the mining projects or on a road crew. But according to the supervisors of those projects, few of the locals remain long. As one explained, "The jungle does not teach a man to save or worry about tomorrow." There may not be a lot of food, but there is always just enough for someone who knows how to find it. That same lesson seemed to apply to all living things in the jungle.

So if Eladio didn't want to talk to us, we understood. Besides, we were in a pleasant daze. Conceicao is close to the Equator so the sun seemed to come up fast and linger overhead for a long time. Even now in the late afternoon it hung high and milky yellow. Under a hat and with a breeze rushing up the river, to us the ride was delightful. The humidity had become less noticeable as the weeks went by and the 90-degree temperature was hot but not unpleasant.

We lay back on our luggage and felt the gentle rock of the boat as it slipped through short swells. Through half-slit eyes we watched the occasional nature show and the monotonous green bank. It had turned into one of those days that make the heat, the bugs, the dirt, the unfamiliar food worthwhile. The scenery and sense of isolation— no one could ever find us—were a blissful sedative.

We finally sat up when, as we turned a bend, a sudden swatch of white loomed across the sky 100 feet over us. It was a bridge, but it seemed like an abstract sculpture: brilliant white stone sharply defined against the deep blue background. Two great sweeping arches set on caissons high enough to withstand 40-foot floods. The artificial earth banks at either side were likewise high—too high to see if any traffic was crossing. The bridge stood alone, its purpose unseen, an intrusion of the landscape so incongruous it hardly seemed insulting. It was, in fact, the new lifeline connecting Conceicao with the Amazon highway system and the world. And from the perspective of the town, it seemed quite logically placed. But approached from upriver, it looked only like an absurd monument to man in the Amazon.

CONCEICAO

The Taruma Tropical Hotel, a low-slung green and gold plaster-of-Paris castle, looked down on a sloping, rocky stretch of shoreline. Off to the left, just upstream from where a sewer spewed grayish green gruel onto the sand, a cluster of women was, once again, beating and twisting laundry on boards jutting into the river. Eladio tossed our bags on the shore and we climbed out. We paid him the $50 we had agreed upon, which, after paying for gasoline up and back, would leave him with about $4 for his pocket. We asked where he was staying and he seemed puzzled.

"Home," he said simply.

It was almost sundown. He was going all the way back up that treacherous river?

"Of course."

What about waiting a day and seeing if he could find paying passengers? He laughed once at the suggestion as he pushed the boat off the shore. He was already turned away from us when he waved, his thick back bent over the tiller in the position he had held all day.

The Taruma was obviously used to queer sights because the arrival of a couple of grimy, sunburned Americans hardly caused a raise of an eyebrow.

"Here to buy land?" presumed the owner. "Everyone else is," he said pointing to the lobby area, which was empty. He had a brusque, self-important manner that broke down only on the last day of our stay when he gave us Taruma Tropical souvenir key chains with extras for our friends, "so they'll stay here too."

Our anticipation at seeing a true Amazon resort hotel, whatever that might be, had quickly faded. The Taruma was not much to speak of. The rooms were concrete cells with a lone window set high on the wall. The single light was a lamp between the two beds which were soft and squishy—stuffed with God knows what. A parade of tiny red ants ambled from somewhere in the wall, across the floor and back into the wall with no apparent objective in view. But there was, as in almost every reasonably good rooming house in the Amazon, a functioning toilet in a clean bathroom. The Brazilian innkeepers of the jungle consistently demonstrated tidier bathrooms than the French or the Irish, to pick just two examples from the supposedly civilized world.

There was also an air conditioner, up on the wall, next to the window—a big gray box the likes of which we hadn't seen since Brasilia. When switched on it produced a low rolling din like a piece of construction equipment and a weak breath of cool air. We tried to nap, but the machine was too loud, so we headed back to the front desk.

The lobby had become a busy place with several groups of what looked like ranchers checking in. The hotel is a staging area for many of the properties that spread out to the west of town. Absentee owners from the south fly to Brasilia then catch the milk-run plane up the Araguaia Valley to Conceicao. If they time it right, they can go from the office in Rio to the bush in a day. They spend the night at the hotel and head out early the next morning, making a great racket as they load up their Chevy pickup trucks. All seemed to have considerable girth and paraded about the hotel lobby in neatly pressed, tight-fitting tan bush shirts.

We ordered a couple of liter-sized Brahma beers and slumped in chairs on the porch to watch the sunset. The orb that had scorched the air all day was now an orange smear down and to the right of the river. It tinted the sandy beaches on the far shoreline pink. A cool breeze whipped across the river and when the beers came—very cold —we had to wonder if it wouldn't be just fine to live one's life in this place.

What happened next wasn't exactly an answer to the question, but the cool breeze was quickly followed by a stiff wind and a line of dark storm clouds that appeared from nowhere and began to march down the river toward us. The sun was swallowed and the whole scene took on a bluish hue. The river pocked with white caps and churned into deep swells. Lightning bolts drove into the forest on the far side, followed by thunder that seemed to roll right into the hotel lobby, and finally sheets of rain came at us horizontally.

Then, in ten minutes, the squall ended, an unfitting climax to such a dramatic introduction. We ate fish for dinner and worried about Eladio.

We woke early as the sun overpowered the laboring air conditioner and turned the room into a cauldron. We were immediately aware that in this enclave of civilization named for Our Lady of the Immaculate Conception, heat was going to be a problem. By 8 A.M., as the town was coming to consciousness, the sun was already burning the back of our necks and starting a perpetual trickle of sweat down our spines.

We went looking for the cathedral where the bishop resided and figured it wouldn't be hard to find. We stopped for a soda at the first lunch bar we came to—the first of many lunch bars and many sodas —and the tiny woman who served us lukewarm orange soda said the church was all the way at the end of the main street.

Conceicao was something of a boom town with people and money pouring in to cash in on the push into the Amazon. We found it hard to imagine what the place was like before the boom. Conceicao was a picture of how Hollywood has portrayed every backwater South American town. A skinny mule, its sides rippled by rib bones, snorted as it tugged a two-wheeled cart full of what looked to be garbage down the rutted dirt street. The driver of the cart mechanically flicked a long, stiff whip, oblivious to his target because a straw hat was pulled almost to his mouth. Babies wailed in nearly every one of the pastel-colored adobe houses while plump mothers in tattered housedresses stood in doorways, hands on hips, to watch the passing parade. Radio announcers competed with the babies, yelling rapidly in that distinctly South American echo-chamber style, then introducing songs dominated by loud trumpets. Dogs of indeterminate parentage lay in the road, limp and uncomprehending.

The sun quickly drew an appropriate scent from the scattered piles of garbage and the grayish green muck that ran in a natural gutter alongside the road. The flies, of course, arrived in droves. All of which made no difference to a dozen barefoot boys who chased a deflated soccer ball up and down an empty lot. One dog joined in the chase.

But underneath the stereotype of lassitude, we saw signs of the boom. Everybody on that main street was selling something; every house revealed a front room with a pool table or a counter and walls lined with bottles of soda, rum and cachaca; every store—usually just a house with a bigger front room—displayed piles of new merchandise: TVs, refrigerators, clock radios, bedsprings. Halfway down the street we had to lift our heads to take in the tallest building in town, next to the church, the three-story House of the Rancher, a sort of Abercrombie & Fitch for the cattle crowd. We saw displays of saddles, bits, rifles, crisp new straw cowboy hats and all manner of tools.

And we were aware of construction all over. On the new highway out to the new airport, mud huts even on the outskirts of town were being replaced by brick buildings.

Conceicao was about two miles long and went back from the river about eight or ten streets deep. Surrounding it was an ever-growing ring of shacks and huts put up by new arrivals, some seeking a fortune in the Amazon and others fleeing the jungle after their farms had failed.

The Church of the Immaculate Conception between the main town and a ragged slum of primitive houses is the dominant building, though compared to other churches in South America it is something of a dowager. Its stucco walls are painted gray with white trim. In front, two modest spires preside over a long open park that runs down to the river. A wall alongside the park was painted with the slogans, "Enough Hunger!" "Land For Those Who Want It!" and "Out Figueiredo!"

We found a new rectory in the back. Bishop Joseph Patrick Hanrahan, sitting behind a desk in his book-lined office, was surprised to see two visitors.

"Well, you know, I'm of course happy to see you," he stammered. "But I do wish you had made an appointment." He wasn't kidding. We actually thought he was going to send us away because we hadn't called in advance. He pondered for a moment in silence then took a pinch of snuff from one of a collection of tins on his desk. He sneezed and said, "Nasty habit." Then, properly composed, he said, "Very well, what can I do for you?"

We said we wanted to talk about the Catholic Church in the Amazon. We had been led to believe it was very much a part of the process of change.

"That is a quite, quite large question," he said, sighing like a man who often finds it regrettably necessary to reduce complex problems to simple responses.

"Let's understand a little recent history," he said, and began a long pedagogical narrative. Throughout Brazil, the church has ceased to sit on the sidelines and has become a participant in the political process. It has renounced centuries of traditional support for the ruling class and has come over to the side of the poor. As Hanrahan put it, the change came, in effect, the day the church decided it would no longer preach that prayer alone would vanquish hunger. Since then it has become in many ways the staunchest and best organized opposition to the military government, and in the repressive years from 1968 to 1974 it was the only dissenting voice not completely stifled. Top church officials have formed a sort of shadow government which frequently speaks out on matters of economic policy, labor relations, social welfare and land reform. The power of the cardinals and bishops in this country—96 percent of whose citizens are Catholics— is overwhelming. Merely the threat of a popular uprising has forced the government to back away from numerous potential church–state

confrontations, though harassment of individual priests is not un-
common.

The clearest watershed in this revolution within the church,
Hanrahan said, was the Bishops Conference in Medellin, Colombia,
in 1968.

"The mandate of that conference was that the church in Latin
America was no longer to be a church of sacrament but it was to
become a church of deed," David Regan, an adviser to Brazil's National Conference of Catholic Bishops, had told us in Brasilia. That
policy was reaffirmed at the conference in Puebla, Mexico, in 1979.
The Brazilian clerics say their own even more radical course was reaffirmed by Pope John Paul II during his 1980 visit here when, among
other gestures, he presented his sacred ring to a congregation in Rio's
most notorious slum and firmly embraced Dom Helder Camara,
whom some call the most radical bishop in Brazil. The photo of that
embrace, ripped from a magazine, adorns the walls of many homes
we saw across the Amazon.

For the bishops, the vast Amazon wilderness has become a priority area, Joseph Patrick Hanrahan said. The question of who
should own the land is starkest here. And, since so much of the
Amazon is unoccupied, there is a sense that action should be taken
before the problem becomes insoluble. In a report emphasizing its
concern over land problems, the Bishops Conference wrote: "Everywhere we hear the cry of the suffering people, who are either threatened with the loss of land they have, or are powerless to get any."

Dom Jose, as the locals call him, stands in the front lines of that
fight; his sprawling diocese spreads from the Araguaia River far to the
north and west and includes many of the areas where small farmers
are fighting large landowners for a piece of the Amazon. His diocese
takes in, if not the leading edge of the frontier, at least some very wild
country.

A scholarly, fastidious man, the bishop appeared comfortable
discoursing on the "liberation theology" that provides intellectual
roots for the church's new activism. But he balked at discussing his
own views or activities because the government had recently begun a
crackdown on the church by expelling an Italian priest for making
"subversive statements." Several weeks earlier, two French priests
assigned to his diocese, Francois Gouriou and Aristedes Camio, had

been arrested and jailed for their involvement in a dispute between the federal police and squatters in Sao Geraldo, north along the river.

"They were arrested for the crime of 'consciousness raising,' whatever that is." The bishop shrugged. "They will go on trial in a few weeks to see if they should be deported." The incident—an increasingly typical one, he said—ended in a shoot-out between the posseiros who refused to move and the police. Four policemen were wounded and a man who was apparently working for the police was killed.

The portly bishop, who with his pink face and wispy white hair reminded us of a benign, beardless Santa Claus, said that before we could understand what the church is trying to do, we needed to understand the problem of land in Brazil. It is, he explained, quite simply a mess. The country had long been run on an almost feudal basis with peasants working in the coffee groves or sugar fields of the giant *latifundios* that were controlled by a few wealthy families. It was a system derived from imperial Spain and Portugal where large tracts were bestowed upon the court's favorites; huge landholdings still characterize Latin America. In contrast, the United States made deliberate efforts—the most notable being the Homestead Act—to open up land areas to landless settlers.

The legacy in Brazil has been a concentration of ownership with perhaps 3 percent of the people controlling two-thirds of the land, and at the other end, half the population—60 million people—owning less than one-tenth. Ten million people have no land and want some. It is a pattern that exists all over settled Brazil and is repeating itself in the Amazon as that region is opened to settlement. As one deputy minister told us in Brasilia, "The little guy never gets a break in Brazil, and the situation isn't changing."

The ownership issue is further contorted by the fact that as far back as 400 years ago, the Portuguese crown was doing a sloppy job of keeping land records. Particularly in the Amazon, giant grants were made to noblemen, often with unclear or overlapping boundaries. Some held title only to the Brazil nuts or timber the land could produce. And many deeds were simply forgeries. That messy situation has never been corrected.

The unwitting victims of this confusion are the posseiros, immigrant families in the Amazon in search of land primarily for subsistence farming. The posseiros are at the vanguard of settlement of the region, often hacking their own paths to unoccupied land that is pristine forest. Either because they are in a hurry, or they are unaware of legal formalities or unable to believe that anyone actually owns the forest, posseiros settle, or possess, land without having legal title. Their own work to clear and till the land is, they feel, their entitlement. Of course their work increases the value of the land. Once an unscrupulous landowner hears that squatters have provided access to previously untilled land he either finds out who owns legal title to the land and buys it, forges a title for it, or makes a claim with more legal basis than the posseiros. What inevitably ensues is a conflict over ownership, resolved in court or, increasingly now, by violence.

"I'm afraid money makes the real difference in how these conflicts are resolved," said the bishop. When a new landowner surveys his property, the first question is how many squatters must he evict? Under official Brazilian law, if the land is without legal title when the squatters occupy it and they work it for a year and a day, they become the rightful owners. Under the unofficial law of the Amazon, "legitimized" by a fee into the right hands, squatters can either accept the new owner's offer of a small payment and leave, or wait to be burned out or shot by his hired guns, known as *pistoleiros*.

"His deeds, of course, are always correct, having been authenticated by the proper authorities," the bishop said with mock severity.

When we pressed him to go into specifics about corruption, he smiled, folded his short fingers on the desk and said, "You're not going to get me to talk about that, so don't even try."

Bishop Hanrahan also expressed concern with the violence that seems endemic to the region. As he was describing it, a young, freckle-faced priest entered the rectory.

"Ah, fine. Father Peter," the bishop called, "save me some trouble. Tell these gentlemen about your little incident."

Father Peter McCarthy, not yet 30, was the assistant pastor. He walked into the room with a collegial smile and an extended hand, and he invited us across the hall to his office, to the obvious relief of the bishop who, despite his best efforts, could not conceal the fact that he had other matters to attend to. Father Peter spoke with only a slight brogue and struck us more as American-Irish than the Dubliner he is.

McCarthy said his troubles came in the same town where the French priests had been arrested for "consciousness raising," and about a week later. The problem arose when the government, after the Frenchmen's arrest, brought in a substitute priest to preside over a series of feast days. However, the government did not ask the bishop's approval. Such a request probably would have been a waste of time, because the government's substitute priest once had been accused of diverting church funds for his personal use, though prosecution was dropped.

"They had also promised the townspeople a 'Papal Mass' which turned out to be one of those videotapes of a Mass the Pope said in Rio. They put the television on the altar. That's a sacrilege."

Bishop Hanrahan's response had been to dispatch Father McCarthy on a 12-hour bus trip with a letter informing the substitute priest that he was not authorized to say Mass in Hanrahan's parish. Shortly after McCarthy arrived, a group of federal agents burst into the rectory and, at gunpoint, took him and four nuns to their field headquarters.

"My gosh, I was scared," he told us. "I had one gun in my ear and one in my face. I thought they were capable of doing anything. They were very insulting to us and if they weren't very, very mad, they were certainly doing a good job of acting."

McCarthy was sure they were all from GETAT, the acronym for a special force of military and law enforcement officers assigned to keep order in the Araguaia Valley. The group reports directly to the National Security Council in Brasilia and can readily invoke national security laws that suspend the civil rights guarantees of the Brazilian Constitution. Although they are, in effect, a secret police force, much of their presence is open and they can often be seen patrolling towns in jeeps and trucks painted black with a white stripe and with the name "GETAT" on the door.

"When they got me to the headquarters, they beat me up a bit—not too bad, but enough to hurt. Then they stood me up against this wall for a few hours. One fellow kept coming up and putting a gun in my ear and pulling the trigger. Click. It was empty."

McCarthy told the story like a victim in a precinct house, in a slow, dispassionate, just-the-facts monotone that made it more credible and more chilling. It was easy to become blasé about tales of random violence and cruelty in the jungle; there were so many. But this was, after all, a priest. And while nobody actually put a bullet into him, having a revolver cocked and released next to your ear is about as horrible a mental torture as we could imagine.

"Well, about 5 o'clock in the morning they let me go. No explanation. Just, 'You can go.' I was a little shaken up and bruised, but otherwise O.K."

We asked if he'd ever go back up there.

"Sure I will. That's just what they want is to keep us away. The church is a moral force they do not know how to deal with . . ." He paused. His nostrils opened slightly and his eyes set in a distant stare. He hardly moved his lips as he finished his sentence softly, "The bastards."

That evening there was a Mass in the cathedral, the start of the feast days in honor of Our Lady of the Immaculate Conception that would occupy the town with dances, bazaars, fairs and ceremonies for most of the week. Long before Mass began at 7:30, the church was so full that people seemed to be oozing from every opening. A huge crowd gathered on the steps to listen to the service over loudspeakers. On the sides, people flocked to the tall windows, some clinging to the wire screens to get a better look inside.

We couldn't get in and headed down the quiet main street, stopping at a small corner barroom which displayed two of the Amazon's standard, undersized pool tables. On the wall hung a movie poster that boasted "Matt Dillon" over a reasonable likeness of the actor James Arness. Underneath it said in Portuguese, "History of the Far West." Two young men chatted noisily as they played at one of the tables and gulped beers; they belonged to the two lumber-laden Mercedes trucks parked out front.

We played them for a beer and won. They took the loss well enough, but insisted on another game. We had long since figured out that, on these short tables with small pockets, you had to hit the ball softly. This idea somehow went against the masculine grain here, and quite a few of our opponents' well-aimed but hard shots bounced into the pocket and back out. We dropped a wimpy assortment of nicks and caresses into the pockets to win game after game. The truck drivers stood, shirts unbuttoned, cigarettes dangling, shaking their heads and paying up graciously—but refusing to change their style.

On the way back to the hotel, we noticed the insides of many houses flickering with a familiar bluish light. In front of some houses, people stood in the street and stared into the window. The light was television. The townspeople had settled in for a night with the tube. Their less-fortunate neighbors who couldn't afford TV stood in the gutter and watched—whole families at a time. A few even brought folding chairs to set up in the street.

After gazing for a few minutes at one of the wildly popular soap operas that captivate Brazil we continued on. The stores were all shuttered and few of the bars had customers. Street lights, dim anyway, were more and more widely spaced as we went on. Through one doorway, we could see a man leaning on both forearms and spooning something into his mouth from a bowl. A few doors down a furniture maker was working late, sanding a headboard. Through another door a girl who looked to be about 14 knelt with her back to us. She was putting a bow in a child's hair. She wore a skirt, but no shirt. Her straight brown hair came just to the top of her naked back.

We found another priest in town the following morning who was not as reticent as the bishop to talk politics. Father Ricardo Rezende, a Brazilian, works for the National Bishops' Conference in its land reform office. His headquarters, in a cluttered room of the Catholic school, had file cabinets filled with records of land disputes. He said he was following almost 100 disputes involving 4,500 families and 18,000 people. But Rezende does more than monitor the disputes; he encourages them.

"This is a class war," he said calmly. "The church is the most important force for change, but we must help the people take the fight into their hands."

The dark, bearded priest, tall and thin, was articulate and intense. He sounded untroubled by doubts about his work, despite the specific words of the Pope that year that priests were not to "promote class warfare."

"You cannot preach the gospel to a man with an empty stomach," Rezende said, echoing a slogan expressed by much of the liberal South American clergy. "He must have basic human dignity and in this part of the world that means a piece of land where he and his family can grow food to live on."

Rezende, from the government's viewpoint, is a very dangerous man, not so much for his ideas—which are only slightly more radical than those of many other priests—but for the fact that he carries them out. Rezende does not just preach from a pulpit; in fact, he rarely preaches at all. He organizes.

"Where the church is most effective is in bringing the rural workers together, helping them to realize they have common problems and that together they are strong," he told us. This activist priest has helped organize a series of Rural Workers Syndicates that elect representatives and are beginning to make demands on the government for land reform. That afternoon, Rezende took us with him to a meeting of officials of the syndicates in his region, held in a remote church retreat in the jungle outside of town. There were 50 people there, sitting on small school desks set in a semicircle. A naked baby played on the concrete floor near her mother. Strewn about were copies of the group's newspaper, *Free Land*, which features the symbol of an angry farmer with an upraised hoe breaking through a barbed-wire fence.

Rezende sat in the back of the room and observed as the group discussed the upcoming elections, efforts to sign up new members and the status of some of the currently most violent areas. From time to time one of the participants would come back to consult with Rezende. They all displayed great respect for the young priest and listened gravely to his words.

"The church is the only one who defends the worker in Brazil," he said, turning to us. "That national security group the government sent here . . ."—he was referring to GETAT—"has no interest in settling disputes, only in keeping the violence down."

The church, too, has an interest in keeping the violence down, but, by Rezende's account, not to the exclusion of justice. He is not a man who is repulsed by talk of bloodshed. At one point a straw-hatted, nearly toothless farmer came up and the priest introduced him as a man who had recently been thrown off his land, but had returned with a neighbor and gunned down one of the pistoleiros. Rezende patted him on the back gently in a sort of gesture of absolution.

"If the government does not give the people land, there will be lots of deaths. The center of the problem is now here, but it will spread," the priest said.

Rezende described how in the early 1970s as many as 20,000 government troops had difficulty flushing out of the jungle a small band of guerrillas, primarily radical students from the south who had chosen the Amazon as a staging area for violence against the military junta. The guerrillas never realized their goal of organizing a workers' rebellion in the area. "The government has never said how many guerrillas were involved, but we know it was about 70. They were students and professionals from the south. The leader was a basketball player. If they could cause so much trouble, imagine what 600 or 700 posseiros could cause!"

Already that year, Rezende estimated, 34 people had died as a result of land disputes in the municipality of Conceicao. Some had been killed by Indians, some by gold prospectors and the rest either by posseiros or pistoleiros.

"I will not tell someone to kill, but I will not tell him not to," said Rezende in trying to explain the apparent departure from Christian doctrine. "These posseiros have suffered as much as they can. They have been moved off their land eight, ten times. But they will move no more. We will give them legal help. But Brazilian justice does not favor the common man. It would be possible for a lawyer to win, but it takes so long, four or five years. Also, there is tremendous corruption. There is sometimes only one alternative left. I cannot be the one to say, 'No, you cannot use it.' "

As one of the candidates in the front of the large room gave a speech, Rezende, in a whisper, concluded his, though on a somewhat less assured note than he had started. "Every day more and more people come here to look for land. It is a powerful attraction that I think no one can control. I do not know what will come of all this."

Then the group wanted to hear from us. One of the farmers told Rezende that everyone wanted to ask the American journalists some questions. We stood in the front of the room and tried to explain what we were doing. No, we were not necessarily here to support them, but we were interested in finding out about them. We didn't really know if the church was absolutely correct and if the government was absolutely wrong. We agreed that organizing into elected groups was important, but it remained to be seen what they would or could do.

It was a wishy-washy answer. We had been caught unawares. Even as we sat in the large dark room we hadn't taken this congregation seriously enough. The bedraggled group, obviously poor and intimate with hardship reminded us of the countless antiwar and other radical discussions American students had participated in during the 60s; but to what avail—a group of reasonably affluent college students who took themselves very seriously but whose destinies really were decided elsewhere.

Here was a group of people—most of them unable to read and write—who were talking about friends who had been murdered and crops that had been burned. These posseiros were tired of ceding their destinies to someone else. The church was telling them that they had to be accountable for their lives, for feeding themselves and their families. This was dignity. This was salvation. This was the deed God meant for them to perform.

Battle lines had been drawn and we were straddling the lines, we told them. We argued that it was important to be objective, because we believed that if the facts were known the truth would win out. If land titles were false, that had to be proved and not assumed. If titles were good and landowners had paid for their land, then posseiros really were trespassing.

They were upset with us. This was not what they wanted to hear at all. Journalists, in their minds, are partisans and either we were for them or against them.

"We want land," one woman implored. "Isn't that enough for you to want to help us?" Another man came closer to making their point when he said, "If only you tell people our story, they will agree with us, because we are right."

And then the woman with the naked baby asked the question which showed how simple and how complex was this whole discussion. "You are Americans so you will know," she began. "Tell me why it is that Ludwig, an American, can own so much of my country and I can have none of it?"

There was no answer. Or, at least we had none. Rezende began to talk about Daniel Ludwig, the multimillionaire owner of four million acres of the Amazon, as a symbol to rally support against the government. We left.

On the way back to town, we talked about Rezende. He, like

many other activist priests, was unlikely to be a Communist, although
the big ranchers and the military undoubtedly called him that. His
language sounded similar to Marxist rhetoric, but here it didn't mean
the same thing. Many of Rezende's words seemed born of a legitimate
frustration with a system that allows no dissent and rigs the rules in
favor of a very few people. He had given the people a certain hope
that they can change their lives. But he had also imbued them with a
single-minded self-righteousness that allowed little to intercede in
their path. They were not to be denied what God says is theirs. And
they knew God said it because Father Rezende and the other priests
had told them. We knew why the government was scared.

Conceicao is in the state of Para, home of the king-making Jarbas
Passarinho, president of the Brazilian Senate and a leader of the
government party. A retired colonel, Passarinho is one of the few
civilians to wield true force in the federal government, and Giovanni
Queiroz, the boyish mayor of Conceicao, had run into him head on.
The story we heard reminded us of some bayou do-gooder taking on
Huey Long at the height of his majesty.

The Mayor's particular misdeed was switching party affiliation
and aligning himself with the governor of Para, a sworn enemy of
Passarinho. In light of the predictions of a massive defeat for the
government party in the November, 1982, elections, Queiroz apparently decided to weather two years of Passarinho's wrath in order to
be with the expected winners in the country's first free elections since
1964.

A few months before Queiroz's defection, the government had
built a grand new airport 17 kilometers from the center of the town to
replace a rocky, dirt strip that was as much a football field as a
runway. The new tarmacked field secured Conceicao's future as the
size of commercial planes visiting the area increased; the runway
could accommodate a *Boeing*, the Brazilian word for jet and one of
the bellwethers of progress on the developing frontier. But that
progress was now threatened because of Queiroz's switch of allegiance. The government's hammer of retribution descended swiftly
upon Conceicao, and the airport was the victim.

We hired a taxi to take us out to the facility, and about seven kilometers out of town we learned first-hand how the game of politics is played in Brazil.

The road ended. The smooth, black macadam that was an exquisite luxury compared to the normally bone-jarring thoroughfares suddenly stopped, leaving a particularly hideous stretch of rocky, rutted and washed-out road that took fully three times as long to travel as the first half. At the end was the airport itself, an empty blockhouse with no telephones, functioning washrooms or even radio for incoming airplanes. Practically the day Queiroz switched parties, the government contractors were ordered to pack up and leave.

When we talked to Mayor Queiroz he was a little sheepish about how swift the retribution had been, but clearly it was not a decision he had taken lightly and all the advantages were in his favor. If democracy is coming, he is going to ride the crest. As the Mayor of Conceicao, he is responsible not only for the town but for the 30,000-square-mile municipality that spreads to the west. When he came to Conceicao in 1972 as a young doctor who had taken someone's advice to "go west," there were 2,600 voters. Now there are close to 115,000 people with the number growing at 15 percent a year.

"It is an avalanche that we cannot control," he said. "There is a *corrida* for land."

He was sitting in a dimly lit, carpeted office that took up one end of the city hall building. The air conditioner was loud and cold. His outside office was lined with constituents seeking favors. Three or four aides regulated the flow, occasionally letting in one who had a particularly urgent problem. Queiroz told one old man, who was wheezing noisily, to "go to the drugstore and put it on my bill."

The Mayor's medical skills were still in demand though he practiced little. He came from the prosperous state of Minas Gerais when he was about 30, calling himself "gynecologist, cardiologist and psychiatrist." Handsome, with carefully coiffeured hair and manicured fingernails, he still affected the white costume—shoes, slacks and embroidered shirt—of his former calling. He was not at all like the old, sepia portraits of former mayors that lined his waiting room: stern, mustached faces staring down from above an assortment of stiff collars, white double-breasted suits or puffed-chest military tunics.

Not that Queiroz did not have some of the traits of those old

caudilhos. He was a rich man, by the standards of Conceicao, owning, with a collection of relatives, several large ranches to the west.
Rich and powerful in the lexicon of Father Rezende and the posseiros
meant evil. Queiroz had been the object of much of their derision. So
it was surprising for us to find out that the Mayor supported the
church and, as we already knew, warred with the very government he
was supposed to be using to manipulate the little man. Queiroz, we
realized quickly, was a politician. With a few modifications, the same
species can be found chomping on a cigar and cutting a deal in one of
the anterooms of Chicago's city hall. The Mayor represented not
some monolithic, all-powerful central government, but rather his own
self-interest kept in check by those of his constituents who exercised
their vote. In that sense he was accountable. He was also clever
enough to realize that to get ahead his actions no longer had to be in
lockstep with Brasilia. Attacking the federal government was not a
bad way to win friends, especially since he knew the 1982 elections
could be expected to draw an outpouring of antipathy against the
government and 18 years of military control.

"The government is the cause of our problems here," he said.
"The laws permit the latifundios [large landholdings] to remain
unproductive while I have people coming back from the jungle every
day because they could find no land. The people get no support from
their government. A road is cut with no idea of the consequences:
people rush into the new area only to be turned back. The government doesn't provide the infrastructure to take care of the demand
for land. They have no process for documentation of titles. They
don't even have maps, and the ones they have are wrong."

Those who were profiting from the opening of the Amazon, he
charged, were the big corporations—another mandatory target for a
populist candidate. Queiroz talked at length of one project by a large
construction company that purchased land for 35 cruzeiros per
hectare, improved it with roads and the creation of support services
like schools and hospitals, and sold it to farmers for 15,000 cruzeiros
per hectare. "That price can only be paid by the middle-class farmers
from the south, not by the people who must have land. The problem
with Brazil is that the top has always been at the top and they don't
know what it's like to be on the bottom."

He said he supported the church when it opposed policies that maintained the hard life of the lower classes. "Someone must be shouting for the abandoned minorities. No one is in a position to shout louder than the church. They have made the government realize the problem and maybe there will be a solution, although right now I think this government considers even the discussion too painful for the country."

We visited Bishop Hanrahan again before we left and told him of our conversation with Mayor Queiroz. He appeared bemused. He told us that the Mayor had helped save his life the previous year when he had a massive heart attack. His personal view was that the Mayor, to whom he was abundantly grateful, was a better doctor than a politician.

We had other thoughts. Political skills aside, Giovanni Queiroz may represent an optimistic harbinger for the country. He switched parties because he was concerned with popular opinion; his conversion had come about because of his fear of an election defeat. That he was no more principled than many American politicians—pro-government one day, anti-establishment the next—may be of minor importance. What matters is that Queiroz felt the need to change his views to respond to his constituency, to align himself with the posseiros. Another stall had opened in the marketplace of ideas. Whether opposition to the government will be effective in relieving misery remains to be seen. Giovanni Queiroz thought so. That in itself is a first step. The bishop was bemused, but we suspected he was also encouraged.

CUMARU

When we went to see Conceicao's former airport, the football field lookalike, we noticed an unusual entourage of men earnestly huddled in conversation.

One of the group looked especially menacing. He was wearing black leather boots, a white T-shirt, and blue jeans held up by a belt dangling a conspicuous wood-handled Colt .44, a gun more vicious than practical. He also wore intimidating mirrored sunglasses that hid the eyes of an acne-scarred, thin-lipped face. Unsurprisingly, the other four men allowed him to do most of the talking.

We, too, were conspicuous in the Amazon, and before long one of the men came over to us. We introduced ourselves, and we asked who they were.

"We are with the government. National Security Council."

We asked what they were doing.

"Visiting."

"What?"

"The region."

So much for their itinerary. Our interlocutor seemed more adept at asking questions than answering.

He asked us if we wanted to meet Colonel Ary Santos, the man behind the sunglasses. We shook hands with Santos, but felt uncomfortable staring at our own reflections in his glasses, the alternative attraction being his gun.

He, too, asked us what we were doing. He said he had heard about us and asked if we wanted to visit him at Cumaru, a remote gold mine which is under government control because of the potentially violent presence of 18,000 lusting prospectors. Santos told us he was in charge of keeping the peace at Cumaru, a job for which he appeared to be eminently well suited. Apologizing that he could not talk longer with us because he had to discuss problems with "my men," gesturing toward the other four in the group, he told us to contact the Caixa Economica, the government bank in Conceicao, when we wanted to fly to Cumaru. They would radio our request to him, and he would send a plane for us.

There are advantages to making friends with the military in a country run by the military. When we accepted Santos' invitation we witnessed an efficiency rarely seen in the jungle. Within days, the clerk at the bank searched the town to find us. He implored us to hurry, an unusual request in that languid atmosphere, and barely let us stop at the Taruma Tropical for our toothbrushes before setting off at an accelerated rate to the airport. He told us he was hurrying because Colonel Santos "doesn't like to wait." The ride to the plane was swift, but so jarring on the unfinished part of the road that we cursed the day Mayor Queiroz left the government party. The propellers of the plane were already spinning when we arrived at the airport, and the pilot, with a shooing motion, shouted, "Hurry, hurry" over the din of the engines. Even before we had fastened our seatbelts we were launched out over the jungle.

Or what once was jungle. West of Conceicao was no better than elsewhere in the Araguaia Valley. Plumes of smoke were as prevalent as trees, even as Conceicao dropped out of sight and we passed over places on no one's maps. Land wars burn through this territory, and the unavoidable victim of the struggle for ownership is the jungle, which is seared to plant crops and to recycle those already planted. We passed over the ironically named Redencao (Redemption), a town that didn't exist five years before, but which now sprawls like oozing mud on a green carpet. Other spontaneous towns—Rio Maria and Xinguara—sent clouds of dust into the air as we overflew them. The reputation of the three towns is as notorious as the embattled land around them. Violence from the jungle turf chokes each of these places, because they serve as havens for pistoleiros waiting to kill, posseiros running from being killed, and the police, some allegedly so corrupt that their rates are cheaper than the gunmen's.

There would be law and order where we were going; we couldn't imagine Colonel Santos having it any other way. Who would be foolhardy enough to disrupt this imperious man's regimen?

At Cumaru his command was 18,000 miners—grubby, hungry men. They live abjectly alone in an angry jungle that gives up its gold only at a high price: malaria, dysentery, loneliness and malnutrition. The lure of gold has lost none of its luster since the coming of the conquistadores. As new roads open easier access to the jungle, tens of thousands of Brazilians, mostly poor laborers but also some lawyers and businessmen, come to try their luck. Spurred on by reports of mines like Serra Pelada, where men reportedly make millions by the minute, they bid good-bye to sorrow on the land in the drought-ridden Northeast and assure their families they'll come back rich. It is estimated that there are 250,000 prospectors in Para, most of them from the northeast states. Here men have found an outlet for their relentless optimism, which they have kept alive during years of famine and despair, and they are willing to endure a life as tough now as it was 400 years ago when Midas-struck men first starved and died in the search for gold that has only now been found. Simple rhyming poems of self-celebration amid suffering have emerged from these garimpeiros, and they are adored by the comfortable chic in Rio and Sao Paulo who gather on Friday nights for samba, cachaca and these readings.

The camaraderie revealed in these laments often is shattered when gold actually is discovered. Rumors sail through the Amazon—

even we knew constantly what spots were promising—and a strike brings thousands into an area overnight. This is what happened when gold was discovered at Cumaru on November 21, 1980. Shortly thereafter, miners began dying in fights over claims, over women, over alcohol. When the government deems a strike significant enough it sends in administrators like Santos to impose law and order and set up health facilities and a warehouse for necessary supplies. In return, miners must sell their gold to the government for 25 percent below world market value. In the first year of Cumaru's existence, the government bought 1.6 metric tons of gold, which is a lot at once, but a meager living when divided among 18,000 miners.

"This is a socialized mine," Santos joked as we toured his base camp. "Everyone is poor."

He ordered a jeep for us to go to the nearest mine—dozens of mines are scattered over 550 square miles—and ordered the driver to let us "go wherever" we wanted and talk to "whomever" we wanted. Santos is sensitive to a nasty public image of these mines as cordoned-off national security areas where miners are enslaved by the military.

At a clearing in the jungle, a hundred men were trying to squeeze something from a sprawling mudhole that was actually the remains of a stream bed that had been ripped open and gouged. Men were hauling bags of muck or squatting near the water and swirling big metal pans. The center of attention was a long wooden chute that sloped down the side of a hill. Dirt and muddy water are added at the top of the chute and flow over a series of barriers. The water and dirt drains off while the heavier gold particles stay behind. The technique of sluicing is probably as old as the act of mining, and, caked as they were in beige mud, some of the miners looked that old, too.

Dirty and ragged, wearing a collection of rubber thong sandals, soccer shorts, torn T-shirts and turned-down hats, only a few of those we talked to seemed to have wrested much treasure from the earth. Always someone is finding just enough gold—a spoonful washed from the mud, tiny particles to hold in one cupped hand, the lure which keeps most of them there. But for the vast majority, the months of living in black plastic lean-tos and hauling bags of dirt until their bodies can't stand anymore are for naught.

After almost a year, Francisco Carvalho had found 20 grams—worth about $250. He traveled here to become a rich man but found that no one was handing him anything. "I have three children and no job. The drought in Piaui is very bad this year so I came here. Now there is a drought for me here."

A sallow, skinny man of 30 years, he was not working that day, a bad sign. Instead, he was sitting around with some friends in the dirty white bakery tent of Jose Angelo da Silva, an unsuccessful prospector who had had the idea of making bread. Da Silva employs many of the hard-luck miners to turn out the slightly sweet rolls and cakelike bread that is the staple of most diets there.

The bakery tent is a popular gathering place, if only for the cheering smell of baking dough. But da Silva, the baker, offers another attraction. The tall, muscular man once worked in the fabled Serra Pelada mine. This is where men reportedly find gold rocks the size of their fists. *Everybody* at Serra Pelada is rich, the miners told us. Most can only guess, though, since the mine at the top of a small hill about 300 miles northeast of Cumaru is tightly controlled by the government. After the initial rush of 20,000 prospectors, the government closed off the site to keep it from becoming more chaotic than it already was. To get in to mine you need a permit, issued only after some other miner leaves.

Jose Angelo da Silva was there in the early days when men in the deep pit could be heard exploding in screams of joy as they unearthed nuggets of precious metal. He sits back in his tent and tells the tales slowly, with windy digressions born of the assurance of a storyteller with a captive audience. For his part, da Silva found nothing. He was only there a short time when he learned his wife was very ill, and he went home to the state of Maranhao. When he returned to Serra Pelada, they wouldn't let him back in.

The conclusion to da Silva's tale made Bernardo Mendes, a fellow Maranhense, snort with laughter and slap his leg. He came here to escape a wife and 10 kids at home. Never mind the gold, of which he has found none. "It was the noise at home which bothered me. It's so quiet here."

At lunchtime we meandered back to camp. In addition to the bakery, we saw a series of small shops set up around the various mining sites. As poor as some of these miners are, there is money around. Even if they are just hauling dirt for someone who has made a strike, they are earning more than they did back home; the day laborers take in about $5 a day. A traveling society of entrepreneurs follows them around, setting up shops that sell meals to miners who have found enough gold to celebrate, and rubber boots, hats, souvenir T-shirts, even plastic attaché cases to carry their goods around in.

We stopped at one of these sheds, about twice the size of an outhouse, run by a swarthy man wearing a stained University of Arizona T-shirt. When we asked what he had to eat, he gave us that "Have I got something for you!" look and began to load things on the counter—a loaf of bread, a round casing of pink meat, a huge white onion and a knob of cheese that had been hanging in a net bag.

"Mortadella, cheese and onion sandwich. Magnificent."

Little Italy in the jungle. It was the first meat we had seen in weeks that was recognizable, so we said to pile it on. He handed us two thick sandwiches. They were delicious with garlicky meat and crunchy pungent onion.

"You're the journalists, right?"

We were surprised he knew.

"News travels fast here. Everybody lives for rumors."

We told him we were just plain old garimpeiros.

He laughed. "There will be real wealth here. These men will be rich some day. The Amazon is giving us what is ours."

It began to rain heavily, one of those sudden violent downpours that were becoming more frequent as the rainy season in the eastern Amazon progressed. We stood under the overhang and talked to the Mortadella Man. His story had the same theme as a hundred others we heard. He picked up and came to the Promised Land with an idea for making money but with no skills more specific than a willingness to work hard. His business was built around an electric blender that he used to mix *vitaminas,* fruit milk shakes. The mortadella and cheese sandwiches were an afterthought. We had no idea what the demand for such things is in the bush, but he seemed happy enough. He had taken a risk and was surviving, and not in a Rio slum, fearing the moment someone would come in and put a gun to his face. That happened all the time in Rio, he said, but not very often here. "Here, no one will kill you for this," he said, patting the mortadella.

The rain stopped. How much, we asked.

He flipped his palms up in front of his face in that bartender's gesture that says, "On the house."

"You just tell people that Brazil is the land of the future. You tell them that this country is going to be great."

We left with mixed emotions, grateful for the kind gesture, yet suspecting that everyone we met had been hustled there in advance by the country's public relations department. But there are too many people in too many different places who say the same thing—though not all gave us free sandwiches—to think that they are anything but sincere. There is a real team spirit. The Brazilian dream is a serious topic of conversation and a venerated ideal. Maybe it was just our American-bred cynicism that made us think their optimism naive and odd. This sort of spirit has become so co-opted by politicians in our country as to be meaningless and no more than a shibboleth heard around election time. Yet, in the aftermath of an Amazon rainstorm—in a setting of natural grandeur and mystery, among men searching for a dream—these words sounded convincing.

Colonel Santos stood in front of his office, having a stern-faced talk with a couple of miners when we approached. He is close to six feet and light-complexioned, as are most of the Brazil officer corps who come from the states in the south, mostly Rio Grande do Sul, a continent away. The miners are typically five feet one or two and the color of creamed coffee. They looked small next to him, like children, and perhaps appropriately, because Santos, as we found out, has a real paternal regard for them. They are always getting into trouble—fighting, wandering onto private property, getting bitten by snakes—and Santos always bails them out.

"Now I don't want you prospecting over that ridge, Pedro Lima. Stay on this side. I'm warning you. I know you think there's gold there, but that is Indian land. If you go there I will expel you from Cumaru. O.K.?"

The men nodded their heads rapidly as Santos spoke. "Yes, Colonel." "Yes, Colonel."

It was an unconvincing demonstration. They walked away like schoolboys from the principal's office. We were tempted to offer Santos a wager on how long it would take them to get over that ridge but decided against it. He already knew.

"I don't need this problem," he sighed as he rubbed the sweat from his hairless neck. "The last two times miners have gone onto

Indian land, a war party has captured them and brought them back to the camp. Those were some very scared men. The first time I gave the Indians—the Kayapo-Gorotire—the weapons the miners carried, but the second time I was worried that if this kept up, the Indians would have an arsenal. We destroyed the guns in front of the Indians so they would trust us."

Indian borders are a perpetual problem for Santos, as they are all over the Amazon. Tribes are supposed to be kept in specially designated parks or on their own traditional land, areas all neatly demarcated on maps, but whose boundaries exist nowhere else.

This neat arrangement is another instance where the ideas promoted in Brasilia are far from the reality of the jungle. The Indian boundaries are paper ones and no one is there to enforce them. Settlers, ranchers, miners, timber cutters—all have ignored Indian land and continue to do so when they think it profitable. The Brazilians have invented a word for supervision of a growing civilization: fiscalizacao. Fiscalizacao is a military man's fantasy. The jungle, by man's own definition, opposes order; no matter how well meaning the government is in establishing Indian boundaries it is practically impotent to fiscalize them and punish trespassers. Often the intrusion is inadvertent; the Indians have vast areas they don't use or sometimes claim more than the government has granted them. But just as often the intrusion is deliberate and the result is bloodshed—the Kayapo-Gorotire, the neighboring tribe to Cumaru, massacred in September, 1980, more then 20 settlers, including women and children, who had invaded Indian land, according to press reports.

"I think it would be interesting for you to visit that tribe," Santos mused. "I like to go there regularly so that they know I am their friend and they can ask me for help. Perhaps the miners don't respect their land, but I do, and I want them to know we will protect it. If not, there will be a war."

That Santos could be a father figure to the miners and guardian of the Indians was a testament to his devotion to order. Rules are rules, to be obeyed. "I don't take sides," he told us often. Everything about him smacked of his struggle to instill discipline in this place. The camp at Cumaru was a neat square with a parade ground and flagpole behind it. Staff attendance for flag ceremonies was mandatory, and Santos asked miners to raise and lower the flag to encourage them to attend too. "It's important that they see that they are not alone," he said. Wooden barracks for the administrators and a garrison for ten soldiers stood on one side of the jungle clearing; a hospital, mess hall and offices on the other. Every soldier's boot was polished. They wore white T-shirts with blue piping and the word "Cumaru" on the left breast, making them look more like camp counselors than secret police. We never ascertained Santos' exact status with GETAT—we believe he was a liaison between the field troops and the National Security Council in Brasilia. We tried to talk politics with him, but he didn't appear interested. He said he was a military man and his goal was to command an infantry battalion, not to preside over internecine conflicts whose only victims were his countrymen.

In light of Santos' clear allegiance to order, we were flabbergasted when he invited us to visit the Kayapo with him. FUNAI has strict rules governing the entrance of visitors to Indian tribes, and since the massacre the Kayapo had been completely off bounds to all outsiders. Recognizing a serendipity, we eagerly accepted his offer.

"This is the same tribe as the one that massacred the women and children?" we asked.

Santos said it was. He also warned us not to ask them about that incident. "It is history," he said. "They do not talk about it."

Unfortunately, the massacre was all we knew about this tribe, and unsurprisingly our imagination ran riot. We recalled Lewis V. Cummings' *I Was a Headhunter*, that 1930s classic of bad taste with a remarkably detailed appendix containing a step-by-step account of how to shrink a human head. The Kayapo aren't headhunters; in fact, head trophying never was a sport of Indians in Brazil's Amazon. But most of the tales of adventurers from earlier this century never made this clear, leaving the world to believe that savage bloodthirsty people wandered through the bush. It's either them or us was the alternative posed by these bogus accounts. Because Indians clearly are from another culture it is readily assumed they are hostile, a sad commentary on every visitor to this region from the Portuguese to us. The image has been further popularized by picture postcards available throughout Brazil of naked Indians carrying bows and arrows or clubs. The postcards are a not-so-subtle statement that Indians "are different from you and me," suggesting that these people are freaks.

Such racism is born of a cultural gap so wide that only a few anthropologists have been able to breach it.

We climbed into an American-made Brazilian Air Force Huey helicopter. One of the pilots, Major Tito, a compact, muscle-bound figure, bragged he could have rescued the American hostages in Teheran and wouldn't have ditched his chopper in the desert. He wore a shiny green flight suit, bulbous orange helmet and scuffless black boots. Two soldiers with M-14 rifles slung over their shoulders sat with us and Colonel Santos in the cabin.

The rotors started with a pneumatic whine and Tito lifted the copter off the ground. He turned it 180 degrees with a sharp jerk on the joystick and roared off straight at the looming tree line. At the last instant, he hopped the machine up and over the trees.

Tito flew about 25 feet above the trees, occasionally jumping over a particularly high one. We saw the gold mines snake through the forest below. At a few points prospectors had opened up a great, wide wound and the mud was dotted with the black plastic squares used to cover lean-tos.

Yelling above the clatter of the rotors, Santos explained that Pedro Lima, the miner he had been lecturing, was one of his favorite prospectors. "Very brave, that one. They call him Tarzan. He discovered gold on a hillside that others were afraid to try. Now the others are all over the hill and he wants to go on the other side. He's not a bad man. Just eager."

Santos told us a little about the massacre. "We don't really understand what happened," he said, using his hands like a megaphone. "The Indians won't talk about it with us. We think they were telling the settlers to get off their land when somebody insulted them. The witnesses said it seemed to happen all at once but that can't be true. The Indians came at night, in war paint and with war clubs. What the people from the Indian agency can't figure out is why the Kayapo killed children. They never do that, but this time they beat children and pregnant women to death. We don't understand them. They are very unpredictable. . . ."

Tito pointed to a notch in the Gradaus Mountains ahead. They looked really more like hills, rising perhaps 1,000 feet and completely covered with trees. The notch, though, was a steep cut filled with mist. It looked ominous. Tito was going to shoot through it for laughs.

Between the mist and the green mountainsides a few yards to either side, it felt as though the copter was actually in the tree canopy. Rain spattered the front windshield and wind bucked the machine. Tito was enjoying himself; Santos was impassive behind the mirrored sunglasses; everyone else held his breath. We went through the gap. The mist dissipated and the tree tops were much farther below us. Ahead was a river, flowing north in a wide sweep of crystal blue to match the suddenly blue sky. There was a brown clearing visible on the edge of the river.

Santos pointed. "Kayapo-Gorotire."

The copter made a slow circle over the village which seemed neatly planned with rows of thatch and mud huts and fenced-off yards. We could see people running out of the huts and pointing up.

Tito landed the chopper softly in a whirl of dust. All around, out of range of the rotor wash, stood hundreds of Indians.

It was all very sudden, disorienting. We had been planning to visit an Indian tribe, but not so soon. We hadn't prepared, hadn't done our homework. Now as we disembarked our senses were in overdrive, trying to absorb so many new sensations.

Five shapes approached us. Piles of straw with feet. As they got closer we could see eyes and mouths cut into the straw and designs painted on it.

From among them, a man wearing brown shorts and a plaid short-sleeved sports shirt, unbuttoned, emerged. Santos and he shook hands and patted each other on the back in the traditional Brazilian greeting. A second man, similarly attired, walked through the hay bales and also greeted Santos. They looked like two caboclos, except for a certain authoritative manner and rough friendliness that they had learned to express in white man's gestures.

The two were Kanhonk and Totui, chiefs of the Kayapo-Gorotire, one of several villages of Kayapo along the Rio Fresco and Rio Xingu. Both chiefs spoke Portuguese well and were quickly laughing with Santos and clapping him on the back. At this sign of friendship, some Indians clustered around us and others went to examine the helicopter. Santos had told us that he visited the village at least once a month and every time was like the first.

Standing around us two towering, pale Americans were mostly small children. Mothers suckling babies stood a few yards away and beyond them some men in their early 20s eyed us suspiciously. The children did not seem to be all from the same tribe. They shared the same brownish yellow skin and Mongolian features, but some had bowl-cut hair that made them look almost Chinese while others had shaven heads with topknots and an assortment of colorful feathers and beads. Still others wore shorts and T-shirts and would have been indistinguishable from the hordes of children in any South American city.

The faces of some of the children were painted bright orange and their bodies ornamented with intricate designs. A teenage boy who spoke Portuguese explained that this was the festival of the anteater, a joyous occasion for the tribe. The boys dressed in straw who first greeted us were the anteaters. Apparently an outgoing personality was a necessary attribute to be picked as an anteater because the boys followed us around in costume the whole time we were there, shaking hands, posing for pictures and talking away—sometimes in Ge, the tribal language, sometimes in Portuguese, but always in the disguised, hoarse voice that is the prescribed way for an anteater to speak. One introduced himself as "Colonel Santos" and offered a hand and a giggle.

London busily snapped pictures of the children. They had seen cameras before and were not shy. The mothers, though, demurely turned their backs.

While Santos went off with the chiefs, the anteaters led us on a tour of the town, followed by a Pied Piper procession of children. The houses in this village were laid out on a grid of dirt streets and appeared more substantial than we had expected, with mud and wattle walls with high-peaked thatch roofs, doors and window awnings. No grass huts at all. Behind and in front fenced-off yards were shaded by large trees. That too surprised us since in so many of the white settlements every tree in sight had been hacked away. The village was also cleaner than some of the other river towns we had visited. We failed to detect the usual pervasive odor of rotting garbage and we saw pigs kept in pens.

The whole site of the village was beautiful—a bank about 30 feet above a curve in the Rio Fresco—the river would rise almost that far by the end of the rainy season—with the green-cloaked mountains behind and a clear vista of treetops, connected like a rolling meadow, in front. Unlike many jungle sites, the Kayapo-Gorotire village did not feel swallowed by the forest.

As we were beginning to realize, the 560 or so Kayapo-Gorotire Indians are no longer a primitive tribe. First contacted by white men 50 years ago, they have had numerous anthropologists, government Indian specialists and missionaries living with them ever since. They had been known as a violent tribe, like the Xavante to the south, and in the early part of this century slaughtered a group of missionary women who had come to teach them. They have periodically ter-rorized the whites around them, though Indian experts who work with them say the tribe has done a relatively good job of coping with white society.

Although the village seemed quite isolated approached in a heli-copter, there are numerous ranches nearby and the town of Sao Felix do Xingu is 75 miles downriver where the Fresco joins the Rio Xingu. Altamira, a major trading center, is another 200 miles be-yond. The Kayapo's main source of income is *castanhas*, Brazil nuts, which they collect from the ground around the tall trees and sell to white traders. This commerce enables them to buy hunting rifles and outboard motors for their fishing canoes as well as medicines, tools and various trinkets like jewelry that the traders sell. Because of the efforts of Colonel Santos, a percentage of Cumaru gold is returned to the Indians through FUNAI.

Overhead we noticed strands of wire running between poles. The government Indian agent told us the Kayapo-Gorotire had electricity, from a gas-powered generator, though television had not yet arrived. "They are a part of Brazilian society," he said.

An old man joined us. Thin and bent, he wore a turquoise shirt and beige swim trunks. His lower lip was distended about three inches by a wooden disc that stretched the skin tight, once a common custom of tribes in this area. Except for some large holes in the ears of the young men, for inserting dowels or earrings made of feathers, the old man's lip was the only sign of traditional body ornaments among the adults. He walked along, grumbling and sometimes shout-ing in Ge. The children laughed at him. He wanted his picture taken, but didn't want to speak into our tape recorder. At least our micro-cassette recorder was something new to some of these people. The teenage children were fascinated to hear their own voices played back. The anteaters were delighted and insisted they be allowed to sing some of their festival chants.

Chief Kanhonk, however, was apparently no stranger to tape recorders. "I will send a message to your chief in my language," he said.

"President Reagan," Santos told him.

His message expressed a hope for peace everywhere and particularly here so his people could continue picking castanhas without fighting. We had the message translated much later on, so clearly it was not meant to impress Colonel Santos, who did not speak Ge. As unpredictable as we were told they are, the Kayapo apparently have very universal human emotions. Frightened, they strike back; but what they really want is nothing more than peace.

Santos said it was time to go. Calling the Indians over to the helicopter, he hauled out a few cases of still-cold *guarana*, the Brazilian fruit soda. A cheer went up as the Kayapo scrambled for the shiny silver cans. Some hoarded armfuls and caused fights; others distributed them among the crowd. Most of the Indians skillfully popped the aluminum tops and began to slurp the soda. Someone had to help the old man open the top of his can. He struggled to drink with the lip disc.

A sudden rainstorm whipped over the mountains and sent the Indians scurrying from the open field to their homes. A few stopped to pick up empty soda cans.

While we waited in the steaming helicopter for the sky to clear, one of the soldiers returned, covering a brightly colored parrot which he put on Kelly's lap for safekeeping. It was a beautiful bird, rare even in the jungle, the kind that might sell for $1,000 or more in an American pet shop. A few moments later, the woman who had sold the bird knocked on the side of the cabin. She was with her brother. She had sold the parrot for $6 and wanted a little more, the brother said.

"No, no, no," the lieutenant said with a scowl. "We made a deal."

They talked on. We realized that the woman had no idea how to place a value on a bird, or what $6 meant. The brother, while vaguely aware that the bird should command something more, was no skilled bargainer. The lieutenant laughed and kept saying, "No, no, no."

Finally Santos, who was sitting in the back, spoke up. "Lieutenant," he said in a sharp voice that made the remainder of the sentence unnecessary. The officer handed over $3, and the woman and her brother walked off, smiling.

The helicopter took off. The flight back was rougher because of the storm, but thankfully Tito had lost his zest for joyriding.

If we had been disoriented when we started, we were worse off now. We didn't know what we had really seen. The trip was like a stop at one of the Disney World exhibits. Impressions abounded in our minds, but we really couldn't make any sense of them. Everything had happened too quickly.

One thing was certain—this tribe seemed safe for the time being; they had Colonel Santos to protect them. But we wondered for how long his paternalism would be enough. The Indians occupy the single most valuable commodity in the Amazon—land. As the hunger for land and gold grows so too will greedy designs on the Kayapo territory. And only one man stood between them and those who would kill them for it.

XINGUARA

The paternalism of the toughest man in the Amazon, which we had seen directed at the miners and the Indians, now was bestowed on us. We had told Colonel Santos of our plan to go to Xinguara where there was a land war. According to Father Rezende in Conceicao, four pistoleiros recently had been killed, and we were eager to learn about these battles firsthand.

"Be careful," Santos said.

"Don't worry about us."

"No, I am serious. If you're not careful, you'll end up dead." We laughed at the silliness of anyone wanting to kill us, but Santos didn't see the humor.

To instill discretion in us he told about his arrival in Redencao, the town we had flown over on the way to Cumaru and whose reputation was as bad as Xinguara's.

Santos called it "the most violent town in the Amazon, perhaps in the whole country, once they found gold in this region." News of the strike spread so quickly that "70 planes were working out of Redencao almost immediately." The extraordinariness of this fact hit us: there wasn't even an airport at the time. The main street was used for buses, cars and planes; landing and taking off was a kind of bumper pool. Coming in on these planes was a pernicious assortment of miners, pistoleiros, whores and entrepreneurs. Where there is a buck in the Amazon there always is a squalid squadron to fight for it.

To inspect Redencao, Santos had dressed in his civilian clothes, although he brought along his conspicuous Colt hip piece, which is as commonplace an adornment there as a hat or earrings. With no specific destination in mind he ambled through the dusty streets trying to understand the lawlessness. From one of the hastily thrown up wooden buildings a man stumbled toward Santos, contortedly grabbing at a long fish-scaling knife stuck in his back. Then he fell on his face.

"No one did anything," he explained to us calmly as we sat around the wooden table in his bunkhouse. "I couldn't believe what was happening. He wasn't dead yet, but no one moved to help him. If I did something they would have known that I was from another world."

Killing wasn't anything unusual in Redencao then; the average was a murder a day.

"Weren't the police doing anything?" we asked.

"The police were part of the problem. They were corrupt. They were killing for money and looking the other way for money. There was no order."

Of the twelve pistoleiros, hired gunmen with names as colorful as their reputations, he said Pedro Parana, known by his crooked nose once sliced by a knife, and Zezinho de Condespar were the most feared, proprietors of a Murder Inc., of the jungle. For $50 they'd kill a nobody; for a lot more they'd kill a big shot. Someone had been paid much money to put a bullet in the head of a local landowner who had kept prospectors off his land; his body was left to decompose behind the wheel of his pickup truck as it sat on the hot and humid main street of Redencao.

The day Santos was there another man was murdered at one of the 17 weddings taking place around town. Marriage is how miners keep a woman waiting for them in the nearest town. That they already are married makes no difference to these men, and wealthy miners who have claims in several areas may have as many wives at convenient locations. Perhaps two husbands met that day. To kill for a woman in the Amazon is considered justifiable, and although the police weren't functioning it's doubtful there would have been any arrests if they had been.

Land and gold also are sound defenses for murder. A refrain we often heard, like the ravings of a pulp novelist, was that men kill for three things—women, land and gold. When the people in Campo Alegre recited the code it sounded like a commercial for the next Matt Dillon program on their Betamax; when Colonel Santos said it, and backed it up with evidence, the caricature became real.

Santos organized a secret meeting with leaders of the town—the doctor, some of the merchants and ranchers. All said they wanted Redencao cleaned up, and they would do what they could to help. Santos promised to be back in two weeks with ten soldiers and said that he'd need a truck to pick them up.

"I didn't trust them," he told us. "A pistoleiro was at the meeting and I knew he'd tell everyone what our plans were."

As he left the meeting Santos passed the body of the stabbing victim. Now he was dead, and the knife had been removed from his back. Dogs were sniffing at the body.

A week later—and a week before he had promised to return—Santos and 60 agents from GETAT descended on Redencao in two bulky Buffalo cargo planes. "I wanted everyone to see we were coming," he said, explaining his choice of transport. Within 24 hours they captured 11 of the 12 known pistoleiros operating in the town. Zezinho de Condespar "gave up peacefully, like a gentleman" when he was surrounded, but Pedro Parana tried to fight his way out. He and the wife who was with him at the time were wounded in a shootout.

"We held all of them in jail for two to three months," Santos said, "but nobody would testify against them. They were afraid. So we had to let them go. But I told them clearly if they ever came back I would be there waiting for them."

Xinguara is a town like Redencao, busy and dusty. It had grown from a few huts to 20,000 people in the five years since roads were cut through to Conceicao, Maraba and the west of Para. On some maps it is called Xingu Junction.

Big Mercedes trucks own the wide main street, mostly hauling sawn lumber or cylindrical logs that look like overgrown sections of pipe. Sometimes a procession of trucks goes by, stirring up so much red dust that it is impossible to see across the road. This is the center of lumber country and the town is ringed with three dozen sawmills. The hard, reddish brown mahogany wood is the most valuable timber the Amazon produces. Sawn into long boards here and trucked north to Belem, it is then shipped by boat to southern Brazil or Europe where it becomes cabinets, paneling and furniture. World demand for fine tropical hardwoods brought hundreds of small logging operations here in the late 1970s.

We found a room at the Rio Vermelho—Red River—Hotel, a mound of stucco across the street from the tin-roofed church. We inspected the cans of kerosene the bed legs stood in to keep ants and termites from crawling up. We had become experienced enough to tell the quality of a hotel by the freshness of its kerosene. This stuff looked pretty old. Also, the toilet had no seat, the sink dripped thick orange water, and the room had a pungent smell, more like a barn than a hotel—a pigsty was beneath our window, we discovered. But for $4 a night we didn't complain.

As we walked about the town, we thought we might best have prepared ourselves by taking in a John Wayne double feature. The dustiness of Xinguara, the dry goods stores, the card games—these struck us as backlot props and not a new, original frontier in the jungle. We felt at first that everyone was playing a role stolen from the silver screen, full of lawlessness and incessant talk of a man's honor.

Magazine kiosks featured the latest in the popular "Dangerous West" series: *Question of Honor,* as well as *Guns Speak Louder,*

Shadow of the Noose and *Every Coward Has His Place*. The most recent issue had a Boot Hill style cemetery on the cover. The Amazon is even called the *Faroeste* of Brazil. Movie theaters, a term we found applicable to any building which can hold more than 20 people, always showed Randolph Scott's B movies or, of course, John Wayne. Westerns are called "Bangy Bangy's." "A man's got to do what a man's got to do" at once exemplifies the mindlessness and seriousness of the violence here.

Yet, the melodrama is not entirely plagiarized from Hollywood. Brazil has had a frontier before, and it, too, spawned such extreme codes to live and die by. Jorge Amado, the most popular author in the country, could also be found in the kiosks. Although he has become much more of a modern social critic in recent years, his early works did not spare lurid blood-and-guts and lavished praise on manly achievement with a gun.

"Blood fertilized these lands," he begins the introduction to *The Violent Land*, his novel about the larger-than-life men who staged Brazil's cacao rush in the early 1900s. The book describes the affection one of Amado's characters, a hired gun, had for his rifle, which he always kept at night at the foot of his bed. "He loved the weapon and kept it bright and shining; he liked to look at it." To Americans like us, the parody appeared as a double image: on the one hand, a land imitating movieland's glorification of our West; on the other, 20th-century Brazil recreating its own frontier.

The aping of the West was more noticeable in Xinguara than along BR-364 because the population here is largely composed of the dispossessed and perpetual have-nots of the poor Northeast, where their tradition is similar to that in Jorge Amado's rough-and-ready chronicles. Rarely did we see the light-skinned European descendants who farm the land in Rondonia. We were beginning to sense more desperation and less rejuvenation among these settlers, which was understandable, because they had fled a drought only to run into a gun pointed at their heads.

Our own plight was becoming less and less comfortable. Besides the psychic discomfort of our dangerous errand here, Xinguara was splattered with insects and filmed with a brown fungus that seemed to grow on everything. It would have taken a full-time crew of sailors to keep things clean, but with new residents arriving in droves, the town could hardly keep up with housing demands. The Brazilian passion for cleanliness had ebbed here; there was mud on the floor of our hotel room and dead bugs in the beds.

And our diets were beginning to change.

The frontier towns of Xinguara and Redencao grew because of roads, not rivers, and few of the inhabitants are caboclos. Meat, not fish or vegetables, is the accustomed diet, and it was in evidence everywhere: bloody carcasses strapped on donkeys walking in the sun; stringy joints hanging from hooks in open-air butcher shops; gore-spattered slaughter pens near the front gates of ranches, the floors strewn with steaming intestines, hides and heads. The smell was everywhere, greasy and decaying. It stayed in our nostrils for weeks. Yet the tough gray meat, unpleasant in color and texture and rank in flavor, was what we had to eat if we were to eat at all.

The bigger problem, though, was parasites. Almost surely some were to be found in each piece and, in spite of ordering meat as well done as possible, there was no avoiding parasitic disease. The tropical climate is an incubator of strange organisms and stranger illnesses. Besides the big-name ones like malaria, hepatitis, typhoid and river blindness, dozens of others haven't even been named—and we got a lot of them. Bottled water—like well-done meat—proved to be a merely fabled protection: we more than once saw a waiter filling from the tap a bottle of supposed spring water.

From Xinguara until the end of our travels months later, one or the other of us was sick with stomach flu, sore throat, dysentery, chills, runny nose, fungus, rashes or animals burrowing through the skin. We would trade back and forth and sometimes be sick in tandem. The symptoms ran together. When one ailment began to dissipate, another would emerge. Still, these illnesses were only debilitating. Although their unfamiliarity worried us, our lives were not at stake. This was not true of the posseiros we had come to see.

"People are dying," Father Rezende had said of the land war in Xinguara. "Go see for yourselves." This land war already had claimed four lives and was threatening to break into open warfare. So far, the dead men were pistoleiros, but it was said no posseiro killed and got away with it. We could have seen the pistoleiros for ourselves; the other hotel in town was booked solid with them. Father Rezende had advised us to go there to watch the card games—"the police and the pistoleiros play together every night"—but Santos' story about Redencao was fresh in our minds and we decided to avoid the police. We were afraid they would impede our visit to the posseiros or follow us. We carried a letter from Rezende to the local priest, a Frenchman, and had been warned to keep our destination a secret.

Xinguara was a small enough town that anyone who really wanted to could find out everyone's business. Word was around that the families of the gunmen who had been killed wanted revenge, and that Ruy Jacinto, the man who claimed ownership of the land, still wanted the posseiros out. Something was going to have to happen soon, before the rains over the next few weeks made all the roads into the posseiros' enclave impassable.

Word was also around, Father Clemente told us when we delivered Rezende's letter, that two American journalists wanted to go see the posseiro families. He said it was anyone's guess what effect that would have on the pistoleiros, Jacinto and the police.

We were told to find Cleuza Oliveira, whose family was one of the more than 60 families who had barricaded themselves in a forest hideout rather than surrender their land to the hired army of Jacinto, who spent most of his time 600 miles from here. She had been staying in town at the church rectory, because her husband had had a heart attack and she wanted to be near him. His condition, however, had not stopped her from taking a three-day bus ride to Brasilia to plead with the President of Brazil to stop the violence. Needless to say, she was rebuffed at the door of the palace, and the killing went on.

In the movies you'd probably see Jane Fonda in this heroine role, but there is no glamour in the real story. Cleuza proved to be a tiny, undistinguished woman—under 5 feet, with tight eyes, a sharp nose and smooth skin the color of polished mahogany. A close-mouthed smile almost never left her face. The day we met her, she was wearing rubber-thonged sandals and a short pink dress that gave her the appearance of a little girl, although she was over 40. She looked like a large walnut, and was about that tough.

Yes, she said, she would take us to the squatters if that was what Father Rezende wanted. Did we know it was very dangerous? We said we did.

"Come back tomorrow," she said. "I will find a truck and driver. One who's dumb enough."

As promised, Cleuza found us a driver who was dumb enough to go—but smart enough to be scared. His name was Genaro and for

$40 he agreed to drive us in his Chevy four-wheel-drive pickup to the general vicinity of the posseiros' encampment. We would then have to walk a few miles through the forest, and Cleuza insisted that part of the deal was that Genaro would leave the truck and walk with us. She was afraid he'd take off; he was afraid he'd get shot, but $40 was $40 and Genaro consented.

We set out west on the road from Xinguara. After an hour or so we turned off to a much narrower and, hard as it was for us to believe, much worse road that ran north through pasture land.

The fields of these ranches were like those we had seen in cattle country to the south, with two differences: they were smaller, a hundred acres at a time instead of the thousands at, say, Volkswagen, and they were forested with termite mounds. These mud mounds, colonies of billions of termites, looked like stalagmites growing up from the ground. The rows of gnarled cylinders varied in size to as high as six feet. In some fields, the mounds were stacked so close we wondered how the cows could move without bumping into them.

We drove through this odd-scape for an hour: gray mounds; tufts of bright green grass; huge charred tree trunks, most lying flat but some still standing, stripped and twisted; white cows, big-humped, with their hide hanging in pendulous folds. It was a scene from another planet and, combined with the heat and the alternately muddy and rocky road, turned our thoughts not to the question of who owned this land but who would want to.

The road got muddier as we went along. Genaro would bravely charge into wide brown puddles, their depth and contents unknown. He may have feared for his life from pistoleiros, but no one would call him a coward in his truck. Finally we came to a giant puddle with an old flatbed truck stuck in the middle. The driver had been fearless, or foolish, and ended up snapping his front axle on a submerged log. The forest came close to the road here, and there was no way around the hole until the truck was moved. The driver would be lucky to get out before the dry season started again.

Cleuza said it was a 10-kilometer walk to the posseiro camp. We set to work trying to lay a raft of fallen logs on one side of the hole; just maybe Genaro's truck would fit by. But the logs kept sinking in mud that seemed to reach to the center of the earth.

Four men came up to the truck, two on each side. Two carried axes, one carried a rifle, and all had pistols in their belts. Open-mouthed, we stared at them for a few seconds. Genaro went white. Cleuza, still in pink dress, hopped down from the cab of the truck and walked up to the man who held nothing and hugged him.

"These are the Perreira brothers," she said, waving an arm to include them all. The name meant nothing to us, but the hug was a good sign. Cleuza spoke to the brothers rapidly, out of our hearing.

The Perreiras came to the side of the truck and with a fury set to work hacking at the forest which here impinged on the road. Axes, machetes and a hoe that had magically appeared cut into roots with syncopated thuds and clangs. The two with machetes wielded them with particular skill, moving the blade from side to side of the small tree trunks like swordsmen and drawing an explosion of wood chips.

They worked nonstop for a half hour while we stood ineptly by and watched. The brothers had stripped off their shirts and in minutes were slicked with sweat. Three of the four looked like the gold miners at Cumaru: dark, small and wiry. Hamilton, taller and fair, stood out. Jose, the oldest at 27, was in charge. Julinho, 23, liked to joke around, but Joao, 25 and looking 45, said little. Their proper family name was Jesuinho Perreira, the last a common Brazilian name; the first meaning "little Jesus."

Soon the four brothers had cleared a half-moon around the mudhole. Jose told the bewildered Genaro to get in and drive. He gingerly picked his way on the narrow strip of firm ground until he was back on the road. Cleuza explained that the Perreiras would take us to their farm. They piled in the back and bounced along with us for a few more miles until Jose told Genaro to turn onto a path that looked wide enough for a bicycle. After a half-mile of branches slapping the truck—we were certainly getting our money's worth out of Genaro—we came to a swollen stream.

"We walk," Jose announced.

On either side of the well-trodden path the forest was gloomy, high and surprisingly cool. A lush forest, better than what we had seen to the south along the Araguaia River and almost like Rondonia, it was also silent. Suddenly Jose stopped.

"Here is where the ambush was."

The path here was a long straight stretch wide enough so that a man would have to take a few precious steps to get to the cover of the underbrush.

Julinho and Joao crept off into the forest to reenact the shooting. After a few yards they were as invisible as had been the 60 posseiros lurking that way a few weeks ago when Jacinto's band of gunmen came up the trail. Cleuza said the pistoleiros had come this route before, when they burned the squatters' huts and threatened to rape the women and kill the children if they didn't leave—methods that had always worked in the past and a time-honored tradition of eviction in the Amazon. But these posseiros were tougher and stayed on, so the pistoleiros had been told to try again, and to be harsher this time. Cleuza said everyone in town had heard the bounty for a dead squatter was $500, adult or child.

Four of the 30 pistoleiros had fallen dead with the first volley and several were wounded. After a couple of minutes, the posseiros melted into the forest while the gunmen crawled down the trail. For the survivors, the shock must have been almost as painful as the loss of their comrades; miserable farmers weren't supposed to fight back.

We walked on. "If they come back, we are ready for them," Jose said. "We have guards in the forest." We saw no one.

"Raimundo," Jose shouted, "stand up."

A man who looked like another Perreira brother stood and waved about 20 yards back from the road. He held a rifle in the crook of his arm.

Finally the jungle fell away and we came to a field of tall corn. Beyond that was a house and behind it a field that looked as if it had been cleared in the last year. "These are our fields," Hamilton said. "That is my house. That is why we came here."

Hamilton Perreira, the youngest of the five brothers, was 20 years old the day we met him. He realized that his hope of turning 21 was anything but certain. "There's a $500 bounty on my head," he said, "and someone is going to come for it. I am waiting for him." Putting his left arm around his voluptuous 18-year-old wife, Rosa, he held her close. With his right hand he leaned on the muzzle of an old black .22 caliber rifle. The late afternoon sun radiated in shafts through the palm fronds of the damp, high-ceilinged shack, like light through a stained-glass church window. The shadows made a series of lines across Hamilton's face that hid a deep frown and hard stare.

Somewhere else, maybe, things wouldn't have been so tough for him. Hamilton was a handsome man, tall with ropey muscles and large calloused hands. From under his crushed straw cowboy hat, brown curls struggled out to hang over a sunburned neck. With his gleaming blue eyes, thick mustache and the sort of easy white smile that opens doors in places where people pay attention to such things, it was the kind of face you might expect to find on a glossy magazine page, offering a cigarette, or, cleaned up a bit, tossing a football on the front lawn of a University of Texas fraternity. Look at that face and you'd think, "I bet that guy does all right for himself." Put him next to his wife and you'd be sure of it.

We had a hard time not looking at her. We hadn't seen many— any—good-looking women for quite some time and Rosa seemed to invite glances. Even in this sickeningly humid insect paradise, her white shirt and tan shorts were clean and alluring. Despite cooking for five men, her burnt-orange fingernail polish was unchipped.

But here, 30 miles out of the civilization of Xinguara, their appearance only made Hamilton and Rosa Perreira more conspicuous targets. They came, the five Perreira brothers and two of their wives, to the jungle to look for a new life. Instead they found a war. They found themselves in conflict with a cattle rancher they had never met who said he owned the land they were now trying to cultivate. They feared Jacinto would kill them if they didn't leave.

"But we're not leaving," said Hamilton Perreira. "We have left before and we're not leaving again."

This was the third time the young family had faced expulsion. They had been gradually moving eastward near the leading edge of the Amazon frontier, but the moves were never voluntary.

The Perreiras were from the northeastern part of Brazil where people are poor as dirt and the dirt is dry, cracked and useless. Like thousands of other families they were lured to the Amazon by the promise of lusher land. Because they were hungry, they put aside the stories of 40-foot snakes and murderous Indians and cut their way into the empty land. But just behind them was a wealthier class of farmer who also wanted more and better land and who had the means to get it. As this second wave caught up with them, the Perreiras and their neighbors were forced out and pushed farther into the jungle. It was here near Xinguara that the Perreiras had decided that they would move no more.

They and several other families had settled here four years ago.

Since then, their number had swelled to more than 60 families and 300 people, all of whom farmed similar 120-acre plots separated from each other by deep stands of forest. They grew rice, corn, manioc, beans, bananas; recently they had started to plant cacao trees.

"The land is good," Jose explained. "People had told us to be careful of that, but we can grow anything here."

The Perreiras and the other families admitted readily that they didn't buy the land, but each had cleared 120 acres, planted it and brought in three crops in a row to fulfill the legal requirements for land ownership—if the land were free of title. Then Jacinto came.

"I said to him, 'If this is your land, why have I not seen you in the four years I have lived here?'" It was Cleuza talking now. She was angry. "No one has come in four years. And now he says it is his land. Jacinto said he would make us leave anyway."

Jose interrupted, inviting us to sit down in his living room. He set out two tiny wooden stools on the clean-swept dirt floor and told his wife, Raimunda, to make some cafezinhos. The proprieties would be observed even here.

The house was well built but primitive, with walls made of thick, bamboolike stalks and a high roof thatched with leaves. A small kitchen area was dominated by a brick stove on which sat several steaming black pots; on one wall hung a shelf holding the family china, a mismatched set of cups, plates and bowls. In the main room was a bed with a mattress and blanket over it. A crucifix hung on the wall above. Jose and Raimunda had no children yet, though she was visibly pregnant.

"This is our land because we worked it," Jose said after the coffee had been downed. "We came here with nothing and built this . . ."

"Nothing but the courage to work," interjected Cleuza, who had a gift for rhetoric and a resoluteness to punctuate it.

Hamilton spoke softly. "We don't have the money to buy land anywhere else. We must stay here. Where else will we go?"

"I have given my life to this," Jose said.

"The land is not Jacinto's," Hamilton continued. "He has never cut a single tree. The land is ours, because we are right. We will stay."

They all nodded. Hamilton spilled water from a clay urn into a coffee cup with a broken handle and sucked it down noisily. Droplets clung to his mustache and he wiped it with the back of his hand.

Hamilton went on: "The church tried to get all the women to leave when this started, but everyone decided to stay and fight." He glanced at his wife, now bent over the smoking stove, sweetening another pot of coffee. She lowered her eyes and said nothing. "Before we came here, we weren't farmers. We were laborers. All my brothers worked on the land of other people. We came to the Amazon so the land we worked would be our own."

Wasn't there another way to solve this than gunfights?

"The church has given us a lawyer," Jose said, shaking his head. "It takes a long time. We don't think anything will come of it."

"We will have to resolve this another way," Hamilton said. "I think the pistoleiros will return and we will have to fight."

We wanted to take a picture of the family, so they posed outside —Hamilton, Jose and Julinho; Rosa and Raimunda, and a young boy who helped out on the farm. They set their faces in stern expressions and displayed the motley collection of weapons they had accumulated. They stood in front of their shack with the pigpen in the back and scrawny pecking chickens in front. Around them were their fields with stalks of corn growing among charred logs. And behind the shack and on all sides was the jungle, growing very high and making the Perreiras seem very small.

MARABA

We traveled on to Maraba with some distrust of our feelings about the Perreiras. We had been charmed by them, their courage and simple faith in what was right and wrong. Their goodness seemed so pure as to be almost unreal in the world as we knew it. This conflict over land had to be more complex, the lines between right and wrong more ambiguous.

So we decided to start over again. The land problems reportedly were as violent around Maraba as around Xinguara.

Maraba was said to be one of the worst towns in the Amazon, where gold miners, ranch hands, truck drivers and construction crews came to blow off steam and con artists and petty thieves came to prey on their paychecks. We had been told it was a good town in which to mind your own business. We jumped when the taxi driver turned around and snarled, "Which church?"

We didn't understand. *The* church is the big building in the center of every Brazilian town where everyone seems to find that God is with him, although only an incredibly flexible Supreme Being could be with the Perreiras and GETAT at the same time. The taxi driver waited for an answer. The better question would have been, "Which Maraba?" Like some kind of shell game, there were three Marabas. Three of everything, including churches. A few years ago some of the people of Old Maraba got tired of evacuating the town every rainy season to escape the increasingly harsh floods. Many of them began to stay put on high ground when the floods receded and they established a town across the unpredictable Itacaiunas River called New City. Then, when the TransAmazon Highway reached here in the early 1970s, a city called New Maraba came into existence, largely a series of government-developed projects—small, poorly ventilated boxes on scraped-bare hillsides farther down the peninsula that held Old Maraba. Until 1981, the only way to move between the cities was a series of roads atop dikes ending at slow barges and passenger ferries which made the river crossing. A bridge now links New City with the other two Marabas, and a colossal railroad–highway bridge to join the TransAmazon Highway across the wide Tocantins River is under construction.

Despite the town's surly reputation, confused traffic pattern and bedraggled appearance, it may soon be one of the most important towns in the Amazon. It is prime real estate, bisected by the Trans-Amazon Highway, the only east–west road in the region. When we were there, that section of the TransAmazon was a dusty path through fallen jungle in the dry season and a muddy, nearly impassable stretch in the wet season. But plans are to pave 150 miles of it to the connection with the north–south Belem–Brasilia Highway to the east. When the Tucurui dam about 125 miles north of Maraba is finished, scheduled for late 1983, the Tocantins River will be navigable all the way to Belem, where the Amazon River meets the Atlantic. A railroad being constructed to carry ore from the Carajas mining project to the port of Sao Luis, on the Atlantic coast, will pass right through Maraba. The Brazilian government insists it will spend $60 billion on the Carajas project by the end of the century; whatever the final sum, a substantial amount is sure to find its way into the economy of Maraba. Land in the area is becoming very valuable.

We told the taxi driver to take us to Old Maraba, where there is a bloated turret cathedral—three circular stories of stone and no apparent entrance.

A face peeked through a crack in the door we at last discovered. It had begun to rain hard and we stood in the mud, drenched, trying to explain who we were to a tall, thin man who spoke Portuguese with what sounded like a French accent. Apparently we dropped enough names from our by now impressive repertoire of Brazilian clerics because he finally opened the door. We followed him silently up a narrow, winding set of stairs to a bare third-floor sitting room where he showed us to two green plastic chairs.

We wanted to know about a place we had heard about called Pau Seco—Dry Stick—a fazenda where the owner and an encampment of squatters were said to be at war.

"No names," said the priest, setting ground rules for the interview. He didn't offer even his own. We nodded in agreement. "I know very little of Pau Seco. The parish is big and we all have different responsibilities. Two people were killed there in the last month: a 6-year-old daughter of one of the posseiros and the brother-in-law of the alleged landowner. Many of the posseiros' huts have been burned."

The death of the little girl was not unusual since children are a prime target in these cruel wars; their murders are meant to discourage their parents and drive them away in sadness and defeat. The reprisal killing of the brother-in-law broke the usual tradition in which hired pistoleiros, but not the alleged landowner or his family, were vulnerable. The priest also said squatters from other areas were coming to the aid of those at Pau Seco, an unprecedented joining of arms that he said the church knew about but had not organized.

This priest knew a lot, more than he was saying; and we told him so. He thought for a moment as he sucked on the end of the eyeglasses he twirled in his hand. He arose and left the room.

"The bishop will see you tomorrow morning at 7:30," he said upon returning. "That is all I can tell you. Now if you will excuse me."

We found our own way back down the dark stairwell and out into the black, rainy night, made blacker by the looming fortress behind us.

Finding the bishop the next morning was another exercise in triplicates. Maraba has only one bishop, but it has more than one parish house and we were confused about which one he inhabited. As we roamed New City in search of the bishop's residence, taxis repeatedly stopped, offering rides. When we refused, a look of incredulity came over the hacks' faces; no doubt they wondered how anyone with our look of tidy prosperity could willfully choose a precarious stroll through the stuff of Maraba's streets—rotting fruit, chicken carcasses, auto parts and mud.

Coming at us was a dazed procession of people we assumed were going to work. Everyone looked clammy in the early morning heat; all the trees have been sheared from this once-jungle, making it hot, dusty and without discernible perimeters. New City by day looks like a refugee camp, which, in a way, it is. This is where the escapees from the perpetual famine of the Northeast have come and where those who cannot enter the land of promise have stayed.

The bishop's house turned out to be in a fenced compound with several smaller structures and a modest, practical main house—airy and open, designed in the Spanish hacienda style that makes so much sense but is so rarely seen in the Amazon. His office was on the left as we entered, a book-lined room where the bishop sat at his desk, halfway through a stack of paperwork even at this early hour.

"Yes, there is a serious problem at Pau Seco," said Dom Alano Pena. "It would be a very good case for you to study. The man who is causing all the trouble is named Nelito. He is a dangerous man."

Dom Alano, the bishop of all the Marabas and much of the surrounding area, described Nelito as a *grileiro*, a term used in the Amazon to describe a land packager, someone who illegally puts together titles for large tracts of land and sells them to willing accomplices or unsuspecting buyers. Sometimes grileiros sell small parcels to squatters who one day will have to do battle with the real owner. Grileiros are expert at falsifying documents, turning 1,500 acres into 15,000 by the skillful addition of a zero or a well-placed bribe in the land registry office.

The bishop said Nelito had purchased only the rights to harvest

Brazil nuts on 15,000 acres in the jungle to the east of Maraba, but he was claiming that he had purchased the land itself. Posseiros, some of whom had been on the land for a decade or more, said the land was theirs because they had worked it.

"There are 164 families involved, about 400 people," said Dom Alano, a round little man with a round, balding head punctuated by a very heavy pair of black-framed glasses that he continually repositioned on his nose. "Two months ago, Nelito got the police to go in there and throw the posseiros off their land. But now they have gone back. The situation there is very grave. I pulled out Father Humberto, one of our priests, because the police threatened to kill him. He had been working with the posseiros. I believe he's the priest you met yesterday."

We thought it odd that Father Humberto had denied knowing much about Pau Seco. We tended to believe everything priests told us, but we were beginning to realize that these priests were not only on the sidelines making judgments but were very active participants.

The bishop continued: "I think the police want something to happen. They want an excuse to come in and act against the church. They want to catch us doing something they can put us in jail for. Then they will have won, they think. We are discovering there is no way we can co-exist with this government because the church puts human values above all. It is not a question of one bishop or one priest, but the entire system."

The arrival of Father Humberto, who was indeed the lean Frenchman from the night before, and another man interrupted the bishop. He joined them in another room and as we waited we could hear urgent but unintelligible whispers.

When the bishop returned he wore a deep frown. He sat down quickly and said, "I must warn you that if you go to Pau Seco it will be very dangerous. I just received reports that the police have been there and there are many pistoleiros in the area. Perhaps today they are trying to goad us." He ushered us out and went back to consulting with his lieutenants.

We decided to head out toward Pau Seco right away to see what was up. We ferried across the Tocantins on a tipsy boat, overstuffed with children and chickens. On the other side, we found a driver to take us 20 miles down the powdery TransAmazon Highway to the town of Mourada Nova where Nelito lived, 10 miles from his land claims in Pau Seco. When a town in the Amazon is named Something Nova it usually means that it is a replacement for a place that has washed away during a particularly heavy rainy season. We were amazed at the rapidity with which these new towns age. We had seen five-year-old Nova Barreira that looked like an archaeologist's dig. Mourada Nova, only about seven years old, had the appearance of a ghost town left to rot in the humid air. Paint, or at least that part visible under the thick coat of red dust, had faded and chipped; beams sagged; door jambs were warped; the dirt path sidewalks were overgrown with weeds. Yet the town that morning was crowded and active.

We had no trouble finding Nelito's house. Everyone knew him and seemed proud of that acquaintance. Having marked him for a villain, we imagined he cut a wide, mean swath through this ramshackle town. The image we had of the Perreiras' unseen enemy—Ruy Jacinto—was a man who took lemonade on the patio of a million-acre cattle ranch and offhandedly issued execution orders to his henchmen. We assumed Nelito would be of a similar mold—smooth, well dressed with an attentive senhorita on each arm. We were not prepared for the simple concrete house in a row of concrete houses a block from the main street.

Manoel Cardoso Neto (Nelito's full name) looked broken down. A large swelling protruded from his forehead. His eyes were underlined with deep circles and a heavy mustache forced his mouth down in a perpetual frown. Given a tin cup to go with his dark sunglasses, unbuttoned shirt and soiled shorts, he could have played a panhandler somewhere other than Mourada Nova, where he reportedly was the richest man.

His house was a series of small rooms set on a shiny cement floor. The only signs of affluence we noted were a new television and a shiny set of pots and pans hanging incongruously in the hall. He invited us to sit on vinyl chairs broken through with use. A collection of children screamed and tugged at him for attention while several women peered shyly from the kitchen.

Finally Nelito roared, "Get out!" and seemed almost surprised that his command was obeyed. "Fifteen people live here," he said—his wife, six children, mother-in-law and assorted nephews and nieces. "It was sixteen until they killed my brother-in-law." He said he was eager to talk, that the story of his dispute had been in many newspapers, but he had never spoken to a reporter.

"Who killed your brother-in-law?" we began.

"The invaders."

"I thought they were posseiros."

"How can they be posseiros if the land is mine? The police say it's mine. They threw the invaders off because they know it's mine. But now the invaders have come back."

"The church says all you have are the rights to the Brazil nuts on the land."

"The church lies. The land is mine. The church is responsible for this problem because they lie. They are Communists."

The tone of the conversation had taken a decidedly prosecutorial air that Nelito seemed unflustered by. We asked if he could prove it was his land. He left and came back with a fat folder of papers. "These are the documents."

We looked through them. Legal descriptions of real estate in the United States are often incomprehensible in English, and it therefore took a while to make some sense of these papers in Portuguese.

"It says here you have 7,200 hectares, but you told us before you have 6,000."

He didn't hesitate. "The documents are not right. I am only claiming 6,000 are mine."

"But aren't these just the rights to pick Brazil nuts?" London asked, pointing to a phrase which he thought referred to that.

"No," Nelito shook his head. "I own all the land. The government told me it was the best title in all the state of Para."

The cross-examination went on. There were discrepancies in dates, plot lines and amounts of money. One receipt showed payment of 50 cows, 50 calves, two bulls, 1,000 sacks of rice, cash and a promissory note. Nelito was an impressive witness. Whatever imperfection we could find he acknowledged and calmly explained. If the documents were forgeries, we had no way of telling. They were stamped and notarized.

Nelito sat quietly while we discussed these matters in English. We were beginning to believe that maybe he had been duped, that one day he realized he hadn't received what he bargained for. He thought he owned the land but only owned the nut concession. A tradition dating back to colonial days when the Portuguese crown would give away certain rights to a piece of land but retain ownership, the practice has endured as one of the absurdities of Brazilian land law. Nelito might very well have been hoodwinked and now he was running scared. He was also angry, arguing his case in the voice of a man who thought he should be entitled to what he paid for.

He had arrived here five years before, he told us, from the south of Brazil where his brother was a congressman.

"I thought this was good land to develop. I was going to farm some of it and sell some."

"Did you ever farm it?"

"I started to, but they threatened to kill me."

"Who did?"

"The invaders."

"But, weren't they already there when you bought the land?"

"Some were."

"Then why did you buy it if people were living on it?"

"Because they told me the title was good."

"Who?"

"The government."

Nelito is a Catholic. He said it hurt him to make accusations against the church. "The church orders that you do not invade, you do not rob and you do not steal. Father Humberto did not listen to the mandate of the church. This is not religion. This is subversion."

"The bishop of Maraba says you threatened to kill Father Humberto."

Nelito continued to frown. "Father Humberto was here, but the people of Mourada Nova threw him out. He incited the invaders and told them that the land belonged to God. The priest left by himself when the people turned against him."

We asked who shot the 6-year-old girl and he said he didn't know, but that she had not died. Then he said someone shot at him last month when he was leaving his home. They missed but wounded a friend. "I don't go out at night. My wife doesn't go out at night. I am scared."

When we asked if he was armed, Nelito delivered a line that had to have been stolen from the script of a bad movie that had played

Mourada Nova. He said, "No, I don't carry a gun. I carry the law."

Melodrama aside, we were confused by Nelito's performance. The mere fact that he felt the need to explain his position—and willingly submitted to intense questioning—seemed a civilized response. He used documents to support his claim and even made an offer of compromise. He showed us affidavits of an offer he made to the posseiros to give them half the land, but said they wanted it all. The Bishop found it easy to assign the good guys and bad guys in these sprawling land disputes; to us, it was not so easy.

The driver we finally found to take us to Pau Seco was a friend of Nelito's brother-in-law. He wasn't happy about going near what he called his "friend's murderers," and we weren't happy about taking him. But finding anyone willing to make this trip was difficult, and we had discovered a crevice in his loyalty called a big tip.

His cab looked as if it had been pulled off a Rio street during Carnival. Its windshield was so covered with decals that there was only a small space to see out. In the middle of the window was a large black-and-red emblem of Rio's Flamengo football team, and across the top was a slogan, "Flamengo is fire, the rest is smoke." On the bottom of the windshield were two examples of self-expression in ornate white calligraphy: "I am happy because I love you" and "Live and let me live." The inside was done in various pieces of fake fur and hung with little fabric balls.

The ride along the one-lane path was only 10 miles, but it took 45 minutes because we had to negotiate through slow cattle herds and around great puddles. There were a few clusters of weathered wood and thatched roof houses. The driver pointed out one house as having a generator, which meant to him cold beer, "if we come back." We didn't know if he meant "if we come back this way" or "if we come back at all." He was a sullen, fatalistic sort, so we assumed the latter.

The road ended with a puddle the size of a pond. Announcing he would go no farther, the driver got out and walked to a shack, clapping his hands three times in the uniquely Brazilian way of saying "Yoo hoo, anybody home?" A young man, about 20 years old, coal black and wearing a purple sleeveless shirt and white pants rolled up to his knees, limped from the side of the house.

"These two want to go to Pau Seco," the driver said.

The man pointed down the path.

"How far?"

"It starts in maybe 200 meters. The houses are all over."

The road on the other side of the puddle was now just a path trampled through the high grass that ran to the edge of the original forest. There was no way to see over the grass or into it. The image of the Perrieras laying in ambush came to mind. We asked the purple shirt if he'd take us in.

He shook his head.

"We'll pay you."

He shook his head again.

"Why not?"

"I hate the posseiros. They know I hate them. They told me if I go there they'll cut my tongue out."

We walked cautiously, vigilant of every movement in the tall grass; it probably took ten minutes to walk 300 yards until we came to a single mud-thatch hut in a clearing. We stood still for a moment, not sure how close to go. Then we clapped our hands. Five women emerged, one by one. They stood in front of us and glared.

"The police were here today looking for our men. We thought you might be them coming back," said the oldest. She wore a worn red cotton dress, and tarnished round earrings. Her name was Maria Nonata Souza.

"We are not posseiros," she said after we told her why we had come. "We live here. This is my land. I have been here 22 years. Nelito wants to take all that away."

"That's right. It's our land." Maria Souza's echo was a small woman who looked to be in her mid-30s but probably was much younger. She wore a loose green tube top which sagged with the weight of her breasts and a red skirt that looked like a towel wrapped around her. Maria Nazare Gomes Santos said she had lived there for seven years.

"Where are the men?" we asked.

"They went into the woods when the police came."

"When will they be back?" The women weren't volunteering much information.

"Three, four days. We don't know."

One of the women was heavily pregnant and two naked infants

crawled in the mud at her feet, tormenting a scrawny chicken. It was hot here; the clearing was like a bowl that held steam. Everyone's face glistened with sweat and hands were in constant motion to sweep away a swarm of gnats. We were about to ask why the men would leave the women and children behind when Benito Teodoro Silva, a man about 30 years old in an open blue shirt and black shorts, walked from the hut, his eyes squinting, getting used to the light.

Benito spoke right away, as if he had been eavesdropping. "The pistoleiros came here a month ago and burned our houses. They will not catch us again. If they come back, we will fight them, but they won't know where we are."

The police had come that morning with summonses for five of the men. They delivered the documents to the women at 6 A.M. with an order to appear in court at 10 A.M. in Maraba—at least a half day's journey away. When they saw the police coming in their jeeps, the men drifted off into the forest which, as the police know, is an impossible lair to penetrate.

"I came from the Northeast because of the drought and now I have land to plant. I will leave here only to go to the cemetery or in chains," Benito's neighbor had told a Brazilian reporter. Benito told us most of the others felt that way and that he had been joined by posseiros from the nearby countryside in what sounded like a budding guerrilla army. "There are 300 of us in the forest. If they want one of us they will have to come and take all of us. We know the roads; we know the woods. The police are afraid and Nelito is afraid of what we can do."

The prospect of violence did not seem to trouble these people as it had the Perreiras. Nelito's brother-in-law had apparently been killed in cold blood as he rode a tractor.

"He was clearing our land," said one of the women.

"We didn't kill him," said the man. "He was dead. Only God knows who killed him."

"Nelito can find other land," the woman in the green top said. "He is rich. He is a baron."

They based their claim on the fact that Nelito had false documents to the land, but they were unconvincing as they tried to explain how they knew this to be true. "People who live in the jungle know these things," was how Benito explained it. And when we pressed the point, he dismissed the question with a wave of his hand and the response, "We just know." He knew, it seemed, because of the age-old theory of ownership that possession is nine-tenths of the law.

"Aren't you scared?" we asked the pregnant woman.

"I am not afraid, but I do not sleep at night. I say 'Father, how can this be?' "

We glanced out the doorway to a small football field laid out in an overgrown clearing alongside the hut. Fruit at the base of trees planted here and there was rotting. The whole place had the look of a bunker, and the tension was clear in these people's faces and their reticence.

"If things are so bad then why didn't you accept Nelito's offer of half of the land?"

The woman in green spoke. "It was terrible land he offered us, dense forest. He wanted this land, which is good land, and he didn't want to pay us for our services. It was jungle when we came here. Now it is ours."

The pregnant woman said they would prevail ultimately because they were "with Jesus" and because "we have rights, and the law is strong."

"But if you believe in the law, why did the men run away from the police today?" we asked.

"The police are not the law. The police are Nelito's," the woman in the green top answered.

"But at least the problem could be resolved in court without violence."

Their uneasy silence suggested that despite their rhetoric, it was too late for that.

We left the hut under their watchful gaze. These people did not seem to us to be like the Perreiras. The posseiros of Pau Seco seemed meaner, uncompromising and self-righteous. There was no self-perception of a desperate yet unbroken faithful flock about to make its last stand. Instead these people had spoken with utter disregard and contempt for any rights Nelito may have had. Because we saw him almost as pathetic, we were not so hasty to dismiss him. We discerned no heros here, only victims. We saw no hope unless a third party intervened, but both church and government had taken sides and were not trusted.

The taxi driver and a few others sat on the steps of the shack we had passed on our way in, clinging to a thin strip of shade beneath the overhang. We sat and rested with them, unburdening our sense that a peaceful solution did not seem likely.

"Things are very bad right here," said Cleo Osvaldo Oliveira, the man in the purple shirt who had been threatened with the loss of his tongue. "Right here," he said, pointing to the ground for emphasis.

His mother nodded. "If the posseiros win we will die slowly because they will force us out. If Nelito wins, we will die quickly because he will throw everyone off his land and then take ours." The Oliveiras showed no sense of community with the posseiros; they had documents to prove they owned their land.

Cleo and his mother showed off bullet holes in the mud of their hut. They said the posseiros had shot at them because they thought Cleo had told the police where they hid. "Or maybe just because they wanted to use their guns," Cleo added.

His family had been there for many years, he said, long before the first posseiros came and long before Nelito came. When the posseiros arrived they stuck together. Every year more came. They wanted nothing to do with Cleo and his family, even though they were neighbors in a harsh land.

Jose Bispo Santos, whose land adjoined the disputed territory, spoke up. "I mind my own business, but you see 15 people walking through the land with guns, like a battalion. You don't know who they are. Others come from far away. They organize to help each other."

Cleo's mother added, "They hate us. The posseiros hate us because we don't support them. Nelito came with the police a few weeks ago. He said to me, 'Give them milk.' I said to him, 'Who's going to pay for it?' Everybody wants something for nothing."

But the price being paid at Pau Seco was absurdly high.

"Why does a country with so much land have land problems?" London asked Jose Bispo Santos.

"I don't know and I don't care. All I want is civilization so that a man can get on his horse and ride around and so his wife can be safe."

SERRA PELADA

From the problems of Brazil to its promise—we were on our way to see the gold of Serra Pelada. Everyone told us we had to go there— businessmen, prospectors, prostitutes, the man who sold mortadella sandwiches. Serra Pelada, where the vaunted promise of the Amazon became something Brazil could put in its pocket. The gold mine about 60 miles southwest of Maraba was proving that the Amazon is as rich as everyone from the conquistadores on have predicted. And the 20,000 miners there were celebrating the common man's arrival at those riches.

We had received permission to visit the mine, which, like the Cumaru mine, was sealed off as a national security area, but we had not yet found a plane to take us there. The Maraba Airport was crowded with decrepit flying machines, all of them abused by the heavy traffic to and from Serra Pelada. Bush pilots here act as taxi cabs for rich miners seeking a respite from the gold mine. Maraba newspapers decry the leisure activities of relaxing miners, claiming that they pointlessly shoot people and recklessly infect the local women with venereal disease.

Walking through the squadron of planes, we came upon a pilot tinkering with his single-engine Cessna, high-winged and visibly rusty. On the tail was a decal with two geese urging us to "Fly United."

The pilot's name was Copila, a bulbous greasy character with an avaricious grin. We asked him to fly us to Serra Pelada.

He asked us how much money we had. It was a buyer's market, and Copila agreed to fly us for $250, which he said was the standard rate for one hour's flying time. The round trip, he said, would take close to one and a half hours. "But I will not charge you more, because I like America. I like Ronald Reagan. A good cowboy."

He told us to come back in the afternoon to ride his "horse of the sky" to Serra Pelada.

When we returned some hours later we found his plane tied down and buttoned up for the night. Copila had left an hour before. Another pilot told us where he was staying. When we found him, he was deep into a bottle of whiskey. We asked why he wasn't at the airport.

"Not today. It is very late. Impossible to fly now. Tomorrow morning," he said.

We reminded him of our deal to leave that afternoon.

He flashed that unscrupulous grin. "There are no schedules in the Amazon. Come back in the morning."

We knocked on his door the next day at 5:30 A.M. After 10 minutes, Copila appeared, looking very bad. "Whiskey," he muttered hoarsely as he stumbled along the street. One pants leg was tucked in his sock. His shirt was out, and his face and hair dripped with the water he had used to revive himself. "Do not speak to me," he said.

The sun was just beginning its quick, vertical climb as Copila started to get the plane in shape. "I had a Scotch," he finally offered.

"One drink did this to you?" Kelly remarked.

"Not one drink. One bottle."

We took off into the sun then headed west with a sharp turn that must have been hell on Copila's stomach because it was bad on ours.

He was sweating heavily as the sun glared into the cabin. The Cessna droned on.

It would be wrong to say that flying over the jungle in single-engine planes had become monotonous to us. True, we had done it often, but there was always that sense of suspense when the engine sputtered. Still, the sameness of the jungle canopy did have a tendency to lull us, and we stared out the window glassy-eyed and began to doze off.

It was Kelly, sitting in back, who first noticed Copila's eyelid. It was closed. He assumed the other one was also. Then the large, lubricated head began to bob forward.

Oh, shit. He's dead.

Kelly shook London whose reaction was instant: an elbow to the pilot's ribs. Startled, Copila looked around, then quickly regained his composure and pasted the lizard grin back on his face.

The awakening process was repeated several times during the trip, as Copila kept slipping into a coma. Each time London poked him in the ribs Copila assured us he was fully aware of what was going on and that we had nothing to worry about.

What loomed ahead of us finally was enough to keep even Copila awake. The green carpet had been bunched and buckled into a series of high ridges and deep valleys. Somewhere in there was Serra Pelada. Copila assured us he could find it.

"I think it's there," he said pointing to a jungle-covered mountain. "On the other side."

He was wrong. On the other side were just more jungle-covered mountains.

He looked at his compass, then smiled at us, his eyelids barely open, the sweat flooding down his fat face. "The instrument, it is wrong."

We asked him if that was a problem.

"No," he said, pointing to his head. "Copila is more intelligent than instruments." With that he banked the plane and started looking anew for Serra Pelada. In the distance we saw another plane, and Copila took off after it.

"Now I know," he announced.

We climbed sharply over a ridge, then pitched forward in a dive. Copila was working hard now. In front of us was a thin short landing strip that looked like the deck of an aircraft carrier, beginning at a plateau above the trees and ending at a mound of dirt. People swarmed over it, oblivious to our approach. It was surrounded on all sides by green ridges, hidden like Edgar Rice Burrough's lost world. Just as it looked as if we were going to slam into the jungle wall at the edge of the runway, Copila leveled off and touched down. As we rolled along, people scattered in front of us; crowds parted down the middle and recongregated quickly behind us. We came to a stop no more than 10 yards from the dirt mound.

Copila parked the plane off to the side with other beaten machines.

"Serra Pelada," he proclaimed. "The jewel of Brazil."

One day in January, 1980, on a small hill in the jungle, distinctive only because few trees grew on it (hence it was called "Naked Mountain"), a giant tree fell over during a rainstorm uprooting tons of earth. In that soil, according to eyewitnesses, were rocks of gold— not what emerged as shiny specks of metal after arduous hours of washing at Cumaru, but real rocks. Within a month 20,000 prospectors swarmed over Serra Pelada like ants in a sugar bowl, addicts of ore desperate to gain entrance to the vein, and they passionately dug away Naked Mountain. With each shovelful, some of the miners found more money than they ever had seen before.

Serra Pelada is run by military officers from a special task force of the National Security Council trying to establish some order among the multitude of men crowded into little more than a square mile. They exuded the same enthusiasm we had heard outside the site, marveling to us about the wondrous nature of this place. "You have to see it to believe it," they told us as we sat in the wood barracks alongside the runway. "You have to talk to the miners, but don't be surprised if they don't always tell the truth."

As if to concede that they had no control over the magic of Serra Pelada, they told us to walk about as we wished. We didn't need a guide to be awestruck, they said.

On a platform supporting a flagpole outside the barracks we saw a young man, well tanned with a beak nose and mournful expression. His name was Clerton Condeiro. We asked him how he was doing, and he told us his life story. It was our luck to come upon probably the most desolate man in all of Serra Pelada.

"My father is a rich man from his trucking business, and he always said I would be nothing in life. I don't know why, but he said it many times. So I came to Serra Pelada to prove that he was wrong and that I could be a rich man, too. But I have been here six months, and I have found nothing. I am beginning to think that maybe my father was right."

He shook his head and looked up as if he were seeing us for the first time. "I speak English, you know," he said. "I am an educated man."

We asked him why, if he was educated, he was poor.

"Sometimes I curse God and say this is not fair. If you look over there, where those men are standing, you will see Jose Maria. He is the king of Serra Pelada. One day he had nothing. Now I think he is the richest man in Brazil. Go talk to him. See if he is any smarter than me. I am sure he can't speak English, and I am not sure he can write. Go over there and see. I will wait for you. I am going nowhere."

Clerton, we thought, must have seen us as arbiters of human worth. In Serra Pelada, gold determines a man's value. Now he had found two outsiders, who he hoped would not be so shallow and would announce that poor Clerton, too, was a king.

Jose Maria stood only about 50 yards away, but it was a perilous run. He was on the other side of the runway we had come in on. Every minute or so a loud piercing siren screamed from a dangling green loudspeaker attached to the air traffic control tower, a listing shack atop wood stilts that doubled as the projection room for nightly movies. At the sound of the whine the men, milling about, scattered and ran for their lives. Once out of the path of the planes, they stood waiting for the imminent crash, transfixed like fans at the Indianapolis 500. There was ample opportunity for disaster; we counted eight takeoffs and landings in 10 minutes.

Our first attempt to cross the runway was aborted because, cowards that we were, we fled instinctively at the sound of the siren before the plane even touched down. As we scurried back to safety we saw Clerton smile, the first time in our short acquaintance that he hadn't looked morose. He yelled, "Courage" to us, and on our second

attempt we ran right through the whine and barely felt the breeze of
the departing plane.

The group congregated around Jose Maria was oblivious to the
chaos around it. The miners hung on every word spoken by the small
brown man with the white cowboy hat. It was easy to pick out Jose
Maria from the crowd: he was clean. Most of the small men enrap-
tured by him wore flip-flop shoes, short shorts and no shirts. They
were caked with mud a shade lighter than their skin. Jose Maria wore
a clean white shirt, neatly pressed black pants and beige cowboy
boots. Even his nails were manicured and polished. He glowed. His
front teeth were gold; he wore a pile of gold chains around his neck,
an oversized gold watchband on his wrist, and a diamond, attached to
a gold band, sparkled on his left hand.

He was telling a story about two girls which, of course, delighted
these sex-starved prospectors, but he could just as easily have been
reciting actuarial tables, and they would have laughed if he laughed,
yawned if he yawned. Jose Maria didn't raise the volume of his voice
to compete with the warning sirens and plane engines, and it didn't
seem to matter that his words were lost.

We didn't have to interrupt to get his attention. No one else
there was tall, white and, in Kelly's case, wore an alligator on his
shirt. Jose Maria finished explaining what lengths the two girls went
to in order to protect their virginity while trying to please him at the
same time, and then he nodded to us.

"Jose Maria," London said, "everyone tells us we must meet
you, because you are the king."

When Jose Maria smiled, the hot sun glistened off his front
teeth. "Everybody here is a king," he said, inadvertently borrowing a
line from Huey Long, the Kingfish of southern American politics. We
started to laugh, but we realized the prospectors were seriously nodding approval of what Jose Maria was saying. There was a camaraderie
among them, each aware that at Serra Pelada the difference between
a king and a pauper is not a stroke of genius but of luck.

London clarified his statement: "In any event, they say you are
a very rich man today."

Jose Maria said that everyone was a rich man, but this time not
everyone nodded.

"He found 327 kilos of gold in one day in September," one of the prospectors told us. We made some calculations in our notebooks and figured that at the prevailing world price that would be about $6 million. Not bad for a day's work.

The other prospectors took up the rest of the conversation as if they wanted to protect Jose Maria from questions and to make sure the truth be known; also, it didn't hurt to ingratiate oneself with the king. In the meantime, their hero greeted well-wishers who passed by; occasionally he smiled as some incredible anecdote was told. Jose Maria was 34 years old and had prospected all through the Amazon for six years without much success. When he arrived at Serra Pelada he used all of his savings to buy a claim from the man who owned the land, and he employed some prospectors to help him. He had to borrow food from others. "I'll pay you back when I find gold," he promised. He made good on his word.

"He has pulled out 1,300 kilos of gold since he is here," one of the prospectors said. In 10 months, all the prospectors together had extracted 10 metric tons from Serra Pelada, more than all of Brazil had ever previously produced in a year. It was no wonder that President Figueiredo, a tough general, broke down and bawled in front of the miners on his visit to Serra Pelada, calling them one of the country's symbols of hope.

We asked him what he was going to do with all that money.

"He divorced his wife," one of the prospectors offered. "Then he bought a new house and asked a nightclub singer to live with him. He wanted to fuck her before, but she said no because he was poor. Then he was living with her, then he stopped. Now he fucks so many girls, young girls. So many."

Jose Maria was listening to this part. Then he added, "I am going to take care of my friends." He nodded around the circle. "I am building the greatest motel in the Amazon so that all of my friends can bring their girls there and fuck like gentlemen. With whiskey and air conditioning. A clean place." A motel in Brazil is not a roadside Holiday Inn, but a place to bring girlfriends, friends' wives or hookers. With large extended families that make privacy difficult to attain, Catholic demureness that dictates extramarital affairs take place on neutral territory, and a male chauvinism that regards most women other than one's wife as whores, Brazilians flock to motels with the abandon of teenagers to Lovers' Lane. Rooms are rented by the hour, or the night if a man wants to make an impression.

"I suppose he told you about the motel," Clerton said when we returned to him "I really hate them, the way they talk of sex, sex, sex. You know, one of Jose Maria's friends stole my wife." Clerton seemed able to match every one of Jose Maria's tales of success with an equally depressing saga.

Clerton had arrived at Serra Pelada after the government restored order to the hill, putting an end to claim jumping, woman stealing and shootings. The rule of law was won single-handedly by a Major Curio of the National Security Council who decreed that no women and no alcohol would be allowed at Serra Pelada. "They only bring confusion," he had said. Clerton, therefore, left his wife in Maraba where the miners go—the rich by plane, the poor by foot—when they are in need of sex or booze. He said he should have left her with his parents, but his father hated her. Anyway, she was pregnant, and Clerton wanted to be near her. In the course of setting up, Clerton spent all his money to acquire a plot of ground and on workers to help him dig it. Whereas many prospectors quickly recoup their investment by sifting out a few vials of gold dust, Clerton accumulated a large pile of dirt. He eventually had to hire himself out as a laborer to another prospector, to sift somebody else's mud.

"I couldn't afford to fly to Maraba to see my wife, and she met a miner named Cara who had much, much money. He took her to Itaituba with him, and she got malaria and had a miscarriage. Now my baby is dead," he said with the same sad monotone that he used for all his stories.

We offered to help him out with the air fare to Maraba. We hadn't known him an hour, and already we were depressed.

"It wouldn't matter," he said. "She's living with Cara, and he'd kill me if I went there. It's over. You know, today is the first day I ever took off my wedding ring. I feel naked."

He handed us a sheaf of papers and told us to read them. "It's a letter to my wife. I'm not sure I should send it," he said. It was 17 pages long, full of threats to kill her, her boyfriend, and himself; full of remorse and pleas for forgiveness; full of accusations of infanticide; full of descriptions of her body and what Clerton once did with it—a cry of a man caught in a maelstrom of craziness, out of touch with what had been real for the first 22 years of his life.

"I saw a priest today, and he doesn't think I should send it. He told me I should pray harder. I never used to believe in God, but I will pray because I have nothing else to lose," he said.

In the hope of getting this infectiously distraught man's mind off his problems, we asked Clerton to give us a tour of the place. What we saw was mind-boggling. When the government arrived to restore order in the spring of 1980, it froze ownership of land at 4-square-meter plots or about six and a half feet on a side. Technically, only that square of surface belongs to the miner, because in Brazil all subsoil belongs to the government, unlike the English and American system where private land ownership traditionally has been from the center of the earth to the blue sky above. But at Serre Pelada, the government keeps only the commission of 25 percent of gold mined, in return for providing order and medical services. The result is a hole the size of a meteor crater gouged out like an amphitheater for Gullivers but populated by perpetually moving Lilliputians. The three-dimensional checkerboard effect comes from the uneven exploration; successful miners dig their tiny square plots 200 feet down while their neighbors, lazy or unlucky, stop far short of that depth. Thus, two men working adjacent horizontal plots of earth can be 50 or 75 feet from each other vertically. "They fall often and die," the gloomy Clerton observed. The only way to exit from the deeper plots is by an intricate system of handmade ladders which cross-hatch the area. Men are in constant motion—shoveling, picking, carrying full bags of wet dripping dirt up ladders, empty bags down them, and visiting deeper plots to see what the future might bring. Because of the different depths the hole is many-colored, from gray rock at the bottom to light brown rock to red clay to dried topsoil to the green of the remaining vegetation.

Cries, yells, and the sound of a thousand tools echoed from below. It was as if Hieronymous Bosch's chaotic, multidimensional painting of the "Garden of Earthly Delights" had been brought to life.

We told this to Clerton, an educated man who knew the 15th-century Dutch masterpiece. "No," said Clerton, nonplussed even at this wonder. "It's like the Hanging Gardens of Babylon. That's why we call it Babylonia."

We were excited and wanted to talk to someone other than Clerton, the black cloud. Nearby stood a man with a thick dark beard, a red bandana around his neck, and a red cap. He also had a leather shoulder bag and a wristwatch, the accouterments of the successful miner, according to Clerton who constantly asked people what time it was.

We walked over to the man, on the way falling twice in the mud; our shoes had picked up so much mud they had quadrupled in weight.

"Joaquim Almeida," the man introduced himself. We asked what he was doing just standing there. "You see that plot over there," he said, pointing to one of the 4-square-meter boxes of land near the bottom of the crater. We thought it impossible for anyone but a proprietor to distinguish one plot from another; there was so much activity and so many depths, rhythms and paces. For the sake of moving on, we said we recognized it. "That's mine. Those are my boys." He spoke with the pride of a scoutmaster.

A psychologist living in Rio, Almeida was watching the news one evening with his wife and three children and saw a report of the Serra Pelada strike. A wakeful, soul-searching night followed. By morning his bags were packed; he kissed his family good-bye and headed off to the jungle seeking his pot of gold. "I took a bus to Maraba then got a ride then I walked the last 14 hours through the jungle."

"Were you scared?"

"Sim, Senhor," he answered. "I had barely been out of Rio in my life and here I was in the Amazon jungle. I saw two men dead on my way in, but I think they must have been on their way out and were hijacked."

"Has it been worth it?" we asked.

"Life here is terrible. I miss my wife and my children. I haven't left this place in five months. My house is some black plastic held up by sticks, and when it rains it falls down. I'm always picking bugs off myself. Sure, it was worth it," he said, winking and rubbing his thumb and index finger together.

Almeida, 32, had been making $240 a month in Rio; his wife, also a psychologist, made the same. At Serra Pelada he was clearing $300 a day after paying his partner and the 16 men who carried dirt for him and searched it for gold. There are different arrangements for workers—some are paid by the day (about $12), some by the bag (about $1, which was Clerton's wage), and some get a percentage of the find (Almeida gave his workers 50 percent and he split 50 percent with his partner).

"I don't mind him making more money than I," said Clerton as we navigated our way up and down ladders to meet other miners. Our feet were too long for the rungs, too wide for the narrow tree limbs serving as bridges, and Kelly's 170 pounds were almost too heavy for the entire rudimentary maze. His khaki pants felt as if they had been coated with lead; his Sears construction boots were hidden under mud cakes at the end of his legs. Clerton continued talking, although he easily outdistanced us. "At least that guy's intelligent. But 90 percent of them are illiterate, and they're going to leave here rich men."

Clerton pointed out one of the lucky ones. "He's another friend of Jose Maria. See how much he's made."

Antonio Gomes Souza, 44, was indeed a friend of Jose Maria; in fact, it appeared they shared the same dentist, although the toothman was more creative with Gomes' mouth. Instead of solid gold teeth, his mouth was an abstract sculpture of gold flowing through the enamel with gentle curves, exclamation points, and commas. It was as if someone had needlepointed his teeth with gold nuggets.

We asked him how much he had found. He said 17 million cruzeiros, about $275,000. Because the main meeting place in Serra Pelada is called the Plaza of Lies, we asked Gomes to prove his net worth. We were having a hard time believing these numbers.

Gomes produced a receipt from the Bank of Brazil, apologizing that it was the only one he had with him. We examined it. The miner was wrong. The bank receipt was not 17 million cruzeiros, but 173 million; about $2.75 million.

"What are you going to do with the money?" London asked, wondering if Gomes knew he had ten times what he said he did.

"I'm going to buy big cattle ranches," he answered. When he spoke, he smiled, and we were slow with follow-up questions, so taken were we with his teeth.

"What did you do before this?"

"I was a laborer, picking Brazil nuts," he said. He told us of another miner friend who also was very rich and who was going to buy five airplanes. "He's crazy," Gomes laughed. "He doesn't even know how to drive a car."

Clerton seethed when we told him what Gomes had said. "God

doesn't know about justice," he said. We asked him who else had made it big. He pondered this for a moment and stood his ground, blocking the path of grunting miners bent double like beggars with 60-kilo sacks of wet dirt on their backs. By this method they already had carried away many thousands of tons—an entire mountain. They cursed Clerton as they passed. He cursed them back and took off his green baseball cap and beat the bags, telling them to hurry up.

Clerton mentioned Dr. Renzo. "You go there yourselves," he said. "I need time to think. I will meet you at the Plaza of Lies in two hours."

Left alone, we stumbled badly through the mud. We constantly feared a sack of dirt or an errant miner would tumble down upon us, and, as we climbed higher, we imagined ourselves losing our footing and coming to rest upon the head of some unsuspecting miner.

"The newspapers say I have 650 kilos," Roger Renzo, the doctor, told us. "I don't even know how much I have, so how do they know? Let's just say I have no complaints."

Renzo, 30, a London-trained surgeon from Sao Paulo, spoke English as well as we did. His brother, also a doctor, had been practicing medicine in Maraba when news of the toppled tree reached the town. He rushed to Serra Pelada and bought up as many mining rights as possible, promising the landowner 10 percent of his find.

"My brother knew nothing about gold except it makes you rich. He hired a lot of these prospectors, set up this camp and started mining," Renzo said. The camp was a wood shack, one of the only dwellings at Serra Pelada not made of black plastic and tree limbs. His men had constructed a neat barbed-wire fence around the perimeter, and the 50 laborers were divided between those who carried gold from the hole to the compound and those who sat in pools of water, cleaning the dirt and extracting the gold.

Renzo offered us a soda from a refrigerator he had hooked up to a homemade generator.

"A lot of the press comes to me because they think I don't belong, that a surgeon who could be a rich man in his profession must be out of his mind to be here. But we have many professional people —lawyers, businessmen, even a priest. Face it, where else in the world do you see change overnight? It makes everyone, as you would say, good press."

"And look where it's coming from—great universities? scientific advancement? No, from the center of the earth by a method that's as old as civilization itself," Renzo continued. "The geologists say that you lose 50 percent of the gold by mining by hand. But the government puts up with it, because if you boot out 20,000 men you're going to have a problem on your hands. This is a great social experiment for this country. It's the first time they've let the people have access to these natural resources."

At first there was talk of evicting all the miners, declaring the area a national security installation, and bringing in the government-owned mining company. Waste resulting from primitive mining methods was only one reported justification; the other was that too many people were dying.

"I wasn't here at the beginning, but my brother said it was very bad, real violent. There was so much shooting you couldn't sleep at night." He took a sip from the soda can.

That had all changed, however, with the arrival of Major Curio, who alit from a helicopter on May 20, 1980, walked to the center of the runway, pulled out his gun, aimed toward the sky and pulled the trigger. "While you can stay armed don't forget that the gun that shoots the loudest is mine," he shouted to the assembled throng. Within a month, thousands of guns had been laid at his feet. He issued the no-woman/no-alcohol edict; broke up the large landholdings such as Renzo's brother and Jose Maria had; he gave everyone already at the site a prospector's work card and promised to bar any newcomers, unless plots were unmanned for 72 hours in which case they would be redistributed. He tossed out one aspiring prospector who had sneaked in through the jungle 42 times before relenting and issuing him a card. The Brazilian Senate President wrote a personal letter to Curio asking him to issue a card to a friend, and, the story goes, Curio returned the letter to the sender with instructions to stuff it.

"For us, God is in Heaven, and Dr. Curio is on earth," one miner said.

T-shirts with Curio's likeness flourished in Serra Pelada. Alongside the letters in his name was a motto, a slogan of manhood barked by high school football coaches every autumn: C(oordination), U(nity), R(espect), I(dealism), O(rganization).

For all his fame, Curio isn't even the soldier's real name, Renzo informed us. He was born Sebastiao Rodrigues de Moura, but he must have felt that a great warrior needed something better, like Stonewall or Black Jack. He got his *nom de guerre* from colleagues who were impressed with his interrogation talents during Brazil's attempt to quell guerrillas in the Amazon region from 1972 to 1974; after listening to his questions the subjects were said to have sung like a bird whose name in Portuguese means curio. Despite having led the army in a guerrilla war in which 20,000 soldiers were rumored to have been involved, he remained a shadowy, James Bond figure.

Because of Curio's experience in the region, the government began to use him as a troubleshooter to resolve the myriad land and social problems on the frontier. He became a GETAT unto himself. He used the titles Dr. and Major interchangeably, and he wasn't beyond inventing pseudonyms. One of the bishops in the Amazon refused to keep an appointment with him, saying he didn't meet with birds, so Curio sent word that he wasn't a bird but Major Marco Antonio Luchini, a name he borrowed from his wife's family.

Renzo said emphatically that this soldier, who never wears a uniform, was a hero to the miners. Many credited him with keeping the government's digging machines out, at least for the time being, and they were delighted that he was seeing to it that a town would be constructed nearby so they could house their wives, whores and bottles. The town's name would be Curionopolis, and the founder has considered representing it in the federal Congress.

When he finished his yarn about Curio, Renzo told us it was fortuitous we heard it from him. "You'd never get the truth from any of them," the doctor said, pointing to his workers half submerged in water as they cleaned the dirt. "They'd tell you he can walk on water."

Clerton was waiting for us at the Plaza of Lies. He was the only one listening to a miner with a megaphone expound on the virtues of the Assembly of God. "Well, I've made a decision," he told us when we asked him if he was thinking of converting. "I'm going to start smoking again. So what if it kills me?"

Together we crossed the runway again to see why a crowd had gathered in front of the infirmary.

"I don't think we should go near them," Clerton said. "There's

supposed to be a meningitis epidemic, and they're probably all waiting to see the doctor." Were the rumor true, the dreaded disease
could spread like a brush fire through the area, because 20,000 men
without running water or sewers co-habit like sardines in a can.

London volunteered to find out. It was easy for him to see over
the heads of the congregated miners, and he saw that they were not
patients waiting to see the doctor, but an audience watching a man in
a white coat lance the purple and green penis of an abject prospector.

"I know who he got it from," a miner said in front of London.
"I was with him in Maraba."

"No, you don't know. It's impossible to tell. All the bitches in
Maraba will give it to you," another responded.

"If you want to see something really bad, come with me," Clerton announced. After the scene at the infirmary, we wondered what
awaited. Clerton took us to another queue outside a wood frame
building with three large open windows.

"This is where they sell the gold to the government," he said.

"It doesn't look so bad to me," Kelly responded, although Clerton might have been referring to the government's commission, a fact
of life so glum a man might view it as exploitation.

"You're not looking at what's bad," he said, pulling us to the
front of the line. We watched as a miner took film canisters out of his
shoulder bag and dumped them on a scale. A government inspector
on the other side of the window ran a magnet through several times in
case metal filings had been used to adulterate the gold, then carefully
pushed the yellow dust into a pile: 786 grams. He punched numbers
into an adding machine, prepared a receipt for the money to be
deposited in the miner's account, and asked him to sign it. The miner,
expressionless despite his new wealth, reached in the window to grab
a stamp pad, placed his thumb on it, then pressed his thumb to the
receipt.

"This hurts me more than that would," Clerton said, nodding in
the direction of the medical shed. "He cannot write, but he is a rich
man and I am not."

We left our lugubrious friend to accept an invitation to eat with
the Brazilian army unit that kept order at the mine. The men discussed who found what that day and reminded us Americans that we
had just trudged across the land of opportunity.

It was dark when we started back to the Plaza of Lies. The runway was quiet. A light was on in the control tower, where there would be a movie in an hour or so, and hundreds were gathering in front of the open-air screen. The hillsides were dotted with small fires and files of flashlights carried by men who were invisible at this hour. It looked like a quiet religious procession, the serenity in marked contrast to the day's movements. Some took bucket baths by candle-light, others huddled around stoves. The clinking of tin cups and plates echoed off the tree line.

The Plaza of Lies, however, was bustling. The stores were as busy as Macy's on a pre-Christmas night. When there was daylight there was work, and nighttime was the only opportunity the men had to buy soap and other supplies. The Assembly of God preacher had attracted a half-dozen bored miners. A miner with a guitar had drawn a crowd: he was singing a homemade song about a *forao*, the un-authorized miner who sneaks in through the jungle like a hungry dog looking for scraps.

Clerton stood with four other men passing a small yellow book among themselves and speaking to about 30 men crowded around. As we got closer we heard what was being said; the book contained poems in celebration of the miners. One miner was reciting:

> In the first place
> Is the farmer who produces food
> For all the population
> For Brazil and the exterior.
> In the second place
> The prospector who produces various minerals.
> The best is gold
> For Brazil to move ahead.

We listened to others recite poems about cures for snake bites and homages to the pilots who fly the dangerous skies of the jungle, making even the most isolated mine accessible to those who can pay. Clerton recited one about taking leave of the family before going off to the jungle.

We recognized one of the audience as the miner who had incurred Clerton's wrath earlier at the cashier's window with his thumbprint.

"Good evening," he responded to our greeting, looking down and smoothing the soil with the rubber sandal on his right foot.

"I saw you today at the bank. Do you remember?"

"Yes."

"How did you make out?" asked London, who had seen the receipt.

"Not so good," said the miner.

"It looked good to me."

"Fifty or sixty grams. Not so good," the miner said, still smoothing the ground of the Plaza.

It was again Clerton's turn to recite:

> Don't say that the prospector
> Is a vagabond.
> The prospector is of the class
> That works most in the world.
> Besides working so much
> The suffering is profound.

We figured he was the only one in the Plaza telling the truth. It was ironic—Clerton being poor—because he was one of the few who seemed to understand what money meant away from Serra Pelada. Others would build brothels, buy airplanes and let them rust, or cattle ranches which one day would become desert. Yet, this is their prerogative. They have suffered, Clerton told us in his poetry. For a fleeting moment in history El Dorado has been reached. It is theirs, to revel in and to squander.

PARAKANA

We moved on from Serra Pelada to find out about a land takeover of monstrous proportion, more tragic than violent, where the line between right and wrong is nearly imperceptible. The land-grabber in this case is one of the highest priorities on the national agenda—the $3 billion Tucurui dam, about 125 miles north of Maraba on the Tocantins River, which will flood out 2,200 square kilometers of forest. The entire industrial development of the eastern Amazon depends upon the construction of this mammoth dam, to be the world's fourth-largest when completed. On the soon to be inundated land live the Parakana Indians. Like posseiros, they have no legal title to their land, though the Parakana have lived there longer than the concept of legal title has been extant. Of course, the Parakana can refuse to move, but once the gates of the dam close they will drown.

We first heard about the plight of the Parakana from Joao Pacheco, the Indian rights activist in Rio. He recommended we try to visit them because they symbolize the clash between indigenous cultures who live harmoniously with the jungle and the modern Brazilian assault on the Amazon. He warned us that access to the tribe was severely restricted because of FUNAI's sensitivity to reports about a small tribe victimized by a giant dam.

Thus, we were completely taken aback when Ivan Zanoni of FUNAI told us in Brasilia that there'd be no problem in visiting the Parakana. He summoned his assistant, who brought forms for us to complete, certifying that we did not have small-pox or tuberculosis, and told us that when we got to the town of Tucurui, we would meet our guides. It seemed so simple, we became suspicious. After extending the invitation Zanoni laughed heartily. We asked him what was so funny and he said, "Nothing." But his reaction was odd. Such requests, if they are granted at all, take six months to process, even when serious anthropologists make them. Why was it so easy for us? Why had Zanoni, the rumored former "interrogator," laughed? The sound of Zanoni's laughter lingered in our minds.

Before visiting the tribe, we sought out the man who had discovered them. Raimundo Nascimento, a FUNAI employee who works at a regional office along the TransAmazon Highway, was somewhat of a legend within the Indian agency because of his discovery of the Parakana and his subsequent work on behalf of the Kayapo-Gorotire. Nascimento welcomed us into his stifling kitchen to listen to his story.

Nascimento removed his shirt and stood there naked but for tiny ochre bathing trunks. He grabbed a glistening steel machete in his right hand. A middle-aged wisp of a man, he began to talk so excitedly that his oversized saucer eyes seemed on the verge of popping out of his head. Sitting on wooden stools around a table covered with yellow vinyl cloth and dotted with small black flies, we listened to the re-creation of what Nascimento called the greatest moment of his life—the discovery of the Parakana Indians.

It happened at 10 o'clock in the morning of December 23, 1970. Following a routine he had established after three months in the jungle, Nascimento went out to gather Brazil nuts for the eight others in the government team sent to locate the Indians. His shoelace came undone. "I went to tie it," he said, kneeling on his kitchen floor to pantomime the effort. "Because I had stopped walking there was complete silence. Then I heard a rustling. Then I saw them. The surprise was so great I couldn't move."

Perched on one knee and holding his left foot with both hands, Nascimento repeatedly shook his head back and forth as if ten years later he still couldn't believe the vision. "They were walking in a single file with arrows in one hand and turtles in the other. They were beautiful. All their hair was shaved off, and they were naked except for a thin string around their waists and a pouch there." He pointed to his genitals.

"I got up, and I stared at them. Then the Indian in the lead saw me and came over. I handed him my machete, handle first." Nascimento stood up and took the machete from the kitchen table and placed it in Kelly's hands. "I waited to see what he would do. Then he gave me his turtle."

Nascimento said, "*Obrigado*" but then realized that they didn't understand him. The Indians spoke no Portuguese, and he didn't know any Tupi, the language group of the Parakana.

"I was afraid they would leave, so I gestured to them to follow me, and I started running through the woods yelling as loud as I could, like this." We cringed as he let out the high-pitched squeal of an excited animal. He didn't look at us for a reaction; he was back in the woods. An unpretentious man, he was reliving this moment as an assertion of self-worth, not to impress anyone else.

"The camp was about two kilometers away, and I was yelling and panting because I was running so hard," he said as he began to run in place on the kitchen floor.

"Happily, the people in the camp heard me, and they threw their guns away. The Indians followed me into the camp, and they started dancing and we . . ."—he paused to take a breath, and his jogging style changed into a modified jig—"started dancing. Then every time a white man jumped in the dance the Indian would jump higher, then we would jump higher, and they would jump higher, and we did this for 40 minutes, and we were exhausted."

He walked over to the sink and drew a glass of beige water and downed it quickly. "You want some?" he asked, putting the glass before us. We declined, as we always did with tap-water offerings.

When the dance ended there was an uneasy silence and gawking by both sides, Nascimento remembered. Everyone in camp realized there was not much to talk about. Although there were three interpreters, finding the proper words to let naked, hairless people know they had just walked into the 20th century was not an easy task. One anthropologist, with the bitterness characteristic of many who worked with Indians, had told us earlier that he would have greeted them, "Now, you're fucked."

Nascimento's team decided to forgo trying to explain everything to the Indians and instead seduced the Indians to return by inviting them to carry off whatever they wanted from the camp. In many Indian cultures, such offerings are commonplace expressions of friendship. "They took everything—utensils, clothes, even the pictures of our wives and girlfriends. We were left with nothing but the clothes we had on. Then they went away."

The head of the camp told Nascimento to follow the Indians back into the jungle, but when he started after them, the chief turned around and held up his hand. Nascimento stayed put.

"That night we cut palm leaves to sleep on because we gave our hammocks to the Indians. Then we went back for more supplies, but on January 6, 1971"—the dates were very clear to him—"the Indians returned and again we gave them everything but the clothes we were wearing." He had calmed down by now and joined us at the table. Oddly, he was not sweating, although we were quite moist in the sweltering kitchen.

The Indians' enthusiasm for claiming the government team's belongings brought them back to camp five or six times during which they stayed only long enough to gather up the available goods. They disappeared into the jungle each time, insisting that they not be followed. At any time they could have failed to return and the process of finding them would have started over. Nascimento had no idea where they lived or if indeed they lived in one place or were perpetual wanderers.

"Finally, the head of the camp asked the Indians to bring their women and children to the camp, but the Indians said they would do this only if the white men would do this too. We had no women in our camp and asked two women from another Indian agency camp if they would help us, and they did.

"The Indians came back, but still it was only the men. We were surprised. They surrounded our women, and they ripped open their shirts and grabbed their bosoms. They examined them very carefully to make sure they were real. Then they left.

"The next day the Indians returned with their women and children. They all were completely naked and without any hair. It was as if they were shining and aglow, they were so beautiful."

The visits continued, and all went smoothly until a day the Indians nervously complained to the white men about an imminent peril. "We had built shelters for the women in our camp so they could go to the bathroom and bathe in privacy. But the Indians thought we built them for an attack, that we were planning to shoot arrows at them from the shelters. When the head of the camp found out about this he had them torn down."

Nascimento left the camp on February 25, 1971, and he spent most of the next ten years living in the jungle with various tribes. In this time he achieved the honored status of *sertanista*, a term which is used to describe discoverers of previously unknown tribes or people who have performed some extraordinary feat on behalf of Indians. It is the ultimate honor for the professional Indian agent.

Yet this honored man was uneasy, even on that night as he sat performance-fatigued in his kitchen, elaborating on his career. Not many people in Brazil or even the world have had the opportunity to introduce others across thousands of years of time. He had performed a special task usually reserved for God, he said.

Time had sobered Nascimento's euphoria and tarnished his self-image as a *sertanista*. Discovery of the Parakana was a moment of individual glory, and "I am still very proud," he said, "but I think about what has happened to them, to the Parakana, and it is not good, not something to be proud of."

As we set out from Tucurui in a government jeep we could sense a hint of the expectation Nascimento must have felt as he walked through the jungle ten years earlier. Unlike our impromptu shocking descent among the Kayapo-Gorotire, we had prepared ourselves for this visit. We could find the tribe's location on a map, and we had learned a good deal about the Parakana's recent experiences after contact with FUNAI.

We soon realized to our distress that we even knew more about the Parakana than did Lucia Helena Soares, the government anthropologist accompanying us. She had been assigned from graduate school to be a government liaison with the Parakana after the FUNAI's controversial dismissal of 28 professional anthropologists who objected to the government's plan to integrate Indians into mainstream society. Lucia Helena, as she liked to be called, had visited the Parakana only three times and, when we asked what they were like, she said, "*Simpatico*"—nice.

The other three members of our group were Celia Ferreira, a government nurse who told us that the Parakana were very sick; Claudio Fabio Moraes, a representative from the government's dam building company who tried to dissuade us from going because it was "too hot and too many mosquitoes," and the driver, who drove dangerously enough on the rutted roads to make the statement that he had no respect for our lives.

As we approached the Parakana reserve, the road deteriorated We eventually encountered a seemingly bottomless puddle and had to get out and walk. The path was narrow but well trodden, and the jungle alive with color and sound. The whooshing screams of howler monkey sounded like a great gale among the trees.

Although we were certain there was no lurking danger—except an errant snake or malarial mosquito—we still were apprehensive as we approached the village. According to Nascimento, the Parakana had fared miserably since their discovery, and we thought it logical that they might be bitter and hostile. Their land had been invaded by a behemoth construction project and the army of workers attendant to it. They were going to have to uproot and move; we knew enough to understand the bond between these Indians and their land—they worship it, for it gives them life. Moving from traditional land often is catastrophic.

Two young boys, neither of them more than 10 years old, joined our single file. They were carrying antiquated rifles, and when we turned to them to smile, they smiled back and snorted a hoarse laugh through their noses. They stayed in the rear of the line as we walked, chuckling to themselves. We asked Lucia Helena what they were saying.

"I don't know," she answered. She hadn't learned their language.

Balancing like the Flying Wallendas, one by one we tightroped a narrow log bridge over a muddy stream and climbed the bank into a clearing. We saw a large thatched-roof community building and a wood shack, painted pink. A line of seven women sat on a log in the shade of the thatch, nursing babies and chatting to each other in what sounded like a slow, deep chant. Some men were in T-shirts and shorts, walking about carrying logs and machetes and doing assorted chores. Our arrival here was not greeted with the enthusiastic reception shown by the Kayapo.

The anthropologist announced, "The Chief sees us. Here he comes." We looked around and saw nothing but heard a scraping noise as if someone were sweeping a dirt floor with a heavy bristle broom. Then out of the shadow of the large hut came a man with muscular arms dragging himself along the ground on a board. His withered legs, like bones with the meat picked off, flopped uselessly in front of him. Approaching the anthropologist, he offered his hand. He was smiling, which made the white bone plug that protruded through his chin all the more prominent on his deeply lined face. Lucia Helena bent and tried to explain in Portuguese that Americans had come to visit, but it was clear that Brazil's current expert on the Parakana couldn't communicate with the chief of the tribe.

We introduced ourselves. The Chief said, "Piaui," which we took as his name, although it also is the name of a state in northeast Brazil. Then we followed him at an uncomfortably slow pace toward the center of the hut. Watching the Chief struggle to pull himself along, we recalled Nascimento's words ". . . they were shining and aglow, they were so beautiful. . . ." We were beginning to understand the nature of his guilt.

Piaui yelled something that brought all those present into a circle around us. The faces were placid, broad and copper. Many of their eyes were watery, and their noses ran. Their easy smiles suddenly contorted to stifle the symptoms of an epidemic cold. Most of these suppressions were futile, and the 15 or so Indians broke the air in a chorus of cacophonous sneezes and bronchial coughs. Although it was only a small group around us, the humidity and heat was oppressive. We felt none of the freshness and physical comfort that we had at the Kayapo village; in fact, this seemed an unhealthy place where germs might feel welcome.

Nascimento had suggested we bring gifts. Lucia Helena took the package of gym shorts from us and began handing them to the men and boys. We had spent $50 for the shorts and for brightly colored cloth, which Lucia Helena gave to the nursing women. They didn't seem to realize the cloth was from us. The Indians looked at us with faces that displayed disappointment, but not anger, over not receiving gifts from us. Piaui scowled at Lucia Helena because he felt the side vents in his shorts were tears in the seams. A man named Felipe, who was introduced as the representative in residence from the Indian agency, assured Piaui that the shorts were in vogue.

Like the Chief, adult men wore bone plugs through their chins, the evidence of a rite of male puberty. The young boys had shaggy western-style haircuts and faces alive with mischief. Their wardrobe was a ragtag collection of worn shorts and T-shirts, one of which proclaimed "Indian Life" and had pictures of tepees on it.

Most of the women paid no attention to us. They stayed on the logs and nursed tiny children, some of whom had skin sores and rashes that were painful to look at. The expressions on the faces of the Parakana women were those of resignation and self-absorption, and we were uncomfortable looking at them, because they seemed to hurt too much to care about anything beyond their breasts. They were despair on display. The Kayapo women had modestly turned away from our cameras; these women seemed oblivious to our picture taking; they didn't change expressions nor did they turn away. Anthropologists had told us of women from another tribe who had aborted their babies to spare them the agony that civilization had brought. An almost incredible statement at the time, now it was becoming less hard to believe.

"What do you think they think of us?" London asked Celia, the nurse, as she tended to a young malaria-stricken patient in a hammock outside the pink shack infirmary.

"They probably think . . ." she was interrupted as the boy vomited on her feet. She took a wet cloth and put it on his forehead. Her feet stayed soiled. "They probably think you're as strange as you think they are. But I'm not sure they care so much anymore."

The community hut, well constructed and airy, was for the Indian agency representatives, as were the living quarters attached to the pink infirmary. On the other side of a barbed-wire fence and down a slope we could see where the Parakana lived: eight huts made entirely of thatched straw. We asked Felipe to show us around. We went into one hut and gagged from the sickening smell, as if someone had forgotten to take the garbage out for months. There were no artificial lights, and in the narrow rays of sun which penetrated the straw, we could make out an intricate web of hammocks and drying meat hanging from the ceiling.

Felipe saw us recoil from the sight and smell and said, "They do not live well."

"But why?"

"They do not live well because they do not know how to live in one place. They are wanderers, and now they cannot wander. Every night they return here."

As we walked through the huts, all of them with the same putrid smell, Felipe explained the plight of the Indians. This particular group of Parakana had not been discovered until January 12, 1976, five years after Nascimento's first contact with the tribe. They were found near the city of Altamira on the TransAmazon Highway, where they had lived for centuries hunting, fishing and migrating through the jungle.

A short time after contact with whites, the Indians became very sick. They didn't have immunities to the common ills of the 20th century. Colds became pneumonia; measles meant death. The Chief contracted polio. Within six months of their initial contact, eleven Indians had died. The government insisted that the Indians move to a healthier environment, because the government medics attempting to cure the Indians were themselves becoming sick with malaria. The tribe was reluctant to move because they knew the land where they had lived for so long.

In October, 1976, the government moved the group to the camp, since abandoned, where Nascimento had lived when he was trying to contact the Parakana. The move was made by bus, which must have been for the Indians like entering H. G. Wells' time machine, a journey through centuries in a matter of hours. No plans had been made to receive the Indians in the new location, and they had to live in the abandoned shelters and eat food trucked in by the government. During this time another group of eight Parakana Indians arrived, but five of them died within months, so difficult was the transition to living in permanent housing on unfamiliar land surrounded by people carrying unfamiliar germs.

This latest site had been cleared in February, 1977, and the surviving Indians were transported again to learn a new life-style on new land. But even this new home was not to be for long.

"You know they must move again," said Felipe. We knew.

"They will be flooded out when they close the gates of the Tucurui dam. They must move, or they all will die," he added.

It seemed to be a Hobson's choice: stay and die, or move and, if the pattern continued, die. This was not the barbarity we had heard about in Rio from Indian rights groups—the smallpox blankets and dynamiting from planes. There didn't seem to be anything you could call murder. Yet, the Indians were dying just the same. They keep getting in the way. There were 700 to 1,000 Parakana Indians in three groups when Nascimento first met them in 1970. A decade later there were no more than 300, of whom 35 were under Felipe's care.

Felipe, 54, was living with the Indians during the week; on weekends he went home to his wife and eight children in the town of Tucurui, about 3 hours away by foot and jeep. We noticed several scars cut deep into his bronzed torso, the reminders of five poison arrows from the Gavioes Indians with whom he had lived for five years. One day they attacked him, chasing him from the village and leaving him for dead. He spent 20 months in a hospital recovering.

"Why did they do it?" we asked.

Felipe shrugged his shoulders. "Only God knows," he said.

"Are you afraid of the Parakana?" we asked rhetorically, as if anyone could be afraid of this helpless bunch.

"I have some fear. You never know."

"Then why do you work with them?"

"For the money," he said. He was making about $750 per month.

As we walked back to the FUNAI hut, Felipe introduced us to Maritowa, a well-built, healthy-looking young man, about 25 years old. When we came upon him he was stooped over a smoldering fire, turning the unskinned head of a wild boar on a spit. Flies swarmed around the head, and the fire hissed as blood dripped into it.

"Dinner," Felipe said matter-of-factly. "I am sure they will ask you to eat with them."

"You know, Maritowa has three wives," Felipe said as we continued on. "Most of the men have more than one woman, but Maritowa, he has three. He is the strongest man, the best hunter. And one of his wives is 5 years old." Polygamy, he explained, was not licentious, but a matter of survival. There just weren't enough healthy men to go around. The parents of the 5-year-old girl were buying protection for her future—assuming, of course, Maritowa lived long enough to consummate their marriage. Even the strongest Parakana have died or been stricken with polio.

Felipe arranged for an interview with Ceara, one of the older men, about 40, who had two wives. He wore a tattered blue and gray rugby shirt, green gym shorts and one sandal. Living on hand-me-downs, the Indians take what they can get, including incomplete pairs of shoes. Ceara had oily black hair and probably had never shaved, as he had a peach fuzz mustache and assorted long whiskers sprouting from his puzzled countenance. He, too, was named after a state in Brazil. Someone with an odd sense of humor or strong sense of nationalism had renamed these Indians, substituting familiar sounds for the names given to them at birth, which were strange to most Brazilians. Because only a local woodsman who had happened by spoke Portuguese and Tupi, our questions were not very deep. After Ceara introduced each young man who stood around, London wrote the name on paper and asked if it was the correct spelling. The Indians could not recognize their names, read or write.

Piaui invited us to dine with the tribe, but we could not. Our reluctance wasn't due to the whiskered head on a spit, although we found it unappetizing, but to our self-consciousness and frustration at our own inability to communicate. We felt penned in at the monkey house of a zoo; either we or the Indians were the monkeys, it didn't matter. After ogling each other for five hours we hadn't even begun to understand what made these people tick. We sensed doom, and surely this was a mischaracterization because the Parakana flourished only a few years ago, according to Nascimento. Maybe we were beginning to understand Zanoni's laugh. It was knowing, not diabolical. How many times had he heard well-meaning journalists or anthropologists ask to visit Indians, thinking that by uncovering awful tales to broadcast to the world they could rescue these sorry people. Yet, in spite of good intentions the Indians still were dying. Hug them, kiss them, shake their hands and still they get germs as deadly as bullets and poison blankets. Zanoni must have understood this, that all of us, not only he, are the enemy.

The Indians' physical incompatibility, which they might overcome after years of contact as the Kayapo-Gorotire apparently have done, is only one part of it. They live in a different cultural world from us. Polygamy, which we thought unusual, is common. These Indians have no books, movies or orchestras and don't seem bored. In fact, they apparently thrived, shining and aglow until the day Nascimento met them. Since then they have stumbled badly in trying to learn a life-style, routine and values completely alien to them. It is as if they are deaf-mutes in our culture and we in theirs. And no matter how sensitive we are to their plight, it really doesn't change things one bit.

That Felipe and Celia could live with these people amazed us. We had seen that they couldn't speak more than a few words to the Indians; Felipe showed them how to hunt and farm, and Celia tried to make them well. But no one had the language to tell them they were about to be washed away. A fundamental communication gap existed, and its very existence seemed to be a telling statement.

"You could just as well have been from the moon," said Lucia Helena in the jeep on the way back. And so could she, for all the Indians knew. Her dilettantism and what it meant to the Parakana came through when she gaily kissed all the women when they gave her a present of a hunting bow and quiver of arrows. The gift would be her stamp of authenticity among her schoolmates at the university. She jumped in excitement, then waved "Bye, bye" until the next time. Lucia Helena was supposed to be their last hope, their buffer against a world that was crashing down on them, and she couldn't even talk to them.

Sensing our scorn and trying to break the ice, she pulled out a colorful map. "This is where we are going to move this group," she said, pointing to an area in the middle.

"What is this?" Kelly asked, referring to an area in red.

"This is where pioneer families will live."

"And this?"

"That is a road."

"And this?"

"That is another group of the Parakana," she said.

Kelly looked puzzled. "I thought those two groups don't get along."

"They're going to have to learn how," said Lucia Helena. "There is no more land for them."

Antonio Carlos Magalhaes, an anthropologist who had been deeply involved in relocating the Parakana, pointed to the same map. "It is like they're being put in a room with the walls closing in on them," he told us. "The posseiros will try to steal their land. People from the road will try to steal their land. And they will fight with the other group.

"This will be the graveyard of the Parakana. And for whose benefit is this move?" he asked, not really expecting an answer.

Magalhaes lived with the tribe from 1975 to 1979, when he was fired in one of the periodic government purges of dissident anthropologists. Although he speaks Tupi and considers individual Indians as his personal friends, he was expelled from the village by the government, which charged him with misappropriating funds earmarked for Indian relocation. He claimed he was dismissed because he opposed the planned move of the Parakana.

With a full dark beard, in jeans and a work shirt, Magalhaes looked like the stereotype of the American student radical of the late 1960s. He had studied the Parakana because of a strong belief he could influence their fate. "These people had no idea what was happening to them. I said—and they trusted me—that the dam would kill them, that they had to move.

"You know what they said to me? They said they'll leave when the waters come." He shook his head as he recollected his frustration of trying to make the Parakana understand what was about to happen to them.

"We wanted to build a model of the dam to show them what would happen when the gates close. If they could visualize it they could make their own decision to leave. But the government refused to go along with the idea."

Magalhaes explained that he had picked out an appropriate site for their relocation, one large enough to keep the two warring groups of Indians from each other. But there were squatters on that land who would have had to be moved.

"This is where the bureaucracy killed the project. FUNAI [the Indian agency] asked INCRA [the land agency] to help in this, but they paid no attention. The squatters actually had title to the land, and we wanted INCRA to find substitute land for them so they'd move."

Before the bureaucracy could respond, 22 new families moved into the area, and the influx made relocation of the settlers impossible. Other land had to be found for the Indians.

"At this point our relocation project was bankrupt. The company which was building the dam wouldn't give us any more money, and we still had to find new land and clear it," Magalhaes said. The Indian agency decided to funnel money into the project by purchasing the rights to the Brazil nut trees on the Parakana's land. "It was a hold-up. They offered to pay way below market price for the nuts, but we had no choice. We had no other money. We used those funds to pay off debts, and that was it. The project stopped."

Although he was fired when the project's funds were exhausted, Magalhaes continued to serve as a gadfly consultant to the committee deciding the Parakana's fate. He got lost in the same bureaucracy that had done him in, and when we met him he was the representative to the committee from the Anthropology Department of the Goeldi Museum in Belem, which is funded by the government. Magalhaes vigorously opposes the new plan and instead proposes the creation of a 6-million-acre reservation for four Indian tribes totaling about 1,000 Indians. But he didn't give his own plan much of a chance.

"The general political vision in this country is a murderous one in ethnic terms," he said. "I don't see how the Indians can be integrated into the Brazilian culture."

"But with all this pressure for land and minerals, can they be left alone?" we wanted to know. Magalhaes' plan calls for an average of 6,000 acres per Indian. And the Perreiras were risking their lives just to have 120 acres.

Magalhaes shook his head. "You know your government called its program in Vietnam pacification. That's what our government calls their program of contacting Indians. But they're both the same, and I call it murder."

TUCURUI

The small stream alongside the village of the Parakana empties into the Tocantins River, which in the advancing rainy season had become a dark, swiftly moving torrent. We left the jeep and took a boat downriver. We could feel and hear the river's strength; it rushed with a sound like breath exhaled through clenched teeth. Even when the sky was clear, the waters looked angry and stormy, whirling and chopping into vicious whitecaps. At this section, the Tocantins is among the most powerful rivers in the world, flowing, according to information we had picked up at one of the ministries in Brasilia, at 51,000 cubic meters a second.

We swept downstream in the small boat for a few miles until

ahead of us we could see the place where the will of man would bring
this natural force to a halt. It was as though a mountain range had
suddenly boiled from the river bottom—a 200-foot-high roadblock of
concrete and steel. If the bridge at Conceicao had been absurd, this
was awesome.

This was the Tucurui dam, at once the hope of the Amazon and
the doom of the Parakana. The dam, which the government says is
due to start working in December, 1983, was still a massive skeleton
only partially filled with concrete. On top, towering construction
cranes with steel-girdered legs moved back and forth like giant pray-
ing mantises, dangling concrete buckets from their snouts. We could
see where the river had been diverted to the east to allow the making
of the massive spillway, which we passed to our left. To the right was
a 6-mile-long earth dam that will restrain the river during flood season. The two parts of the dam made a deep canyon through which
our boat bobbed as we headed for the main loading dock on the
downriver side.

We were once again to be suckled at the corporate breast—often
the only way to see what is happening in the big projects that lie like
an archipelago across the jungle. We either dealt with the authorities
or we didn't go. Executives of Eletronorte, the government electric
company in the Amazon, had invited us to see the dam and promised
that "all your needs will be taken care of."

The Tucurui dam occupies center stage for a town that spreads
above and around it like an amphitheater. Moving up the hillside in
order of the importance of their occupants are layers of houses,
schools, stores and shopping centers for the 40,000 people and their
families employed building the dam. As we drove up the hill, the
scene grew closer and closer to pure California suburbia: neatly paved
and curbed roads, stop signs, fire hydrants, identical white houses
with clipped front lawns and driveways, healthy dogs, kids kicking
soccer balls that were neither lopsided nor deflated. A shopping plaza
that bent around a blacktopped parking lot contained the Roxy
Cinema showing "Star Wars" and a glass-fronted supermarket with
specials pasted in the window. Only a woman balancing her grocery
bag on her head suggested we were not in the hills of San Diego.

There were practically no trees in the town; only the far-off
jungle scenery and the oppressive heat and humidity suggested that

this was a town in the rain forest. The few remaining trees were coveted by workers on their lunch hour and strollers, all nearly desperate for relief from the glaring sun. The lack of trees seemed odd. Conceicao and Xinguara had grown helter-skelter without a bow to esthetics or any sense of luxury; their treeless state was understandable. Tucurui had developed according to a master plan, and the reasonably affluent citizens easily could have foregone a patch of sidewalk for a shade tree. There seemed to be a meanness in the town plan, a purposeful denial of the sense of place.

Tucurui was the first big-money government project we visited. As with any organization that has a budget for public relations, our initial information about it came from a slide show staged for us at the executive offices. The narrator, speaking in Portuguese but in the soothing resonant tones common to taped slide shows everywhere, told us that Tucurui would soon be the fourth-largest dam in the world. Then he began to brim over with statistics to prove it. Tucurui will produce 8 million kilowatts of electricity—4 million when it starts up and another 4 million by 1990. This will put it behind Itaipu, a joint Brazilian–Argentine–Paraguayan venture in the south, soon to churn out 12.6 million kilowatts; but only slightly behind Grand Coulee in Washington State with 9 million, and Guri in Venezuela, also 9 million. Tucurui, started in 1976, will be 12 kilometers long, including the earth dam, and will create a 2,200-square-kilometer lake. The spillway, where the dammed water will overflow to drive $500 million worth of French-financed turbines, is 570 meters, the longest in existence. By the time the dam is finished 80 million cubic meters of earth will have been moved and 5.2 million cubic meters of concrete poured. The price tag, which started at $1.6 billion, was up to $3 billion when we were there and probably will go higher.

Although the dam is spectacular in its own right, especially to those who appreciate a difficult construction job, it has much greater significance as a Brazilian symbol. If Serra Pelada is the success story to offer the masses, Tucurui is the one for the businessmen and the international bankers. The dam has been planned as the cornerstone of an Amazon industrial state, a $60 billion scheme to exploit the mineral resources of the vast Carajas Mountain region which spreads to the southeast of Tucurui. It will provide the power to run steel mills, copper smelters, aluminum refineries and a host of subsidiary industries that are to be encouraged by the government once the mining operations begin. The whole area is to become the Amazon model, integrating farms, factories, towns, highways and railroads in a pattern that its planners hope will multiply across the jungle. To the grand-design planners in Brasilia, Tucurui is the first step.

There is a good deal of logic to this master plan. As Kerman Jose Machado, a top executive of Eletronorte, explained to us, Brazil has rare opportunities in the Amazon that could make it the nation's industrial heartland. At Carajas and other jungle sites, staggering reserves of minerals, especially iron and bauxite, are being discovered which will require tremendous amounts of energy to refine to a usable state. At the same time, Eletronorte is learning just how much potential for hydroelectric power the dozens of major rivers in the Amazon basin offer.

"We could be the Saudi Arabia of hydropower," Machado said. "We think eventually we could produce 40 percent of Brazil's power from the Amazon—at least 100 million kilowatts. We have already studied 23 dam sites but we think we could find over 50 or 60." Work had already begun on one near Manaus, Machado added, and another near Porto Velho. Plans were being completed for a dam larger than Tucurui on the Xingu River, the next river to the west.

"It is the combination of energy and minerals that will make Brazil so important," Machado continued. "Much of the cost of turning bauxite into aluminum is energy. Nations like Japan cannot afford to keep bringing in raw materials and refining them because the energy cost is so high. But we have the cheapest, cleanest, best form of energy right here, right next to our minerals."

The way Machado explained it, there seemed no doubt of Brazil's eventual success. He had obviously communicated that feeling to the trenches because, if the workmen were to be believed, it was only a matter of months before Brazil became the next world superpower. Our random interviews with what passed for the man on the street revealed a consistently fervent outlook.

Working at the base of the dam, carrying buckets of nails and boards for the carpenters, was Gionato Marchao, a 20-year-old from the state of Maranhao. "This is opportunity," he said. "I came for the money but now I don't know if I will leave. This is the future." As an unskilled worker he was earning $150 a month for working 16-hour shifts—about 40 cents an hour. He also got a bed in a company dormitory, three meals a day and laundry. "In the south you don't get as much. In the Northeast, where I come from, you get nothing."

Antonio Carlos da Silva, 21, another laborer from the Northeast, wore his hard hat on top of a straw fedora which reminded him of home, he said, but he had no desire to go back. "When I came here, I knew nothing. They have taught me to work and they are teaching me to read." He was participating with many others in after-work classes. Besides academic subjects, he could also learn trade skills such as welding and carpentry. The program is part of Eletronorte's particular view of this project: Tucurui is a social experiment as much as a construction site.

Gang foreman Zillo Tucanduva, 36, was amazed at what had been accomplished with what began as a ragtag work force. "What we've done is a marvel. We've taken people who didn't know how to work, who never received a paycheck in their lives, and we built this. And it is all Brazilian, you know. Designed, engineered and built by Brazilians. You may not think that means much, coming from the United States, but this is one of the first all-Brazilian projects."

Behind Zillo, his crew of ironworkers crawled over the skeleton of what would be one of the concrete vaults for the spillway. Other crews of welders, sheet metal workers, carpenters, masons, cement mixers—all with colored plastic hard hats designating their jobs—swarmed the oval mold. Sparks showered down and metal plates clanged into place.

"One day, two months ago, we poured 7,082 cubic meters of concrete," Tucanduva told us with precision. "That is a national record."

For $1,500 a month "and a chance to be part of a great project," he moved his family up from Sao Paulo. We asked if they liked it. "They accept it," he said, sounding like a career military man. "They know what I do is important."

Such optimism was common, but not pervasive. "This place sucks," Ed Albuquerque said. He had once been an English teacher and though his diction had deteriorated, he remembered the right slang. Albuquerque, the public relations director for Eletronorte, was drinking with us at the company lodge—Scotch for him, beer for us—and getting mad.

"Brazil will fail here because it is being crushed. It is a colony of America and Europe and it won't try to escape. We talk of all we have, then we give it away like some African colony."

Albuquerque was perhaps more emotional about it, but he made a point we heard many times: Brazil is mortgaging the Amazon in a rush to develop it. Already much of the early production of the Carajas mines has been sold to West Germany and Japan. A plan is ready—but forestalled by political pressure—to lease giant forest tracts to foreign timber companies. Foreign investment in the Amazon is regularly courted by teams of top ministers. The idea is to use the production of the Amazon—the iron ore, cattle, timber, bauxite—to get cash to eventually build refineries and factories to ship finished goods. The fear of Albuquerque and others we talked to is that international banks and industrial companies will gain a stranglehold over the resources and control the method of development. We remembered the glossy pamphlet we had found on an official's desk in Brasilia, the P.R. piece selling the Amazon to the foreign investors of the world. Apparently, this is a risk the government in Brasilia has decided to take.

Through his Scotch, Albuquerque could see only disaster in this approach. "We talk big but we're nothing without foreign money," he said bitterly. "We build this dam like good boys so we can show the foreigners that it is all right to give us a little more money."

As the Chivas, worth about $8 a glass but free to him, began to disappear, the complaints became more personal. "Who would live in this goddamn place? It is a failure. Right here—a wasteland. There is no culture, no intelligence. This is no life here. Who would come to the Amazon?"

The public relations director of Eletronorte need have looked only about two miles downriver for an answer to his question. There on the banks of the Tocantins is another town called Tucurui, a boomtown populated by anyone who ever had an idea on how to sell things to 40,000 dam workers and their families. This Tucurui is the antithesis of the engineer's master-planned creation. Pandering among chaos and filth is the industry here; the town is a smaller Maraba and a textbook case of growth gone wild. It had 800 people five years before and by the time of our visit almost matched the new town with 35,000 residents. This Tucurui is where the dam workers come to buy things and feel the life that has been disinfected away by the technocrats' practical plans.

We walked down the main street that dropped sharply to the river. A film of red dust clung to our sweat, and we quickly became gritty and grimy. Noise was everywhere, a cacophony of American discos and Latin rhythms blaring from record shops and speakers strung on poles that seemed to form the municipal sound system. We passed dozens of tiny hotels, bars and stores with their wares piled in front: mounds of gaudy shirts, ranks of plastic shoes, leatherette handbags, straw hats, comic books.

Behind the main street we came upon a jumbled mass of bamboo houses built on stilts and linked with a flimsy boardwalk. Beneath them ran streams that receive the waste of each house through its floor in one of the oldest sewage systems known to man. But as bad as those traditional river dweller houses looked to us, they were at least protected from the fate of the more substantial mud brick structures built by newcomers. All the walls of these newer, more modern houses had that bathtub ring we had seen elsewhere, a brown stain that went as high as six feet. The flooding here, far down the Araguaia and Tocantins rivers, had been catastrophic in recent years, washing away whole sections of the town and claiming many lives. No one seemed too concerned with the problem; when the dam is finished in a few years, they reasoned correctly, there will be no more floods in Tucurui.

Six miles out of Tucurui on what may be the worst single stretch of road in the Amazon, closer, really, to an amusement park ride than a highway, is still another section of the boomtown called, simply, The Quarter. According to our guide, 2,000 prostitutes live and work there—The Quarter is not so much a red-light district as a red-light city. Once the harlots mingled in the mainstream of the town, but they inspired too many fights and too much diversion for the Eletronorte workers. By some arrangement, which our guide wasn't able to specify, the dam-building company paid for a mass exodus of the women to their own little suburb. The move happened overnight, and the prostitutes reportedly were reimbursed for the work they missed.

We pulled up opposite a pink building. The women in front of it flirted with us and giggled. One was fat, her belly protruding from her shirt where the buttons had popped off, and she picked her nose intensively as we talked. Another had oriental features, very long black hair, and she wore a faded, stained basketball shirt of a Sao Paulo high school, perhaps a souvenir from one of her customers. The third woman wore a pink leotard and white slacks. She would have been pretty anywhere.

We talked with the three prostitutes about what it was like to have sex with 22 men in a night, about the diseases they constantly feared (they showed us wrappers of pills which they took with every meal) and about their cleanliness. They showed us six women—big, flabby and many years past the proper definition of girls—who were bathing in a scummy stream that ran beside the shack.

"This is a man's world," Robert Milne, the rancher, had said and we were seeing a cruel result of that fact. If one day the company decides that these women are to be rounded up like a cattle herd and moved, then so be it. This is what the men want. Initially we misjudged the role of women in the Amazon. Silvana, the beautiful cosmopolitan farmer we met in Sao Paulo, was among the first people we met, and we assumed that women played a public role as they do in our own country. But as we traveled along BR-364, through Sinop, into the area of the land wars and even in Tucurui we saw only men at the forefront, and there didn't seem much reason why. Cleuza, the tiny posseiro woman, was as tough as Hamilton Perreira; she didn't wield a gun, but she traveled three days to see the President of Brazil. Alfonso Andrade's wife bore eight children and ran a general store, while he dreamed of cattle ranches.

That there would be no development of the Amazon without women is contrary to the myth of machismo. So women are degraded or ignored, but still these women are as courageous and resilient as the men who boasted about themselves.

We asked the woman in pink if we could take her picture, and she was flattered. Her poses were professional, as if she were a *Vogue* model on location. We asked if we could see where she lived and she agreed.

Walking back in the whorehouse on the damp, creaking boards down a narrow dark corridor where the walls didn't meet the ceiling, we felt none of the excitement that an illicit rendezvous is reputed to bring. That a score of men had had sex with her 12 hours before had something to do with it, but more noticeable was our guilt over the slavishness of these conditions. The Quarter is no more than a zoo for sex, and women are condemned to it. There is no challenge, no romance, and no escape.

Well, no physical escape. Inside the woman's pink room were piles of soap opera magazines, black-and-white photos, the dialogue in bubbles. There was a picture of a baby boy ("My son," she said, but she didn't say where), and a collection of snapshots of herself. There was a make-up table, a bed, and nothing more.

She jumped on the bed and began posing in positions from early *Playboy*, contortions that accentuated her figure, and facial expressions evincing a willing participant. Assuming we were interested in more pictures, and more sexual ones, she removed her white slacks and began another series of poses. Once she stumbled as she tried to stand still on the soft mattress, her hands on her hips and her breasts proudly thrust forward.

We thought she intended to pose topless. She shook her head "No" and struck another series of poses, cross-legged, her elbow on her knee, her chin in the palm of her hand.

Embarrassed, we thought she was annoyed because we were not paying customers, and offered her money. "No." Now she was adamant, like a teenage girl following her mother's instructions to save herself for marriage at all costs. No customer paid her a fourth of the $20 we held out, yet "No" she repeated.

"You make me famous," she ordered. She picked up a soap opera magazine and showed us advertisements featuring women in poses like we had just seen. "Famous. You make me famous. Like them." Her body perhaps was for sale, but not her self-respect.

Pigs rooted around the scattered houses. There were many dogs, ill or limping on three legs. The houses stank from excrement. A huckster in sunglasses roamed the dusty streets selling pictures from his Polaroid camera ("Better than a mirror," he bragged). Some groaning came out to the street, but mostly we heard giggling and tinny Roberto Carlos songs wafting out from Victrolas which had once been used to pay for sex. Yet we had found a touch of dignity.

At every level, Tucurui displayed to us a pride that can overtake reality. Nilo Miranda, head of the project to clear the forest to be flooded by the dam, was an extreme example, but nonetheless a telling one. We met him in his office at CAPEMI, the acronym for a military pension fund that is one of the most cash-rich enterprises in the country. Miranda had been assigned to oversee the immediate logging of 2,200 square kilometers of trees, a task similar to clearing the state of Rhode Island in three years. Miranda greeted us from behind his desk in his cramped and dirty office. He had been reading a book. There was one other man in the room and five empty desks.

"The clearing is a job that must be done quickly," he said. "If the trees are not taken out they will eventually rot and clog the dam mechanism."

The pension fund and the Paris office of Lazard Freres, the prestigious international investment banking house, expected to put up about $500 million to finance the clearing project, which was to include 200 sawmills and 10,000 loggers. "We think the timber is worth $2.5 billion. Not a bad profit, eh?" Miranda said with a wink.

"No one has ever stripped land like this. A Canadian company said it would take 10 to 15 years. So we got the job. We'll do it in three years."

We asked if CAPEMI normally did this sort of thing.

"No," he said. "But it is good for us to get a start in the Amazon." At the Tucurui guesthouse we had met a Frenchman calling himself a "deforester" who had told us, "Getting wood out of the Amazon is going to be one of the best businesses of the future."

"And how much has been cleared so far?" we asked Miranda.

Nothing had.

CAPEMI was just getting organized. They had some troubles. They could cut the trees, but they hadn't figured out how to get them out of the forest. The last we heard CAPEMI was contemplating using Agent Orange to defoliate the area, but the government vetoed the idea.

We might have been stunned by the discrepancy between Miranda's plans and his accomplishments if we had not already begun to notice a certain disjointed quality in even trivial events here. The guesthouse where we stayed had two beautiful tennis courts. When he saw our interest, our guide scurried off and soon returned with two tennis rackets—and one old ball. He seemed surprised at our surprise.

"Tennis balls are very hard to get around here," he apologized.

"I don't know why that is, but we never have any. It is important that we have the courts. It is not important that people play tennis." The courts stood like monuments to a conquest. Unused, they still served their purpose.

The tennis-ball problem got us thinking about another odd thing we had noticed—the maps. Every Brazilian map printed since 1978 showed a vast blue lake immediately behind what was labeled as Tucurui Dam. We knew for a fact the lake wasn't there and wouldn't be for some years to come. Asking about it got mostly puzzled looks for answers.

"I know what you mean," one of the Eletronorte engineers said finally. "It bothers me too. Sometimes I think we get a little ahead of ourselves in Brazil. We dream things up and consider them done. We forget about the doing."

On our way from Tucurui to the surrounding mining areas the dam is to support one day, we turned off at a side road, marked only by the tracks of heavy trucks that emerged from the forest wall. We went for five miles on a narrow path that was like riding in a green tunnel with a mud floor. At its end, we emerged into a perfect square clearing that seemed seared into the forest by a surgical laser. On all four sides, walls were formed by smooth white tree trunks.

The inside of the square resembled one of those black-and-white World War I photos taken the day after the battle of Verdun. Broken trees were everywhere, some smoldering, some still flaming. Off to the left was a lone black stalk, a hundred feet tall and looking like a twisted licorice stick in the heat-distorted air. The field was covered with a thick deposit of snowy ash that clung to our boots when we walked. The only things that survived were the bugs, small clouds of which had returned after the holocaust to swarm anything standing still.

On the far side of the field we could see a man. Atop a raft of 6-foot-diameter logs, hands on hips, he shouted commands to a dozen sweating men loading sawn boards onto the bed of a red Mercedes truck. Things weren't moving fast enough for him. His voice competed with the high-pitched whine of a bandsaw. He wore only a pair of dusty leather cowboy boots and green shorts, sagging under the push of a comfortable middle-aged belly. His chest was spotted with insect bites and smudged with mud; his sunburned face shadowed with a three-day's beard. Only the razor-cut hair, designer eyeglasses and Rolex watch gave away his pedigree.

Alceu Abreu didn't come to the jungle because he was hungry. A pioneer of another sort, a man who had followed Brazil's earlier frontier booms like a bookmaker follows the thoroughbreds, he was betting that the Amazon would be the next winner and he planned to make his latest fortune cutting it down.

We had met Abreu at Tucurui where he sometimes went for supplies. He readily invited us to come see what he had made. "Come and I'll show you what the Amazon is all about," he said with a high, nasal laugh.

Now we shuffled and swatted our way across the clearing that was the center of Abreu's domain. Trees were strewn over the 100-acre field: to the left were the worthless ones, charred and still burning; to the right the valuable hardwoods were trimmed, stacked and ready to be pushed into the glistening saw blade. The long, smooth boards of multicolored tropical wood that emerged from the saw were the object of Alceu Abreu's attention.

He jumped down from the logs when he saw us approaching. "Ah, my friends, welcome to my estate," he said with mock seriousness.

It looked more like a smoldering parking lot. Besides the sawmill, there were two rough wooden barracks. No stately manor house with white-coated butlers. No neat split-rail corral. No barn. No guesthouse.

"As you can see, we have much to do. Now we are selling the trees. Soon the cattle will come."

Abreu, who wanted us to call him Al, was a hyperactive man of a thousand gestures. No phrase went unpunctuated. He was constantly lifting his eyebrows, slapping his chest or head, exploding in laughter. "The work here is very hard. A struggle." He grabbed the sides of his throat with both hands and tugged the flesh in opposite directions.

As Al supervised the loading of boards onto the truck, he explained that he had come upon a businessman's dream: an investment that pays for itself. To cut, saw and ship one of the logs—about

6 feet in diameter and 10 feet long—costs about $60. He was selling the resulting boards to a lumber company for about $200. The beautifully grained and hued wood—mahogany, cedar, jacaranda—eventually will find its way into someone's dining room table, while Al takes the proceeds and uses them to clear more forest.

"My investment in the sawmill was $30,000. I got that back in two months." Now, he said, the logging operation was taking in $50,000 a month.

But that won't last forever, because the trees on his 7,500-acre property won't. "When we have a big enough pasture, we'll bring in those big ugly white cattle and set them loose. I'll sit back and watch for a while, then move on to the next site."

The scheme seemed foolproof to us. Al agreed. "I said I would show you what the Amazon was about," he began in Portuguese. He switched to the few English words he knew. "Amazon is money."

Al giggled when he said this and performed a peculiarly Brazilian gesture. Holding his thumb and middle finger tight, he shook his wrist violently, causing the index finger to flap against the other two. *Slap, slap, slap.* It was his all-purpose gesture, but it usually meant, "Let's get moving. Time's wasting"—which was what Al was all about. We started calling him Big Al, more in tribute to his overwhelming drive than to his average stature.

"Rio is for comfort." He laughed, enjoying his new command of the English language. "Amazon [*slap, slap, slap*] is for work. Amazon is for money."

If there is a war to conquer the Amazon, then Big Al ranks as one of the front-line generals. While the government and the naturalists bicker about a policy to save the forest, Al—and hundreds of entrepreneurs like him—are methodically chopping it away. Snapping his fingers, pounding his chest and shouting orders to his workmen, Al showed us he was wasting no time. He displayed to us what was good and bad about these go-getters, about the enterprising spirit on the frontier. This man showed energy, ambition and cleverness as well as a lack of concern for the effects of his actions.

From Big Al's perspective, he was just doing what an entrepreneur is supposed to do: find the most profitable business. The government wants to make the Amazon a very profitable place and here Al was doing it.

With the truck loaded, he asked us to come in and have coffee. His office–bedroom, which he was sharing with his son-in-law, had two beds, a clothes cabinet and a shower, cold water only. A short-wave radio was his contact with the world—in this case, his office in Belem.

Big Al called himself an "adventurer–entrepreneur." In 1959, he headed to the frontier town of Brasilia at a time when the govern-ment was desperate to attract businessmen, and no one wanted to go. He invested in real estate and a car dealership and, when Brasilia was force-fed its population of bureaucrats, Big Al made a fortune.

He puffed rapidly on his cafezinho, then downed it in a shot. "If you were willing to take a chance on Brasilia—on Brazil—you made money," he said. "I made money."

By the early 1970s, the new frontier was the Amazon. The TransAmazon Highway had been inaugurated and the prospects were for a dozen Brasilias. Al could have spent his time in a plush Rio condominium, gaping at string bikinis, but he chose instead to risk his cash, his comfort and possibly his life on a remote patch of steaming jungle.

First he went to Altamira, a major stop on the TransAmazon Highway. He bought a sawmill and learned the lumber business, but wasn't satisfied with the area—too many struggling, small-time farmers and not enough money. He wrinkled his face in an expression of agony as he explained that he lost money on the Altamira venture. The grimace conveyed dishonor and shame. He determined to recoup his pride and money.

In 1972 Abreu had bought almost 35,000 acres near Tucurui from the government at a cost of $2 an acre. When he decided six years later to move his operation there, he sold 25,000 acres to a Japanese company for $30 each.

The new site was slow getting started, but now looked to be a gold mine of another sort. Al paced the room steadily. His success, he felt, was inevitable.

"God has given us this forest for us to take advantage of," he said. "We are to use it as we need it." Big Al didn't trample on the pleas of the environmentalists, he didn't even care they existed; he was simply taking what had been put out there for him, and there was nothing to be embarrassed about. Sure he knew that if you didn't plant the fields at the right time they would erode to desert clay, but only someone stupid would do that with perfectly good land. There were no apologies to be made.

Big Al prided himself on not taking any of the loans or incentive payments available to Amazon businessmen, the incentives that are the only reason for the existence of the giant ranches in the southern Amazon. Not wanting to deal with "the corrupt bureaucracy," he was using his own money.

While Abreu felt his enterprise to be between him and the God who gave him the forest, it is the Brazilian government that has made that forest accessible. He wouldn't have been there if it hadn't been for the government-built roads. And his land might have been worth nothing if it wasn't for the government-planned Tucurui dam project. The giant enterprise, 30 miles northwest of the clearing where we stood, had, by putting in such an enormous infrastructure, spawned hundreds of smaller projects and inflated land values.

Tucurui gave Al another benefit. In a coals-to-Newcastle scenario, Al was selling wood to the contractor who was building the dam. Vast quantities were needed and, he told us, CAPEMI was having more than just "a little trouble" getting started clearing the forest.

"They trip over each other." Al smirked. "It is a government pension fund, what do you expect? They have all the wood in the world and they don't know how to get it out. So they buy my wood [*slap, slap, slap*] at a very high price." And, he admitted, he even knows of people who cut the government's own wood and sell it back to them without their knowledge.

And there it was. The whole point of Big Al—the positive and the negative. Such men are skilled, motivated businessmen who get things done—like taking down a forest. The giant corporations are nothing next to a thousand men like Al figuring the cheapest, fastest way to get the job done because that is the most profitable. For an environmentalist, Big Al is the true enemy. As long as there are no rules governing his conduct or no ways to enforce them, he will do what is best for him regardless of the consequences for anything else.

At the same time, his efficiency is what makes Big All so important to Brazil. He is the man between the corporation and the squatter families, a man who can be greedy and useful. He brings his own wits and his own money; the government can't, the poor farmer can't and the atrophied corporation can't. He is willing to take risks and his success induces others to try the same.

The only question we weren't able to answer was how many Big Als there are in Brazil—and how many will it take. Without this entrepreneurial class—their spirit and efficiency—the development of the Amazon will probably go nowhere. Yet if there are enough of them and they are allowed to run free, the destruction they can bring about will be astonishing.

"Come look at this," Al said with a *slap, slap, slap* as he took us on a tour of his lumberyard. The logs all looked the same from the outside, but their round hearts were a spectrum of brown and with intricate grains in hundreds of concentric rings. One was a Spanish cedar and its scent permeated the pile, pungent even amid the smell of charcoal.

Al bounced up on one of the logs and threw his arms out. "Look what God has given us," he said, sweeping his hands even farther apart. We couldn't tell if he meant the green forest in the distance or the smoking rubble around us.

The Serra dos Carajas is a group of ridges and plateaus about 100 miles southwest of Tucurui. Averaging only about 1,000 feet above sea level with the tallest rising to 2,500 feet, they are among the least imposing mountains in the world; but if they are judged by the mineral wealth they contain, they may prove the most impressive. These ridges are probably the single most important asset in Brazil today and the nation has committed itself to an ambitious project to scoop them out.

We had had our fill of slide shows and chamber-of-commerce tours at Tucurui. But the cry we had heard in Sao Paulo and Brasilia was "Carajas, Carajas." It had to be some project if they were spending $3 billion on a dam just to service the mining and refining operations. Without much enthusiasm but with a curiosity to see what the fuss was all about, we joined some government engineers on a twin-engine Fairchild and flew to Carajas.

As we approached, the trees began to drop away as a mountain with a sheared-off top rose in front of us like an eruption on the jungle skin. Barely dipping the plane's nose, the pilot slid in for a soft landing on the airstrip. Only it wasn't your usual airstrip; it was closer to a rusted waffle griddle. The top of the mountain is made of hard, red iron ore. In fact, the whole mountain is made of it, as are a few of the adjacent mountains, all with sheared-off peaks and sparse vegetation where the iron pokes to the surface, like a scar on an animal's hide. Eighteen billion tons of iron ore, Brazilian geologists told us, one of the two or three largest deposits in the world and, with 66 percent iron content, the purest.

This same sight had confronted a young geologist for U.S. Steel in 1967 when his helicopter was forced down for lack of fuel. There had been talk about the strange mountains that distorted compass readings, and the treeless patches that showed up on aerial photographs. When the geologist, Breno dos Santos, jumped from the copter onto one of those patches, he knew immediately that it was iron. The ore had been there for a billion years and it took Western man more than 400 to find it, but the Brazilians began to say that this, at last, was the real El Dorado the Amazon had been holding from them.

It has taken more than a decade to figure out what to do with Carajas. U.S. Steel held a half-interest in the mineral rights and started development plans, but ran into an uncertain Brazilian government that wasn't sure what to do about the industrial giant's participation. Beset with economic problems of its own and not desperate for iron ore, U.S. Steel backed out and left the Brazilians to stew, assuming the project would never happen. Not until 1980 was a commitment finally made to launch an all-out effort to develop Carajas.

As geologists roamed the treacherous mountains, the mineral inventory continued to grow. According to estimates from Companhia Vale do Rio Doce, the Brazilian national mining firm, a dozen other valuable minerals have been found, including manganese deposits estimated at 60 million tons; copper, a billion tons; bauxite, 40 million tons; nickel, 47 million tons; tin, 100,000 tons; gold, 100 tons, and smaller amounts of zinc, lead, cobalt, molybdenum, tungsten and tantalum. Uranium and chromium have been hinted at but not confirmed. The deposits, which occur on the northern edge of the ancient rock that forms the Brazilian Shield, are a colossal array of minerals, the likes of which exist only in southern Africa and in Australia. More than 100 million years ago, those two areas were connected to the Brazilian Shield, before the supercontinent of Gondwanaland broke up.

This is the treasure chest that is going to pay for putting Brazil into the 21st century, or so the Brazilians are betting. Once again we had a slide show—this time in a flimsy wooden barracks—to tell us how it is going to be done. The magic date is 1985, when the first commercial loads of ore are due to move. It will cost $5 billion to ship that initial carload, and the screen flashed with pictures of what the money is to buy: giant shovels; 150-ton dump trucks; crushers; screeners; washers; a 550-mile railroad through the jungle; a new deep-water port at Sao Luis on the Atlantic Ocean and finally conveyors to dump the ore into the 280,000-ton VLOCs (Very Large Ore Carriers) of as many foreign countries as can be signed up. Thirty-five million tons a year are supposed to drop into those holds, making Brazil the world's leading exporter of iron ore and returning it badly needed foreign exchange. And it should all happen at just the right time, the Brazilians are predicting, just when the world is beginning to have a substantial shortfall of iron ore. In fact, the Brazilians figure that most of what they have the world will want very much by 1990. By then the iron treasure of the Serra dos Carajas will be worth $10 billion a year, according to government projections.

The other minerals, except gold and bauxite, will be mined later, as foreign capital is attracted. Gold already attracts all the human capital the region can stand. Bauxite is finding a life of its own. Even before Carajas, gigantic deposits of the red dirt from which aluminum is extracted had been found in the north central Amazon at Trombetas. Those ores are already being exported and several companies are now taking advantage of the soon to be completed Tucurui power plant to build aluminum smelters in the region. Alumina, a white powder that comes from the intermediate refining stage, has a market of its own as an additive to such products as paint and explosives. Alcoa's Brazilian subsidiary, partly owned by Hanna Mining Co. of Cleveland, is investing more than $1 billion in a 500,000-ton-a-year alumina plant as well as a 100,000-ton-a-year smelter in Sao Luis. Nippon Aluminum Co. and the Brazilian government have formed Albras and plan a 900,000-ton-a-year alumina plant and smelter just north of Carajas.

Alongside these projects the social conquest of the region is supposed to take place. The iron project alone is building six towns along the railroad route. Other cities are expected to spring up as civilization and dollars flood into the area. Maraba, that hell hole, is destined by planners to become another Pittsburgh. Farms to feed the masses are considered a necessity, and prosperity, it is hoped, will extend as far away as Campo Alegre's slaughterhouse. At least that is the way it is supposed to work.

The vision of what Carajas is to become takes imagination. Helio Siqueira stood amid the guts of the unbuilt city. Toilet bowls, sinks, windowsills, pipes and beams were piled about; stakes with white flags marked where the roads were to go. "There is not much to see yet, but this will be the main city. Eleven thousand people will live here. My wife and I will live over here," he said as he walked to the concrete base of what would be a four-room house, picking up and tossing a stray bent nail from his living room. "In a few months all these houses for the technical people will be up and then this place will be alive."

Eventually Carajas will be much like Tucurui. Now, though, Siqueira was right; there wasn't much to see. The whole project seemed tentative to us, and we were incapable of the large leap of faith between the unfinished shell of a four-room house and a $60 billion project that was so automatic to Siqueira.

Siqueira, a 28-year-old construction engineer, seemed to believe everything that is said about Carajas because he was helping to build it. Wearing a baseball cap that said U.S.A., he took us on a tour of the mountaintop. He proudly pointed to the pilot crusher plant, a collection of gleaming yellow steel towers, bins and conveyor belts that is a miniature version of the eventual processing plant.

"We built this thing in 18 days last month. It was like a war with planes flying in all day and trucks shuttling back and forth. We worked day and night. This is where we will process the sample ore so we can show the world what we have."

Siqueira said the whole project had a wartime intensity with everyone working long hours building roads, preparing the mine sites and searching for new minerals. "We get the best equipment and the best people in Brazil—whatever we ask for."

For now, everyone lives in a row of wood barracks clustered along the airstrip. The same rules as Serra Pelada—no alcohol, no women—apply. Every night a different movie is shown and the sight of a celluloid female—any female—causes excited howls.

"If you're looking for fun, it's not an easy way to live," said Siqueira as he invited us to his room, shared with another engineer. Both slept in hammocks. There was an elaborate stereo system and the walls were pasted with nude pinups clipped from magazines, giving the room the appearance of a male dormitory. We listened to some Beatles records.

"I can put up with this because I get to do things here that I'd wait years for in the south," he said. "I built all the electrical systems in that plant you saw today and I'm in charge of running it. The supervisor of the whole mountaintop is only 40."

The mining company put us up in the guest bunkhouse— "Where Robert McNamara stayed when he came to lend us the World Bank's money," Siqueira informed us. In the morning we stood on the porch and saw that the house perched on the edge of the mountain which dropped in a steep, wooded slope of more than 1,000 feet. Across the way two other peaks formed the sides of a valley, a deep, mysterious cauldron, steaming with morning mists. Cries of birds echoed from the abyss. The roar of howler monkeys, like a cheering football crowd, erupted far below. An iguanalike lizard sunned itself on a rock a few feet down the slope. Two long-tailed birds, bright blue and bright red, flew just above the mists. It would not have seemed at all out of place for a pterodactyl or some other prehistoric beast to emerge from there.

Siqueira said the geologists hadn't yet searched that misty valley. "Eventually they will and I'm sure they will find something. But we have so much already."

At lunch in the mess hall with Stefenson Pena, another 28-year-old engineer, we ate beans, rice, noodles, potatoes and grilled meat. "You need some carbohydrates when you're doing physical work all day," Pena explained as he heaped his plate. What Siqueira saw as an opportunity, Pena saw as a challenge. "It's close but not the same thing. I'm not so much concerned with getting ahead as with finding new things. We know maybe five to eight percent of the minerals in the Amazon. Who knows what else could be out there? We didn't know there was bauxite until we started to build the city and someone said, 'Hey, this red dirt isn't like the other red dirt.' "

Pena particularly would like to find oil and coal, the two great treasures the Amazon has thus far withheld. Brazil needs both desperately, and in his desire to look for them Pena is like many Brazilians we met who have tied their own destiny to that of the country. They consider their own success to be Brazil's, confirming that the dream of Grand Brazil that the government has been trying to sell for years is finding buyers. In a nation where celebrity means about as much as in the United States, Pena, Siqueira and others like them see themselves as minor national heroes—not exactly soccer stars, but people the whole nation is watching. The glossy magazines from the south frequently run long picture stories about the exploits of the brave men conquering the Amazon. We learned more about building an ore crusher than anyone short of an engineering student would want to know just by reading *Manchete*, the Brazilian equivalent of *Life*.

After a while, it was hard for us not to get caught up in the enthusiasm. Listening to intense, adventurous men like Pena and Siqueira—both about our age, motivated by some of the same ideas that moved us—it was easy to identify with them and imagine, 10 years down the road, a Grand Brazil. They have the intelligence, energy and sense of purpose that could make it happen.

True, Carajas is a gamble that hinges on some great intangibles, like world commodity prices and the ability to raise foreign cash—and the political consequences of doing so. For Brazil, an enormous amount of resources are behind that bet—more than 10 percent of the country's gross national product over the next two decades, according to an estimate by the *Wall Street Journal*. And the greatest intangible of all is the Amazon jungle, which has provided confident exploiters with unexpected and unpleasant surprises for centuries.

But the spirit of this enterprise was so infectious while we were at Tucurui and Carajas that the dream at times seemed not only logical, but infallible.

BELEM

We needed to rest. The Amazon so far had been like a jigsaw puzzle of which we had many pieces but were missing the picture on the box lid that would show us how to put them together. We were exhausted from gathering the pieces, and both of us were sick. London had lost considerable weight and was wracked by an angry rash that did not respond to the ointments and powders we bought willy-nilly in pharmacies. Kelly had some type of virus that left him hoarse, weak and in constant need of a bathroom.

In Belem, where the Amazon meets the Atlantic, we looked forward to hot showers, clean linens and medical attention as well as sober interviews with professionals who might give us needed perspective.

We decided to travel by bus, to see the countryside and to unwind from our hectic pace.

"The bus comes at 6 o'clock," the kid behind the counter said, sizing us up, "the bus that you want to take. The other bus comes an hour later."

We asked what the difference was.

"Well, senhores, the first bus is the sleeper. It makes four stops and takes 12 hours. And what is best is that no one stands in the aisles. The people are all clean."

And how many stops did the other bus make?

The kid laughed and said, "As many as the driver wants. The passengers will bet on what time it reaches Belem. You do not want to take that bus."

He couldn't sell us a ticket; we had to buy it on the bus. We waited at the side of the road where it meets the Tocantins. The bus, and a steady stream of truck traffic, had to be ferried across the wide brown river.

A makeshift village of bamboo stores and restaurants had sprung up along the riverbank to cater to ferry passengers. When there was a lot of traffic, people sometimes waited hours to get on the ferry. They whiled away the time eating skewers of barbecued meat cooked by women squatting at tiny charcoal grills and reading photo novellas.

We read photo novellas, too, and teased the small pigs that romped in garbage piles. Bored with waiting, we thought we might hitch a ride with one of the truckers, but every one we asked turned us down. They either had no room or, unbelievable as it seemed, were concerned about their insurance liability. The sun was just start-ing its rapid descent when a distinctive honk down at the dock started travelers around us scrambling. Some who already had tickets lined up alongside the road.

In a few moments a modern white bus groaned its way up the hill. "Belem" it said over the windshield in neat block letters. It looked comfortable, with curtains on the smoked-glass windows and an air conditioner in back. There were empty seats. But when we stepped into the bus, the driver shook his head.

"No room. We have reservations for all seats." He was as adamant as anyone we'd seen in Brazil. No room for compromise, no bending the rules or any hint that bribery was called for. Just, "Get off because I'm losing time."

So we stood and watched the red dust of the departing 6 P.M. sleeper to Belem, perversely admiring the principled driver.

The bus we didn't want to take was an hour late. When it arrived we didn't realize immediately why we didn't want to take it. It looked the same as the first bus, though somewhat battered and dirty. But there was no air conditioning, and the bus was more crowded. We bought tickets and found two seats.

Before starting off, one of the two drivers who would spell each other during the long drive went to relieve himself. He left the over-head lights on and they attracted a swarm of black flies that filled the bus and covered the lights so they glowed only faintly. The flies covered the faces of the passengers and settled thickly on babies slumped in their mothers' arms. No one moved. These people were oblivious. While we rummaged frantically through our bags for Vietnam-issue bug repellent, everyone else sat glassy-eyed.

The bus started, the lights went off and the flies disappeared. A cool breeze came through the window; the road was smooth, the aisles empty. But at the next two stops, entire villages seemed to get on. The aisles became packed with sweating, lurching bodies. People carried suitcases, baskets and cloth-wrapped bundles. To add to the confusion, someone in the back of the bus invariably had to get off at every stop. The bus became a living organism, constantly consuming and disgorging people while its innards reeked of humanity.

In the back, a group of four very drunk Brazilian college students sang college songs. They had come for an adventure in the Wild West: the bus from Belem to Maraba and back. In front, stop by stop, a fraternity of workmen was organizing. Laborers on big construction projects and ranches who were heading to Belem for a holiday, they all knew each other, or knew someone who knew someone. They, too, got progressively drunker and louder.

At each stop—and there were many—the laborers left the bus for a shot of cachaca, followed by a bottle of beer. The college boys tried to keep up and came to a bad end, vomiting in the road then, mercifully, passing out sometime around midnight.

About then a preacher started up. But for the fact that he spoke Portuguese, he could have been selling his wares on any Greyhound

in the southern United States. The preacher worked on two young
women, telling them that they had to accept God, let him in all the
way, if they ever hoped to be saved.

While this was going on, the co-drivers made their first shift on
the fly. Doing about 50 miles an hour on a straight stretch of road,
the driver with the Frankie Avalon-style, slicked-back, duck's-ass
hairdo stepped behind the driver with the Ramon Navarro, pasted-to-
the-skull hair and took the wheel. Then Frankie maneuvered himself
into the seat as Ramon slid out, exchanging feet on the gas pedal at
the last instant. The boys in front cheered and Frankie took a bow.

The drivers carried themselves like 747 pilots, as if to advertise
that it is no mean thing to be a bus driver in the Amazon. They wore
brown uniforms with light brown shirts and ties they kept knotted.
Hair seemed an important asset; they coiffed it frequently. Under-
standably, both Frankie and Ramon flirted with female passengers
and women waiting at the bus stops.

At one point, faster than the eye could follow, Frankie Avalon,
who even had the lean chin and dark eyes of the 1950s pop star,
made a score. The next thing we knew he was cuddled in the first row
with a brown-haired girl in a loose cotton dress. She rode for a few
stops, then, at some point during the night, disappeared.

The night ground on like the bus's gears, slowly and painfully.
The bus jolted over bumps in the road, slamming passengers against
the plastic seats. Even when the bus was moving at 50 miles an
hour, the breeze from the window stopped before it got past the window seats. Whoever sat on the aisle or in the aisle roasted. The towns
along the road took on a surreal sameness—a row of store fronts, a
big, garishly lit bar and a few small restaurants. Two or three buses
were pulled up at every stop. Crowds milled around, twisting necks
and arms, stamping circulation back into their feet.

We ate bananas and packaged cookies and drank Cokes until
our tongues felt furry. After midnight, we made these stops once an
hour.

At about 2 A.M., the bus came to a sudden stop in the middle of
the road. A pickup truck loaded with some kind of merchandise had
broken down. The bus drivers and some of their friends up front
started to load the cargo into the storage bay. When that was full,
they brought what remained to the front of the bus and stacked it on

the floor. It was big white slabs of cheese. The driver of the pickup paid his fare and sat on top of them. The cheese smelled bad.

At 4 A.M. we arrived on the Belem–Brasilia Highway, the magnet for more than a million settlers along its 1,500-mile length, the first road to have linked the Amazon and the south. The sky began to lighten to a steel gray and the countryside slowly emerged from the night gloom. The land was desert on both sides, as far back from the road as we could see. Hard, cracked dirt was broken only by sparse patches of grass and small trees. Most of the land was fenced with barbed wire. Occasional groups of cattle clustered around the larger trees. Paragominas, the center of the first Amazon cattle boom along the Amazon's first highway.

We gazed out the window at evidence for dire predictions of what would happen to the entire Amazon if it were cleared. The stampede into the jungle here had begun only two decades before with the completion of the Belem–Brasilia Highway. Rapidly, trees had been cut and burned to make way for pasture. Crops of grass sown in its place had grown sparser each year until it quit growing altogether. Thin cows wandered miles between meals. The desert of failed ranches went on for an hour—gray sky, gray dirt. It was 50 miles of moonscape.

In Santa Maria, a village where we stopped at about midmorning, one of the passengers went berserk. The sun was heating the bus, cooking the cheese to stinking ripeness when we rolled to a halt. A man, only about 20, stepped off the bus, turned and, with a roundhouse swing, socked the middle-aged woman he was traveling with. The blow was badly aimed and caught her on the shoulder. The man had reared back again when another passenger popped him in the jaw with a right cross and sent him sprawling. An instant crowd gathered and the mad fellow responded with a tantrum, removing his trousers and ripping them to bits.

A passenger and the Frankie Avalon look-alike coaxed him back onto the bus and we continued on. But after fifteen minutes he blew up again and tore off all his remaining clothes and threw them out the window. Stark naked, he paced the aisle while female passengers looked away and Frankie Avalon looked in the rear-view mirror dumbfounded.

The men up front who had drunk beer and cachaca the night

long wouldn't allow the driver to throw him off the bus. "He is a man, not an animal," one of them said. The passenger who had slugged him earlier got him into his seat and sat next to him to keep him quiet. The driver pulled his whole busload into the Castanhal police station.

The sergeant on duty scratched his head at the problem and said that he would arrest the naked man. The crowd, and even his female traveling companion, pleaded for mercy in a display of community compassion we found puzzling but heartening. The sergeant told everyone to stay put; he was going to call in the chief of police. Casually dressed, as if he had been attending a neighbor's barbecue, the chief listened to everyone's story and then came up with a solution. He tied the madman, buck naked, to his seat in the bus.

"Deal with this when you get to Belem," said the Solomon-like chief. The passengers were satisfied and off we went, yet another hour late to Belem. We arrived in Belem at 2 that afternoon, making the total trip 18 hours to cover 250 miles.

We awoke early the next morning, still tired yet like schoolchildren on their first day back. We had an appointment that we had been looking forward to for a long time. It was with the Amazon River. That we had spent so long in the Amazon jungle without seeing the lifeline itself was testimony to the river system's breadth and influence.

Walking through the quiet, littered streets of Belem we felt the heat begin to rise, and absorbed the peculiar lethargy that even rush hours have here. There was a biological reason for not rushing: it was too hot.

The main avenue of the town spills out into a dock area, and it was there that we first saw the river, brown and wide. "River Sea" is its common nickname and it is deserved. The water is colored with silt it has carried nearly 4,000 miles in its journey from the Andes. Its brownness is not a sign of pollution, but strength, proof that the river can still alter the topography of the continent. For the next 150 miles, far out into the Atlantic, the ocean itself is stained brown because of the power of this river.

At Belem the Amazon looks like an ocean. We were unable to follow the shoreline on the other side. From some angles it appeared there was no shoreline; no doubt, it had once been there until it gave way to the incessant flow of the river. *The Mighty, Mighty Amazon* is the title of a book about the river, and it was easy to appreciate that homage to the river's power. We felt its calm omnipotence: "I am the mighty, mighty Amazon, and I go wherever I wish and take with me what and whom I desire."

The docks on the bank were not the stuff of foggy farewells in a Maugham novel. Lumber was piled neatly in barracks of open warehouses; it was here that Big Al's fallen trees would begin to earn money for Brazil. Large cranes, still asleep that morning, drooped over ships from the south of Brazil and Europe—old, rusting vessels, for the most part. Fences encircled the loading areas, but the watchmen were listless and content to let curious Americans roam freely.

We watched the tide surge in, jostling the 40,000-ton *Benedict* visiting from Liverpool as easily as it rocked the two-man *Esperanca* carrying fish to market. The port for the *Esperanca* and the other fishing boats of the area is upriver from the large commercial docks, a sprawling fish market whose very name, Ver-o-Peso, is a warning to consumers: "watch the weight." To get there we had to slink through a ribbonwide opening between lines of rickety wooden stalls offering everything from essence of turtle perfume to smoked dolphin vagina, a mythic delicacy in that region. The stalls were so close together they blocked out the sun, and wares were displayed in eerie dimness— dried boa skins, tapir skulls, large rubber monkeys masturbating. When we stopped to marvel at a curio, a voice chirped from the rear of the stall, "*Diga*"—speak. We could make out a pair of hungry eyes. "*Nada*," we said and went to the next stall. How do you bargain for piranha teeth? What is the right price to pay for jaguar's testicles? We strolled and stared and remembered easily that this was the strange Amazon that, long ago in Chicago and Washington, we had expected to see everywhere.

Into the small slip at the Ver-o-Peso came boats providentially named, like the *Esperanca* which means Hope, *Sonhos* (Dreams) and *Life Is Tough For Him Who Is Soft*. From these ships tumbled a potpourri of the remarkably varied fish life of the river—small silvery piranhas with sharp deadly teeth; shiny pirarucu, at 6 feet long the largest freshwater fish in the world; tambaqui, tucunare—delicious fish with beautiful names. We watched men with towels curled on their heads balancing wood cartons of fish, crossing back and forth from boats to the market. Fruits and vegetables were being sold, too, adding a blossoming springtime of color to the steady, determined activity.

This place which sells crazy ornaments and exotic fish was, for that morning at least, the real Belem to us. The highway from Brasilia, the airplanes flying overhead, and the apartment houses we had walked by could not distract this town from the real source of its life. The Amazon River did not disappoint us.

On our first day in Belem we ate *pato no tucupi*, a regional favorite consisting of duck and greens that seems marinated in novocaine, for it numbs the mouth. Tucupi is prepared from the soft white pulp of the manioc root, in which, according to legend, the beautiful daughter of an Indian chief was hidden after her death. But that starchy root alone cannot explain the effect of the dish. Our mouths were rendered senseless from it; the after-meal coffee trickled out of the side of London's mouth, so incapable was he of controlling the deadened muscles. As a prelude to a siesta stroll through Belem, the meal had no equal. It made us high and nearly oblivious to the heat. We repeated the experience on other days.

Soon we discovered that the high could be enhanced by ice cream, which we consumed in great quantities after eating pato no tucupi. The flavors offered by the multitude of ice cream parlors were from fruits with untranslatable names and so difficult for us to remember that we ordered by color, our favorites being dark purple and light orange. Light-headed and licking ice cream cones, we spent early afternoons ambling on shaded, uneven sidewalks, waiting until the sensation had passed.

Walking through Belem was a surprisingly comfortable exercise. Belem is one of the few Amazon towns where the founders left some trees, and many of the streets, laid out in a grid pattern downtown, were mercifully shaded from the sun by high, well-placed leaves. The architecture is an eclectic assortment of Colonial Portuguese colorfully tiled buildings with dark wood door frames and shutters, jungle Arabic alabaster buildings in pastel hues with archway entrances, and 20-story concrete and glass apartment houses. The epidemic of apartment houses—there were no signs of the building boom subsiding—is a uniquely Belem phenomenon: river people traditionally like to live near the river but in Belem there are just too many people for each to have his own house near the water, so they must pile atop one another instead.

Belem, unlike many of the towns in the Amazon, owes its success to a recognizable geographic factor: the meeting of river and ocean. Originally a fortress guarding the entrance to the Amazon, Belem developed into a busy port that reached its zenith during the rubber boom of the early 20th century. There still are reminders of the fantastic wealth which flowed into Belem in those days. The most conspicuous is the baroque Theatre of Peace, a fluffy pink building with white frills like an architectural high school prom dress, where Anna Pavlova once danced. On the main square with the theater is the Hotel Grao Para, which used to be an overnight resting place for travelers from the United States to Rio in the days when planes refueled in Belem. Xavier Cougat and his orchestra, Zsa Zsa Gabor and a procession of Carnival-bound playboys who have shone in Rio sprinkled a little glamour along the way in Belem. Brazil nuts and mahogany and other exotic woods passing through the port kept the town solvent even after the rubber boom fizzled. And the airfield was strategically important in World War II to Americans who were preparing to jump the Atlantic to meet Rommel in North Africa.

To call Belem a town seems insulting, because anything with a million people ought to be a city. Yet, the place has only a handful of movie theaters, a few decent hotels, and six or seven good restaurants, perhaps because only a small percentage of the population can afford these amenities. The downtown is old and fixed; the jungle yesterday–jumble today effect of Ji Parana and Xinguara is missing. Belem's downtown can accommodate only a finite number of stores, though the area is stuffed with people. Because it can't expand, Belem is really only a big small town despite the size of its population. Most newcomers live outside the town, along flat muddy streets in colorful wood shacks that have gone up in a hurry.

The grounds of the Goeldi Museum and the nearby city forest are Belem's only reminders that this modern city once upon a time was jungle. From the air these enclaves of trees stick out like broccoli bunches planted in cement; they are the remaining tropical landscape whose boundaries are determined by square city blocks. This topography is what some cynics predict for the entire Amazon, when the rain forest replaces man as the curio of the jungle.

For Joao Murca Pires, this landscape must be symbolic. As we spoke with him in his office at the Goeldi Museum, he appeared wracked by angst to see his beloved jungle go up in flames. Pires is one of the world's leading experts on the flora of the Amazon. A soft-spoken botanist with a craggy face, etched with worry lines, he wore his hair short and frequently ran his hand over it as if he were mining for the right answer. He seemed to take the destruction more personally than anyone we had met.

"We had an experimental plot about 200 kilometers south of here, of about 11,000 hectares. We had the land for ten years, and it took us the last five to get our research project approved. This year we finally got approval, and we went out to see the parcel of land. It was devastated, destroyed. Nothing on it. A grileiro had moved in, burned it and then sold false titles to pioneer families."

The land-hungry pioneers could not be moved without creating another war, and Pires' project was shelved. He blamed the government. "There is so much land in this country. Yet we have land problems, and have policies to destroy the land. That is crazy." He wrung his hands as if he were trying to sever the flow of venom.

"The trees aren't the only things going up in flames," Pires mourned. "There is the loss of species. We're losing this biological reserve. Many species are being destroyed before they are known, and people don't understand this. There is great concern in restoring monuments and art, but no concern over the natural things that are being lost."

With at least 10 percent of the earth's stock of species, the Amazon contains between 300,000 and one million forms of plant and animal life. Most of these still have not been discovered. Among the products derived from those native Amazon species that have been discovered are rubber (imagine life without rubber!), Brazil nuts, linotol from rosewood for the perfume industry, powerful drugs such as curare and a myriad of other useful pharmaceuticals. Scientists like Pires are certain that valuable food crops, pulp woods and sources of new drugs remain to be recognized. But this may never happen.

Pires told us of a car trip he had made the previous year near Paragominas, the moonscape of our bus trip to Belem. "I drove for hours," he said, "and I didn't see a tree, not one tree. Why are we doing this?" What is needed, he said, is a Three Mile Island of the Amazon, something nearly cataclysmic that will bring the potential dangers to the surface before it is too late.

"What we need to develop is not the Amazon but a program to win time. And we need to develop methods of controlling development." Then Pires stopped and looked shell-shocked, as if he'd had a horrible vision that he couldn't communicate. His face contorted with pain, and he shook his head and stood up. He didn't excuse himself or deliver a pithy summation; instead, he offered a limp handshake and shuffled from the room.

The very richness of speciation that fills such men as Pires with anxiety to preserve the jungle causes an altogether different sort of concern for scientists at the Chagas Institute, the tropical disease research center in Belem. We visited the Chagas Institute to find out about our health problems and those prevalent in the Amazon. In keeping with the rampant speciation of other forms of life in this jungle, 423 known viruses in the world occur in the Amazon and so do an incredible number of disease-causing funguses, bacteria, parasites and the various creatures that spread them. We decided to concentrate on one particular ill—leishmaniasis, caused by a parasite-carrying fly.

We waited in the office of Dr. Ralph Lainson, an Englishman who had spent 17 years in Brazil studying leishmaniasis, and is considered the world's expert on the disease. We examined photos on the wall and were horrified—a man's face with a scab where his nose was supposed to be, a scrotum with what looked to us like wine corks pasted on it, and a woman's hand with tiny volcanos growing out of her knuckles.

"I had a pimple on my calf, and I thought it was a mosquito bite so I didn't pay any attention to it," an American researcher we met had told us of his own case of leishmaniasis. "After about three weeks it began to grow and grow until it looked like a golfer had taken a divot out of my leg. What was worse, however, is that once they diagnosed it they told me there was no cure. They gave me a metal-based serum, a poison, and I gave myself injections for nine months. The problem was that if I made the dosage too large not only the parasite would die, but I would, too."

"Leishmaniasis doesn't have the drama of malaria. Whereas malaria can kill in a matter of weeks, leish is a more insidious killer. And quite disfiguring, as you can see," explained Dr. Lainson, after he had settled into a chair in his office. He wore a white laboratory coat and had disheveled gray hair and eyeglasses that kept slipping down his nose. He was delighted to tell us about his specialty, because although 400,000 people around the world get leishmaniasis every year, almost all in the tropics, the disease still is relatively unknown.

"There are two types of this disease," Lainson said. "There is the visceral which is the type that kills, and the dermal whereby the parasite spreads through the lymph system to the mucus membranes in the nose and larynx."

Both forms are transmitted by tiny sandflies that first bite a host animal, sucking in the infected blood which is transformed in the fly's gut into what Lainson called "something hideous" that the sandfly then injects into an unsuspecting person. Lainson characterized man as "the accidental victim of this process and because of this he reacts badly. But one thing is certain; it is not transmitted man to man. It goes from reservoir animal to the fly to man."

Were those small red bumps we had the early stages of a lifetime of horror? We showed Lainson a variety of bites we had acquired in recent days.

He laughed hard, but told us our concern that they might indicate leishmaniasis was not farfetched. "The bite is often confused with tropical sores and bacterial infections, and in some cases the bite mark simply disappears, although the parasite doesn't. Years later you can see the results." He pointed to the man without the nose.

"Who gets it?"

"Mostly it's poor people, but this disease doesn't respect your social bracket. The flies congregate on the trunks of trees, millions of them. And when you disturb them, especially at night, they're going to bite you. I say mostly poor people, because they are the ones most likely to work or live in the forest."

Leishmaniasis is one of the oldest known tropical diseases, discovered in 1889 by a self-effacing Russian named Borovsky, who neglected to name the guilty parasite. David Leishman confirmed Borovsky's findings in 1903 and took the opportunity to christen the causative agent, thereby gaining the appreciation of generations of medical students spared the chore of pronouncing Borovskyiasis.

Lainson said that anyone who wants a disease named after him ought to come to the Amazon. In 1980 in an epidemic of oropouche virus in Manaus, 90,000 people were stricken with chills, fever and severe body aches, courtesy of a small mosquito. The hemorrhaging syndrome of Altamira killed several immigrant children in 1971 before doctors realized that a black fly was the culprit and steroids the antidote. Other newly discovered diseases include Mayaro fever, Micambo virus and Guared virus. Each year a new vector—usually an insect capable of carrying the disease—appears, and epidemiologists race to identify it in order to minimize its damage. Detailed reports are prepared for medical journals to alert other physicians to symptoms and effects. The reports carry prosaic names such as "An Outbreak of Oropouche Virus Disease in the Vicinity of Santarem, Para, Brazil," but the illnesses themselves are quite mysterious, because they are so new. Known viruses combine with other known viruses in mosquito carriers, and the result is an unknown virus, which usually carries the benign generic name "arbor virus" until further identification can be made and the organism is named after its discoverer, its symptoms, or the place in which it was first observed.

"We are learning that when you open up the jungle, you release viruses and parasites we've never seen before," Lainson said. "We are constantly playing catch-up."

In addition to fostering outbreaks of new illnesses, development of the Amazon has created increases among many diseases already known. Chagas disease, first identified by the man for whom the Chagas Institute is named, continues to be troublesome. It is another parasitic disease, in this case carried by a beetle and causing slow, insidious damage. The victim's heart and esophagus atrophy so slowly and imperceptibly that apparently healthy people drop dead 20 years after the parasite invaded their organs. *Onchocerca volvulus*, a disease related to malaria, is a blinding illness caused by a small worm that is injected into the skin by a carrier mosquito. The worm eventually works its way up into the head, inside the eyes, destroying vision; the popular name of this disease is African river blindness. A related disease, also spread by a worm-carrying mosquito, is *wuchereria bancrofti,* which causes painful, disfiguring elephantiasis.

Lainson, himself, patient as he was enumerating these diseases for us, has little time to study them. Leishmaniasis cases have increased frighteningly in the latest wave of Amazon development. When an outbreak of 300 cases occurred one year at Daniel Ludwig's Jari project, Lainson sent out 12 researchers to study the problem. All 12 scientists became his patients. Every soldier who went through Brazil's jungle warfare school near Manaus got leishmaniasis. And shortly after the discovery of the Carajas ore deposits, there was a violent outbreak of the disease.

"Is there a cure?" we asked, remembering the words of the American victim.

"No, not really," Lainson said. "Chemotherapy of this disease is in a poor situation. Drugs of choice are antimony derivatives, which can knock the patient about a bit. There have been no significant advances in many years. The treatment is not as efficient as we want it."

"What about killing it at the source?"

"You can't. The large-scale insecticide programs that would be necessary to eliminate the many varieties of sandfly are impossible without destroying the entire ecological system. Even if we learn how to protect people against the parasite itself, there are as many varieties of the parasite as there are types of sandfly. And you can't very well bump off all the wild animal hosts—opossums, rodents, sloths, and anteaters."

We thanked Lainson for his time, and he said he was delighted his parasite finally was getting the respect it deserved. He walked with us to the photographs one more time and stopped in front of us to offer his assistance. "Remember if you need me I'm here."

Somewhat shaken, but reassured that our present complaints were not any of these dread diseases, we walked out of the Chagas Institute onto the main avenue and were happy to smell exhaust fumes and dodge traffic, pests we were used to. We tried hailing a cab, but it was raining hard—as it always does between 3 and 4 P.M. in Belem—and all the taxis were full.

We went back into the institute until the rain let up and then tried again. This time a pickup truck stopped for us. The driver, a big man, rolled down the window and said in perfect English, "Hey, you guys want a lift?"

Kelly said "Sure" and we climbed into the back of the truck.

The man's invitation so smacked of familiarity that each of us assumed the other knew him. We looked through the rear window of the cab at the back of a prematurely balding head and the outgrowth of a salt-and-pepper beard, looked at each other and said almost simultaneously, "I don't know him." Nor did we know the passenger who shared the front seat of the pickup.

But they knew us. The driver stopped the truck across from the Hotel Grao Para, in front of a large plaza with benches and shade trees. He jumped out of the cabin and said, "You turkeys are Kelly and London. Right?" He lifted his cowboy boot onto the tire and scraped it over the edge. "I think I stepped in dog shit."

We asked him to introduce himself. He laughed and said to the man in the passenger seat in Portuguese, "I told you they didn't know me." Then turning back to us, he said, "I was going to drive you guys to the police station and pretend to arrest you. Wouldn't that have been funny?"

His name was Rafael Lesco, which meant nothing to us.

"I'm the guy who runs the big ranch next to Volkswagen." He hit London in the shoulder as if the jolt would bring recognition.

We wanted to know how he recognized us.

"I heard you guys were supposed to be in Belem. Not too many people look like you. You're not hip enough to be drug dealers and too hip to be scientists."

The mystery solved, we told Rafael Lesco we were delighted to meet him, but were on our way back to the Equatorial Hotel. Still exhausted, we had taken to napping in the hot afternoons.

"Okay, I'll stay there with you," he said. "You seem like pretty cool guys." He spoke English as if he had learned it from "Happy Days" or hanging out at the basement bar of a college frat house.

Lesco arrived at the hotel a day too late, because the monthly

increase had just taken effect, raising the room rates 50 percent overnight. He had to pay $60 for the same room we had for $40. Prices
don't rise gradually in Brazil's inflation-battered economy, and there
occasionally are angry demonstrations when periodic fare increases
or food price hikes are enacted to keep pace with the 100 percent
inflation rate. We kept ahead of the cost of living by changing our
dollars with everyone from hotel elevator men in Brasilia to record
store owners in Manaus. Greenbacks proved to be the best hedge
against inflation, and popular demand for them was so great that the
newspapers printed the black market rate ("parallel rate" was the
euphemism) alongside the official rate of exchange.

We asked our new friend to leave us alone for three hours to
shower and rest. Just as London fell asleep the door began shaking.
Rafael Lesco was back.

"Hi, I got lonely and decided to see what you guys were up to."
He stormed past a towel-clad Kelly, pointed to a sleeping London
and said, "Come on, you assholes; let's go pick up chicks."

Lesco grabbed the pillow out from under London's head, placed
it against his posterior and loudly broke wind. Laughing hard, he
said, "That'll really put you out." Then he threw the pillow back to a
startled London.

At last, we had discovered the primeval man of the jungle. Educated at Lehigh University and Dartmouth Business School, Rafael
Lesco was a Cuban immigrant, whose vision of America at its best
was freshman rush week at fraternities across the country. He practiced at being a frat man as assiduously as English teenagers try to be
mods or rockers. He bragged about how many brews he could drink
before he puked, described in detail his predilection for anal sex,
hinted that farm animals were fair game and refused to call anyone
by his proper name. We both became "Bro"; repeating the word often
was an obvious source of pleasure to Lesco. And, of course, we were
to call him Bro.

Bro had married a rich Brazilian "broad—she lived with me and
the guys in the house at Dartmouth." He chose to ignore his own
father's remarkable success—from shipping clerk to the presidency of
a major American corporation—and he went off on his own. But the
big New York accounting firm that hired him out of business school
was not the rocket Lesco wanted to launch him to the stars. "I always
wanted to be a big shot, my own man," he confided in us. His wife

had a baby, and on the trip to Brazil to show the new grandchild to his in-laws they decided to stay. "My father-in-law made me an offer I couldn't refuse." But Bro was to learn that sons come first in Brazil, and instead of being his own man he worked for his brothers-in-law. "They're a bunch of idiots. They know about as much about business as you two do." He was a master of insult. Life on one of his father-in-law's ranches agreed with him, and there he decided that he would become a cattleman. "I always loved the outdoors, shooting and shit like that." But his persistent insults strained family relationships to the breaking point, and he had to look elsewhere for a job. "They're going to lose everything, because they don't know what the fuck they're doing. At least they can't blame it on me."

The new job had come in the guise of a large concrete company that wanted to buy land in the Amazon in order to acquire an asset with available government subsidies. "I did it on my own," Bro insisted, although the contact was his father-in-law's. "I hunted around for them, and I found a large piece that had been abandoned. I found the owner and bought it. I'm finally taking risks," Bro said, almost in the same breath with which he explained that the purchase of land with public money is practically risk free.

We had dinner at a first-class Japanese steak house.

"I'm here to reap the fruits of my labors," Bro proclaimed of his visit to Belem. He was on his fourth beer and already had called London, who lagged behind by two, a "wimp."

"I'm going to arrange for my incentives for the year. The accountants from SUDAM"—the agency responsible for Amazon development—"were at the ranch last month, and I set the whole thing up. Now, I just need their approval. It's no sweat." He was expecting approval for 67 million cruzeiros in incentives, about $600,000; we wondered how he could be so sure.

" 'Cause I bribe the motherfuckers. And one of the sons of bitches had the nerve to fucking complain that the boots I gave him weren't the style he wanted. You believe that? A $300 pair of boots!"

We asked to learn more about bribery techniques.

He smiled, telling us that we had come to the expert. "These guys I gave cases of whiskey and work boots. A guy from INCRA I gave 10 percent of the real estate taxes I'd save if he forgot we were cheating."

We thought he was kidding.

"Hell, no. You go into some of these people's houses and look at the stereos they got and look in their liquor cabinets and see how their wives dress. These fuckers steal like hungry Jews."

Lesco yelled at London for hogging all the steak, then resolved the dispute by ordering more. But when the check came, he told London to pick it up. "Hell, you ate it all."

We objected.

"Okay. I'll pay one-fifth. That's about my share. And what the hell do I care, the company's paying for it."

Outside the restaurant, Lesco stopped at a newsstand to buy a copy of *Taurus*, the magazine of horses, cows and buffaloes. "My Bible," he called it. Kelly gave him the money for the magazine after Bro claimed to have spent everything on dinner.

"You know, you guys are all right for a bunch of faggots." London told him he wasn't such a bad guy for a buffalofart. Bro took that as the highest praise and asked London if he wanted to "slap-fight" right there on the darkened streets of Belem.

"Hey, what are you guys doing tomorrow? Maybe I'll come along."

Our plan was to see one of the lawyers for the posseiros.

"Well, count me out. I'll just read my magazine."

We suggested maybe he should come, to see how the other half lives. "Are you shitting me?" Bro bellowed. "Those fucking Communists are a fucking pain in the balls. I told them any one of them comes on my land I shoot his fucking dick off."

The lawyer, Egydio Salles, was on his way to becoming the best known lawyer in all Brazil for a cause Bro thought subversive. The two French priests charged with "consciousness raising," inciting squatters in the incident that had left one man dead, were his clients, and they were on the front page of every newspaper in the nation. By the time we met Salles in Belem the trial had become a forum for many of Brazil's profound social questions: the government's tolerance of the church's social activities, the role of foreign priests and, of course, the rights of posseiros, the little people in a big land.

Only the day before our appointment Salles had scored a major victory in the courtroom. The government had claimed that the dead victim in this land dispute was the foreman employed by the rightful owner of the land, but Salles had proved that the foreman was alive and well on a nearby fazenda. "The government was lying. The dead man was an army reservist specializing in guerrilla warfare," he told us. "I'd like to know what he was doing fighting on the side of the pistoleiros."

One of his colleagues interrupted to ask Salles to help him for a moment. The office he shared with two other attorneys was dignified but dark and musty in the style preferred by aging English barristers. The thriving commercial practice of Salles' father, the senior partner of the firm, allowed the son to follow his principles without regard to fees.

We asked Salles about Pau Seco, the other land war which we had seen. He shook his head knowingly and pulled off his wire-rimmed glasses, wiping them clean while he talked. "It's hard to believe what is going on in the jungle. It's so far away that people can kill quietly. No one notices."

We told him we had come to him to find out if the rule of law had yet arrived at the frontier. We expected that he'd tell us that it had, that there was an arena where the truth would win out. But Salles said "No" very clearly.

"First of all, the government is not neutral here. It opened the roads saying land with no men for men with no land. And now the government is killing those men."

Even if there were honest judges and police, Salles continued, there still would be a problem trying to decide who owns the land. The land registry is in shambles, and Salles blamed the document mess for the confusion over ownership. "At first the land belonged to the federal government, then to the state. Then when they built the federal roads, land for 100 kilometers on each side of the road went back to the federal government. It's at the point where it's impossible to tell who owns what. There are so many overlapping titles we call it a 'house of cards.' "

If he had his way, Salles told us, he would expropriate all land in the Amazon and give titles to the people working on it. He said that in the present confusion the balance of justice tips in favor of the wealthier party. "They can buy judges and they can buy policemen. The rule of law cannot exist when it is up for sale."

We asked Salles about the resolution of these conflicts; was a class war on the horizon? We told him about the apparent influx of neighboring squatters in Pau Seco to bolster the defense against Nelito. "Do you think it's a sign of organized rebellion?"

Salles doubted it. "No," he said. "The question today is not one of ideology, not similar to the guerrilla warfare of the 70s. This violence does not have political goals. These squatters are fighting in defense of their land and in defense of their lives."

We should have known that Belem could not offer us the perspective we longed for. Each person pastes his own picture on the puzzle-box lid. Looking at identical pieces, Pires the botanist saw beneficent life choked off, Lainson the doctor saw pestilence unleashed. Bro saw himself as big and Salles saw how small others really are. The lethargy of Belem's streets at noon, the pleasant sensations of pato no tucupi, our own need for rest should have held another message for us: Slow down, take the magnificent shock of the Amazon one lick at a time, like the strange-flavored ice creams whose names we had trouble learning, but of which Belem's residents are so justly proud. Instead, we gobbled away at our itinerary, continuing to think the answer would be in the next bite.

TRANSAMAZON

The headquarters of the Superintendency of the Amazon, SUDAM, is the most important office building in the Amazon. If Interior Minister Andreazza is Santa Claus in the jungle—having jurisdiction over Indians, highways, land and all government subsidies—then SUDAM is his elves' workshop. It is an agency with one purpose behind it: to develop the Amazon.

Pires, the botanist, called SUDAM's programs a "deadly mistake." Bro, a significant beneficiary of SUDAM's money, characterized the agency and its bureaucrats as "jokers" and "greedy motherfuckers." We visited the offices, fenced off and guarded as vigilantly as a military base, to find someone who would defend

SUDAM's programs and make good on Andreazza's promise to let us see the results firsthand.

The SUDAM program for development is divided into three parts: outright grants and loans, forgiveness for taxes and reinvestment of tax money owed the government, and duty-free imports of certain materials on which Brazilian tariffs are high. Virtually every large project in the Amazon—from the ranches to the slaughterhouses, from luxury hotels to private colonization projects, from the duty-free zone of Manaus to the very private Jari project—benefit in one way or another from these incentives. In the first 15 years of the program, about $1.8 billion was made available to private enterprise, although precise figures are difficult to come by because of the wildly fluctuating currency.

Raimundo Monteiro, who is in charge of the subsidy program, told us the money had been well spent. "Fifteen years ago," he said, "the Amazon was a jungle. Now it is a place where people can live and work." He admitted that mistakes have been made, citing SUDAM's promotion of large cattle projects that had resulted in the stark deserts we had seen. He insisted, however, that the agency's achievements are impressive, considering the short time it has been in operation and the lack of available precedents.

We told Monteiro of a frequent criticism we had heard—that the SUDAM programs have made the Amazon a colony of the south with all of the money going to large corporations who use the Amazon as a tax dodge.

He was not apologetic about this. "Those who make a lot receive a lot," he replied. "It's the natural law." Monteiro subscribed to the trickle-down theory that interesting giant companies to invest in the region enabled the small people to ride in on the companies' roads and work in their factories. But he also acknowledged that SUDAM has virtually no programs to directly help small farmers and immigrants from other areas of Brazil, those who take the greatest risk.

Although Monteiro's explanation was reasonable and the results of SUDAM's programs are remarkable and visible throughout the region, the agency remains a tremendous focus of derision, even to its beneficiaries. SUDAM's reputation is that of a vehicle for patronage within the Interior Ministry; it is reputed to be a receptacle for brothers-in-law and chums of Interior Ministry officials. It is seen as the ideal home for incompetence, because whatever damage the bureaucrats cause, the Amazon is large enough to absorb it.

"We have nothing to hide," Interior Minister Andreazza had told us. "You want to see the Amazon. Go. You will have our airplane, whatever you need." We expected to arrange our Grand Tour through SUDAM's press secretary, known as the Secretary of Obstruction among foreign journalists we had met. Maria Brigida, we were told, kept visitors like ourselves waiting for days for appointments before explaining that the appropriate bureaucrat was on vacation. She didn't return phone calls, although her secretary called back to say she was too busy to talk.

When we finally met Maria Brigida we were, therefore, not surprised by her reaction. She refused to extend a welcoming hand upon introduction; she merely nodded at the mention of our names and walked away. She was angry with us, because she had seen a telex from Andreazza that was on the desk of all the high officials of SUDAM: Receive them! The press secretary, accustomed to being the guardian of SUDAM's gate, had been emasculated by her boss in Brasilia.

We had to find a replacement bureaucrat. We needed a guide and, since the Interior Minister had decided we were important enough to merit the Grand Tour, SUDAM needed a spokesman. So we arranged to see the Assistant Superintendent, but had gotten no farther than his waiting room when Skaff came into our lives. "Dr. Joseph Skaff, at your disposal," he said. He ordered "three cafezinhos in a hurry for my American friends" and sat down.

Skaff immediately told us that he, too, was in the newspaper business as editor and publisher of *Flash*, "the only independent weekly in Para." "Sweethearts, I am one of you," he said.

He apologized for the delay in seeing the Assistant Superintendent, but added that "It is not a bad thing. It will give us time to exchange ideas."

Skaff clearly was working hard at instant friendship, apparently convinced that his fluency in English and status as journalist would catapult him into our hearts. But we were wary, as much because of his sudden coziness as his appearance. Skaff did not look chummy. No matter how much he made his thick lips grin, a scowl stayed sewn on. He had a dark, stubby, 5 o'clock shadow. An intense squint managed to distract attention from a receding hairline; the hair that remained sprouted wildly as if he had used LSD as a hair tonic. His suit, a double-breasted one of a large black-and-white check, suggested that he had draped himself in the morning's crossword puzzle.

"You know I'm also an oral surgeon who enjoys quite a good practice here in Belem." Skaff didn't want to hear from us; friendship, he felt, would come from our being bowled over by his talent. He had spent his youth with an uncle who owned a barbershop in Pittsfield, Massachusetts, but he left there after high school because "there you are all numbers. Here I am an important man." In fact, Skaff was such a legend in his own mind that he was puzzled how he had escaped widespread recognition, but that would be rectified. "You'll write about me, of course," he instructed us.

We wondered how he managed to be an oral surgeon and publisher and to work at SUDAM at the same time; it was a question Skaff had been waiting for.

He smiled and said, "Nada." Then he added in English, "It's simple." As he sipped his coffee, his pinky pointed toward the sky. "Here I do nothing. I am an adviser to the Superintendent, and he is my friend. I take care of him, and he takes care of me."

The secretary was beckoning us; Skaff nodded. "Look—we must arrange your schedule. But we will have plenty of time to talk on our trip. We will become good friends."

The Assistant Superintendent, a grandfatherly man with white hair slicked back and a thin mustache, walked from behind his large desk, piled high with papers, to greet us. He introduced us to four men sitting around a coffee table, not one of whom showed any pleasure in meeting us. "The Minister wants you to know that we are here to serve you," the Assistant Superintendent said. The four men nodded weakly; Skaff winked at us and laughed.

We expected all sorts of caveats, leading to such frustration that we'd cancel the trip. But we were wrong. "Amazonia is yours," Andreazza's aide had assured us, and now the Assistant Superintendent was confirming that the Interior Minister was a man of his word.

Confronted with such power, we conferred and hastily concocted an elaborate itinerary—a 2,000-mile, 2-day whirlwind tour to a remote Indian tribe and three cities on the TransAmazon Highway.

The Assistant Superintendent said the program sounded "ambitious"; Skaff said it was "exciting." We thought it was ridiculous, not to mention impossible, and had proposed it only as a negotiating tactic; we were willing to accept a lesser excursion.

While the Assistant Superintendent was mumbling to himself, fretting over how to accommodate us, another man entered the office. He wore dark sunglasses, a tight beige suit, and had a deep tan and long wavy hair. He was introduced as Paulo Cesar Abreu, the Belem representative of FUNAI, the Indian agency. Abreu looked more like a Rio real estate salesman, which, we later learned, he had been until he was hired by a friend in the Interior Ministry. The Assistant Superintendent told him about our desires.

Abreu said, "That's crazy." The Assistant Superintendent showed him the telex from Andreazza.

Abreu realized he was outranked and barked at us. "Indians. What kind of Indians do you want? big tribes? small tribes? I have all types of Indians."

We told him we preferred a tribe that spoke Portuguese. We wanted conversation, not just observing a few daily activities and leaving at dusk.

A burly man in a white shirt with epaulets, presumably our pilot, interjected, "We need a tribe where we can land." He explained to Abreu the type of plane we would be flying and the required length of the landing strip.

Abreu closed his eyes and nodded as he hit his chin with his fist. "I know," he said. "The Kayapo-Gorotire. That's where you'll go."

We told him we'd already been there.

"How were you there," he demanded to know.

When we explained that Colonel Santos had taken us in his helicopter, Abreu appeared mollified, or at least humbled.

"Well, it's impossible then," he said. "Anyway tomorrow is a holiday."

"For the Indians?" we asked.

"No, for me. It can't be done."

The Assistant Superintendent again waved Andreazza's telex and explained to Abreu that it had to be done. We felt obnoxious, but powerful.

"There is another tribe," he finally said. "The Apalai."

The pilot asked about the airstrip and seemed satisfied with the answer.

Abreu arose and said he would find someone to accompany us. "For me it is a holiday." He shook hands with the Assistant Superintendent and left.

The visits to the cities on the TransAmazon Highway were easily arranged, because each of the towns has an airport. The itinerary was finalized, and we agreed to meet the next morning at the airport at 6 A.M.

We arrived at the Belem airport at its busiest hour when the damp dawn begins to give way to a morning so hot the air over the runway wobbles like jelly.

Skaff and the others were late. When they straggled in, their appearances suggested they were expecting an outing to Lion Country Safari Adventure Park. Skaff, his fat-lipped, humorless smile fixed on his face, wore a rumpled pink polo shirt, designer jeans and white loafers with no socks. Arturo Reis, a portly well-meaning bureaucrat from SUDAM, who acted confused by all this and whom Skaff treated as his staff aide, carried an armload of prepackaged chicken dinners. Napoleon Vitorino, a half-Indian, represented FUNAI and would have preferred to stay home; he, too, was supposed to be on holiday. The SUDAM pilots were as spotless and courteous as tour bus drivers as they led our small band out to the twin-engine executive aircraft with soft leather seats that was to take us for this government's eye view of the Amazon.

Skaff held the itinerary for what we had requested—a round trip of 2,000 miles in 2 days. We were to fly about an hour north to Macapa, the capital of the Territory of Amapa, for refueling then head northwest toward the border with Surinam where the largest of nine Apalai Indian villages is located. We then were scheduled to visit the TransAmazon Highway towns of Itaituba, President Medici and Altamira.

Skaff passed out copies of *Flash* as we settled in. "Now you read it so we can exchange ideas about journalism," he said.

On the front page was a lengthy tribute to SUDAM, citing the great work done by the agency and especially the current superintendent in conquering the Amazon—past tense. On the back page was a sizable advertisement from SUDAM, making the same points as Skaff's piece.

"Usually we come out on Mondays, but sometimes Fridays," Skaff said by way of unrequested explanation. "Sometimes not at all. A schedule is not important. Everyone always is waiting to read *Flash*."

Reis had been brought along to explain the SUDAM programs, but couldn't compete with Skaff.

"Listen, sweetheart, let me tell you about my trip to the United States last year. I go a lot you know; I know the place. I spent 45 days with my family. First class. When it was over, I was so tired, I needed a vacation from my vacation so I went to the Bahamas. I could go live in the United States, but why should I? I live like a king," said the oral surgeon–publisher–political consultant.

The refueling stop in Macapa was extended by the disappearance of one of the pilots. He wanted to visit an old friend in the city, a maneuver that made us realize we were far from the finger-snapping efficiency of Interior Minister Andreazza in Brasilia.

When we took off again, the dry scrub plain that surrounds Macapa changed back to the green carpet of the rain-forest canopy but with the addition of hills—dozens of them, even more than around Carajas. One of the most uninhabited parts of the world extends from Macapa to the border with Surinam, an area without any towns or roads and few houses. Dark brown rivers twist their way through the jungle, sometimes meandering back on themselves in wide sweeps, other times cutting straight gashes between ridges. It was the most remote landscape we had seen, no clearings anywhere. To us, every hill, ridge, river and tree looked like one we had flown over a minute before.

Apparently the pilots had the same impression. We were lost.

The pilots admitted they had confused the compass readings and were looking for a landmark on the map or some feature that they could recognize. One choice was to find a river that matched the outline of one on the map, assuming the map makers had done a good job and such precision even existed and that the river hadn't changed its course since the map had been drawn.

The two pilots hunched over and conferred in strained whispers, jabbing at each other and the charts. Five heads were craned toward the cockpit until one of the pilots finally pulled the door curtain shut. The plane made wide circles, dipping sometimes to get a closer look at the terrain. The engine drone seemed to get higher and higher pitched. Skaff started to sweat; the corners of his already sour smile turned down even further until his face looked as though it had melted. We flew like this for almost an hour until one of the pilots spotted an Indian village, apparently abandoned, with a partly over-grown runway. The pilots decided it was too short and talked about turning back to Belem. Clearly they wanted to, but they were faced with the perhaps more serious dilemma of how they would explain to the bosses back at SUDAM that they had gotten lost.

An hour and twenty minutes after we had been due to land, the pilots spotted the Apalai runway, a long dirt clearing at the end of a cluster of huts that Napoleon Vitorino immediately recognized. The landing was flawless, and as soon as we had taxied to a halt, Skaff pushed his way out the door ahead of everyone else.

According to Napoleon there were 241 Apalai in all, living in nine villages—119 in the one we had landed at. We were on a plateau above much of the surrounding jungle; it was more like grassland up here with sparse trees and dry dirt. Below, maybe 100 feet down a bank, a swift river snaked through the forest. The air was clear and sunny and this was not at all an unpleasant place to be. But there were no Indians to greet us.

Napoleon said the next village was a three-day canoe trip and inaccessible to airplanes. Skaff was unfazed, and the pilots were sug-gesting a side trip to Manaus—about 600 miles out of our way—so they could do some Christmas shopping at the duty-free stores. At about this point, a man came toward us, two small children at his side, followed by a woman in a red skirt with a small baby busily suckling her breast. The man wore only a red loincloth, but he had tinted wire-rim glasses, wavy dark hair and sharp features that made him look not so much a jungle Indian as a Brooklyn accountant who had dropped out of the rat race.

Napoleon recognized him: Toranque, chief of the Apalai. "But he prefers his Brazilian name, Joao Aranha," our guide said.

The Chief's greeting was surprisingly perfunctory, as if a plane-load of visitors were a daily occurrence. He shook hands limply then started complaining to Napoleon about the price of gasoline. Na-poleon put up a hand. "We'll talk about it later," he said. "These are two journalists from the United States. They have come to meet the tribe. Where are they?"

"They've gone hunting," Chief Aranha said in good Portuguese. "We do not have gasoline for our boats so they took canoes. They will be gone three, four days." He turned to us. "This life is very hard."

The only ones left at the village were the Chief, his three small children, one of his wives and his brother-in-law, an older man with long graying locks who also wore a red loincloth.

Skaff walked up and gave the Chief a copy of *Flash* and told him to write a letter if he had any news he wanted printed. He handed the Chief his business card, saying, "Joseph Skaff. I'm a very important man in Belem. I can be of help to you."

Chief Aranha admitted he needed some help. "You see we have wires," he said, pointing to the overhead electric lines as we walked through the village, "but we don't have fuel to run the generator. When FUNAI comes they bring visitors, but the generator cannot run with visitors. It needs fuel."

The Apalai were first contacted in 1935 by the government, but because they had met gold prospectors and rubber tappers in the area decades earlier, they already spoke Portuguese and often wore Western clothes. Napoleon said the Chief had been to Belem about ten times as one of FUNAI's showcase Indians. Officially, Aranha used this forum to assert how much FUNAI meant to his tribe and how their life had been better since FUNAI came. The tribe now relies on FUNAI for many things such as gasoline, medicine and hunting rifles. The Apalai village pays for these goods and services by making souvenirs for the FUNAI tourist shops around the country—bows and arrows, beaded necklaces, headdresses of parrot feathers.

Chief Aranha, though, complained to us. "FUNAI is terrible," he said, "they give us nothing and we need so much." He talked about gasoline and food, and claimed that FUNAI would not give his tribe any motorboats.

"That's right," said Napoleon. "We make them buy the boats. Because if we give them boats, they will die." Napoleon, one of the few Indians who works with FUNAI, spoke sympathetically of the Apalai. He feared they will become so dependent on FUNAI that they will forget the considerable skills they have always used to survive in a hard world. Their culture, he said, makes them prone to such dependency.

"It's not that they're lazy. But they have learned to fish when they are hungry then dance when they are fed and happy. They do not save for tomorrow and they do not want to create a lasting industry. When we contacted them, we introduced them to a consumer society because it was what we knew and we thought why shouldn't everyone else? But they cannot understand this way of life."

Napoleon was one of a few FUNAI employees we met who seemed to understand these subtle differences between modern society and the tribes. As glib and worldly as Joao Aranha made himself out to be, Napoleon guessed he had only a tenuous hold on the edge of modern Brazil.

As a chief, Aranha was used to receiving gifts—motorboats, gasoline and tools from Westerners and other sorts of tribute from his own people. But he didn't seem to understand FUNAI's *quid pro quo*—that he had to be a good boy and not make waves. He was supposed to do so by becoming industrious, by transforming his subsistence culture into a capitalist one. FUNAI expects Indians to understand that certain values—permanence and security—are the cornerstones of a successful life. Yet, the Chief told us he had done well before FUNAI came along. And, his complaining implied, who were they to tell him the model life-style for the jungle? FUNAI brings visitors when he needs gasoline.

"Ask him about his sex life," Skaff interrupted with a burst of sincerity, as if the answer would reveal a secret to the tribe's existence. "He has two young wives."

Chief Aranha was nonplussed. "More than two wives is no good because they would fight," he said with a shrug. The Chief took us through the village of mostly well-constructed thatch-roof houses, far more substantial and airy than the fetid straw mounds of the Parakana. As we conversed, we realized that Aranha was not unaware of his tribe's dependency on FUNAI. "They have things we have learned to like," he said, but his perception did not include the necessity of joining Brazilian culture in a deeper sense. He added that he felt it was the Indian agency's duty to give gasoline, boats and guns to the tribe because the Indians were an important part of Brazil's history.

However, the Chief did know that his people's survival is imperiled. "Half the children born in this village die of sickness," he said. We asked what were the other causes of death.

"Snakes sometimes. Jaguars are not a problem. The biggest danger we have is ghosts." It was the first irrational thing he had said, this modern-looking matter-of-fact man. We looked at each other, suppressing smiles. The Chief caught us in the act and knew what was up.

"I know you don't believe me. White men don't believe in ghosts because white men can't see them, but I know. A person meets a ghost and a person gets up and screams and dies. It can happen day or night. Sometimes they are sick for a long time, sometimes they die right away."

However easily people from alien cultures can notice one another's emotions—our skepticism was so instantly recognized—cultures are not so easily shared. We believe in invisible germs; they believe in invisible ghosts. Standing there, chatting in Portuguese, we had to realize that the Indians will not in this or the next generation share the culture whose artifacts they adopt any more than a tourist in a FUNAI shop comes closer to an inner sense of Indian culture when he buys a parrot headdress. Convergence can come about only through response to a similar environment, but no one knows what sort of environment the development of the Amazon is creating or how long a time people will have to forge workable responses to it.

A thought had been stirring in us, and now it surfaced. Always, we had been warned that it was the Indian culture that would have to give way before development, but that is only one side of the coin. Traditional Brazilian ways of life—plantation farming and cattle ranching—will also give way before the onslaught of the Amazon. This is a unique land which treats its guests to hardship without regard to wealth or social class. The land has a face that does not bend. Its message, as we were reading it, was "you must learn to live with the kind of place I am." Settlers and natives are in this together, though they believe themselves on opposite sides.

We ate lunch at the FUNAI post, a five-room house set behind barbed wire—as prescribed by FUNAI policy—on the edge of the village. Two young graduate anthropology students assigned to the tribe served up a meal of wild boar and rice, and showed surprisingly little knowledge about the tribe. We talked with the girlfriend of one of the FUNAI agents who had come up to spend her summer vacation. Breathlessly, she told us how Brazil owed so much to the Indians and it was important to give them as much help as possible. "We try to do as many things for them as we can," she said.

We waited in the plane as Skaff bargained with the Chief for a small monkey—"for my son." He put the hunched, whimpering beast in a cardboard box in the back of the cabin. The Indians did not stay to watch the plane take off.

Our itinerary called for us to fly two hours to the southwest, crossing the Amazon River and landing in Itaituba, the midpoint on the TransAmazon Highway. For the whole trip, the earth beneath us was obscured by clouds. We flew as if in a windowless room until we dropped down to see the sparkling blue Tapajos River, a smudge of a town pushed into the jungle and a landing strip.

As soon as we banked toward the Itaituba Airport, we could see the red strip of the TransAmazon Highway beneath us. It looked fresh and well tended, a long surgical incision in the green skin of the jungle, stretching off into the misty horizon. Though not as imposing as the river itself, the road in its own way is more important. Its completion was the first real indication Brazilians had that they might actually be able to conquer the Amazon. And it is this road and all it signifies that has caused environmentalists to predict the destruction of the jungle.

In 1970 Emilio Medici, then President of Brazil, responded to the effects of the devastating drought in the Northeast with the declaration that he would open a "land with no men for men with no land." The sight of famine gnawed at the sentimental side of the general but his response was limited by his training: he was a military man and the solution had to be an assault on something. Ten days after his declaration, the TransAmazon Highway project was announced, a grandiose scheme to cut through 3,000 miles of jungle to allow the entrance of a culture alien to the rain-forest ecology.

Medici's technocrats devised a settlement pattern of planned communities, population clusters of varying sizes called Ruropolis or Agropolis and built at predetermined intervals along the highway route. Each town was to have electricity, water, hospitals and schools. Each colonist received 100 hectares—247 acres—of land. For the first six to eight months the government supported the newcomers with cash subsidies and attractive credit terms for housing and farm equipment purchases. Medici predicted that within 10 years, 100,000 families would settle on farms along the road. However many settled, we had learned that only 8,000 families remained.

By many standards, the road has been a dismal failure. Farmers from the Northeast were used to a very different environment from that which confronted them in the jungle. Soils are of a different chemistry, the climate here is wet and not drought-prone. Although most of the first communities were placed on fertile soils, and the initial high yields were encouraging, further penetration along the road was on poor soil and the settlers who went out there came up empty. Probably more significant, when something goes wrong for a farmer in the Amazon, the government has no answers, because there are no answers. As with so much about the Amazon, the textbooks are silent about what farm techniques will work in a rain forest. So far, only the Indians have developed an agriculture compatible with this environment, techniques that work well for very small groups who meet their needs one day at a time.

Yet the road has been a symbolic success in affirming that the nation could raze a rain forest and draw international attention to the area. A material success in that excavation crews uncovered a number of important mineral deposits, it has also been a scientific bonanza of information on topography, geology and soil composition.

Today there is even a revisionist school, mostly a collection of American scholars, that claims Brazil wrote the highway off too quickly. Professor Emilio Moran of Indiana University contends in a recent book that while the whole project did not provide the crop yields the government had expected, many individual farms did well. But because the government felt the overall project was a failure, it cut off subsidies for many who were feeling out the new ways the Amazon requires. Mario Andreazza had told us there was much recently begun unsubsidized farming in the area, and the vast stretches of cleared land we could see on either side of the highway tended to confirm this. From the air, at least, the TransAmazon Highway has the appearance of a permanent fixture.

The madness of Itaituba was immediately apparent as we climbed from the plane. The airstrip was lined with almost 100 small aircraft, most of them, it seemed, in the process of taking off. In fact the strip was so busy that planes took off in opposite directions, often at virtually the same time. Two planes would sit at either end of the runway, gunning their engines until some unseen authority said they were cleared. As the wheels of one plane left the ground, the second would charge ahead into the prop wash.

The reason for the high-risk acrobatics, we discovered, was gold. A substantial find had been made 50 miles south and men were tumbling over each other to get to it.

Skaff found a truck to take us into town, and insisted on having the front seat to himself because his tooth hurt. It was dusk and the heavy traffic kicked up clouds of dirt that put the whole town in soft focus. The main intersection was a scene of barely controlled chaos with thousands of people in the streets, cars honking and swerving, music blaring. On one corner was a record store and from a speaker over the door came the Beatles singing "Yesterday," plaintive, low and totally out of place; on the anniversary of John Lennon's death a Beatle maniac of the jungle was paying his respects.

Skaff had some personal business to tend to so we went along. He had written an article in *Flash* about Ze Arara—the Parrot—the gold baron of Itaituba who had made one of the first big strikes: "Ze the Modest says, 'I am the largest taxpayer in Para and I am going to be the largest contributor to Brazil.' Ze has the results of a secret French study that shows that the mine on his land will yield more than nine tons a month. Ze is an interesting character who gives a gold visitor's card and a small piece of gold to those who come to visit him."

Skaff had come back for a bigger piece of gold. With a copy of his flattering profile under his arm, Skaff planned to ask the Parrot to put up some money to set up a *Flash* printing plant in Itaituba. SUDAM, he knew, would match whatever the Parrot put up.

We drove out to the Parrot's ranch that night, past the gate area where two cowboys were hacking up a dead cow in the slaughter pen. The eyes of the severed head greeted visitors with a dull stare.

Ze's wife greeted us, giggling at Skaff's unctuous attempt to kiss both her hands. Her husband was in Belem for a few days, she said, to the visible deterioration of Skaff's features, but she would be happy to have us take the cool evening air on her patio.

The main house was an amalgam of various sheds that had been added on over the years as the Parrot's prosperity increased, and the patio was a *louca*, a traditional Indian building, round, open-sided and covered by a cone-shaped thatch roof. Though oddly planted next to the rambling, air-conditioned house, the louca had been acculturated by festoons of blinking Christmas tree lights. Underneath was a very middle-class gathering: the mother-in-law in a new flower print dress, a toothsome relative from the south of Brazil and his pudgy wife, and a collection of children playing with the remnants of toys.

Skaff did not pause in his torrent of ingratiating remarks, directed at the wife but absorbed by her mother-in-law, who smiled and nodded approval. "A genius," he called the Parrot, "a family man dedicated to the future of Brazil." Holding forth like an Oxford grad among the natives, Skaff spoke of society in Belem as something Mrs. Parrot must get to know. "You and your husband must join me for a tour of our delightful city," Skaff said. Sipping her beer in the shade of her Indian louca, Mrs. Parrot asked Skaff where he thought the swimming pool should go.

The airport in Ruropolis President Medici, named for the founder of the TransAmazon plan, was suffering from the opposite problem of Itaituba; it had been three months since a plane landed. One rusted wreck lay crumpled at the end of the runway, but otherwise the field was as neglected as those of the remote Indian tribes. A few of the locals came to witness the rare landing, and again Skaff collared one to truck us the less than 500 yards into town. He said it was too hot to walk and because it was so hot he was feeling weak and again needed the front seat of the truck to relax in.

Ruropolis President Medici seemed no more than a dusty square of identical prefabricated buildings, more like a stage prop than a town; on one side a school, on another a telephone satellite disc, the remainder lined by stores connected with wooden boardwalks, their wares advertised by overhanging signs done in fading pastel paints.

In the center of the square stood a row of rusted, flagless flagpoles. Grass had not grown through the cracked dirt of what was supposed to be the civic center, although there were browned patches that let us believe someone had once tried. On February 12, 1974,

President Medici had come here to open the town. The plaque com-
memorating his appearance was tarnished and rusted, but still bore
witness to the magic moment: "To inaugurate this Ruropolis with the
presence and name of President Emilio G. Medici the Brazilian people respond to the challenge of history, occupying the heart of
Amazonia."

Then, nothing. The trek from the Northeast for "the men with
no land" was too arduous, and after the initial discouraging reports it
was not worth the upheaval. The government's promise to support
settlers for six months was fulfilled, but nothing permanent remained.
Neither the farmers nor their technology could adapt to the foreign,
unknown soil in such a short period of time. This Ruropolis that was
paraded before a nation was abandoned, a failed prodigy.

In a popular Brazilian movie—*Bye Bye Brazil*—the TransAmazon
town of Altamira is the symbol for a tropical paradise that exists in
the minds of Brazilian citizens when they think of the Amazon. "Go
West, young man" Horace Greeley told a restless, hungry American
generation; "Altamira!" a slovenly truck driver on the TransAmazon
Highway advises the greedy wandering Brazilians in *Bye Bye Brazil*.
Their trek to the town is fortified by visions of lushness, a life so easy
pineapples will fall into their laps. Although the journey along the
way is laden with harbingers of a topsy-turvy world—hitchhiking
Indians, television antennas in towns without running water—the pil-
grims remain blind. Altamira, after all, is their dream, their personal
conquest of the riches Brazil has to offer. But the town in the movie is
like the town in real life—filthy, populated by misfits, crooks, and
despairing settlers; and in the end the optimists are forced to ac-
knowledge a bye-bye to a Brazil that existed in their minds but really
never was.

In the real Altamira, the concession seemed to us tacit; yet the
people have stayed. Altamira's population rose from 15,000 in 1970
to 50,000 in 1980, and its surrounding jungle has gone "pfft." For
miles and miles around the town we saw no evidence of forest, although an occasional plume of smoke let on to what had happened to
it.

The city is on a major Amazon air route and jet planes roar

regularly into its airport. The Xingu River becomes navigable at this point, clear down to the Amazon. Maraba is 200 miles to the east; there is talk of paving the TransAmazon Highway between the two cities.

You can abandon a little town like Ruropolis Medici, but Altamira is too big to die so quickly. It is a place that matters, not only in the lore of the Amazon, but in the future of its growth. For whatever reason, lack of funds or lack of pessimism, the settlers of Altamira have endured. The American West wasn't settled overnight, and in spite of a television society that now makes 30-second judgments of success or failure, the residents of this frontier town seem determined to prove that ten years is an awfully short time to declare the frontier a failure, pack up pots and pans and move on. The official decisions that affect their lives are made too quickly, without even time for trial and error to find out what works. The settlers themselves are more patient and more hopeful. They must all have seen *Bye Bye Brazil*, and perhaps they feel the eyes of their country on them. But because of the magnitude of this recent foray into the jungle many observers feel that failure, if it comes, would be a mess that couldn't be obscured as easily as the cemetery of the railroad workers in Porto Velho. The pressures to succeed are so great that there won't be a forest left along this highway to obscure automobiles as the Mad Maria's locomotives were hidden.

Skaff was as hot in Altamira as he had been in Ruropolis and he told us he would wait in the air-conditioned SUDAM office for us if we wanted to tour the town. Because he wanted to get home in time for dinner, we had two hours, no more; what was supposed to have been a guided tour from the government had turned into a version of bureaucratic tag-along. We tried to see the Assistant Superintendent for the TransAmazon Highway to find out more about the building of this road that had spawned such an assortment of cities, abandoned by their planners or poised for plans of their own. He wasn't in. We rejoined Skaff at the airstrip in midafternoon.

We, including Skaff's monkey which had nearly suffocated in the box, headed back to Belem. Skaff thought a celebration was in order, and he invited us to "take a whiskey" at his home. At 8:30, the appointed hour, we appeared at his home. Skaff wasn't there.

"He's gone to see his brother-in-law," one of the maids said.

"It must have been an emergency, because he invited us over to take a whiskey."

"No, it wasn't an emergency. He just went."

"But didn't he know he invited us over?"

"Yes," the maid said. "He told me to expect you, but to say he wasn't here. He does this all the time. He says he has no choice. He is important, and has so many things to do."

JARI

In the very early morning before the rains pelt Belem the airport bustles at a rush-hour pace. The morning after our aborted celebration with Skaff, we arrived there at 5:00 A.M. while the stars still winked over the wide river, and already the tempo was frenetic. From Rio, from Miami and from Manaus jets came to shatter the sultry air. The noise, the movement and the strong cafezinhos from the coffee bar brought us to full consciousness even at that ungodly hour. We began to brim with anticipation. We were on our way to Jari. In our search for symbols to simplify what was happening in Brazil and the Amazon we chose Jari, for it seemed to engage on a grand scale almost every obstacle we saw arising from the jungle. The world's richest man had challenged the world's greatest natural resource to a *mano a mano*. The global implications of Jari's success or failure were enormous, because for millions of people in tropics around the world this project was to signal their Industrial Revolution.

In the lore and reality of the Amazon no endeavor has matched that of Jari in terms of vision, energy and size. Named for the Jari River, the dark Amazon tributary that loops sinuously through the property, this agro-industrial project is nearly the size of Connecticut and Rhode Island combined, and was, when we first saw it, the world's largest private landholding, the property of Daniel Keith Ludwig, the 85-year-old self-made billionaire with world-wide holdings of enormous diversity and worth, who started the project in 1967 to create the first significant renewable source of food and fiber in the tropics.

For Ludwig, a visionary business genius, his Amazon dream was to be his legacy; he never had children, never even had any hobbies. Jari never was meant to make him richer; already 70 years old by the time the project got under way, he knew he'd be in his grave before a profit was turned. He had no head for fame; his sense of privacy verged on secrecy and earned him only the notoriety that was to be his undoing. But on this visit, that end was in the future and we were to see Jari moving at top speed toward Ludwig's ambitious goal: to tame the Amazon jungle, to give an ever more populated world a new frontier for food and fiber.

Ludwig's effects on the Amazon were visible almost as soon as our plane crossed into his airspace. For the first time in our travels we saw disciplined, orderly forest. The same type of tree repeated itself over and over; this was the only homogeneous forest in the Amazon.

As we drove from the airport to the corporate headquarters we passed the first forests Ludwig planted in the late 1960s. They were conceived even a decade before that when Ludwig became convinced that a shortage of wood would grip the world before the end of this century. Land use in developed countries was moving away from trees and toward development. Increases in population meant that demand for forest products would rise, but pressure for land for commercial and residential use meant supply would dwindle. A new source would have to be found.

Ludwig's solution for the shortage was to find a fast-growing tree suitable for plantations in underdeveloped areas where land was plentiful, and which would yield the lumber and pulp the world would soon so badly need. He hired scouts to roam the world, among them a chemical engineer named Everett Wynkoop, who was told to find a tree that could grow quickly in a tropical climate. It took him nearly ten years, but Wynkoop came back with a candidate—the melina tree (*gmelina arborea*). A native of Southeast Asia, the tree was transplanted to Africa by the British, who used it for fuel and mine shaft supports. Wynkoop swore that the tree grew a foot a month, and Ludwig sent him to Nigeria to gather seeds, which then were taken to Ludwig's properties in Costa Rica and Panama for testing. Confirming Wynkoop's observations, the trees grew almost exponentially. Ludwig set about searching for sufficient land on which to grow them.

His search came to the attention of Roberto Campos, Brazil's Ambassador to the United States, who convinced Ludwig that his country could meet the four prerequisites that he had set for the project: a large uninterrupted expanse of land, a source of cheap labor, proximity to a deep-water port and a stable government. That the land was in the Amazon, notorious for snuffing out dreams of grandeur, was inconsequential to Ludwig. He had never failed at anything.

Businessmen in Belem had told us that Ludwig responded to Campos' invitation by chartering a plane, touring the property by air, disembarking in Belem and handing a $3 million check to the owner. Although characteristic of Ludwig's impulsive business style, the story is apocryphal; the deal actually was consummated in Brasilia between Ludwig and President Humberto Castello Branco. What Ludwig actually bought in 1967 always has been subject to dispute. A 1976 government report stated that the project had 943,320 hectares (2.33 million acres), but according to a 1975 SUDAM proposal, the size was 3,654,491 hectares (9.03 million acres). The most widely accepted figure is 1,632,121 hectares (4.03 million acres), which makes the purchase price about 75 cents an acre.

The trees we passed on the way to town from the airport were the second generation of melinas on plots first planted in 1968 and 1969. They were nothing like the stately trees we had expected as the cornerstone of Ludwig's green revolution. At four and five years old, they resembled awkward adolescents, gangling and crooked, and because they were alongside the dusty road, they appeared to be choking on red dust.

Charles Briscoe, whose horn-rimmed glasses and casual shorts made him seem more like a high school biology teacher on a field trip than a forester for a fabled billionaire, thought the fact they had survived at all was a testimony to Ludwig's determination. The plots along the airport road had been cleared of jungle growth by tractors and bulldozers, an acceptable method in temperate climates. But here the heavy machinery compacted the thin layer of nutrient matter on the surface of the jungle floor or completely shaved it off. Most of the original melina seedlings had starved to death. The mistake cost Ludwig $20 million, but he learned from it. By 1971, tractors and bulldozers were replaced entirely by hordes of men who cleared the land by hand with chain saws and axes. That early sign of this cryptic man's willingness to roll with the punches was augmented as the blows came harder and faster.

Now, there wasn't one type of homogeneous forest, but three. As we drove along the dusty roads Briscoe barked, "Melina," "Pine," or "Eucalyptus" to identify the groves we were passing.

We entered a pine grove and left the VW hatchback to walk around on the thick bed of soft pine needles. The forest was quiet, soft and tame. "It's nothing but a pine forest," Briscoe said in his Texas drawl. But what was it doing in the Amazon, where there had never been a pine grove before?

Briscoe explained that original plans for Jari had envisioned only the melina, which achieved its miraculous growth in clay soils. "At the time Mr. Ludwig bought the land everyone thought the soils would be clay, and they were for the first plantations." Upon further development of the project it turned out that over half of Jari's soils were very sandy, and not at all conducive to the melinas' needs.

"We came up with a solution, the Caribbean pine tree, what you're standing among," Briscoe said. "But Mr. Ludwig said no. He said anybody could grow a pine tree; there was no challenge to it. You know, it's great to have a challenge, but in the meantime we needed a tree."

The pine, however, did fit Ludwig's requirements for rapid growth and he ultimately agreed to try it. It could be cut for long-fiber pulp in 11 years and for lumber in 16 years, only four or five years longer than it took melinas to produce pulp or lumber. But although the pine took well to the soil, so did the shrubby secondary growth that takes over when primary forest is cut, and within a short time the trees were competing with rampant undergrowth. Ludwig tried to fight back, but his options were few. He could not use chemicals because the pines also would die. He could not use his cadre of workers to cut away the weeds, because the vegetation multiplied faster than the sickles could eliminate it. Finally, he decided that the only way to beat the jungle was to eat it, so to keep down the undergrowth he brought in 5,000 cows to graze among the weeds.

The melina and the pine did well in their respective niches of clay or sand. "But," Briscoe continued, "there were mixed soils, part clay and part sand." Still another tree was needed. This time Ludwig planted a eucalyptus native to the Phillipines, another tree known for its rapid growth. "We're still experimenting with many varieties of the eucalyptus," Briscoe said, "always looking for the right tree for the right soil."

The groves we saw all were in different stages of destruction and creation. Some of them, burned after felling to return nutrients to the soil, reminded us of the battleground of charred stumps and powdery ash which Big Al had created near Tucurui. Other plots bore the first hints of new life as the melinas regenerated themselves from their blackened trunks. The serene pine forests were a setting for campfire marshmallow roasts; they looked as though they had had no beginning, and would never come to an end. From atop the fire tower the trees below us seemed to be growing like corn. How could this be, when plantations had never before worked in the Amazon?

Environmentalists at first predicted certain doom for Ludwig. They were right to a certain extent. In 1974 an unidentified larva quickly killed off 700 acres of melina trees. A menacing fungus appeared in 1976, and young trees constantly ran the danger of being devoured by leaf-cutter ants. But, Briscoe claimed, Ludwig's plantations were mostly protected from devastating blights because the trees he chose were not native to the region. Unlike the rubber tree, the melina and pine had few enemies native to the Amazon. Also, Ludwig's rapid turnover of trees meant that he would lose only one crop and not an entire plantation at a time.

When they weren't foretelling doom for Ludwig personally, environmentalists had railed at him for what he was doing to the jungle, and to the world. They accused the mogul of killing off thousands of undiscovered species for speculative personal gain. They warned that he was depleting the oxygen supply by cutting the forest.

Over time this criticism of Ludwig subsided. Ludwig's young forests, it turned out, produce more oxygen than old, decaying jungle. And compared to the cattle ranches in the south of Para or the burn-for-profit ventures of Big Al and his kind, Jari was a godsend. The few environmentalists who were invited to Jari walked away impressed; their articles revealed an admiration for the sheer energy of Jari.

"I remember how excited the Old Man used to be," said a long-time employee who accompanied him on regular tours of Jari. Five or six times a year Ludwig would book three seats across in economy class on a commercial airline, order milk and vodka on the rocks, and fly to Belem. There he would pace in the airport, his mind alive with ideas for the project as he impatiently waited for dawn. Accompanying whatever workers of his happened to be in Belem at the time, he would board one of his 12 planes and fly 250 miles northwest to Jari. En route he would interrogate his employees, seeking information about the project, what they were doing and how they thought the project could be improved. Without resting, he would commandeer the car waiting at the airport and set out to view his domain.

"I was riding with him, and we saw a line of 20 mules lying down. He said to me, 'Look how fat they are. They must not do any work. Whose mules are they anyway?' I told him they were his. So he said, 'Well, goddammit, get them up and get some work out of them.'"

His mania was contagious. Johan Zweede, the tall and handsome Indonesia-born American director of forestry operations, recalled: "We used to work 20 hours a day, 7 days a week. Remember there was nothing here. We had to build a town with all that entailed, bring in machinery, men, you name it. Then we could talk about the forests. And for Mr. Ludwig, of course, it all had to be done yesterday." The deliberate pace of forestry research, the patient years it takes, was not congenial to Ludwig's temperament and not realistic at his age. He was always trying to outrace his own mortality. "We couldn't exactly go to North Carolina State and say 'How do you harvest trees in the jungle?' and wait a few decades for a study. We had to do it. Great if we succeeded. Try again, if we failed." Zweede had seen all the failures. He had worked here since the beginning, and now approached middle age. He took off his glasses to rub his eyes, and called for a driver to take us to Ludwig's industrial complex.

Jari's power plant and pulp mill were the edifices that had signaled the end of the experimental tree-growing stage and the beginning of business operations at Jari. In spite of his secrecy up to that point in 1979, there was no way Ludwig could cut a low profile for these two 66-million-pound, 17-story factories: each was shipped, fully built, to Jari from Kure, Japan, a 3-month journey of more than 15,000 miles. The sight of the buildings on barges had been bizarre, like a modern city cast adrift. The factories lent themselves to metaphor for what was happening to the jungle: the machine was coming to the garden.

The construction, transportation and mounting of the $269 million pulp mill and power plant created a new perspective for industrialization in inaccessible places. The method has been copied a dozen times since Ludwig's breakthrough—for petrochemical plants, power plants and hotels.

The buildings were maneuvered into a holding lagoon whose entrance was shut off and the water level raised. They were then floated onto 3,700 cigar-butt pilings cut from rot-resistant massaranduba wood, sinking into place as the dike was opened and the water returned to its original level. The placement was so accurate that joint connections between the plant and the in-place machinery at the site were never off by more than 0.37 inch. Business operations started at the first melinas that Ludwig's foresters had meticulously nurtured and cared for were cut, mashed and spit out as pulp—at the rate of 4,000 tons of wood a day.

Ludwig's men ran the mill from spanking-clean air-conditioned control rooms that looked to us like the insides of a space shuttle. A new record of 911 tons of pulp produced in one day was set while we were there. The daily average was 750 tons, which emerged in a cool warehouse as 3-foot white cubes labeled "Jaripulp" in green letters. The guts of the mill itself overwhelmed us with the odor of rotten eggs, the deafening noise of machinery, the cruel heat of power to drive the plant. We knew it was much like any mill—except for where it was. The pulp mill and adjacent power plant were a quantum leap ahead of any attempt at industry we yet had seen. Only Tucurui, backed by a determined government, could match what one man had brought to the Amazon.

"If it's development Brazil wanted, this is it," Zweede had told us.

Next to the plants were the gratefully quiet and air-conditioned headquarters of the pulp operation. There we spoke with Cecil Mac-Donald, the taciturn Scotsman who was director of the mill. He had a way of wrapping things up with such considered brevity that it was as though he was reading the virtues of his mill off a list.

"We have the basic ingredients here for a world-class diversified paper operation," MacDonald said. "First, we are independent of oil as a fuel. The power plant runs almost entirely on the trees which we don't use for pulp. The savings between this method and oil burners in 1980 was $28 million.

"Second, the melina gives us a first-class short fiber and the pine a first-class long fiber. And third, we have a first-class transportation system and access to world markets."

If that left us spinning, there was more to come: the port, freight trains, pipelines, rice paddies and the kaolin mine.

The fine, white clay of the kaolin mine rose like a glacier against the verdant jungle. Ludwig has claimed that the discovery of this third-largest mine in the world—after ones in Georgia and Corn-wall, England—was a serendipity. Its quantity—enough for 200 years of production—and quality are almost unparalleled. But what really made the kaolin find a bonanza was that it is so accessible. It was discovered along the river bank, practically under the project's exit sign. An easily built pipeline connects the mine to a $25 million processing plant next to a large silvery lake of kaolin residue across from the pulp mill. From its inception this was a money-making operation. The processed clay, destined to coat porcelain and paper with a fine gloss or, in the form of kaopectate, to soothe the bowels of those suffering from diarrhea, is loaded into freighters at the port of Munguba, where Jari pulp also begins its journey out into the world. We could walk to the port; it was just beyond the mill. A Russian freighter was taking on a load of pulp—no visitors allowed. Across the Jari River from the factories we could see the stilt town of Beiradinho, a traditional jungle river town that had grown up there naturally, without the hand of Ludwig. Children aboard dugout canoes were amusing themselves by banging into the mammoth freighters lined up along the port, jungle kids in playful combat with invaders from the future.

Or at least we thought we were seeing the future of the Amazon. As we rode back to the guesthouse in Monte Dourado, the major town and all built from the wood at Jari, we discovered that we each shared some disappointment in what we had seen. Jari seemed so normal. The pine forests were settled, civilized. We might have seen the mill in America or Europe. A freight train carrying melina trunks ran alongside our Volkswagen van. We missed the raw excitement of Serra Pelada, the towering drama of the Tucurui dam. But the mere idea that we'd consider a 33-kilometer railroad or a 17-story pulp mill to be normal was itself extraordinary. No one—no company, not even the government—had managed to create an integrated, permanent development as Ludwig had. Was this what the Amazon would be like everywhere one day?

We flew from Monte Dourado to Sao Raimundo, another of Ludwig's towns along the Amazon River, to discover another dimension of the project. Here was a pastoral Amazon, emerald with rice paddies, whose rich grain was to feed a hungry world—as Ludwig saw it.

Ludwig's initial idea was to grow rice to support the Jari employees, but he soon became convinced that the Amazon could supply the world. He began to consider his initial view of Jari too simplistic and narrow. It could be much, much more than a tree plantation, he told his colleagues. A long-time Jari employee explained, "It sounds like a cliché, but the Old Man thought the Amazon could become the breadbasket of the world. All the pieces were here—land, sun, rain and a 12-month growing season. It's just that no one had ever tried it before."

The varzea, the fertile land in the Amazon along the river which floods it with rich soil every year, was proving to be an effective growing area. Ludwig planned to grow rice on 45,000 acres, of which more than 10,000 acres had been planted, and they looked to us like the top of the world's largest billiard table. "The key is leveling the ground," explained Han Steenmeijer, another hardy Indonesian-born Dutchman, who had been with the rice operation since its beginning. "Rice has to be on flat land because it must be covered by some water, but not too much." Leveling equipment the size of large snowplows worked to grade new paddies day and night, guided by laser beams which created a perfectly straight line to follow. The equipment was run by Louisianans who spoke Portuguese so badly that the drivers of the machinery begged for Steenmeijer to translate the rich Southern accents.

When a field was properly prepared the results were startling. Almost overnight, Ludwig had devised a highly automated system of planting, fertilizing, and spraying the diked rice fields by air. Speed was essential, for two harvests had to be achieved in the six-month dry season, the only time the harvesting equipment could function. He even designed a floating dragline to dredge canals between the dikes; it consisted of a house mounted on a barge so that the operators could remain on it 24 hours.

"The rice came up very fast. You could almost hear it grow," said Steenmeijer. "We were getting four metric tons per hectare per harvest: that's eight tons a year. Elsewhere in the world four tons for the whole year would be considered very good."

To achieve such crop yields was not easy and not cheap. The first plantings were disastrous; there was a rare sulphur deficiency in the soil which hadn't been anticipated. Leveling alone cost $1,000 per hectare. The reliance on airplanes made the operation vulnerable to increases in oil prices. And it took experimentation with about 300 varieties of rice before the right variety was found.

"Time after time you'd think the Old Man would have quit," said Steenmeijer. But Ludwig kept coming back. He spent $7 million on a state-of-the-art rice mill, intended one day to handle the full harvest from the total number of planned acres, but now being used at only 30 percent capacity.

Thoughts of what might be grown here in the tropics, if only new crops were tried, must have haunted this man. He brought in agronomists from around the world, and spent $17 million on research for foods such as taro and soybeans that would grow well on the varzea. He even grew papyrus.

It seemed at times that all one of his small army of researchers had to do was tell Ludwig about a dream, and he would fund it. "It stopped being a business venture," Johan Zweede, the forester, told us. "It was more than that, much more than that."

When we made this visit to Jari, few journalists had been allowed to see it. We had done our homework. Combing articles, interviewing whoever would see us at Ludwig's headquarters in New York, we pieced together the skeleton of Ludwig's Amazon dream, though we could not flesh out the recondite character of the man himself. He had begun to slip the reins of caution in 1971, when William Wagner, Ludwig's administrative alter ego for 35 years, died. Wagner reportedly saw Jari as a toy for Ludwig to play with and was never convinced that it could become the technological breakthrough that Ludwig envisioned. Wagner's death brought a profound change to the way Ludwig did business. It reminded Ludwig of his own mortality, and it robbed him of the one force that contained his impetuosity.

With no one to keep him in check, Ludwig became obsessed with Jari. None of the major fortunes he had made interested him anymore. He wanted to win in the jungle. In 1974 the dismantling of his empire to raise cash for Jari began in earnest. His innovative salt evaporation plant in Baja, Mexico, the largest in the world, was sold to the Mitsubishi Corporation for $50 million. He sold one of his construction companies in 1974 for $10 million. In 1976 he sold half of his New South Wales coal interests to British Petroleum for $203 million. He sold his 10,000-acre orange plantation to the government of Panama, and when he wasn't paid his asking price, Ludwig called on his friends in government to delay the Panama Canal Treaty. In 1979 Tenneco paid $70 million for Ludwig's oil and gas properties in the western United States, and Christina Onassis bought his newest supertanker for about $30 million. He sold half of his chain of Princess resort hotels for $50 million.

One transaction above all bespoke Ludwig's devotion to and exposure at Jari. In 1976 he canceled orders for three supertankers, and in their stead he built the power plant and pulp mill for Jari. By doing so Ludwig repudiated the one most dependable source of his wealth to pay for his expensive habit. It was Ludwig who had invented the supertanker, and it was with the fortune he earned from that invention that he developed Jari.

We returned to Jari as the very fabric of Ludwig's dream was falling to shreds. The press obituaries of Jari colored the undertaking as a colossal failure. The man who spent over $1 billion in 14 years—about $180,000 per day, 7 days a week—was portrayed as an obsessed megalomaniac.

Only Jari's airport was busy. Salesmen were there to bargain for some of the 12 airplanes in Ludwig's fleet. Moving men were having a field day arranging for the complicated and expensive relocation of scores of personnel. Government officials were arriving to man the newly constructed tax office and the police headquarters; their confident gait conveyed the unmistakable impression that they felt they were rubbing their shoes in what was soon to be a Brazilian project.

We passed the rickety stilt city of Beiradinho across the river from the port. The playful combatants in their dugouts were not in sight. No one was. We drove straight to Monte Dourado to see Zweede, the director of forestry, and Howard King, the 22nd director of the whole project—and its last one. The office building where we had met with them before had burned down and no one planned to rebuild it. The recreation center also had burned down, and there were no more nightly movies. The insistent "Safe Driving" campaign so visible on our earlier visit was moot; there was barely any traffic on the roads. Acquaintances we asked about had moved on. On the desk in King's present office was an article called, "Can You Keep Demoralized People Motivated?" The moments to a showdown were ticking away during our visit. We joined the deathwatch over Jari.

The disease had been incubating a long time, but not in the fields, forests and mills that surrounded us. Those might have succeeded—only a few more crop rotations would tell whether the fertility of the land could be maintained—and Daniel Ludwig had been incomparably imaginative, innovative and flexible no matter what setbacks he had faced. But his extreme secrecy was his downfall, for it lost him the support of Brazil itself.

The first harbinger of trouble appeared in 1973 when President Medici visited the project, but Ludwig ignored the omen. President

Medici's visit provided the Brazilian press with its first report of the project and what stole the show was not the thriving homogeneous melina forest or impressive development but a sign held by workers which said, "We want our liberty." The nation's curiosity about the American's activities was piqued.

Feigning airplane trouble, a reporter from one of the country's leading newspapers, the *Journal do Brasil*, landed in Jari the following year and emerged with the first detailed account of life on Ludwig's land. One worker interviewed said, "Many die, bitten by snakes or of fever from pests, when there isn't a tree the size of a house falling on top of us." Another worker talked of malnourishment and of being under constant guard. The reporter intimated that the land was rich in gold, which was why the capital was called Monte Dourado.

"We should have opened the project to publicity right then," said Zweede. "But we were so busy with what we were doing, we just didn't think publicity was that important or inviting the press was a very high priority. People used to say this was a closed project, but it wasn't. We just didn't have time."

There was no company response to rumors, and the silence made Jari the Garbo of the Amazon. The Brazilian imagination ran riot, and the tales were so tantalizing that the project as a business venture became unimportant next to its symbolic evil.

The political problem took a serious turn for the worse when all land titles in the state of Para, where over half of Jari lies, were voided with a promise they would be quickly reissued. "In 1978, they told us they'd have the whole thing done in 60 days," Zweede said. "And they kept promising and promising." Years had passed, and still there was no reissue. Without title to the land, Ludwig was no more than an elephantine posseiro, ineligible for myriad government programs including subsidies for houses, schools and road maintenance. He had built almost 300 miles of heavy-duty road for 30-ton trucks and 2,500 miles of roads that could tolerate 7-ton trucks. Their maintenance in the rough climate was a significant part of the $5.5 million annual bill for infrastructure.

The infrastructure cost was especially intolerable, because the project it was meant to service never was realized. As fantastic an accomplishment as Jari was, it was only half of what it was supposed to be. "Mr. Ludwig spent $75 million for infrastructure for a project we never became," Zweede said. "We were a penthouse without the apartment building."

Howard King told us about the Old Man's unrealized plans. "They staggered the imagination," King said. "He was going to spend at least another $700 million, and he wanted to do it by himself." Ludwig wanted to double the capacity of the pulp mill. There were accompanying plans to double the size of the plantations to 500,000 acres. The sawmill capacity also was to be doubled because, according to King, "there are hundreds of exotic woods we could market, but it would take a long-term effort to teach people about them." There were plans for a newsprint plant and finished kraft paper plant. And Ludwig was planning to mine extensive bauxite reserves also discovered on the property. The roads were to have been for these gigantic enterprises, and not merely for the cool pine woods and bright green paddies that lay around us.

To power all the new machinery Ludwig wanted to build a dam, and in 1978 he began to seek government approval. It was a time of great change in Brazil, the beginning of the *abertura*, the gradual opening of the political process by the military. The Brazilian press, which Ludwig had treated like a communicable disease, was to assume an important role in abertura, and the hundreds of bureaucrats, whose heads he had gone over, were getting expanded powers in the move toward democracy. These politicians were becoming aware of the public opinion Ludwig had chosen to ignore since his arrival in 1967. The Jari executives and Ludwig himself seemed not to perceive the meaning of the changes, or were blind to them.

In retrospect, King pinpointed the dam permission process as the handwriting on the wall that eventually read "Yankee Go Home." The request got caught up in an administrative haggle between the World Bank, which Ludwig had gone to for funding, and the Brazilian government. Finger-pointing ensued on both sides, and Ludwig finally got the message; no one thought it was wise to come to his rescue amid the floodtide of rising hostility.

"But it wasn't only the government," King went on, resting his gentle face on calloused hands. "We beat ourselves, too. This was always a pioneering project, but we never looked at it as an operation. It was always an expanding construction camp, getting bigger and bigger without shape." Ludwig was becoming surrounded by a plethora of yes-men.

King was hired in late 1979 to pare down the operation while Ludwig contemplated whether he would continue to support it. As director of one of Anaconda's copper facilities in Iran during the overthrow of the Shah, King had learned what it was like to have a billion-dollar investment blow away in the winds of political change.

Although we never met Ludwig (he has granted only two interviews in his life) we imagined King's open and friendly style to be quite different from the no-nonsense approach of his boss.

"I had never heard of Mr. Ludwig before he hired me," King reminisced. "He kept calling me, and I kept avoiding his calls. I thought he was part of a German mining group that I once had a falling out with. Finally, he caught me one Friday as I was leaving the office, and I immediately realized he was an American and someone who didn't waste any time. The next day a chauffeured limousine picked me up and brought me to his Beverly Hills house, and he made me an offer I couldn't refuse."

As impatient as he was publicity shy, Ludwig fired more than 20 project directors before he hired King. One lasted only three days; the jungle apparently confirmed his worst fears, and he fled. But the principal reason the directors were removed so frequently was Ludwig's style.

He was in a hurry, and a director's hurt feelings were irrelevant to his plans. "He'd come down from New York and take the construction chief out and say, 'I want the railroad to go through here.' Then he'd get on the plane and go home without ever seeing the director," King said.

As Ludwig grew restless and fired project directors, administrative problems worsened. Although Jari's finances were a closely guarded secret we knew that the year King was hired operating costs, construction and debt service far exceeded any revenues. Though he hadn't gotten into Jari for the money, Ludwig, suffering from a painful back ailment and bitter at the failures, was tired of treating his project like a spoiled child who continued to get into trouble. King's orders were to make the operation profitable if at all possible. "When I came here," King said, "people were taking the company pickups to go on family picnics. People were taking the planes all over, just to visit grandma in Belem. When I came here they all crawled under a rock and figured I'd be gone in four or five months, just like the others.

"I told my personnel director to stop the waste. He said he couldn't do that, no one would listen to him. I told him to fire somebody, and he said you can't do that in Brazil. So I fired *him*."

By 1980 King had improved the picture by extreme austerity measures: revenues were $90 million, costs $94 million. The number of full-time employees was at a peak of 6,656 in August, when the final chapter of Jari began.

Ludwig wrote a 17-page letter to his close friend, General Golbery Couto e Silva, a one-man shadow government and adviser to presidents for most of the 1970s, telling him that Jari needed help. Specifically, he asked Brazil to bear the infrastructure burden, legitimate aid he had been denied when the government refused to reissue title to most of his land. The land titles had still not come through. Ludwig thought it unfair that he should have to provide schools, hospitals, housing, and roads for 35,000 Brazilians, the population of Jari, without any government help.

"The press said Mr. Ludwig was looking for a handout in his letter," King explained, "but all he was asking was to be treated just like everybody else. The letter was just a plea to the government—get your fingers off our throat and let us breathe, and we'll run a good project for you in the Amazon." The Brazilian press took it as a take-me-or-I'll-leave-you ultimatum.

In response to the letter, the government assigned a group from the National Security Council to look into Ludwig's complaints. The head of the committee was an ardent Brazilian nationalist. He never called any meetings between his group and Jari officials. In January, 1981, when the first of the twice-yearly $17 million payments on the factories' loan was due, Ludwig was promised that he would have clear land titles by June. When June passed, Ludwig felt that his bluff had been called, and he decided to call one of his own. He would put Jari up for sale. He set a deadline for January 1, 1982. If he couldn't sell the project by that date he would take a walk, leaving behind 35,000 people who directly or indirectly depended on his payroll and a $180 million obligation to Japan, which had been guaranteed by the Brazilian Development Bank.

We stayed close to King during days of negotiations. He was

candid with us, because he believed that Ludwig would soon be out of the picture—either by selling the property or abandoning it.

The key figure on Brazil's end of the negotiating table was Antonio Delfim Netto. The roly-poly, owlish Planning Minister of Brazil had put the disposition of the Jari project on the top of his agenda. Rather, it was put there for him.

On a fundraising trip to West Germany for the Carajas mining project, Delfim was asked, "What about Jari?" by the chairman of the Deutsche Bank. He didn't have a good answer, and he needed one. International bankers considered Ludwig a deity, and they were upset about the treatment he had received. Rules had been changed in the middle of the game, they felt, and Ludwig was maltreated after he had maximized his exposure. Excuses of domestic politics or nationalism are very tenuous in international banking circles where a country's idiosyncrasies are supposed to stay out of business affairs. The head of the Deutsche Bank wanted to know what assurance Delfim could offer that the next foreign investor wouldn't share Ludwig's fate. Because Delfim was trying to raise billions in foreign investment for the Carajas project, he felt it important to answer the question.

Upon returning to Brazil he called upon the moguls of Brazilian industry and told them to buy Jari.

"How could he order them to do it?" we asked King as he discussed the latest rumor of a sale.

"He can't order them," King responded. "But there's an old expression in the army: I can't make you do it, but I sure as hell can make you wish you had."

Jari was finally sold to a consortium of Brazilian enterprises. Twenty-two of the country's largest companies each contributed $2.7 million, and Ludwig's close friend Augusto Azevedo Antunes contributed $40 million by handing over the kaolin operation, which Ludwig previously had sold to him. The Bank of Brazil assumed the $180 million foreign debt of the company in exchange for 25 percent of the forestry operation. The other $160 million in debt was assumed by the 22 companies and Antunes.

One of the new owners of the project claimed he invested as "a service to the nation." Another said he signed on "out of obligation." An interview reported his words: "The government thinks it's necessary that I have to do it, and so I'll do it. I didn't spend ten seconds reading the proposal. I accepted and that was that." Other than Antunes, not one of the new owners publicly expressed any interest in the development of Jari. As King had predicted, they had done what they were told to do.

Ludwig walked away from his great achievements with his pockets empty. He had invested $863 million in the project, which at 1981 prices amounted to $1.15 billion. He will receive five percent of any dividends from the forestry operation starting in 1987, then four percent in 1997 and three percent from 2007 until the contract's termination in 2021. Ironically, the money, if any, will not go to him but to a Swiss-based cancer research institute that Ludwig endowed in 1974. Even that gift, however, raised a chorus of catcalls in Brazil. Ludwig was reminded that Brazil, too, had cancer institutes. In response, Ludwig donated his royalties from bauxite reserves to a Brazilian cancer foundation. "He's a man who wants to do it all himself, call all the shots, and then he'll give you the whole thing," King said.

King suggested that before we leave we visit one of the agriculture communities which had been built. A driver took us halfway across the tree plantations and we came to a fence with a bleary-eyed guard at the gate. The community—houses, roads, garden plots —had cost $4 million to build. Plantation workers were to live there, and their wives were to grow food for the community on the plots. The houses were empty. Vines grew through the windows. Tall weeds sprouted from the garden plots. We asked if we could enter this ghost town, and the guard shook his head.

Ludwig's vision was to bring people to the jungle to learn how to sustain themselves there, and to provide for the needs of others. He was not afraid of failure, its costs or the challenges it created. He just wanted to be left alone to stare face to face for the last time with something commensurate with his capacity to wonder. But even here, in one of the most remote parts of the earth, he found that was impossible.

Still King didn't doubt that the project would survive under the new management, but its potential may have been reached, its vision finally capped. For Ludwig, his race against time was over. His dream had died before him.

SANTAREM

We stayed at two hotels in Santarem, and they gave very different perceptions of the city that is the center of commerce along the main river, about halfway between the jungle metropolises of Belem and Manaus, and where the blue Tapajos empties its crystal water into the brown of the Amazon. The Tropical Hotel is a monument to foolishness, a brazen and unsuccessful attempt to invade the jungle with an alien culture and technology. The hotel belongs in Houston, sandwiched between a fast-food stand and a freeway exit ramp. It was built by Varig, the national airline, reportedly so that the President of Brazil would have a grand place to stay when he inaugurated the Cuiaba–Santarem Highway, the road that begins to the south at

Cuiaba's cavernous bus station, runs north past Karlheinz's house and through Sinop, and dead-ends here in Santarem.

The Tropical is about the size and shape of a large drive-in movie screen with terraces. It rises out of the cleared jungle as if it had emerged from a more advanced civilization existing under the soil. It blends with nothing else and its height is very prominent, which must be important, for room prices vary according to the floor although all floors have the same unobstructed view of a blue swimming pool without swimmers, monkey cages without monkeys and a jungle without trees. Dead bugs littered the floor of our room. Unopened, foul-smelling milk cartons sat on the desk among small bottles of whiskey. The cinema downstairs had opened and failed, as had the shopping mall. The night club was boarded shut. Most of the hotel rooms were empty anyway.

The other hotel was the Palace, a clean two-story inn near the center of the city. It looked as congruous there as the Tropical looked weird. From our room was the view of the tropical city we had expected to see from the start of the trip. Long, lazy palm trees bent easily in the breeze. Below them were red clay tiled roofs on newly white-washed buildings which turned pink as the sun set. The brick streets of Santarem are narrow, and they run to the river. In the distance we could see the two rivers meet, the blue and brown waters running side by side and not mixing. When the Amazon's tide rolls in from the estuary 400 miles to the east it beats back the blue Tapajos to the shores of the city, and later the Tapajos rolls out, removing the sight of the chocolate waters from the city's eye.

Sunset is a special time in Santarem, and the civic rhythm defers to the dusk hour. The day starts early but peters out at noon for a break so long that afternoons felt to us like morning starting over. Cabdrivers, unwilling or unable to go home, recline in their seats at the sun's highest hour and snooze. When afternoon work begins, it has a special earnestness and direction. Activities are focused at the cargo docks on the outskirts of town, a busy port with heavy concrete wharves and steel cranes. Santarem is the hub for 200 miles in each direction of the Amazon as well as down the Tapajos and up the Trombetas. The riverines depend on the river's traffic for Coca Cola, cars, beer, spare parts, newspapers, and a market for their produce. With this at stake, the mien of commerce at the cargo area is as serious as anywhere in the region. Everything must be ready by sun-down. All boats depart at nightfall in order to avoid the equatorial sun.

There is a seriousness, too, at the wharf where the passengers embark, but it is tempered by human emotions. Lives are in transit. From 3 P.M. on, a steady stream of people and boxes stops at the crumbling concrete retaining wall overlooking the river. Pickup trucks and vans stop to drop off overstuffed boxes of foam rubber, empty soda bottles, and toilet paper. Hustling, barefoot teenage boys whisk away the cartons and confidently descend the narrow steps to the splintery wood planks embedded in wet mud. Tiptoeing across the mud, boxes piled on their shoulders, they shout for someone on the boat to meet them. The boxes are thrown on deck then stowed below by a bucket brigade of sweating men. The passengers stand in an orderly line. As the sun sinks over the river, its amber glare lights up the queue, and people duck their heads or squint in order to avoid the brilliance. But the sun's color and strength sets them aglow as if they had been painted with radium. Boyfriends and girlfriends hug, rela-tives kiss each other on both cheeks, and traveling businessmen go over last minute instructions with their Santarem contacts.

We watched this scene from the Bar Moscote, an open patio of tables on one side of the town square and across the road from the retaining wall. The waiter unfurled a worn but clean tablecloth for us and brought beers. He shooed away the pack of eager shoeshine boys who mischievously returned whenever he went inside.

We both were wearing sneakers, so there was no work for them, but we figured out another way to compensate them. We had a trivia contest, and the four waifs shone with their knowledge of famous Brazilians and Brazilian geography. One even knew the name of our space shuttle Columbia. We wondered how these kids knew so much. We watched them work untiringly around the patio and noticed their incessant chatter with customers, and their refusal to be shooed away from their livelihood.

It grew dark, and kids their age should have been home and not hanging around a bar on the Amazon River. But like the settlers along BR-364, this was the road they had been placed on, and they, too, were filled with resourcefulness. There was camaraderie among them—no one stole the others' customers—and there was ambition in each of them.

It was nice sitting by the dark, whooshing, restless river with a cool breeze making folds in our red tablecloth. We were in no hurry; here by the Amazon River was a momentary peace, and we felt entitled to do nothing but drink beer and muse.

Against the busy little boys we saw the image of the Tropical Hotel and wondered why Brazil's millions weren't spent on shoeshine boys. They would have made a greater monument to the country than garish hotels or wasted cattle ranches. We saw the unyielding force in Brasilia and the South to make this place like the rest of Brazil, even if it meant destruction. These little boys had no choice but to discover for themselves how to get by. Might cleverness, resiliency and patience prevail where brute force had failed?

Probably the greatest skeleton of the war against this land lies 25 miles south of Santarem, where Henry Ford once daydreamed of the renaissance of the Amazon rubber boom.

Nearly all the world's production of rubber once came from the Amazon, tapped by caboclos and Indians who roved the wild forest waiting for the milky sap of the native *Hevea brasiliansis* to flow into their tin buckets. But in 1910, trees stolen as seedlings from the Amazon 40 years earlier began to produce rubber in the Far East. The soil and climate suited them well; there were no natural pests. Unlike the Amazon, where rubber trees grow singly here and there throughout the jungle, these transplanted trees flourished in large plantations.

By 1923 the British–Dutch monopoly over Far East rubber was artificially manipulating supply and prices, driving industrialists like Ford to look elsewhere for their supplies. Brazil, hoping to find a way to regain its throne of rubber, apparently thought Ford, whose name was synonymous with Yankee ingenuity, was just the man to help them.

Ford was given nearly 2.5 million acres of land in the state of Para on the banks of the crystal blue Tapajos River about 125 miles south of its juncture with the Amazon at Santarem. Besides the free land, Ford was promised that all machinery and equipment could enter duty-free and that police protection would be provided. In return he promised to share 7 percent of his profits with the Para government after 12 years. The final agreement was signed in October, 1927.

There were problems from the beginning caused by the Americans' failure to understand that doing business in the Amazon was vastly different from any method that might have worked in Michigan. The first company town was logically called Fordlandia. Its houses were designed by Detroit architects who probably couldn't envision a land without snow. The sturdy cement structures, which epitomized 20th-century suburban America, were poorly ventilated sweat boxes in the Brazilian jungle. Native workers were taught by their American colleagues that silk stockings were the way to a woman's heart—no matter that the native women wore no shoes and the coveted stockings wore out quickly in the jungle mud. They couldn't speak English, but the local workers were asked to recite Longfellow and sing homey folk songs of Merrie England. They weren't allowed to drink alcohol, and didn't like Detroit-style cooking. The workers objected to paying rent—a strange concept to caboclos who built and owned their own houses—and they complained that West Indians brought in by Ford were taking their jobs.

There were horticultural as well as cultural problems. Ford's will and money notwithstanding, the rubber trees could not flourish in an orderly, plantation manner in this jungle. The openness of the layout robbed the trees of the shelter they needed from hard pelting rains, and in the dry season they baked in the tropical sun. They only grew rambunctiously among other species which could shelter them and whose positioning would prevent a rubber-loving pest—in Ford's case, a fungus called *microcycous uli*—from spreading tree to tree. The Fordlandia site also was hilly, and the rich topsoil, once cleared and unprotected by thick plant life, eroded.

In 1934 Ford traded 703,750 acres of Fordlandia for what he thought was better land 25 miles south of Santarem. He named this second company town Belterra. Ford sent researchers to the Far East for disease-resistant strains of trees which then were grafted onto the native varieties by an expensive procedure. Chemicals were introduced but had only limited success against leaf blight. By 1941 Belterra had 3,651,500 trees, and the initial production the following year was 750 tons of natural rubber. Yet, Ford could not shake the natural enemies of the trees and all his protective methods were expensive. The company had financial problems after World War II and these, coupled with the development of artificial rubber, prompted it to sell Fordlandia and Belterra to the Brazilian government in 1945 for $250,000. The company's investment had been over $20 million.

We went to visit Belterra in—how else?—a Ford, and we were forced to think about rubber tires the whole way. Each time the driver took the car to 60 kilometers, its balding and uneven wheels made it shimmy with the fury of a blender. For some reason, the teenage driver thought that extra speed would quell the trembling, but that solution only brought us into frightening half, three-quarter and full-circle turns. It offended his machismo to have to change the worst tire—the rear left wheel, shiny as a bald man's head. We inspected it after every automotive acrobatic, pleaded with him to mount the spare and cursed him when he refused with a sullen scowl. It was not until the front end of the car whacked a scrawny tree alongside the rocky red dirt road that he consented to change tires. Unfortunately, the replacement was none too tready itself, and the fish-tailing drive took over an hour.

The entrance to Belterra was magnificent enough to make us forget about man-made foibles. The rubber trees that Ford tried so hard to tame and nurture lined the long, winding drive in neat ranks as far back as we could see. They were graceful specimens, the bark an ashen shade, background for perky yellow flowers and pregnant green pods. Near their bases were the angled slashes of rubber gatherers whose knives scar the trunks to let the milky sap run. Young boys on wobbly bicycles had narrow wood poles spread across their necks, metal wash buckets dangling from both ends. They stopped to empty cups of sap belted to the trees into their yoked buckets. Speckled pastel butterflies swarmed in our path, rising and dropping in clouds, then separating in a fluttering natural ticker-tape parade.

We emerged from the rubber forest to find an eerily undisturbed vision of America in the 1930s. It was as if the residents of Henry Aldrich's town had all fled, leaving the place and spirit behind. Paint had chipped and screens had torn and weeds were clinging to buildings. Small bungalows, evenly spaced, lined the dusty, rutted main street with a precision foreign to the Amazon. They had white picket fences before them, neatly squared front lawns, shaded porches and carports. One lesson had been half learned: these were not the cement sweat boxes of Fordlandia, but a compromise between New England quaint and tropical exigencies. Sidewalks outlined the road and ran in front of the houses; the dirt road itself had washed away during 50 years of relentless rains, but those sidewalks were still ruler straight and sturdy sitting atop the soil. Occasionally a rusted red fire hydrant, bearing the marks of Michigan manufacture, sprouted from the earth, the pipe below its apron exposed by erosion. Yet, even the passing of a half century had not altered native predilections, and it was rare to see a pedestrian on the sidewalks; people preferred the jungle dirt road.

After a half mile of identical bungalows, the road burst open on one side to a village green, a wide expanse of scrub jolted by the presence of the gazebo in its midst, the type from which bands play to welcome home war-weary soldiers or mark the Fourth of July in Sousa tempo. Around the green were rambling white clapboard houses. The Judge would have lived here in Henry Aldrich's ordered world. Sheltered garages stood behind the houses, but not a one was occupied. The scene was watched over by an imposing church done in Art Deco curves of concrete.

"Everything. He built everything. So long ago." This was the refrain of our local guide Nicolas Costa, who flagged us down as we entered the town. Costa was born in Belterra in 1936 and claimed to be the only remaining native son. His adoration of Ford was such that he called him "God." The other locals we met told us that Costa's mind, like the rubber trees, baked easily in the hot sun.

Costa took us to the large school building: 12 pink rooms with green trim, one for each grade. In the dark, musty auditorium he showed us the uneven stage and recalled his role as a rubber tree in a seventh-grade play.

Costa, sitting in the back of the taxi with Kelly, was so enthusiastic on the drive that the brim of his green baseball hat nearly touched the windshield as he leaned his lined, weathered face forward. He barked names into London's ear, Americans he could remember: Charles Tons, Gruter, Snall, Rubis—a badly pronounced list of alien beings he once had known. "Pringle," he added to the roster. This one caught our attention, because we had read that the folk hero of Belterra was Curtis Pringle, a sheriff from Kalamazoo who, as a town manager, tempered the Americans' Calvinism and deferred to native customs in planning meals, houses and entertainment.

The executives' homes were remarkably similar to those at Jari, large tropical houses with so many angles and screens it was difficult to figure out which was the entrance, but easy to see that native know-how had contributed to the architecture. They stood together in the shaded, obviously more affluent area near the hospital. As usual, the hospital was crowded that day. The taxi driver told us that he frequently came to Belterra, because its hospital still was said to be the best in that area of the Amazon. Like the school, it was a large ranch house building with a shaded porch where the waiting patients huddled away from the hot sun.

"Everything. He built everything. So long ago," Costa exclaimed again as we passed the sawmill on the way to the pumping station. The sawmill had been neglected, and it was overgrown with weeds, the metal coarsely rusted. Once it was the scene of a titanic struggle between Ford and the jungle which sent forth hardwood trees so tough the best steel Ford's mills could make gnashed and bent against them. The faster the saws ran, the faster they broke down.

The road sloped down toward the blue Tapajos, sporadically visible through the trees, and it ended at a weathered shack that housed the well-greased chortling water pumps from the Square D Company of Detroit, Michigan. Costa still expressed astonishment that Ford was able to send water from the banks of the river 10 kilometers uphill in something other than pails. For feats like these he merited the sobriquet "God."

The Belterra tour ended, appropriately enough, at the cemetery. Costa wanted us to see his father's grave, the second ever at Belterra, and that of Johnny Morrison, who, Costa claimed, was the only American buried there. Out of respect for Costa and any Morrison family that exists we inspected each small white wooden cross, about 400 of them, under the hellish sun, sometimes dawdling for a minute at a site to try to read the name under the erosion of time and chipped paint. The dates of death ran in clumps, many, for example, in the fall of 1942, suggesting that epidemics occasionally visited the area. Costa's father had a heart attack one morning as his son was leaving for school. The act that sent Mr. Costa into the soil was pantomimed for us by his son, who grabbed his chest and keeled over, banging his head against his father's name on the cross. We never did find Johnny Morrison.

The way trees want to grow and the way governments and corporations insist they grow often are in conflict. Ford, for all his money and power, was not successful in forcing rubber trees to behave like a tame plantation of maples in Vermont. The question of whether plantations of any tree species can survive in the Amazon is dealt with at the government's Wood Technology Center in Santarem.

We had heard a great deal about this branch of SUDAM. When government officials in Brasilia say they want to hold off on making decisions about Amazon policy until the facts are complete, this is one of the places they expect those facts to come from. Skaff, on behalf of his SUDAM bosses, had touted the center as "a magnificent example of Brazilian research." From the ghost-townlike atmosphere, we immediately sensed the familiar prideful exaggeration.

"Please, make yourselves comfortable. I have much to explain," Cesar Augusto Carneiro said to us as he patted two deep chairs in the center of what he called "the main laboratory." It looked like a high school science classroom with slate-top counters lined with beakers and Bunsen burners, neater than a classroom, though, with most of the equipment clean and out of the way. Cesar was alone and it was quiet in the lab, except for a ticking clock and the low hum of a metal box that he said was "cooking" a piece of wood.

"We have studies that have been under way here for many years," said Carneiro. "We have a monoculture forest—like Jari— that has been going on for 22 years with 100 native species and 40 foreign species. We'll know what trees can stand to grow next to each other in only 13 more years."

One of Carneiro's biggest tasks is just to catalog the trees and develop a list of their characteristics. He had identified 800 tree species and guessed that there were that many more to be found. "Our studies have not been so detailed as to know much about these trees. We work slowly."

The major reason for slow work is that trees grow slowly. But another reason is Carneiro's staff: nine forest engineers. "We need, maybe, 20. No one new has been hired since 1971," he said in a plaintive voice. "They always tell us we are important, except when we ask for money. Then they tell us we don't count."

Down the river bank from the lab was an open-sided barn of a building. A whining sound came out of it, and busy men walked in and out.

"This is our sawmill school," Carneiro said as we approached. "We teach workers how to cut the most lumber from a log, how to clean a saw and how to sharpen a blade."

The barn was surrounded with piles of sawdust, smooth boards and broken mistakes. Mounds of fat logs were stacked waiting at the entrance. Inside men worked over a whining bandsaw while others drew long sparks from the angled teeth of another blade they were sharpening.

"Companies which are cutting the jungle send us their workers from all over the Amazon. We do a good job." The sawmill, he said, more than paid for itself since it charged tuition and sold the wood. Carneiro said there were plans to expand it; in fact, there were plans to expand the whole center.

Carneiro riffled through stacks of plans for a new Wood Technology Center. The architect's drawings in colored pencil depicted an expansive, campuslike setting for the center. We asked where it would be built.

"Right here. It's already going up." Carneiro beamed. This puzzled us. We had noticed only the slightly lopsided shed the lab was in and a few dormitories, a setting more like summer camp in the off season than research park.

"There and there and there." Carneiro pointed to two half-dug foundations; a third site had a completed concrete base and rising from it a set of concrete pillars, still wearing a mold of weathered timber. There were no workmen.

"Work stopped for a while . . . oh, about a year ago. The money has stopped. But it will start again, I am sure."

Against the background of the highly touted but largely ignored Wood Technology Center, where the work takes too long for many government planners, we went to see the Trombetas bauxite project, where success has not had to wait on patient research. The Trombetas project is based on a very simple concept: find one of the largest bauxite deposits in the world; clear the jungle; dig massive open pits to extract the mineral that begins to appear at a depth of 12 feet; crunch up the dirt; put it in a train to take it 30 kilometers through the jungle; wash it; dry it; send it on a conveyor belt into a ship and deposit the proceeds in the bank. The project is owned by a multinational joint venture of firms from Brazil, Canada, Holland, the United States, Norway, and Spain. The bauxite reserves—600 million tons—were discovered in 1964. The consortium was formed in 1974; construction began in April, 1976, and was finished in August, 1979, at a cost of $400 million. Trombetas was the first Amazon industrial project to have been finished and making money, earning desperately needed foreign currency.

The plane that shuttles engineers, technicians and executives back and forth between Santarem and Trombetas flew us over low green land. Every imaginable shade of green was visible in the low-lying pastures, swamps and forests, from the pale shade of hospital walls to the artificial coloring in plastic St. Patrick's Day hats. The long indolent river went wherever it liked, cutting three channels in some places, 20 in others. At Santarem it was about four miles wide; 15 minutes later at the town of Obidos it was less than a half mile.

We could easily tell when we were approaching Trombetas: the jungle started turning red. In the distance we could see a plume of red smoke, and its residue tainted trees for miles around. The incongruous smokestack coughed red smoke in the process of cleaning bauxite, a red metallic ore. It painted the jungle, dressed it up with a thick coat of rouge. Mauricio Schettino, the director of the project, lunched with us at the Trombetas guesthouse, an American-style roadside motel. We wanted to speak Portuguese with him, but he insisted on English even though he said he spoke it "like a dumb Indian."

"I come here in 1978 to take over the start-up of the project. I work before in steel mill and road construction. Nobody here really knows bauxite in big mines. Brazil has only two small mines before operation of this. This is the first on scale industrial." Schettino spoke slowly and ungrammatically. His wife told him he sounded foolish and should speak Portuguese, but he told her he was a cosmopolitan man.

"The special problems are supply—bring here spare parts, foods, and medicines," Schettino continued. The project often had to shut down after it opened because of the 16-day delay for getting parts. The problem had ameliorated, however, as management learned more about the operation and was able to compile maximum–minimum parts lists.

"Other problem is you need to import manpower. In the state of Para it is not traditional industrial. Now in big numbers you have 12 percent of our people from the south, 18 percent from north and 70 percent from micro-region here." Schettino said the workers from outside the region were the skilled technicians who he said were taking advantage of "a good chance for technical development. I believe in Brazil the new business where there is the most opportunity is aluminum. It is not very difficult to bring people here. Young people want the opportunity. The pay is 20 percent more than in the south and they get free houses, longer vacations, free tickets to return home, free electricity and water."

The local employees puzzled him, however. "There is a high turnover for local people. You try to understand this, but you detect some points. They want houses, they want hospital, they want school, they want relax. And they don't believe so much in money. They believe in exchange. They have no tradition in money. They don't know what they are going to do with the money."

The project has been so successful, he said, that the corporation decided to expand the annual output from 4 million tons to 8 million tons by 1986. The expansion will cost an additional $400 million, and the work force will be expanded from 1,500 to 2,200 workers, increasing Trombetas' population from 6,000 to a total of 10,000.

We heard the loading of the bauxite throughout the night, incessant sounds of rocks hitting rocks, drowning out the insects that had sung uninterrupted for millennia. In the morning, we wended our way to the port area to visit the enormous 37,000-ton ore-carrier *Benvorlich* from Liverpool, England, whose breadth took up nearly a quarter of the narrow Trombetas River.

Captain Donald Macintosh, decked out in finely pressed white Bermuda shorts and a braided captain's shirt, was upset with the native pace. "We should have taken on the dirt at 4,100 tons per hour, but we're going at 1,200 tons per hour instead," he complained as we stood on the bridge and watched the holds being filled. The slow ways of the Amazon meant the *Benvorlich* wouldn't be loaded until 2 P.M. "We're going to have to anchor for the night because the pilot won't navigate the Trombetas River in the dark." Another concession—and a wise one.

We asked him what it was like to navigate the Amazon.

"A bit hair-raising for the first time, really. There is some difficulty in figuring out the mouth of the river when a third of the buoys are gone and a third are without lights. Fortunately, the rest are accurate." About 100 kilometers into the river from Belem the ship picks up a pilot boat that guides it for the next 1,000 kilometers up the Amazon on its way to Trombetas.

"It's quite easy after the mouth," he said, "although you do find that some of the chaps in small boats like to play a game of chicken with you and they cut in front of you to see if you'll turn away."

"Do you?"

The captain looked at us sternly. "Of course not. We're bigger than they are."

Captain Macintosh was disgusted at what the air was doing to his ship, and he compulsively took out his handkerchief to wipe the polished wood railing. "We just came from Norway," he said. "It was 20 below there, but we didn't have a problem with all this dust." His next port of call was Mobile, Alabama, where he was going to unload, then proceed to New Orleans to take on a cargo of coal for shipment to Spain. He was comfortable in many cultures, but the Amazon was strange to him.

He took us on a tour of the spacious, air-conditioned officers' quarters and introduced us to some of the Chinese crew. We invited him to have dinner with us, but he declined, saying he'd stay on board and read a book. "I've already seen all the jungle I wish to see," he said, wiping his brow with the red-stained handkerchief.

The Bar Moscote in Santarem was nearly empty. The waiter told us that was because "Dallas" was on television, and Brazil is a country enamored of soap operas. We thought he was kidding, but Kelly went to check and managed a glimpse into a living room where J.R. was talking sharply in Portuguese.

A lonely man at the next table asked if we were Americans, and we said we were. He ordered a scotch and Coca-Cola and ignored us.

"I am not Brazilian," he wanted us to know about five minutes later. "No, I am from Spain." He said it in Spanish, without asking us if we could speak that language.

"I was the maître d'hôtel at the Hilton in Madrid in the 1960s when we had the banquet for Faisal, the greatest banquet the world has ever seen," he continued without prompting.

It was an unusual introduction. Even the waiter, carrying a tray of french fries and beer, paused to eavesdrop.

"I stayed at that Hilton in 1964," London said.

"I was there."

"Then where did you go?"

"I went to the Hostal of the Catholic Regents in Santiago."

"I stayed there, too, in 1969," London said.

"I was there."

He had been in charge of the Tropical Hotel in Manaus where we were planning to stay in a few days.

"Where will you go next, just so I can plan my life," London asked.

The Spaniard appeared almost drunk. "All of us know where we were born, but none of us know where we will die."

His white tennis hat fell off, and as he bent over to pick it up he muttered, "*Que vida!*" What a life! He was about 50 years old with proof of hard living—watery eyes and untended graying whiskers. He wore long white shorts and a blue windbreaker, no shirt. He introduced himself: Enrique Blanco Gomez. He had been born in a town in northwest Spain that London knew well, and the two began to speak of restaurants and bus routes.

As Enrique realized that London knew this geography well, he hit his head in astonishment. "I love Garcia Lorca. Do you know him?" he asked.

London recited a poem of the Spanish poet, and Enrique began to cry. "I don't believe it," he said. He paused and announced, "The Unfaithful Wife." He set his scotch and Coke on the table and slowly recited Lorca's poem, occasionally brushing away tears. He slapped

London on the back, not really out of enthusiasm as much as to see that this was real and not a mirage. He pulled his chair over to our table and ordered another round of drinks.

"How did you ever get here?" Kelly asked, pointing to the Amazon, which flowed steadily under the gaze of the moon.

Enrique rubbed his thumb and index finger together. He was in charge of the hotel and food purchases at the Trombetas bauxite mining project and had come to Santarem to buy supplies. As isolated as he was in the jungle, he said, it was worthwhile because of the money.

"What about women? Don't you get lonely?"

"Women are the blood of life," Enrique preached. "And I am married to a great one."

"Is she Spanish?"

"No, she is an Amazon Indian. You know what the blood of life is? It is a 50-year-old man from Spain who lives in the Amazon jungle and is married to an Amazon Indian—a semi-savage Indian who makes much fire—and who has a 3-year-old son in order to prove that her husband still functions. That is the blood of life."

He told us he wanted us to know of the greatest moment in his life. "You understand this, I can talk about this." It was the banquet for King Faisal. "It hurts me to talk about it," he said, pointing to his heart. "We had 2,500 people and five rooms and we roasted goats and the King was very, very happy.

"I have given banquets for Trudeau, for Giscard, for the prince who married in the summer, but the one for Faisal . . ."

His eyes began to well up again, and he blew his nose. He said, "You know," but stopped and shook his head.

"Yes," he said, but really to himself. Then he gave us a determined stare. "Yes, you must please put my name in your book because I have many friends, and I want them to know that the man who gave the greatest banquet ever—never was there one better than the banquet for Faisal, the world has never seen better—this man still breathes in the Amazon jungle."

AMAZON RIVER

There were many boats that make the trip from Santarem to Manaus, the so-called capital of the Amazon, and we were determined to choose the most pleasant. The full selection of river transportation was on display at the landing across from the Bar Moscote. Most were ragged wooden affairs, 40 or 50 feet long with a wheelhouse in the front, a flat empty deck in the middle, a cabin with a kitchen and toilet in the rear, and the whole covered with an oval-shaped roof. Passenger decks beneath the roofs were strung with thickets of colorful hammocks, their occupants jammed against each other like smoked sausages in a box for the three-day journey upriver. These lesser craft, each the sole property of a feisty river huckster, were referred to as *barcos*, boats. The *Sobral Santos II*, on the other hand, was known to everyone in town as a *navio*, a ship. The reference was always followed by a thumbs-up sign to indicate that it was worthy of our trade, and that was the way we chose to go. Jet planes fly between Santarem and Manaus, but river people prefer their riverine traditions. The *Sobral Santos* was a celebration of something they could understand and appreciate. It was the best.

Manaus, too, was the best, the Big City, as far as everyone in the interior of the Amazon was concerned. Originally a trading post founded by the early Portuguese explorers and eventually the world capital of the rubber boom at the turn of the century, the city is more than 300 years old. A whole culture in isolation from the rest of Brazil has grown up there, spreading downriver to the little villages that cling to the fertile flood plain. Manaus, at the intersection of the Amazon and Negro rivers, also marks the dividing line between the upper and lower Amazon. Below Manaus, incursions of man have beaten back the jungle; beyond Manaus nature dominates civilization.

"On Thursdays the *Sobral Santos* is at the cargo dock," we were told, and so it was, hard by the concrete wharf with muscular teenage boys shuttling full cases of soda off and empty ones on. A crowd of waifs, many with the ubiquitous shoeshine kits slung over a shoulder, stood and watched, no doubt hoping that someday there would be a place for them on the staff of the *Sobral Santos*. "She is beautiful," one told us.

The ship was white and tall like a wedding cake. Three layers with filigree and railings and a touch of shiny brass. The bow sat high and proud out of the water. On the top deck in front was the pilot house followed by four cabin doors, a smokestack and a wide open rear deck. The *Sobral Santos* was 150 feet long and had about it the height and girth of a Mississippi River sidewheeler.

Captain Kalil Mourao was in his office on the second deck, wetting his thumb and counting a nearly foot-high pile of cash in front of him. Even with Brazilian inflation, it was a lot of money. Warming to us immediately, he said he had much experience transporting foreigners, especially Swedes and Germans. We told him we were Americans. "And many, many Americans," he added seamlessly.

Was a cabin available on the boat? "Ship," he corrected, and walked us out to the deck. "This is a cabin," he said opening the door behind his office. "But I don't think gentlemen such as yourselves should travel this way." It looked fine to us. "Ah, but it has no toilet. You must use the toilet back there with all the other passengers." He held his nose for emphasis.

We climbed to the top deck. "This is a suite," he said, opening another door with a sweep of his arm. The room was identical to the first—two small bunks, a shelf and a mirror—with the exception of a toilet bowl with a shower head directly over it, making it necessary to straddle the toilet to shower.

"And," he said, throwing a switch, "it's air-conditioned." A clanking sound came out of the wall. He quickly shut it off and maintained his relentless landlord's smile. The "suite" would be $45 each for three nights and two days; the cabin, $35. For ten bucks more, we were sold.

"There is no better way to go to Manaus," Kalil assured us. "They are let quickly so you are smart to make the reservation now."

On Friday afternoon the wharf across from the bar was crowded with people waiting to see the arrival of the Sobral Santos from the cargo dock, a major weekly event. The ship glided majestically in with a blast of its horn that was firm but not so long as to be ostentatious, dwarfing the surrounding boats as it nosed in among them to the muddy shore. The river was at a low point, far below the top of the 30-foot-high wharf, so all the loading had to be done by going down a flight of steps to the sandy beach then across a narrow wood gangplank to the ship's hold. When the gangplank slapped down, the first wave of passengers rushed on and began to string hammocks between overhead hooks. We quickly realized that space was going to be at as much of a premium on the mighty ship Sobral Santos as it was on mere boats.

The steerage deck looked ready for defense against shore battery shelling; cartons of empty soda and beer bottles were stacked from floor to ceiling, assuring that the only view passengers on that level would get was of a trademark. The air there was already hot and thick with sweat; the cargo blocked all ventilation. It was nearly impossible to navigate through the catacombs of hammocks swaying from above and the maze of possessions below—suitcases, dining room sets, brightly wrapped Christmas presents.

The passengers were not exotic: no diamond smugglers or fugitives from European financial scandals here. Mostly the boat was filled with residents of various river towns who had paid $20 for the trip to Manaus. We soon noticed that there were two distinct lots: those visiting and those fleeing. The continually hard economic times in the Amazon valley have forced families apart over the years as the promise of work pushed many people far down the river. A family that still considers itself close might be strung out for 500 or 1,000 miles along the Amazon and its tributaries. Along the main river, money is being spent in the bigger towns—Santarem and particularly Manaus—and the selective good fortune of these cities draws thousands of people from depressed river communities. We watched them come aboard carrying huge bundles—burlap sacks, sagging cardboard boxes held together with twine, a kitchen chair, a dresser. Those with arms full of Christmas presents looked more serene.

All, though, had hammocks, the common denominator of river travel and the usual way to sleep among the traditional people here. The generous, brightly striped pieces of cotton were being unfurled all over the deck. Many of the passengers would spend virtually all their time in these hammocks, like larvae in cocoons, for the most part gently swaying with the boat, occasionally slamming into each other when it lurched.

In his office, Kalil was collecting cash and barter. One young man gave him his radio to hold and promised to sell it in Manaus to pay for the ticket. "You take what you can get," Kalil said. "I get chickens, pigs. It's all worth something." Some of the passengers made vague offers to sell unnamed goods when they got to Manaus or to have a relative pay. The approaching spirit of Christmas was infectious; the captain turned no one away.

At sunset on Friday, December 20, the *Sobral Santos* set sail out of Santarem bound for Manaus, a city of almost 700,000 people at the center of the jungle. With an ocean liner's whistle and a pause to throw the gangplank back down for a tardy passenger, it regally turned its back on the admiring throng. We sat in folding chairs on the top deck, smoked cigars and watched Santarem glow in the fading light. The sun ahead of us was a wavy orange ball, sitting at the end of the caramel-colored alley that was the Amazon. As the sun dropped, the streaky sky around it turned purple and lavender.

The cool breeze carried our smoke over the darkening water, a soft samba cooed from the speakers, and we were giddy from having found an image as enchanting as we had pictured.

At 3 A.M., Kalil's voice, urgent over the loudspeaker, warned passengers to stay away from the port side of the ship. If they persisted, he advised, the ship could tip over. Even from our cramped horizontal vantage points in the bunk beds—they were built for passengers under 6 feet and we are both over—we could understand his concern. The ship was leaning hard, driving our skulls into the bulkhead. We were arriving in Obidos, although a thick mist hid the town from view. Only a high pier was visible, seeming to hang suspended in the fog and crowded with a ghostly assortment of figures. The river was calm. The problem was that the disembarking passengers straining over the railing to find friends, relatives and lovers in the humming crowd that was now illuminated by the ship's spotlight could tip the ship over. Kalil repeated his warning in a sufficiently panicky voice, the crowd moved and the boat began to right.

When the gangplank was dropped on the pier, people ran back and forth. New passengers boarded before the old ones could leave, like rush-hour subway riders at a crowded station. New territory was staked out in steerage. Those leaving fought their way back onto the ship to rescue belongings, then off again, then back on. Remarkably no one fell in the water. And in ten minutes, we were under way again.

Kalil's music, which came from a large tape recorder in his office, started up at 7 A.M. with an unusual selection of bad "easy listening" music and good jazz. We guessed the music was one of the reasons for the ship's popularity. Every mile or so when we glided by small houses—straw-colored, palm-thatched, peaked roofs on stilts—people would emerge and wave, their bodies responding to the sound blaring across the water. They ran along the shore as we passed, grabbing the last notes they'd hear until the return voyage on Tuesday.

After a breakfast of cookies and coffee, we went to see Kalil in his office. He wanted to tell us about his plans.

"My father was an Assyrian Christian from Lebanon," he said by way of starting an unprompted autobiography. "He came to Manaus when he heard about the rubber boom. He brought supplies to rubber workers and carried away rubber, Brazil nuts, rice. He became rich."

The captain certainly looked Semitic, dark with an oval face, beaked nose and straight black hair. He was built like a barrel, an image accentuated by the broad red-and-white striped sailor's shirt he wore. With his passengers he seemed part hustler, part scoutmaster. Kalil came across as an intense man and a devout one, convinced that God was going to help him along; a conviction that played a big role in his life, as he finished any statement about the future with "if God wishes it."

Kalil started in the boat business when he was 12. "My father gave me a rowboat and said, 'That's all you get. If you want a motor, buy it yourself.' He had lots of motors, but I rowed rubber and supplies up and down the river to earn enough to buy one." He bought the *Sobral Santos II* in 1978 and converted her from a cargo steamer to a passenger ship. It was the second of his fleet of three ships, all old steamers built near the turn of the century. To buy the first one in 1974 he had traded in his entire fleet of 11 skiffs and small passenger boats. But he considered the risk minimal.

"Business is good. I always have more people than I can carry." On this trip at least, Kalil's combination of generosity and greed had resulted in a badly overloaded vessel. The *Sobral Santos* was meant to carry 300 and now had about 500 aboard.

Anyone who saw Kalil fondle his pile of cash could guess that his dreams did not end with the monopoly of the Santarem–Manaus run. "I'd like to have 200 boats, something moving all the time. In two or three years I hope to have four boats going to Belem."

He crossed himself after exposing his ambitions. St. Francis was smiling at him from over his desk, and the Blessed Virgin hung above his bunk.

We talked about the perils of the river. He seemed to respect it as much as the religious figures. "I have spent years learning her. I have only the best pilots. They have to know how to read her, just as you would a book. She changes every day. Islands move. The bottom comes up at you. The shore falls away. The Amazon has given me what I have but I can never relax."

The Amazon ebbed and surged just like the tributaries we had been on—only the scale was much greater. Kalil told of seeing floating islands rushing downriver during the flood season that were several times larger than his boat; of river banks that looked one way on the trip out and completely different on the way back three days later.

The boats, of course, never stopped. Flood season just forced the pilots, skilled in reading the ripples and currents from a lifetime on the river, to work that much harder. Kalil said he always used two pilots who worked four-hour shifts, day and night, endlessly scanning the river's surface for signs of change. The Amazon was just now beginning to rise and wouldn't crest until perhaps May, so Kalil said he was sleeping well at night.

The other danger that worried him was snakes, the ones that eat men. "There are snakes 200 feet long. Yes. I have seen them 60 feet. Once on the Madeira River I ran my boat up onto one in the water. I thought it was a log. I don't know how I escaped; I think that one was 100 feet long. You can tell by the size of the head."

He spoke gravely. He saw nothing incredible or absurd about this, then he laughed at what he thought were our own fearful expressions. "Don't worry. I don't think any of them are big enough to sink the *Sobral Santos*."

The scenery along this portion of the river is a monotony of damaged green—ferns, grass and stunted trees that look like giant weeds along the flat flood plains. At some points, the flood plain extends for 30 or 40 miles on either side of the river and at high water would more closely resemble a giant lake. Sometimes a fringe of trees cloaks the shore, but mostly the edge is clear. Between the floods and four centuries of civilization, nothing that could be called jungle remains along the river banks. The forbidding wall early explorers saw is gone, sheared off by centuries of habitation. "Any big trees you see left are ones that have grown back a hundred years after the original ones were cut," the botanist Joao Murca Pires had told us. "There is no such thing as original growth on the lower Amazon."

As remote as the Amazon might seem, it is surprisingly well populated—not with many towns, but with a steady string of farms, ranches, and fishing huts. Some of the cottages we saw were well built and neat, sitting in groves of trees set amid bright green grass. One farm had 100 or so head of white cattle in an elaborate bamboo pen almost on the edge of the 20-foot high cliff that formed the river bank there. In a few months the river would come to the top of that bank, or maybe overrun it by 10 feet and, if the flood were sudden, wash the cattle away. Another house was white stucco with a red tile roof, a substantial house built to stay and with a shiny new Massey-

Ferguson tractor parked in the yard. At a third cottage, a mother and her five children, all blond and in evenly descending size, came to watch the boat pass. The smallest child held a cow by a tether.

Life on these isolated farms is geared to a trading economy, often through a relationship with a trading company in the nearest large town that has endured for generations. Just as in the days when rubber was collected from each individual tapper, traders still ply the river, appearing once a month at a farm and buying or bartering whatever is available. Traders in turn sell what they collect to the large trading houses in Manaus or Belem. The farming is subsistence, although the growing population of the cities along the river has created a demand for vegetables, fish and beef that has prospered the cleverer farmers. The flood-plain land is among the best in the Amazon, though it has never been used for large-scale farming and must be carefully cultivated because it is so unevenly silted. Even the most careful farmer could have a whole year's crop washed away if the floods came early.

Our impression was that no one was getting rich along the river. Most families don't make a living by farming alone, but collect rubber, palm nuts, Brazil nuts, jute, timber or any of a dozen other export-oriented products just as they have done for centuries. Such trade allows them to buy staple goods such as sugar, salt, kerosene, rifles or fishing hooks. The caboclos have to be farmers, fishermen, day laborers and gatherers, responding to whatever opportunity presents itself. We saw signs that the cycle might change only in the bigger towns where the largely illiterate caboclos have migrated so their children can get some schooling.

The boat stopped at river towns about every ten hours—Parantins, Juruti, Itacoatiara. These, graced by the *Sobral Santos* because of their size, are the biggest towns between Santarem and Manaus, and the centers of commerce for surrounding municipalities that average 5,000 square miles. Everything tapped from the forest or pulled from the rivers finds its way to their docks or dirt squares, where it is spread out and sold. These towns have the small sawmills, the rubber-processing factories, the Brazil nut warehouses that sort produce for the export companies in Manaus and Belem.

At these stops we saw some signs of the reawakening of the Amazon region since the rubber crash early in the century, but noth-

ing like the boom towns in the southern jungle. Jute, brought over by
the Japanese in 1929, is the increasingly important money crop and
accounts for some prosperity. It grows three centimeters a day in the
dry season; the trick is to harvest it just before the rainy season floods
wash it away, usually in June. Itacoatiara has three jute-pressing mills
that turn the stalky plant into a ropey fiber used for making coffee
sacks in the south. The dock there on the Sunday afternoon we
stopped was quiet. We walked across wood stained with blood and
fish scales to be greeted by some children who had come down to see
the boat—unquestionably a major event. Higher up on the bank,
groups of men peered warily out of open-front taverns. Sunday here
was the day for cachaca and shooting pool.

We noticed some towns had new churches and warehouses;
storefronts here and there were freshly painted; there were new cars
and several main streets had just been paved. At Parantins, a 17-year-
old girl boarded, on her way to visit relatives in Manaus. When we
asked her about Parantins she gave a gross-out grimace that could
have passed muster in the girls' room at any American high school
and said, "It's like living on the moon. There's just nothing there."

From what we had seen, we couldn't argue. Parantins made the
wind-swept Texas towns so favored by American filmmakers looking
for images of desolation seem downright cheerful. Absent were all the
elements that make the life of the small-town American teenager
barely tolerable: movie theater, record store, fast-food restaurant,
shopping plaza—things that are ubiquitous elsewhere in Brazil. The
frenetic atmosphere of the frontier towns was missing. Parantins was
just a boring, if modestly prosperous, small town, and we shouldn't
have been surprised that even in the Amazon a 17-year-old girl knew
it and couldn't wait to get out.

The stops averaged a half-hour and we got off each time, partly
to see the town and partly to hunt food that would provide some
relief from the *Sobral Santos*' communal mess. In contrast to the
elaborate fish preparations of Belem, meals in most river towns—and
on the boat—tended to be boiled fish served with a bowl of pebbly
farina. The blandness was overcome by chopped hot peppers potent
enough to make an unsuspecting gringo gasp. Beef, a novelty until
recently, showed up uninterestingly cubed and stewed—no old family
recipes here. Chicken, which we gathered must be considered a treat

by the approving nods it won when served the first day on the boat, bore little resemblance to the supermarket variety. These birds had legs so sinewy and chests so meager that we reasoned they had been herded to market over a long hard road. Vegetables, not a normal part of most diets here, were in scarce supply, though carbohydrates were as abundant on Kalil's boat as elsewhere in Brazil. No meal was complete without piles of farina, spaghetti, rice, beans and some boiled manioc.

By the second day the sameness of the shoreline had become tedious. Everything seemed out of scale after our past boat trips. Before, we had been right on the water, with trees hanging over us and fish jumping in the boat. Now we were removed, 20 feet above the river, a hundred yards from the shore. The river itself was so big that it lost all meaning as a river. Before the morning mist burned off, we couldn't see either shore. At some points along our route the Amazon was 10 miles wide. At times, it could have been Lake Michigan.

Only the dolphins broke the monotony. Brazilians call them *botos* and they are the enchanted creatures of the Amazon. Of the two species, the pink dolphin and the smaller black one, we saw only the black botos, and only on the least-populated stretch about halfway between Santarem and Manaus. The pink dolphins have been fished out in much of the lower Amazon. Although elsewhere in the world dolphins are social mammals that congregate in schools, typical of the Amazon we saw only single botos break the surface. It would splash out of the water and arch up with a playful air that was all out of character for this deadly serious natural world.

The river people revere the boto for his magic—much of it sexual. During his study of river towns, anthropologist Charles Wagley discovered that a powder made from certain parts of a boto is used as a powerful aphrodisiac. The left eye of a boto, dried and grated into a woman's food, is believed to make her mad with desire. The left eye socket is dried into the shape of a ring which, when a man views through it a woman he desires, makes her immediately attracted to him. The living boto, male and female, is thought to have great sexual power over humans. "The sexual organs of the female are strikingly similar to those of a woman," Wagley wrote, "and they give man such intense pleasure, it is said, that if his companion does not pull him away he will die in continual intercourse." A widespread legend says that the male boto sometimes appears in river towns as a handsome young man dressed in a white suit who seduces virgins. Many an unexpected wedding night discrepancy has been explained away by tales of the white-suited boto.

Despite the blistering sun on the open deck, four men continued a marathon card game—something with three packs of cards, requiring constant yelling and slapping of the table. We were two degrees south of the Equator and in midriver where the combination of sun, constant humidity and no shade turned the ship into a close approximation of a steam cooker. Most of those on the lower decks, where it was hotter, just slumped listlessly in their hammocks, even though they could have come above.

Unless a traveler can spend what for these people is a great deal of money and buy a plane ticket, there is no painless way to travel in the Amazon. The trick is not to fight it—as we continued to do. The more you move, the hotter it gets; the more impatient you feel, the longer the trip. Those on the lower decks knew that lesson well and had settled into a trancelike state, listening to the pulsing diesels and swaying gently as the boat pushed ahead. Even the children—there were only a few—stayed quiet.

We drank a couple of cans of beer—the only cold thing on board. Unthinking, we followed the lead of everyone else and threw the empties over the side. Watching them float away, we were reminded of the tourist brochure we had read in the lobby of the Tropical Hotel: "You can enjoy the beauty of the Amazon, unspoiled, as yet."

Late the third night, we smelled Manaus before we saw it. A sharp scent of chemicals, familiar to someone who grew up in industrial sprawl but out of place here, drifted over the boat. Just before midnight Sunday the shoreline had begun to change. The darkness was broken by an increasing array of lights on shore: floodlit warehouses, sawmills and factories with smoke glowing as it poured from the stacks. An oil refinery, all its pipes and tanks strung with bulbs, looked like a Christmas tree. Ahead the sky radiated a dull orange from the lights of Manaus, and in that dim light we could make out the muddy waters of the Amazon running alongside the ink-black water of the Rio Negro. The two do not mix at this confluence, running in separate stripes for 10 miles because their temperatures and speeds do not agree. The *Sobral Santos* crossed over from the Amazon into the Negro and slowed her engines. Almost silently she slid through the water, black and shiny like a polished floor.

The Manaus dock area looked much bigger than Santarem's. Two crewmen on the bow shoved aside smaller boats with poles while the pilot nosed the *Sobral Santos* to the dock. Fifty-three hours and we were here. Alone among the passengers we had no place to go in the middle of the night, so we slept on board after all the others had gone home.

Some weeks later we heard what had become of Kalil's dream. We were on a side trip far to the south when we happened to see a few-days-old newspaper with a sketchy story about a boat capsizing at Obidos, killing 300. The boat—the ship—was the *Sobral Santos II*. The reports were lurid, and, we guessed, of questionable accuracy, telling of struggling victims ravaged by piranhas and blood-sucking catfish or swept away in the swift, deep channel. The accident happened as the boat was docking late at night. We replayed the scene of our own docking with Kalil's nasal voice desperately asking people to move to the other side and imagined the terror of waking up in a cabin filled with water. Most of the passengers, packed in as we knew they must have been, never had a chance.

When we returned to Manaus, we sought out Kalil. He lived in a crumbling neighborhood of what had been the mansions of second-rate rubber barons, though his own residence looked more like a warehouse. He greeted us in shorts and the same red-and-white-striped sailor shirt. He had not shaved in a few days and his eyes were red.

"Have a beer," he offered immediately. "It's too hot."

Kalil was surrounded by his extended family. His wife was serving dinner to a son-in-law, a cousin and one of the boat pilots. A half-dozen dissimilar children played on the concrete floor in the maze of high-ceilinged rooms and shrieked with laughter when Kalil's infant son fell out of a hammock and landed with a thunk. Outside the kitchen door was a courtyard stacked with ceramic sinks and plumbing fixtures. "One of my side businesses," Kalil explained.

He and his brother-in-law were watching the news on a new

color television set. A story came on about the *Sobral Santos*. The death ship, they called it. The boat that killed 300 had just been refloated and towed to Manaus, the TV said. The film showed the once-gleaming wedding cake with the superstructure crushed and the white sides slopped with mud.

Kalil was outraged. He turned to us almost pleading. "Not 300, not 200. Fifty-one people died. There were only 200 aboard."

We doubted that, though we also doubted the press reports.

"They would find arms and legs and count each as a body. I swear all those people did not die."

But a lot of people died, the pride of Kalil's fleet was badly damaged and he had no insurance.

"I have spent everything I had—$400,000—to bring up the boat, to pay hospital bills for passengers. Now I have nothing."

Kalil wasn't aboard the night the accident happened. His brother-in-law, a bowed, timid man who carried a perpetual open-mouthed look of surprise, had been captaining. As best they could figure, one of the passengers had taken the rope securing crates to string his hammock. When the boat got close to port, people moved to the side as usual. The list caused the cargo to shift and toppled the boat over. In a few minutes, Kalil Mourao's dreams of grandeur were gone.

"It has been a true hell," he said, clenching his hands together and twisting them so tightly it made the knuckles white.

MANAUS

In the warmth from the early morning sun, the odor of fish entered
our cabin and awakened us. The smell came from the nearby fish
market, an ornate iron structure delicately designed by Alexandre
Eiffel. The French architect had come to Manaus, as had many
European artisans, at the turn of the century when rubber-rich
Manaus was like an oil-rich Arab state today. The rubber barons
created an opulent and alien society built on the sweat of thousands
of caboclos and the blood of as many Indians. The rewards can still
be seen in the immense colonial mansions that line tree-shaded
boulevards, constructed in European fashion. In those turn-of-the-
century days clothes were sent to London for a proper cleaning and

children to the Sorbonne for a proper education. In 1910 the jewelry trade in the city of less than 90,000 inhabitants exceeded $8 million. A Florentine opera house, completed in 1896 with stone shipped from Italy, was graced with special performances by Enrico Caruso and Jenny Lind. The Palace of Justice was built to resemble a miniature Versailles. Manaus was the third city in the hemisphere to get electricity and once had a trolley line. The night life was said to be extraordinary.

That grandeur lasted barely a score of years—1912 spelled the beginning of the city's decline. The stolen rubber trees that had been transplanted in the Far East began to thrive at much lower cost than in Brazil. Rubber prices dropped sharply and the great commercial houses in Manaus and Belem folded. The effects were felt down the line, far in the forest by the lowliest rubber gatherer. By 1918 Asian plantations were producing 260,000 tons of natural rubber against the jungle's 30,000 and the pall of failure soon settled over the Amazon.

We examined the fish under M. Eiffel's elegant roof. They were much like those at the Ver-O-Peso in Belem, laid out on white marble counters. Pirarucu and catfish as big as cows; piranha with leering, serrated mouths; coils of eels; unfamiliar species with bulging eyes or long, toothed snouts—all had been lurking beneath the surface we had so recently passed over. An early morning army of women with baskets picked over the display, prying open mouths and poking inside gills to check for the bright color and shine of freshness.

Outside, a less indigenous form of merchandising was gearing up to start the day. Manaus must qualify as one of the world's largest bazaars. Fifteen years ago the Brazilian government made the city a free-trade zone, meaning foreign companies would not have to pay import duty on component products they brought in. The result has been a proliferation of assembly operations, principally Japanese electronics companies that have ringed the city with boxlike buildings where the guts of radios and television sets are put together. The streets of Manaus, an expanse of crumbling European elegance around a core of modern glass skyscrapers, are lined with shops displaying the products of these factories: tape players, stereo systems, cameras, digital watches, clock radios. Strobe lights pop and music pours from the doorways, enticing customers from the jammed streets. What can't be found in the stores is available on the sidewalk where a second-tier economy of street vendors operating from unfurled blankets peddles everything from decades old *Time* magazines to day-old shrimp.

We couldn't figure out how an isolated city of 700,000 people could support such extensive commerce until we hauled our bags into the lobby of the Hotel Tropical. A congregation of Japanese men, neatly dressed in dark suits, chatted in the lobby while their frenetic Brazilian guide argued with the desk clerk. An American in full jungle camouflage fatigues—turned-up bush hat, jacket with shotgun shell pockets and baggy pants out of "Apocalypse Now"—invited us to go hunting. Three Italian men with fresh tans, dressed in well-coordinated golf outfits, asked us if we could translate a travel brochure. And there were Brazilian couples from Rio who had come to take advantage of this advertised shoppers' paradise.

Manaus caters to the world's idea of the Amazon. "The beaches of Rio and a night in the darkest Amazon," an Air France brochure reads. Three times a week a French 747 traveling between Paris and Lima stops in Manaus and venturesome tourists remain for a few days in the "jungle."

The lavish $125 a night Tropical Hotel, on the Rio Negro north of Manaus, was built in 1978 to serve well-heeled tourists. Tourism has not yet quite lived up to expectations, but government subsidies insure its continuing operation. When we were there, the hotel was far more active and well staffed than the Tropical in Santarem, yet it had its illusory aspects, too. The promotional material advertised a nine-hole golf course. We followed the signs along a path and found some areas where the forest was lower, but nothing that looked like a fairway. There was a suspicious bump that could have been a putting green, but it was impossible to tell. We asked the concierge what had happened.

"Our guests didn't play," he said. "I think they were afraid to go out there. Now it's grown over and even we can't find it."

We went water skiing along the black surface of the Rio Negro with Jamie Benchimol, the American-educated son of one of Manaus' leading merchant families. Jamie had a sleek fiberglass outboard speedboat. He picked us up at the beach of the Tropical and we roared upriver past crowded public beaches toward the more exclusive beach clubs along the Rio Negro. Jamie had gone to college in Miami and had just graduated from business school in Berkeley, California.

As one of the heirs to Bemol, the family department store chain, Jamie's financial future was assured, but he worried about his personal future. He had a girlfriend in Miami and wasn't sure how she was going to adjust here. There wasn't much to do, he told us, besides water-skiing. "The women in Manaus play the role. They take good care of their bodies, but not such good care of their minds. There is no one to talk to here."

Despite his American education, Jamie offered a typically Brazilian taunt when it was time to go in the water. "Who has the courage to go in first?" He said it at least half jokingly, but we remained aware of the varied and unfamiliar life beneath these black waters. Jamie scoffed at the notion of anything untoward in the water, and in fact we skied and swam and headed back with no one suffering any discernible ill effects.

The next day we met Jamie's father, Samuel Benchimol, the patriarch of the company and perhaps the best-known folklorist of the Amazon.

The Benchimol family arrived in the Amazon in the 1820s as part of an exodus of Jewish families from Morocco. Many of the descendants of these Sephardic Jews dominate commerce throughout the region. We were told that at one time all the important merchants of Santarem were Jewish, and their remains can be seen in a most incongruous cemetery—Hebrew writing in the Amazon jungle. The Bennsabe family still is prominent in Guajara Mirim, the terminus of the Mad Maria Railroad on the Bolivian border. Benchimol's cousin, Isaac Sabba, is known as the king of the Amazon because of the fortune he controls, from the oil refinery we had seen lit like a Christmas tree to a giant jute-processing plant to a lucrative contract with Wrigley's for chicle, the base for chewing gum.

Samuel Benchimol's father was born in Itaituba but gravitated to Manaus as rubber became the Amazon's money crop. "My father was a rubber baron," Benchimol told us; "not one of the really rich ones, but he lived well." Shortly after Benchimol was born in 1923, his father lost everything in what by then had become the continuing dismal collapse of the Brazilian rubber industry. The price had dropped from £655 sterling per ton and was on its way to £34, where it bottomed out in 1932. The Benchimol family moved to the southwestern Amazon where the once wealthy father tapped trees. "They were years of fighting, of poverty, of misery, of sickness; years that brought him and all of us the indelible marks of penury," Benchimol has written.

Yet Samuel Benchimol's father lived to see the family flourish again. Despite their extreme poverty, all the Benchimol children had gone to college and one of Samuel's brothers is a heart specialist in Phoenix, Arizona.

When we visited the Benchimols, they were again among the wealthiest families in Manaus. Their department stores and an expanding bottled-gas operation employed 800 people. Benchimol told us he was considering major new operations in the Porto Velho area. "The future of Brazil," he called it.

Benchimol defies easy labeling because he is both a successful businessman and an idiosyncratic scholar whose work consists largely of compilations of personal memorabilia and raw data. For example, his major tome, *Amazonia,* contains everything from his high school term papers to his thesis at Miami University to stream-of-consciousness writing on the future of the Amazon economy. He has also chronicled the disastrous government attempt to rekindle the rubber boom during World War II by inducing hundreds of thousands of impoverished Northeasterners to migrate. He has published a useful summary of census data, detailing the growth of the region from 1970 to 1980, and when we met him in his office he was mulling over potential uses for a pile of statistics on the types of fish caught at random towns along the Amazon.

"Someone wants to know how many' tucunares they caught in Tabatinga last March. I'm sure of that. So many numbers. I'll make something out of them."

Unusual scholarship runs in the family. Another cousin, Abraham Bentes, compiled a dictionary of *Hakitia,* the patois used by Jews who have come to the Amazon. We leafed through the pages, but none of the words even sounded familiar: *haq* (truth), *hamur* (important), *jara* (shit), *maggaa* (a bad meal).

During his lifetime, Benchimol told us, none of the previous changes have been so drastic as what he is seeing now. His frequent trips all over the jungle have shown him a world that is out of control. Benchimol pronounced himself in favor of development, but not the way the government is doing it. "The savage ecosystem is diseased. There is no reason it can't be made to work for man, but the means must be changed. The jungle now is a very sloppy place."

He spoke in a gravelly voice, looking over our heads as if lecturing to a class. "What I object to is the giant project. The way to learn is not to knock it all down and start over again. Cattle ranches were the biggest mistake that could have been made. Let's be humble and start with 25 acres instead of 25,000. We don't know enough. I'll tell you what I do know, and that's if you clear the Rio Negro basin—as they're doing in some parts now—you'll be raising camels instead of cattle. Nothing will grow there.

"You have to understand what the Amazon is. It may be the last big piece of good land left in the world. Biologically, it is incredibly rich. It produces almost 500 tons of biomass per acre. You have no right to take it down unless you can produce something more valuable.

"The world is going to come here. I have no doubt. We better be ready for them when they do."

Moises Sabba, son of Isaac the king of the Amazon and the heir to the refinery and jute plant, agreed with his older cousin about the imminence of development. He also had a stern warning for all the expected arrivals.

"Don't treat this like a magical, mythical land. It is a place like any other place. It is not better or worse, if you know how to live here. It is different, so it must be treated differently. We must learn about it. I live here just like someone lives in Hawaii or Oklahoma. I have a family, I go to work every day. I am not a freak."

In his pale blue Oxford-cloth shirt, tailored slacks and Gucci loafers, Moises Sabba could have passed for a Wall Street stockbroker on his day off. He is educated and articulate and has a perspective on the Amazon that has been learned through permanence and roots. His views, while not widely held, were the most reasonable we had heard and stood in contrast to both the unfathomable optimism and the brash carelessness of the frontier. He received us in the headquarters of the family business, an airy, modern two-story structure which is attached to the main house where Isaac still lives. He handed us magazine stories about his father going back to the 1950s. *Time, Newsweek, Paris Match,* Brazilian magazines, Argentine magazines, all took up the king of the Amazon theme and talked about how Isaac Sabba had triumphed over the jungle. The stories predicted great things for the Amazon any day now. Moises said business was good, but not great.

"The myth of the Amazon sets us back. When Ford failed, everyone said, 'Aha, the terrible Amazon has claimed another victim.' When my father succeeds, the stories say, 'Superman beats the jungle.' Now that Ludwig has failed, it will set us back again.

"What we need is less myth, and more know-how. The research the government does is too slow and too small. For example, the way they log in Africa and Asia is not the way to do it here. We must develop ways to log the Amazon that are our own. But the scientists spend their time studying birds and ants. What has been done so far, all the research, is nothing compared to what must be done. Then we will replace the myth and people will say, 'The Amazon is not so bad and not so good. It is just a place.' "

After talking with Sabba we joined Jamie Benchimol for lunch. We asked if he had been doing any more water-skiing. His eyes widened.

"You know," he said, astonished, "a few days after I went out with you I was at the dock. They brought in a girl who had been skiing. Four of her toes and half her knee had been bitten off by piranhas. She dripped blood all over the dock. I never thought it could happen. We all grow up with the stories, but don't pay any attention to them because everyone always tells us, 'Don't worry.' "

The perpetuation of the specialness of the Amazon has a popular new chronicler named Marcio Souza. At a few years over 30, he is the most famous author the Amazon has produced and is on his way to becoming one of a small group of Brazilian writers with reputations abroad. His first book, a fictional history called *The Emperor of the Amazon,* sold well in Brazil and, after translation into English and French, also did well in Europe and the United States. *Mad Maria,* a fictional history of the Madeira-Mamore Railroad, was a bestseller in Brazil and is under contract for a Spanish edition with a first printing of 500,000 copies. A thriller about a right-wing coup in Brazil was to get first-run publication in the United States—because, Souza explained, the censors would never pass on it in Brazil.

Success has not gone to Souza's head. We found him still living with his family behind the pastel blue American Beauty Parlour that his mother runs on one of the shaded side streets of Manaus. A woman with her hands wrist-deep in the red beehive of a customer nodded us in the right direction.

Souza is a slight man whose eyes alternately twinkle and squint behind thick, round, wire-rim glasses. His face draws itself toward a sharp nose, making it seem that he is always bearing down on the person he is speaking to, his head leaning farther and farther forward on his neck. We sat on lawn chairs in the hallway between the living quarters and the beauty shop. A younger cousin watched cartoons on TV in the next room.

Souza began writing film criticism for Manaus newspapers when he was 14. To pay his way as a student in Sao Paulo, he wrote screenplays and pornographic stories for magazines. His novels caused a minor scandal in Brazil because he peopled them partly with real characters from Brazilian history. "People couldn't believe that these heros of the history books would say things like 'son of a bitch' and 'faggot,'" he explained, adding that he had learned such controversy does not hurt sales.

The book he was currently working on was, he said, about "violence, repression and the myth of the Amazon." It started with the dolphin legend we had heard on the *Sobral Santos*, the handsome creature seducing a young virgin and leaving her with a child. "But she doesn't throw the child in the water as she's supposed to. She raises him and he becomes a gangster—sort of an Al Capone of the Amazon."

Souza was not reluctant to talk of his work in progress, as many authors are. He seemed eager to explain it, although we had a tough time following the plot. "It is not actually the narrator writing the story. It is written by a Marxist-Leninist professor, written by his hand. Do you know psychography? It is a ghost or a metaphysical force moving his hand. But he is a Marxist-Leninist who doesn't believe in metaphysics." He laughed at that last, as if the humor was self-evident.

"He thinks he is going crazy, because he doesn't believe in metaphysics. It happened after he was at a demonstration to protest the giving away of rights to cut Amazon timber to foreign companies. He gets beaten badly by the police. Then he starts to write. He thinks he's going crazy so he goes to a psychiatrist. He tells him what he is writing about and that's how the story is told."

Souza had been described to us as a leader of the Amazon environmental movement. His New York publisher told us he writes plays for "an important group fighting for the preservation and defense of the Amazon." The businessmen we spoke with assumed he is a Communist, which seemed sufficient confirmation of his activism. But Souza said he isn't active because there is no movement anymore. "The interest in the Amazon has disappeared, at least some of it. Others have shifted. The discussion is not the Amazon but democracy for Brazil. The Amazon has done its job. When we protested the risk contracts a few years ago [the proposal to sell part of the forest to foreign lumber companies] it was the first protest movement this country had in 16 years. It brought together people fighting for the forest, the Indians, the farm workers. But we all came to realize that the Amazon was not the issue, democracy was. It was a turning point in Brazilian history. And we were heard."

The risk contract proposal was withdrawn. Its defeat was a significant step in the abertura process, the opening of Brazil's political system. If people could be organized to defeat the risk contract plan then they could perhaps shout louder and stop highways from crossing Indian lands or stop an incentive program for rich corporations from the south of Brazil. Democracy could mean a change in direction for development of the Amazon. Small farmers, of whom there are thousands, could vote to disband GETAT and a few weak landowners might not be able to stop them. Subsidies might be redirected away from cattle ranches in Campo Alegre toward housing in Xinguara. No ideas would remain sacred.

Perhaps in view of this the government was, during the months of our trip, rethinking its plans for free-for-all elections in 1982 and was instituting restrictions such as prohibiting ticket-splitting to make it difficult for the opposition to prevail.

Souza was cautiously optimistic about the upcoming elections.

"We're hoping to be more active for the 1982 elections. That will be another turning point. We don't know if the elections will be fixed, but you can see signs of it. The military government is already kidding around, just like the Shah of Iran kidded around."

We wanted to know what that meant for the Amazon.

"You can't talk about the Amazon without talking about Brazil. Unless you see a change in Brazilian society, you can only expect things in the Amazon to get worse. The common man never gets a fair chance; he will be pushed off his land and shot. The Indians will be exterminated. The big companies will come in and take what they want.

"Don't get me wrong. I'm not against technology. I'm an urban guy. I'd rather be in an air-conditioned room all day with the dial set at 68 degrees than in the jungle. What I'm against is the violence —the violence for the sake of violence of taking the trees down, moving the squatters out. That is Brazilian society and that must change."

And if it doesn't?

"Then there will be violence from the other side. Our side. And that will be very bad. Especially for me. I'm a marked man. If there's a coup, I might as well just head for the football stadium and let myself in."

The center of Amazon wisdom, we had been told, is INPA, the National Institute of Amazon Research. INPA had been described to us in glowing terms: the Cape Canaveral of Brazil's moonshot to the Amazon. We traveled through Manaus' cluttered urban sprawl, through streets lined with auto parts stores, junkyards, and super-markets to get there at 8:00 A.M. one morning, the height of the rush hour.

The cabbie zipped his orange Volkswagen underneath a swing-ing traffic light, which was red, with only a brief pause, lifting his foot from the gas pedal for a second then slamming it down hard. It was the stop-and-go move Pele used to do so fluidly on the soccer field. The cabbie did it well and allowed himself a slight smile. The move had been executed to allow a pedestrian—crossing with a green light —the opportunity to freeze in his tracks so the cab could zoom past. We sat in the back seat, automatically braking with our feet as the pedestrian's mouth began to open in what would surely be a foul curse.

We were too far away to hear the oath, but did catch a hand being raised with the fingers circled in the "O.K." symbol, but veteran Brazilianists that we had become, we knew that here the gesture meant the pedestrian wanted the driver to stick something in his lowermost orifice.

"Hah. Son of a bitch," the driver said, glaring in the rear-view mirror. "Red lights don't mean you have to stop."

At first glance, the institute looked more like an abandoned motel. The complex of long one- and two-story white buildings was tucked away just off the road behind a thick screen of trees.

"What do you want to come here for?" the cabbie asked.

"For some answers about the jungle," we said.

He thought for a moment with a disbelieving frown on his face. He finally said, "What jungle?"

The grounds seemed deserted. We wandered along winding concrete paths as a gentle rain began to fall. The trees were labeled and we could see empty animal cages. In front of us was a large round backyard swimming pool, about five feet deep and filled with brown water. We were peering into the curious article when a pair of eyes and a whiskered nose broke the surface. Then another and another. They were manatees, or sea cows, mammals with fat brown bodies and faces like seals sucking on lemons. For some time manatees have been the focus of efforts to breed them in herds for meat. Peaceful and affectionate animals who graze on water weeds, they have been successfully used to keep waterways free of plant growth, but so far have not bred well in captivity.

While we were gazing at the manatees an Englishman stopped to talk with us. He introduced himself: Dr. Roger Shrimpton, a nutritionist studying the zinc content of diets in certain areas. "We have 40 PhDs working here—most of them foreign. We should have 250 PhDs, most of them Brazilian." We watched a manatee come up for air. "There is so much to be done," Shrimpton said, "and so little time and money to do it."

Scientists often complain about shortages of research staff and dollars. Shrimpton told us the INPA scientists feel their lack of staff and dollars all the more keenly because they are so alone. Their work is rhetorically praised by the government but largely ignored. The most striking example is the environmental impact statement that some INPA scientists were preparing for the Tucurui dam; it was not scheduled to be completed until after the dam opens. Private enterprise and government alike seem to have no patience for science. Shrimpton told us that his greatest audience was other INPA scientists. Few journals or symposia exist in Brazil to integrate the esoteric studies being conducted with the larger, more general, needs of government planners and industry.

"Sometimes we feel it's all a little futile," said Herbert Schubart, the ecologist who was temporary head of the institute during our visit. "We're criticized for so much emphasis on pure science while the jungle is coming down around us. But I think that basic research is needed. Without it, we don't have the scientific base to know what we're talking about. It's very frustrating for us. It's as though this problem is being forced on us long before we're ready to deal with it.

"Time, that is our preoccupation," he said. With time, with more scientists, with more money and more places where basic research on the rain forest of the Amazon is conducted, failures like Fordlandia may not have to spawn themselves endlessly across the jungle.

Inadequate as INPA may be to discover alternatives in time, its scientists are grappling with critical questions. It was at INPA that Eneas Salati, who headed the institute for several years, developed his theory of how cutting the forest may affect regional rainfall patterns, perhaps causing the dry storms and lack of rain that the ranchers of Araguaia had begun to notice. The work is probably the most plausible and disturbing argument to be made for restricting forest clearing, but it has gone unfinished for lack of funds.

Rob Bierregaard, a young Yale-educated ornithologist, was running a promising program for the World Wildlife Fund to determine the minimum size of a plot of jungle that must be preserved to maintain its species in a balanced ecosystem. Isolate too small a patch, and no matter how undisturbed you leave it, animals such as monkeys and many birds who range far in search of food will not find enough to eat, and will flee or die. The exposed edges of any patch are vulnerable to drying; species are lost, and their loss leaves still other species unprotected. Bierregaard's group was isolating patches of 100, 200, 300 hectares, counting plants, beetles, birds, marmosets —and waiting to count again. Bierregaard said he expected some usable findings in about 10 years.

Philip Fearnside, a biologist from Michigan, was studying what he called "carrying capacity"—the number of people who can be supported on a given jungle project, a figure that varies with the type of colonization, the quality of the land, the type of productive technology employed, the desired standard of living and the probabilities of failure, as defined by a variety of criteria considered acceptable to planners.

Both of these scientists, the one looking at how to support the jungle intact and the other looking at how to support people in a changed jungle, envisioned a sort of give and take with the exigencies of Amazon environments that was lacking among businessmen, ranchers and government officials we had met. Neither the scientists' perspectives nor their sense of time is easily shared by busy developers in the jungle. "They study bat shit while we're trying to figure out how to grow a tree," Johann Zweede, the Jari forestry engineer, had told us, but now we could appreciate another side to that complaint.

We recalled something the head of a Washington-based wildlife foundation had told us about how most Amazon experts have spent most of their careers concentrating on a small patch of jungle, and usually only one aspect of that—maybe the birds or the soil or the ants. "I myself know all there is to know about a square kilometer near Belem and a square kilometer near Manaus. And not much else," he had said. To know just that, however, may take a scientist's lifetime.

From all the special subjects and all those lifetimes, those who plan the future of the Amazon must weave a policy. Several researchers at INPA argued that the confused priorities of the government prevent any coherent weaving together of research about the Amazon. The result is a scattershot approach with little coordination and little discussion of what kind of research is the most valuable.

"The Brazilian government only funds a part of INPA, the rest has to come from private grants," explained Judy Rankin, a forestry researcher. "We don't know from year to year where the priorities will be so it's very hard to make research proposals. But one area where there has never been very much money available is applied science subjects."

She said, for instance, that there is virtually no cooperation between INPA and private companies, many of which have an interest in exploiting Amazon resources. "Nobody has ever said, 'Let's take a company that wants to harvest trees in the jungle and put them together with a scientist who knows something about harvesting trees in the jungle.'"

Fearnside and Schubart were gloomy about the possibility of even INPA's few results being used by the officials who plan the development of the Amazon. Fearnside flatly stated that the people who plan these projects could care less. "I think the fact that the planners don't want this kind of information leads to a great danger of the projects failing," he said, "both from the standpoint of the people living there and from what it does to the forest."

Public consciousness—or lack of it—also concerns Schubart. He recalled the time of environmental activism, but agreed with the author Souza that it was dead. "There was a big environmental movement for a few years at the end of the 70s. The Amazon was the issue. Save the Amazon. Then it died down. Now no one pays attention. I don't think they cared about the Amazon, I think they just wanted something to protest." The government responded to the criticism by selecting a committee to come up with a draft of a comprehensive forest development policy. "I think they bought off a lot of critics by putting them on the committee. But now the draft sits in some drawer in the President's office. We don't feel very good about it ever coming out."

Schubart was strong in his feeling that the forest policy is the key to properly developing the Amazon and saving the ecology. The document, he said, should tell people what they are allowed to do and where, setting out guidelines for the size of projects; what can be raised on them; restricted preserves for parks, Indian tribes, ecological preservation and scientific study. "It should slow development to buy time," he said, echoing the concern of the botanist, Joao Murca Pires, whom we had met in Belem.

He stressed, however, the chicken-and-egg problem: you can't have a detailed policy without much more study of what the Amazon

contains, but it is unlikely such comprehensive study will be undertaken unless there is a policy mandating it. "So we go around in
circles like that while the smoke from the burning forest drifts over
Manaus," he lamented.

We prowled the INPA offices, empty for the most part because
of the holiday. Each, we could now imagine, held some small clue of
where to look for answers to pressing questions, but the clues eluded
us. Most of the rooms smelled of alcohol and formaldehyde. Some
had frogs or snakes floating in small jars. One was lined from floor to
ceiling with shelves on which rested thousands of containers of fish
preserved in alcohol. Most of the offices had a framed map on the
wall, a 1971 Brazilian government map of the Amazon that was
about six feet by six feet. Venezuela was over our heads, the Amazon
at about eye level and Mato Grosso at our knees. We had seen the
map elsewhere, but had never paid as much attention to it as we did
now, tracing our route over the paper surface. It was an excellent
map, the most nearly accurate of the notoriously inaccurate Amazon
maps, colored topographically in light shades of brown, cream and
green. The darkest green—the low part of the basin—was a giant
splash, covering an uninterrupted square yard of the wall. Around it
were rings of lighter green with some splotches of cream jutting in.
That was all jungle, beyond the tips of our outstretched arms. The
ground we had covered, which had seemed so vast, would only have
made a narrow ribbon across the map.

Yet at least in Brazil, we had now been over most of the land we
had set out to see. We thought about Carlos Marx, the goateed college professor sitting in his paper-filled Brasilia office poring over
satellite photographs with a magnifying glass. Looking at the map, we
could visualize the "danger zones" he had marked on his own map.
We had been to those places, and what we had seen agreed with what
he saw through his magnifying glass. We had seen the checkerboard
of small farms in Rondonia; the blotches of colonization projects
across the north of Mato Grosso; the huge bites the cattle ranches
had taken out of the Araguaia Valley—and the many little nibbles of
the squatters; the desert along the Belem–Brasilia Highway and the
lusher farms spreading back dozens of miles from the TransAmazon
Highway; the sprawling agricultural zone around Manaus and the
great projects—Tucurui, Carajas, Trombetas—with their state-sized

clearings that were flooding and gouging the forest. We had seen the crisscross of highways and the web of access roads that allowed settlers to chew their way back into obscure parts of the forest like ants.

Marx's estimate of 25 million acres—less than four percent of the forest area—was probably right, or, given all the small farms that we had seen that might not show up on satellite images, maybe the figure was 5 percent. That was 54,000 square miles or about the size of the state of Illinois, a staggering area of land but nothing like the 30 percent destruction figure that we had been told before we left and that has been inserted as gospel into environmentalist preaching.

An incomprehensibly huge amount of jungle was left on the map. The land north of Jari was untouched—we had flown over much of it to visit the Apalai Indians—as were thousands of square miles of the Mato Grosso and Para state. And this even seemed small compared to the western Amazon, the heart of the continent, perhaps 300,000 square miles, and, by the account of everyone we had asked, untouched by any development. Then, too, this map was just Brazil. There are substantial portions of jungle in Venezuela, Colombia, Bolivia and especially Peru. How could all this be taken down?

The whole subject had been a continual question, even an obsession, throughout the trip. How much? How much forest do you think is gone? we would ask anyone who seemed in a position to have a reasonable grasp of the problem. Unlike the Americans and Europeans who have written on the subject and blithely toss off that 30 percent figure, the people we met in Brazil knew the difficulty of estimating what they were dealing with and would usually not venture a guess. "Who can say?" they would respond. "There are guesses, but when you are here, you know they must be meaningless." The work of Carlos Marx and his satellite maps was just a rumor to most of those involved with the Amazon. Little of his data had ever been made public, and had it been, it was unlikely many Brazilians would have believed the news, coming as it did from a government everyone considered partisan on the issue.

We believed Carlos Marx, but we didn't know what his estimates meant. Busing through the gray moonscape of Paragominas, where jungle had once thrived, the figures were real and startling; looking at the deluxe Amazon wall map, the numbers didn't seem very important at all.

Then, at a Christmas party, Phil Fearnside, the biologist studying carrying capacity, and his wife, Judy Rankin, were holding for
some of the INPA staff, we were shown an alarming way to look at
the numbers. Phil and Judy are both Americans, PhD researchers at
INPA who live in a Manaus subdivision in a small white adobe house
that could pass for Southern California mission style. The guest list
was a collection of far-flung expatriates, mostly scientists from Europe and the United States. We ate Christmas cookies and drank
eggnog. Everyone sang carols, though it was hard to find melodies
and lyrics that more than a few members of that international group
were familiar with.

When most of the guests had left, we talked to Fearnside about
the tropical forest he had come to love. "Too many people have been
looking at the question of how much has been cut," he began as we
sat around the table with him. "Two percent or five percent or whatever isn't a big piece of the Amazon. What is important is the rate—
how much is being cut this year and next year and next year. The
question is whether we have exponential growth here. I have good
reason to believe that the recent deforestation trends are exponential."

Fearnside, a horn-rimmed, gangly and shy man who often spoke
in impenetrable scientific jargon, was also one of the few people we
met who had taken a broad look at the question of deforestation, who
had tried to compile the statistics and look at the economic and
cultural factors that influence those statistics.

He had a pad and paper out to explain what exponential meant.
Capital N's and little t's and i's were strung about in an equation. It
was Rankin who had the words.

"Exponential means that if present cutting patterns continue,
the jungle will be gone in a very short time."

Her husband agreed. He showed us a paper he had written with
complicated mathematical equations. The figures which he said were
most significant were those of 28,595 square kilometers of cleared
jungle in 1975 and 77, 171 square kilometers in 1978. According to
his calculations, the exponential rate of increase was .33, or a doubling of destruction in just over two years. The total destroyed could
double again in another two years, and again four years from now. In
a very matter-of-fact manner, Fearnside stated that at this rate the
entire jungle could be down in twelve and a half years, by 1991.

Then he added quickly, "That's not a prediction. I'm not saying it will happen. That's just an illustration of what could happen. It's an illustration to say that the Amazon is not infinite, despite how it may seem."

But Fearnside, the cautious scientist, admitted that just such a progression was taking place in Rondonia, an area where he had spent much time. "It's truly incredible there. The speed with which things are happening is awesome. Anybody who says it can't happen just has to go back there in a few years."

Fearnside was convinced that without a forest policy setting out guidelines for development, it is only a question of time before the same happens to the rest of the Amazon. There are too many pressures; Brazil needs the land and the world needs what that land produces. Besides the continual pressure from within Brazil, he felt the next surge of foreign investment would come when the forests of Southeast Asia are logged out. The world will turn to the Amazon for most of its wood, and unless there is a policy for controlling timber and development activities, the Amazon won't be ready.

"And you still have all the old problems. First, the government incentives which make it economical to destroy the forest and use it up as quickly as possible," he said, bending back one finger. "Then," he bent back a second finger, "the roads, the new ones and the old ones that are being paved. We've got a strong correlation between roads and deforestation." He gripped a third finger. "And you have the oldest law of the Amazon, the one that says if you clear a piece of land, it belongs to you. None of this has changed."

But even Fearnside was not totally fatalistic that night. "It is still a very big jungle. There is some time. And think about that part in the west. I don't know of anything going on there. Just that part alone would still be the biggest untouched forest in the world."

Everyone from environmentalists to government officials had told us not to worry because the heart of the Amazon, the great western portion of the state of Amazonas which runs to the Peruvian border, was untouched. Everyone except Dorival Knipboff, a millionaire builder from the far south who was planning to clear a 3.5 million-acre tract in the center of Amazonas.

Joao Carlos Meirelles had mentioned Dorival to us. "He's doing something or other out west. Even I don't know. Go ask him." Dorival greeted us in his office converted from a rubber baron's man-

sion. He was intense and nervous, some of the Big Al energy spilling
out of him as he shuffled through papers on his desk or exploded
from his seat to pace the room as he talked. When he sat still, his left
leg became the exit point for excess enthusiasm as he bounced it up
and down like a fast piston.

Dorival explained that with his partner, a huge pension fund
from the southern city of Porto Alegre, he was developing a palm oil,
rubber and wood alcohol plantation near Caruari on the Jurua River.
All hyperbole aside, this is one place that can truly be called among
the most remote on earth. It is close to nothing and, Dorival said, it
was nothing when he got there. The land is 450 miles southwest of
Manaus by air or about 10 days by river. When the first workers
arrived, they had to be dropped from helicopters into a natural clearing in the 100-foot-tall forest so they could cut trees for a landing pad
and a base camp. Now there were 4,000 people, to be followed soon
by a colonization project. Dorival expected to clear 400,000 acres
and grow rubber trees much as they had been grown at Belterra. "I
know what Ford did wrong," he said, but he didn't elaborate. Natural
rubber is needed because, despite Brazil's onetime dominance, it now
imports from Malaysia two-thirds of the 70,000 tons it uses. The oil
of the dende palm fruit is one of the great hopes of the jungle,
because Brazilians believe that with very little refinement it can be a
substitute for diesel fuel. The wood was to be used in a giant alcohol
refinery that Dorival was hoping to entice the Soviet Union to build.

"The market is there for all this, as soon as we learn the best
way to take it all out," Dorival said. "We will not make the mistakes
of Ford or Ludwig. We have the technology. We will just take our
time. We expect to be there for many, many years."

Only one thing could speed up his leisurely timetable, he said.
Petrobras, the Brazilian national oil company, had recently found
natural gas deposits nearby. "If they decide it is enough to take out,
or if they find oil, then this whole area will explode. There will be
money and people all over. Then we will see a new heart of the
Amazon. Oil is what everyone wants to see."

Not so Dorival. At 57, he said, he had seen most of all he
wanted to. He came to the jungle for a last challenge—leaving behind
his four ranches, his grownup children and "the best swimming pool
in Porto Alegre." He wanted to see the project grow and he liked to

cruise far up the Amazon tributaries in his 40-foot cabin cruiser with just his wife for company.

"I'll stop sometimes and watch a caboclo fish with just a line in his hand. No nets, no fancy gear. Just slow with a single line. It feels like that is all there is to life. Just beautiful."

He saw no contradiction in his clearing so much of the forest he idealized and was puzzled when probed for conflict. "She's so big. You can't dent her." And he had a ready answer when we told him no one knew about his giant project that had been there five years. He laughed. "Nobody knows anything about her."

LIMA

We planned to fly to Tefe then find a boat to take us to Leticia, where the borders of Brazil, Peru and Colombia meet. The girl behind the counter at the bush airline office said that would be impossible. The few seats to Tefe had been booked weeks ago and it would be at least another week before more were available. We tried charm, threats, money. She had heard it all before. There were no seats for a week.

We were not so concerned to see the river between Manaus and Tefe. Those who knew it said it was much the same as the Manaus–Santarem stretch, only a little less populous. After Tefe, the river becomes wilder. Civilization has not penetrated there with much force. The river up there doesn't even go by the name Amazon; the

Brazilians call it the Solimoes. Lush, untouched jungle and rare pink dolphins—we longed for that sense of untrampled ground that we had had only brief tastes of so far. So if we couldn't fly, we'd have to take a boat all the way. We figured it would be 10 days to Leticia.

There were no boats. The world's largest river and there was no way to get from Manaus to Leticia. At the wharves we were told it was possible to hop a series of the rickety wooden tubs that plied between towns. One boat captain said he thought we could get all the way to Leticia that way, but he couldn't guarantee it. Another old riverman remembered that all the proper folks used to go on the Booth Lines, which could book you a cabin on one of their freighters.

Of course, the Booth Lines. Just the name brightened us, the famous Liverpool steamship company that was incidentally mentioned in most of the Amazon literature. It was how anyone who was anyone—from Bates and Wallace on—got up the Amazon. We had visions of a smaller version of the *Sobral Santos,* something a bit more intimate with a roster of British explorers, international diamond smugglers, maybe a missionary and his lovely wife—and good food.

We were about 10 years too late. Captain Eric Bentley, a Booth Lines skipper himself, broke the bad news to us.

"I'm afraid we discontinued taking passengers some years back," the narrow-faced Cockney told us. "We just don't have the demand and it was costing too much. Maybe everyone who wants to see the Amazon has seen it."

The line sends fewer freighters up the river past Manaus these days anyway, he said. "It's still pretty busy downriver, but that Iquitos run has slowed down a lot in the past few years." Bentley looked content, remembering the way it used to be.

"That was a bloody grand run. Wild. A wild place. Sometimes I'd come around a corner and we'd come on a herd of wild pigs swimming across the river. I'd reach down and grab a couple of them by the tail and the cook would barbecue them. We ate well. We were carrying food from all over the world."

He was wound up. "There were so many lovely places on shore. Isolated, like paradise. I remember there were some English nurses working along the river in some kind of health program. We'd put 'stopped because of heavy rain' in the log book and go ashore and visit with them. Bring them magazines, special food, you know, things like that. They were grand girls.

"Nowadays there's not much that goes up that way. The freighters aren't allowed to take passengers and, even so, there's nothing coming through for a week or so. There are some smaller boats, but I'll tell you something now, but you didn't hear it from me. They carry drugs and the like. A lot of smuggling up in that area. I suppose you could take your chances on those leaky old local boats, but I wouldn't. The freighters would have been grand for you two. It's a shame you boys missed them."

We left Bentley with the realization that we had hit our first big snag. We couldn't get to that wild stretch of river from Manaus and that was that. This wasn't like dealing with Greyhound buses. "There are no schedules in the Amazon," Copila, the sleazy pilot, had told us. We decided reluctantly to go straight to Lima and try to work our way back downriver.

Before leaving the United States, we had cleared the way to meet with Peru's President, Fernando Belaunde Terry, at his palace in Lima. The meeting was to have been the last stop of our journey, the last word before we headed home. Peru, with its more than 20,000 square miles of the Amazon jungle, stands where Brazil stood 20 years ago: aware of what the jungle may hold for its people, not yet geared to exploit it. We had been told that Belaunde was a man of many interests, first among them being the Amazon jungle.

We had no trouble booking seats on the Air France 747 that made a fuel stop in Manaus on its Paris–Lima run and sat back on comfortable foam cushions among gaily dressed French tourists, helping ourselves to fresh croissants, Normandy butter, quiche Lorraine and Bordeaux wine.

Far below, when the clouds got wispy, we could see the faint line where the world turned from green to brown. The line is where the Amazon peters out against the sharp slopes of the Andes, choked off in the dry, frigid air. It was a boundary that had provided perhaps the most vivid image of the jungle we had seen: the opening of the film "Aguirre: The Wrath of God" by the West German director Werner Herzog. Herzog based his work on the true story of a 16th-century Spanish expedition that had been sent down from the Andes to tap into the heart of the continent. In a long shot that gradually moves closer, Herzog shows a thin file of men and animals winding its way down the steep mountainside, moving deeper and deeper into the steaming green that is all around them. The camera pans closer still as the men slog on down the muddy, crumbling trail, their armor dragging them down, their beasts squealing, their heavy baggage and cannon falling into the abyss. Among them are the once mighty Inca warriors, now slaves who strain and sweat under heavy loads. The faces of the conquistadores are creased first with puzzled frowns, then wide-eyed looks of terror as they realize that what they are descending into is far more terrible than the hostile place they are leaving.

Where they had started, we were going: Lima, once the wealthiest city in the hemisphere, the seat of the Spanish vice-royalty. Lima sits on a dry plain that runs the length of Peru's west coast. About 90 percent of the country's 19 million people live along this coastal shelf—5 million in Lima alone—with more arriving every day. The problem is a common one in Latin America, subsistence farmers leaving the countryside as the soil wears out and bringing their families to the last hope, the city. In Peru, they come mostly from the Andes, the 1,000-mile-long spine of the country which separates the coast from the jungle.

There is no grandeur in Lima today. There is dust, traffic, tumbling buildings and the smell of urine. Everywhere this old squalid city smells of urine and it is quickly apparent why. As we walked around downtown we saw an old man on a side street, his back turned to us, a wet stream running on the sidewalk between his feet. A few blocks further a younger man emerged from a doorway and finished zipping up the fly on his worn-shiny polyester trousers in full view of anyone who cared to notice. Public pissing, we discovered, is a way of life in Lima, even in the better sections of town. It is a sort of collective gesture of contempt the citizens make at their failed city.

The poverty is intense. Along the highways on the northeast side of the city, people live in whole villages of cardboard boxes and tin shacks. We glimpsed a low stream running between shacks, no more than a dirty froth of water sucked dry by the needs of the slum dwellers. At every stoplight, crowds of small boys ran to the cars waving red rags and offering to clean windshields for a few cents. The drivers shooed them away. Ours, a burly man, did it by cocking a thick forearm and showing the back of his hand. On the sidewalks, Indian women in round-brimmed hats sat on piles made of blankets and all the possessions they owned, begging with outstretched leathery hands. A shoeshine boy in a torn maroon sweatsuit had the face of a 45-year-old man. He was not so unusual; all the children have grave faces. The boys sleep in doorways, huddled together head to toe for warmth.

The town seems half built, or half falling down. Houses of mud and brick have exposed beams on the upper floors, as though the owners ran out of money halfway through construction. Most buildings seemed cracked or faded. Some foundations may date to the 1500s, but earthquakes have long since tumbled any walls that old.

Throughout Lima are elaborate monuments and statuary, dedicated to generals of defeated armies. The only truly imposing cast is the blackened bronze of Francisco Pizarro, the 1542 conqueror of the Incas, rearing up on horseback next to the Presidential Palace. The sculpture is powerful and fierce, with none of the gaudy wedding-cake ornamentation that bedecks the others. Inside the cathedral, across the main piazza, his dry bones are on display in a glass case.

The city offers one other notable class of monument—its cars. Vintage American dreammobiles from the 50s and 60s are all over the streets, preserved by the dry climate and the reverence their owners shower on them. Tearing down the wide boulevards and careening around corners are endless variations of the classic '57 Chevy with its high, haughty fins; the mid-50s Dodges with taillights like ray guns; Corvairs; Studebakers; Ford Falcons and, occasionally, black Cadillacs.

There was one standing among the row of luxury taxis in front of our hotel, a black 1957 Caddy, bulbous and boatlike. A real car. Most of the luxury taxi drivers favor old Dodges or the modern Latin status car, a silver Ford LTD. But Martinez Chaves' life is his Caddy.

"It won't cost you more," Chaves said, sweeping his hand in the direction of the open rear door.

Chaves showed us the town, shuttling us back and forth to interviews in government offices, universities and embassies. He always drove slowly, as if piloting a large ship. "With dignity," said the thin, aging man. He had been a chauffeur and was given the car by its owner after the 1968 coup, when displays of wealth were frowned upon. He kept it gleaming and in perfect working order.

We spoke with Chaves about the President of the Republic, Fernando Belaunde Terry, and we noticed that he and many others we met referred to Belaunde as if he were a prosperous uncle who often came to Sunday dinner. People talked of him familiarly and discussed "his problems," which were really their own. Chaves had followed the career of the President closely and claimed to have met him.

"A good man," Chaves pronounced one day. "Belaunde knows what this country needs. He will shake it and help us get back what we have lost."

Chaves knew of the President's grand plans for the jungle. "The March to the Jungle is what they call it," he told us. "It is a very great idea, but I am too old to participate."

Chaves drove us to the Presidential Palace, in the center of the oldest part of Lima. He dropped us off under the Pizarro statue, next to an outdoor cafe frequented by tourists.

"Tell Fernando that Martinez Chaves of Arequipa is with him," he said as we left.

The palace, which has been the object of many coups, was guarded by a small detachment of soldiers dressed in 19th-century European military outfits, all red and white and brass, but carrying dull black automatic rifles. We were taken through a maze of rooms with carved ceilings, frescoed walls and marbled floors. The heavy dark furniture and hand-painted tiles had been done by Spanish craftsmen centuries ago.

At precisely 4:30 we were ushered by a military aide into Belaunde's office. He did seem to be an uncle, friendly but reserved, casually dressed but with a starched white collar and tightly knotted tie. He wore a tan blazer and dark brown slacks; his white hair was slicked back from a high, wide forehead. Belaunde, a square man, thrust out a large hand at the end of a short arm.

"My pleasure," he said, and pointed us to a semicircle of chairs in front of his desk.

This day, and apparently many others, the President was thinking about decay. It is Belaunde's passion to see Peru become the country it is supposed to be, the true heir to the remarkable Incan civilization and the Spanish genius for order. Much of that wealth and tradition has been squandered over the centuries, largely through internal warfare among competing groups within the country. The decay we had noticed in the capital city pervades the whole nation. Now, for the first time in memory, an elected president had put together a functioning coalition and made peace with the military. It was time to regain the glory and the starting point was to be the Amazon.

"It was the marriage of my two professions—architecture and loving Peru—that got me interested in the Amazon. Architects are frequent travelers, always looking at historic buildings and communities. I have traveled by the usual means of transportation, but I crossed the Andes by mule nine times. Then I went down the Amazon by raft from the origins of the river. Then I made several trips by horse all over the country to places that have had some importance in the past and have no importance now."

But as his books—*Peru: Town by Town* and *Peru's Own Conquest*—make clear, Belaunde was not only looking at structures. He was trying to find out what happened to his country; to the physical and spiritual unity that pervaded the land during the rule of the Incas; to the ingenuity that he saw most stunningly in the imposing walls they built with perfectly cut stone that fit together without cement.

"My question was why? Why this decay?"

A military aide he had called came in with a handful of black-and-white photographs which he handed to us. Belaunde on horseback. In a canoe. On a mule. The always determined look on his face suggested that his search for answers was no trivial quest.

In 1924, when he was 12 years old, Belaunde's father was jailed and deported to Paris for his political beliefs. When Belaunde was college age, his family moved to Miami where he studied architecture, a course he completed at the University of Texas. He came back to Peru and was elected to Congress in 1945, but a military coup in 1948 put an end to democratic government. In the next round of elections, in 1956, Belaunde was a candidate for President, although the military government only allowed his name on the ballot after a massive rally in Lima. But the opposition parties united against him, and he lost the election.

Illustrations of the lengths Belaunde would go to promote his principles emerged over the next few years. In 1957 he fought a saber duel with a congressman who had publically denounced him as a liar

and a demagogue. Both men were slightly injured, but Belaunde enhanced his reputation as a dashing populist.

President Manuel Prado, who saw Belaunde as a menace to the
traditional oligarchical ways of doing business, had him jailed for
defying a presidential ban on political rallies. Belaunde turned this
setback to his advantage by slipping out of his island prison and
swimming through the chilly Pacific to a waiting escape craft. He was
recaptured, but not before he won the imagination of his nation. In
1963, after another military coup, Belaunde finally was elected
President.

Now in a position to implement his ideas, the first thing he set
out to do was join this geographically divided nation. "I intercon-
nected all the provinces of Peru, all the capitals, except for one. Now
some of them are connected by water—by the Amazon system—and
others are connected by road."

But the more Belaunde had looked at the map of his country,
the more he had realized that people were in the wrong place. He led
us over to an easel and folded down a full-color map of Peru. With
the skill of a professor, he telescoped a silver pointer and aimed it at
the middle of the country.

"This is the high jungle, where the vegetation starts to come
down from the Andes to the Amazon. This, near Iquitos, is the low
jungle, where the land is generally considered poor for agriculture. In
the high jungle, it is rich.

"Here you have plenty of water." The pointer went back to the
high jungle. "Here you don't have a drop." The pointer moved to the
coast. "The idea is not to bring water to the people—as we're doing
now—but to bring the people to the water."

Belaunde plans to bring people into the high jungle with roads, a
vast system called the Marginal Forest Highway. He originated the
plan more than two decades ago, and it became a symbol of the
ambition and folly of his first administration. No one from the time of
Pizarro had ever suggested that any place but Lima could be critical
to the national destiny. But in 1965 Belaunde wrote a new perspective for the country: "The construction of the Marginal Forest
Highway . . . will lead to progress and prosperity. The landless will
have fields to till and a home of their own. Peru will once again gain a
balance it lost with the downfall of the Inca empire; roads will be

rhythmically integrated with agriculture. A unity in the mountains will bring a unity to the whole nation. The deserts, mountains and jungles will eventually be laced together in a system that offers hope for all."

In Brazil such talk of national conquest of the jungle was the clarion of Getulio Vargas and Juscelino Kubitschek, two of the most popular leaders of the 20th century. But Peru never has shown any great fervor to integrate within its borders, no frontier spirit, and Belaunde's call to arms was ridiculed by the establishment as the rantings of a populist out of touch with his populace. In 1968, he was roused from bed in the middle of one night by a military coup and shipped out of the country in exile. Talk of the conquest of the jungle ceased.

For the next 12 years, Belaunde lectured on urban planning at an array of major American universities, keeping alive the hope of his return to Peru and the opportunity to march to the jungle. In 1980 the military government, under pressure from the administration of President Jimmy Carter, but more importantly facing the total collapse of Peru's economy, decided to hold elections. Belaunde, the returned hero who evoked memories of the days before the military, easily won.

He came back preaching the same gospel as when he left. Some people in the government told us that exile had sapped much of his original fervor and that now his main concern was simply to finish his six-year term and prove that democracy can work. But if he cares less, he did a good job of fooling us. His explanation of the marginal highway and his two other schemes—all unprompted by questions— was delivered like a sermon. Belaunde was totally absorbed in the map before him, though we knew he must have given the presentation a thousand times.

The aide, a major in a green uniform and heavy gold braid, brought a new easel full of large cardboard maps, some of them looking quite worn. The highway first. It is to snake vertically down the country through the high jungle of the eastern Andes and link up with the TransAmazon Highway system in Brazil's state of Acre. Iquitos, which we had thought of as the center of the Peruvian Amazon, was far off the path. Belaunde said Iquitos had an "African climate" and had written after a trip there that it was "a confrontation with the harsh realities of living with pain and hope not shared by the world of officialdom."

But the land for the highway is not harsh, he said. "It is a Riviera climate, the Saint Tropez or Monaco of South America. This marginal road is in the most promising area of the world as far as energy is concerned. No place can compete. You have Maracaibo [the oil-rich Venezuelan lake], then there is oil in the Orinoco River, and you have oil here in Ecuador and oil here in Peru, then in the central part you have gas, and Madre de Dios in our south is a promising area and in Bolivia, in Santa Cruz, there is a lot of gas. And you have all the hydroelectric potential of the rivers. Add that to the climate and the agricultural possibilities and there is no place in the world like this."

Belaunde envisioned the road, we realized, as a continental venture, linking Venezuela, Colombia, Ecuador, Peru, Bolivia and Brazil. Sixty percent of what he thinks the system should be has already been built, he said. But thus far none of the international connections have been made.

The town of Constitution is the second major part of the President's scheme. It is to be like Brasilia, a city built from scratch in the empty interior, almost equidistant from all the country's borders. Already Belaunde had sponsored a design competition for a city plan—we saw rooms in the palace full of models submitted by architects for many design competitions—but a final decision had not been made. Constitution won't be a capital city, though, only a population center to draw people to the middle of Peru. Belaunde said construction would start at the end of 1982.

"Then I am interested in tying up the river systems," Belaunde said as he shuffled the maps to find the most worn chart. It was a map of South America with lines representing dredging and dams linking the Orinoco River system in Venezuela with the Amazon in the center and the Paraguay and eventually the Plata in the south.

"Think of this," he said, the pointer moving. "If we tie up these systems," he hit the map three times, "and with your system in North America, then with a crossing of the Caribbean, which is not too long, you have the longest waterway in the world, from Quebec to Buenos Aires. The continents will be invulnerable, because if you have this no one can compete with the Western Hemisphere for strategic materials. No submarine could touch you."

We told him the plan sounded similar to that of the Hudson Institute in the 1960s, the think-tank proposal to dam the Amazon that caused such an uproar in Brazil and made the generals think they had better get on with their own occupation before someone else did.

Belaunde scoffed at the political problem we were hinting at. "The idea is as old as the continent itself. I talked to President Figueiredo. He is rather receptive but feels that is not so easy. Personally, I think it is not so difficult." He estimated the cost at $1 billion, which he said was "nothing."

We could see Belaunde didn't like interruptions. It was as if he didn't want to be challenged, that the genius of the plan ought to be self-evident. He brought our attention back to the map and ran his pointer along the squiggly black lines of the rivers. "So, it is a simple matter," he concluded.

Simple, he admitted, except that it hadn't been done. The President assumed the sheepish look of many of his countrymen when discussing their failures. "You have this kind of system in the United States. You move coal and steel. You had a system where nature did half the work and you did the other half. Here, nature has done almost 100 percent of the job, and we have done nothing. You cannot be satisfied with what nature did. Whoever is satisfied with what nature did will not be advancing much."

He explained how the combination of river and highway systems would create a new market for the continent at its center and how Constitution would enable Peru to participate. "You know the whole movement in South America was centrifugal," Belaunde said. "Now we want to turn it into a centripetal movement." Sounding very much like the Brazilian generals, he said, "The world is too crowded and in another world war you don't know what can happen. There are people who need land. If we are not using it, someone else will."

Security is not Belaunde's only concern. He predicted years ago that the dark Malthusian shadow was drawing over Peru. "We had always been expanding our agricultural production until recently. Now it is stable, but with a population growing at almost 3 percent a year, if we stop expanding, we will starve to death. I predicted it 20 years ago and I have lived long enough to see it happen. We have to expand the area we give to agriculture."

So far, though, Peru has largely failed to attract population to the jungle. One of the officials at the United States Agency for International Development branch in Lima had told us the influx of people is erratic and uncontrolled. Families are flooding into valleys in numbers greater than the land can support; yet other valleys not far away are unreachable and empty. Peru is in no position to handle a major migration, but the few who are going in are creating environmental havoc. Preliminary studies have shown that deforestation in the Upper Amazon valleys is causing extreme flooding in the lowland towns. The country's meager settlement effort has been the worst of all possible worlds.

Belaunde said migration would be organized when Constitution was finished, solving the problem of random surges. He was certain the people would go because they would have to. We saw, though, no evidence of pioneer spirit in anyone but Belaunde himself.

We asked his thoughts about the environment. "The ecologists are completely insane," Belaunde answered. "We need space and resources. We are not going to sit back. But we do not mean to occupy the whole area. We mean to occupy perhaps 20 percent, where the land is favorable."

Presence of Indian tribes, another troubling environmental and human problem in Brazil, didn't seem to bother Belaunde. He said about 200,000 indigenous people would be affected by his highway plan. "These people are very important because they know the area. They are prepared to live there, so they can be very useful. They are nomads, but if you give them land they will stay in one place with great benefits for their health, their culture."

We wondered whether the road to hell is paved with good intentions. We had seen, we remarked, what has happened to the nomadic Parakana Indians when they stayed in one place, then another place, then another.

Belaunde responded, "There are people, sociologists, who believe they should stay as they are. That means a life expectancy of 25 years. That means very bad health, losing your teeth and complete illiteracy. So you cannot take them seriously. They want to change the continent to a museum for sociologists, but we have other responsibilities."

We were also curious about the political problems, particularly on a continent that has been notoriously unable to agree on anything for centuries. The border disputes alone are awesome: Peru versus Chile; Ecuador versus Peru; Venezuela versus Guyana; Chile versus Argentina; and everyone suspicious of Brazil. But Belaunde dismissed such problems as "not very difficult. When you have a large neighbor, I think it is safer to have connections than not to have them." He was not bothered by the world beyond his maps. He saw no reason he couldn't get these wary neighbors to agree on a plan that was self-evidently to everyone's benefit.

"I'm used to it. Even the people in Peru say, Belaunde and his jungle plans—craziness!" This time he smiled at the criticism. "I don't have to argue any more. This thing has been proved. I tell them to go to Tarapoto, in the high jungle. The first time I went there I went by mule for three days. I walked for days and canoed for two more. Now you can drive. People are coming."

Later we learned that the city of Tarapoto is in the center of one of Peru's most productive coca growing regions—the raw material for cocaine. There is also some industrial development there and much farming, but the chance that this show of progress is a false promise is great.

We turned away from the maps and sat again in the high leather chairs before his desk. The President circled around to review his appointment schedule which we had set awry; we had been scheduled for 20 minutes but had taken nearly two hours. He apologized that he had to take leave of us, perhaps more from a professorial sense that his students had not absorbed enough. On the way to the door, Kelly had a last question.

"Who's going to pay for it?"

"Who's going to pay for it?" Belaunde responded. He paused a moment, opened his mouth to speak, then paused again. "Well, the community . . . this is a self-paying proposition. When I built the road in my last government to the beach district, it has been paid for 20 times by the users. So those who benefit will pay for it."

But these were not projects where the revenue would be as certain as a road to the beach; subsidies would be needed. And, too, his government now has many more demands on its cash than 20 years ago.

"Oh, there is money. You have banks. You have the World Bank, the Inter-American Development Bank. And the people have money. I remember once a group of bankers came to see me. They were very sad. They said we are going to have a strike of the workers because they want higher salaries. So we are going broke, we have to close the banks. They were so depressed, I wanted to get my pocketbook and give them some money. These were the richest people in Peru.

"Then my aide tells me there is an Indian community, they want to see you. I said to him, if the rich people are asking for so much, what am I going to face now? The Indians came in, they spoke Quecha; I needed an interpreter. They came to ask me to collect what they owed the country. They said they had been given land expropriated from a hacienda and now they wanted to pay for it. So there you have a great lesson."

We stood silently, unsatisfied. Belaunde knew it; he had been called "Belaunde the Dreamer" too many times.

"You said who will pay for it. During the Inca regime, you know, nobody asked that question. There was no money. I told Friedman—the economist, Mr. Milton Friedman—I said we had no problem with monetary theories then because the Incas had no money. Nevertheless, they had an economy. People were fed. Food was stored all over the country. Everything was organized. So, the important lesson from Peru, the only single idea that comes out of Peru that is fundamental, is you can have civilization even if you don't have money."

He talked a little more about the Incas, but time was short and we knew we would get nothing else. We wondered how the right-wing generals in Chile or his friends in Brazil and Argentina with their perpetual triple-digit inflation respond when Belaunde tells them that the Incas built roads with no money.

Belaunde's press secretary offered us a tour of the historic palace before we left. We stopped to look out into the courtyard garden that we had seen from the window behind the President's desk.

"That is the President's favorite sculpture," said the press secretary, pointing to a tall thin man standing next to an overburdened mule supporting a plump shape.

We didn't recognize it at first. The press secretary was surprised. "That's Don Quixote, of course."

IQUITOS

Ahead of us along the road from the airport to the town of Iquitos in northeastern Peru we spotted a glowing green sign. From a distance it was a fluorescent smudge through the rain as we approached, crouched in the back of one of the motorcycle-powered rickshaws that serve as taxicabs here. As we closed in, the sign grew and defined itself into a familiar, jaunty script: "Holiday Inn." Set in a clearing surrounded by unruly green trees in this town that was literally hundreds of miles from any other city was a whitewashed motel with a portico and uniformed doorman to park what, by all rights, should have been a steady stream of rented Fords driven by traveling salesmen. The Holiday Inn was not new to London. This monument to irony had greeted him years before, on his impulsive dash to the Amazon that had been the yeast for our years of ferment and our many months of travel here. By now, there was little of that original buoyancy left in us.

We looked at each other, shrugged, and told the motorcycle driver to turn in. Along one wall of the lobby were four or five booths advertising Amazon tours. One booth advertised direct daily flights to Miami, four hours to the north. That thought had not occurred to us before, Miami so close. We had been gone long enough to feel the United States should have been days, not hours away. We each felt a fleeting temptation to pack it in. The Amazon had proved an exhausting place, not just for the climate and the strain of getting from here to there, but for the difficulty of plucking out any one impression for close examination. The striking contrasts—the blacks and whites we had seen at first—had long since merged into gray-toned subtleties. To notice anything novel or telling now required constant attention to detail. We had to work for our observations and we were tired.

And, too, we were frustrated by a growing sense that the more jungle we saw, the less we knew. The enormousness of the forest, the impossibility of experiencing it all—the way when you were in it you couldn't see it, just as when you were over it you couldn't see it—had begun to make us feel inadequate. If nothing else, we knew we had to see some of Peru just to contrast it with Brazil. And we wanted to go back to Manaus over that great middle chunk of the river, to finish it all, to see everything we had planned to see.

So rather than check the plane schedule, we headed into town.

Iquitos is to the Peruvian Amazon what Manaus is to the Brazilian Amazon: the capital of the jungle. This city, 2,300 miles from the mouth of the Amazon, 600 miles northeast of Lima and clear over the Andes, was where we hoped to get some idea of what the Peruvians are doing with the jungle that covers more than half of their country.

The city of 150,000 is also like Manaus in that its great days were those of rubber at the turn of the century—and those great days are long gone. Even at its best, Iquitos was the poor man's rubber capital with only a couple of grand buildings and no opera house. The rubber companies that operated out of Iquitos were accused of committing the worst atrocities on Indian rubber gatherers. A British Foreign Service officer, Roger Casement, in his celebrated investigation of the treatment of the Indians, concluded that 30,000 were killed in the region of the Putumayo River, just to the north. He documented cases of Indians being savagely beaten, burned alive and chopped up and fed to dogs. His 1912 report caused an international scandal and did much to shape the image of violence in the Amazon. The meanness that marks Iquitos' legacy seemed to hang in the air.

A smoky haze stung our eyes and nose with the scent of burning garbage—something we had not encountered in Brazil. Only the rain cleared the air, and for that reason alone Iquitos is fortunate; it rains here all the time—120 inches a year, which is more than most places in the Amazon. Yet really the rain cleansed nothing. It spattered the dark mud and pounded the rotting refuse deeper into the oozing river bank. As soon as it stopped, the acrid smoke was back.

Iquitos clings to a high bank of the Maranon River, as the Amazon is called here. The river flows north and a little west at Iquitos, just before it makes a wide turn and heads straight east for the Brazilian border. The town has gradually retreated as the river has cut off giant chunks of the bank during each rainy season. It has about it the feeling of a lifeboat, crowded with people and jammed up against the jungle wall. Below the bank, on the squishy mud flats, live the people who cannot afford to flee to higher ground. They live in a stilt-hut and houseboat community called Belen, an area of neither water nor land. From there, out of a collection of flimsy stalls, the inhabitants were selling all manner of goods—much of it floated in from up or down the river.

Above on the river bank, the stalls looked somewhat sturdier, though the commerce was no less frenzied. Despite a few established stores such as pharmacies and stationery shops, most of the selling in Iquitos seemed to be done from outdoor booths. We walked through booth-jammed streets at the south end of town, through a continuous tunnel formed by canvas roofs and lined with stacks of pants, bins of shoes and the backs of diners curled over bowls of fish stew. We sensed no permanence to the market, nor to Iquitos itself. A really good rain, we felt, and the whole sodden city might slip away.

Befitting its location at a bend in the river, Iquitos collects an array of human as well as material flotsam. We saw the posters in the cafes downtown. Photographs of young adults with long hair and American names accompanied by desperate pleas from parents for information of their whereabouts. Generous rewards were offered, but the age of many of the signs testified to the futility. The drifters, misfits and dropouts of the world are comforted by this isolated city wrapped in an anonymous cloak of jungle. Those we met made us think it was not so much a place for a new beginning—as we sensed so often in Brazil—but for retreat.

Paul Hittscher, one of the first of those escapees we met in Iquitos, was a ship captain until his sea ran out here at just about the farthest point a ship can travel up the Amazon. Hittscher, who was born in Hamburg, left home after World War II to see the world. Winding up in Marseilles, he worked as a bartender until he signed aboard one of the luxurious yachts plying the Mediterranean to learn the trade of a seaman. Eventually he captained the yachts of some extraordinarily wealthy men, dropping anchor in the blue waters off Cap d'Antibes with Arab and Greek tycoons. One day he was asked to take a boat to Iquitos where it would be sold to a tour operator. When he got here he decided that, having nothing better to do, he would stay with the boat a while. The boat sank and he went to work scrounging equipment and boats for the oil companies.

When we met him he was running the Tropical Restaurant, a tidy, open-front place with the best food in town.

"We needed a goddamn good steak and a joint where you could get real American powdered mashed potatoes," he told us one afternoon as we sat sipping cold cans of beer on his patio. He laughed with a phlegmy roar that came from somewhere inside his huge belly, and spoke colloquial and thoroughly profane English with a slight accent that made his favorite phrase come out "muddafucka."

"I made a little money around here so I was the one to do it. Open this joint. Besides I got this local girl pregnant so I thought it's time to stay. I bet you bastards think that's the only decent thing I ever did, and so maybe you're right."

Hittscher, a big, blond, crookedly built man with fingers like bratwursts and worn tattoos on his wide forearms, presented himself as a sort of king of the Lilliputians. "Why the fuck should I go back to Germany and put up with all that shit? Here I'm the king. They don't know how to make money here, so I show them," he said with a wink and a spreading grin that threatened to pull his meaty face apart. He was always working on a few schemes: brokering parts for the oil companies, recruiting workers, financing cargo for the trading houses, reselling imported whiskey.

"Senor Paul" raced around town in a dented yellow jeep, scattering the pedestrians in front of him with a steady stream of curses. "Muddafucka kid, get out of the way." One day while touring in the jeep, we pulled up beside his father-in-law, an ancient former mayor of a nearby town.

"Ah, the great and wise Don Roberto," Hittscher greeted him in lilting Spanish as the wizened man brightened. He switched to English, for us: "You goddamn smug old turkey. You know, I have to support this old fucker and all his relatives? They come in like flies. Sometimes I'd like to shoot the grinning bastard."

All the while he spoke, the smile never left Hittscher's lips, matching that of the uncomprehending Don Roberto.

For a few nights we ate grilled fish with mashed potatoes and green chili sauce in the ship captain's restaurant. He would tend to his customers and stop by for a beer to tell us about them. Most were transients here on some kind of business—smugglers, oil men, riverboat captains, a few airline crews, drug dealers. The river town has become a major transshipment point for cocaine grown on the jungle slopes 200 miles to the southwest near Tingo Maria. The consequences can be seen in the way checks at Hittscher's restaurant were often paid with $100 bills, and in the way murder has become an expected event. Sometimes a couple of American women from the increasingly scarce jungle missions would come in, looking pink-scrubbed and out of place in flower print shirtwaist dresses.

Many permanent residents we met were foreigners, a fact that told us something of the difference between Peru and Brazil. Iquitos is more heterogeneous than any of the Brazilian cities, much more Amazonian than Peruvian. Peru has never really made much progress in "conquering" the jungle and integrating it into the rest of the country and, President Belaunde's dreams aside, the Peruvian people are not nationalistic about the Amazon because they can't afford to be. There are no road connections from Iquitos to the rest of Peru; the Andes were long a nearly insurmountable barrier. For many years it was almost as easy to reach Iquitos by coming up the Amazon from the Atlantic as it was to come the other way from Lima.

"This is the right place for madmen," Paul Hittscher told us late one night. "It is really shit here."

"See some guy like that?" he nodded his head slightly toward the table at the rear. "Don't stare. Someone like that. They'll kill you and drop you in the river and no one cares. This jungle digests people like garbage. This is not the place to create something. Only to take something out."

The best taking these days is oil.

In the early 1970s the multinational oil firms decided to investigate the long-held belief that the Amazon once flowed the other way, emptying into the Pacific Ocean. That would mean that a river delta laden with ancient organic matter should once have existed in the region around Iquitos. Like an armored assault, the men and equipment poured in; roustabouts who had worked in Oklahoma and Bahrain came to try their hand at the jungle. Oil had built the air-conditioned Holiday Inn, its red velvet lounge offering the familiar comforts of a stern bartender, an open-mouthed bus boy and a cocktail waitress in a low-cut dress.

Most of the oil men were gone when we arrived. All but one company—Occidental Petroleum—had come up dry, and after battling impassable swamps, disease epidemics and hostile Indians, the losers packed up and left. With them went the loud laughter and huge bar tabs at the Holiday Inn.

But Hittscher told us about a Kentuckian named Jim Ray who was helping to suck the oil from underneath the jungle floor. He was running a construction firm based in Lima and Iquitos that worked for the giant oil companies. Ray had learned some lessons about the jungle, Hittscher told us, and knew how to deal with it maybe better than anyone in Peru.

"Maybe he's the only one that ever got really rich off this bastard," Hittscher said. "I mean millions and millions of dollars."

We met Jim Ray in a hotel. He came through the doors wearing a tan Stetson and walking like he was going someplace in a hurry.

"You Kelly? This joint got a bar? Let's get us a drink."

The words came out in a tumbling, growly Southern drawl so deep and raspy it seemed impossible for a human voice to make the sounds. His face looked like the front end of a dump truck after a head-on collision. The fleshy red nose was creased and off-center, the cheeks lined and sagging, the eyes heavy-lidded and the whole business skewed to the left.

"Let's just suppose I have made a little money," he began the conversation. "Do you think I'd tell you about it?"

A couple of scotches and a half dozen Bloody Marys later, he did.

Ray, 60 now, was a man in the right place when the Amazon finally gave up one of its most coveted treasures. For decades, geologists had punched holes all through the basin and come up empty. In the early 1960s a famous oil explorer, Walter Lake, said, "I'll drink any oil you find in the Amazon." Jim Ray, who would have drunk oil on a dare, was there when they found it, 200 miles northwest of Iquitos near the Equador border. Actually, by the time the first Peru strike came in, Texaco was already in the Ecuador jungles with wells and a pipeline system Ray had helped build. He moved south to work for Occidental Petroleum in the mid 1970s when the rush to Peru was on. The oil company had to spend money to prove geologists' theories about the river once flowing the other way and Ray, a former project manager for Williams Brothers, a big contractor in Tulsa, Oklahoma, was happy to help them.

He built roads and shipped equipment for Oxy, which, as the most persistent of the oil firms, was finally rewarded with a major find in 1976. When the company needed a permanent camp and a thousand miles of roads, Jim Ray from Kentucky horse country was there to build it.

"I did it by treating her a little careful. Nobody's going to beat that jungle. You have to learn to work around her. You go with her. As a general rule you have to remember the good Lord was a fine man, but he picked some godawful places to put oil."

We had been out to the drilling site, which resembled the bivouac of an American battalion in Vietnam, complete with equipment, houses, steaks and beers choppered in.

The oil men said these were some of the toughest conditions they had ever worked under. The initial group had come in by dugout canoe up the Rio Tigre. Their first task was to clear a helicopter pad so the Peruvian Air Force could begin a shuttle service with its odd combination of Russian- and American-made helicopters, ferrying lighter equipment. Pipes, bulldozers, house trailers and even submarine engines to run the pumps were barged in, sometimes starting in Texas and traveling 2,500 miles up the Amazon; the dented pickups bore the sticker of a Houston Ford dealer. A tank farm was built, and then Jim Ray and his team of crusty foremen and rugged laborers went to work on a network of roads and pipelines to connect the dozen or so drilling operations spread over 4 million acres of alternately swampy and hilly jungle.

The roads and the way Jim Ray had built them made the biggest impression on us. Not at all like the straight strips we had driven over in Brazil, these roads twisted and turned and rippled through the jungle. They took constant traffic from heavy trucks laden with loads of pipe, and daily washings from the regular downpours. Yet they were smooth and firm.

"You wouldn't think there would be hills under that tree cover, would you?" Ray said as he downed drinks in the hotel bar. "Well, hell, you can't draw a straight line anywhere around here."

The method Ray had evolved to survey the roads was to take two of the local woodsmen who worked for him, drop them from a helicopter at the point where he wanted the road to go and tell them to find their way back.

"I say, 'Stick to the high ground and mark your trail.' Some college-educated engineer would get himself lost and killed out there. But these monkeys come back in about a week or so with the trees all marked and there's your road. We just go in and follow the trees."

He drained another pulpy red Bloody Mary, wiped his mouth with the back of his hand and called for the waiter.

"Rapido, Bozo," he said, clapping his hands.

"It ain't," he began again, "such a horrible place to work. I'll tell you, in all the 20 years I've been down here, I've never had any problems. I've had the shits a few times, I had malaria once but that's no big deal. A lot of these folks come down here all scared about working in the jungle, wearing these lion-tamer hats. That's a lot of bullshit. It's just a place like any other place. You just have to go with it instead of against it is all."

But Jim Ray made it clear that was not all. Another secret to his success had been money, great gobs of it, that oil companies cough up when they need something done.

"Nothing is as, shall we say, urgent as the oil business," Ray explained. "When they hit oil they say, 'Goddamn, get after it. Build us a damn pipeline yesterday. It might cost more but goddamn get her done."

If it weren't for the money, Ray was not sure the work would have gotten done.

"You have to pay people very, very well for working in that jungle." He said his foremen, mostly Americans, "come into the sunlight at the end of the year with a backpack full of money."

If money runs out, they go. When the wells run dry, they move on. Jim Ray, the most successful businessman in the Amazon, knew the best way to gouge the jungle and was well paid for it, but he also knew that as soon as he was no longer paid to keep up his roads, they would wash away.

The Jim Rays and the Paul Hittschers—there were others we came across in Peru—were the most disturbing people we met on the trip. They were, in their own way, totally charming rogues who have succeeded in a hard land, men full of life and stories. But it was the way they held the land and the people in contempt that we found disheartening—all the more so because we could find no reason to challenge them.

Peru was not Brazil, not even close. There was nothing here to admire. It seemed a worn-out country unable to pull itself together. Those who had come to the jungle had none of the excitement or hope we found on the other side of the continent. Instead we came upon the Hittschers and the Rays, smarter than the people around them, but users and takers. We met a bigoted naval officer who railed about the "Jewish banking conspiracy" that had brought his country to its knees; we saw government agricultural projects that had been turned into cocaine fields; we noticed beggars in jungle towns like those we had previously seen only in urban slums.

And as can happen far from home, our sour feeling began to feed on itself. We saw nothing good, thought nothing good and convinced ourselves that Peru was the end of the world. At that point our gloom was abruptly dispelled by Peter Jenson, a man who looked at the jungle with different eyes.

Jenson washed up in Iquitos with the idea of taking people to see the jungle. He ran by far the most ambitious and authentic tourist camp in the region. An anthropologist from the University of Minnesota, he had arrived here almost 20 years earlier propelled by a dream, and now made his living catering to the dreams of others.

"When I was a little boy, my favorite book was *Chiquita of the Amazon in Faraway Brazil*," he told us. "I read it over and over. The Amazon became the place of fantasy for me; it was always the magical land."

While working on a dig in the Andes, Jenson decided it was time to see the place of his childhood fantasy and took a freighter from Pucallpa down the twisting Ucayali River to Iquitos. The jaunt was supposed to be only a vacation, but Jenson never left, eventually starting his Explorama tour company and building a camp 50 miles down the Amazon near where it meets the Napo River. Business was so good he had recently opened two other camps, much more primitive and so remote they were accessible only by seaplane or a very long boat ride.

One afternoon as we sat in his air-conditioned office gratefully slurping Cokes, Jenson said he was going to inspect his camps and invited us to come along.

As we were about to leave, an angry American woman barged in. She wore a belted cotton dress, canvas espadrilles and, with her freckled face and frazzled hair, looked like she had just finished the 18th hole on Ladies Day. She was, she made clear, the wife of an important Exxon executive in Bogota and she wanted results. Her Colombian travel agent had screwed up.

"The boys want to see real jungle. They're adventurers and they want to rough it. But we just found out it's more expensive to go to your camps farther out. We have to stay at the close one."

Jenson, apparently experienced and long-suffering in such matters, assured the woman that the jungle he would show her boys—a son and three friends, all about 20—would be real enough.

"If they want to rough it more after they get to the lodge, we'll work something out."

Placated, the woman left. Jenson, who was trying to quit smoking, lit up.

"I'm finding I can take less and less time in town. I've got to get out to the jungle because it's the only place I can relax."

The regular guests at Jenson's camp get there by chugging about four hours downriver in a long wooden boat. Jenson moves from camp to camp by seaplane. We flew with him north from Iquitos in a wide sweep. It was a rare clear and brilliant morning and Jenson wanted to see the countryside.

"When you spend so much time under the trees, it helps to get above them once in a while," he said. "This really is a very beautiful place."

We flew low and slow, following the Mazan River. Much of the land beneath was a Peruvian government reserve, unspoiled in contrast to the scarred land around Iquitos. The Peruvians, Jenson said, do well with forest conservation. Others had told us the same thing; Peru may have the best jungle conservation program in South America.

The view was of a palette of greens and browns. The Mazan was caramel-colored, with a rippled surface that in the reflected sunlight had the pattern of human skin. It made looping curlicues and question marks through the forest. The tree tops, monotonously green at great heights and not visible at all from the ground, were individuals at 150 feet and 60 miles an hour. Each shade of green was perceptibly different from the next; leaves and the shape of the crown were distinguishable and for the first time we could see flowers in the treetops, small dots of color that might have been orchids.

We turned south and plowed to a stop on the edge of the Amazon. A motorized dugout canoe brought us up a twisting tributary to a lodge complex so unobtrusive as to be almost invisible. The half dozen buildings were constructed of native woods and bamboo lashed together in the fashion of local huts. All were on stilts and connected by bridges—a necessity since the river sometimes rises to cover the whole campsite. Sleeping rooms were bare cubes with a water basin and a cot shrouded in mosquito netting. Jenson had built a latrine complex and even a lounge area with tree stumps as coffee tables. Generators ran refrigerators and there were soft drinks and beer, but otherwise it was a very rudimentary place. Toucans, parrots, macaws, tapirs, lizards and small deer nosed about as they wished.

The guests were generally a serious lot, most of them Europeans and fairly knowledgeable about nature, if not the jungle. An English couple in sensible shoes—he in necktie, she in turned-down terry cloth hat—made copious entries in their bird journal, burbling softly in the back of the dugout and pointing in all directions. Diane Lowrie from Oregon was doing advance work for her Audubon Society chapter, which was contemplating a trip. She was often up at 5 A.M. with a flashlight, crashing through the forest and crying "Good look, good look" as she charted orioles, spectacled owls, jays, doves, hawks and a mocking thrush. One morning we accompanied her and a guide on one of their forays and found, silhouetted on a bare branch as the sun began to rise, the elusive umbrella bird, just as Bates had described it.

On the dock, we met one of the boys attached to the frantic American woman. His name was Hal. He wore designer jeans and a blow-dry haircut. He wasn't liking the jungle.

"It sucks. It's too goddamn hot, it's too humid, there's too many mosquitoes and there's nothing to do. Got the message?"

We asked if he'd be going on to the more remote camp.

"Fuck no," he said. "We're getting our ass out of here and going to Miami."

We went on in the seaplane to the new camp far up the Napo River. The camp was just a clearing containing two large platforms with open sides and thatch roofs—one for eating, the other for stringing hammocks—an outhouse building and a shower stall. The clearing was deep in the forest where it was surprisingly cool and not too humid. A tiny stream ran nearby and made a soothing sound as it rushed over the rocks.

We had lunch with Jenson and his two top guides, brothers Bader and Alfredo Chavez, who grew up not far from the camp. The menu was smoked piranha, fried manioc and a fish stew that consisted of whole fish and green bananas floating in a soapy-looking broth. The piranha was succulent and delicious; only the Chavez brothers ate the stew with relish.

They said they had killed 50 deadly fer-de-lance snakes while building the camp and that when it was almost up, a herd of wild boar stampeded through and wrecked it. Since then, there had been no unpleasant incidents, and Bader said they tried to spend as much time as they could at the secluded outpost.

The brothers, in their mid-20s, were jungle romantics. Spotting

the umbrella bird had sent Alfredo into grinning ecstasy for an hour.
Bader said he could sit all afternoon and watch ants build a nest.
They saw the jungle with eyes very different from our own. The
subtleties stood out for them. Cruising up a black-water tributary,
Alfredo saw a gray-and-white sloth far up in a tree. He had seen it
immediately; even though it was straight above our heads and we had
binoculars, it took many minutes before we could make it out.

"Look at the way he holds himself in there with his long claws
and how he wraps himself around the branch so you can't see him,"
Alfredo said, marveling at a sight he had seen many times but that
was obviously still thrilling. An orchid moved him to explain its way
of life with the understanding of a botanist but the language of a poet.
And when he noticed a giant Amazon kingfisher skimming along the
glossy black surface of the river, he launched into a dramatic play-by-
play of the bird's feeding habits, correctly predicting when it would
dip its beak under the surface and, flying at full speed, spear a
squirming silver fish.

In this part of the forest, the brothers told us, most animals are
still plentiful. There are only a few Indian villages and *rivereno* settlements in a hundred-square-mile area and the forest preserve nearby
is uninhabited. For those who know how to look there are deer,
ocelots, boars, dozens of kinds of monkeys.

One afternoon we took out a tippy dugout canoe alone and
paddled far upstream on a tributary that was completely enclosed by
forest. When Kelly got the knack of steering the wobbly craft, we
moved gracefully, pushing with barely a sound through the clear
water with long strokes of the oval paddle blades and negotiating
nimbly around tree limbs and rocks. We were so low and the jungle
so close in around us—we could touch both banks at once—that it
felt as though we were gliding on our backsides along the jungle
floor.

It was so quiet, we stopped talking. We listened and watched.

We saw more than we had been able to see before. There was a
deer. It was ten yards away and half-emerged from behind a tree
trunk when it smelled us and froze, only its ears twitching. We slid
by. On the damp mud were a big cat's round paw prints. In a tree
ahead we could distinguish the pendulous nests of orioles, shapes that
used to seem just part of the hanging paraphernalia.

When we stopped paddling, we could hear water fall from leaf to leaf.

In Iquitos, garbage heaps up and stinks or smokes. Here we saw no waste. There is none. It is all consumed, leaving the floor clear and the air clean.

For months we had moved so fast, pushing all the time to meet new things—the next interview, the next town. Time in the jungle—the natural jungle—moves very slowly. What happens here is intricate and minute and must be studied with leisure. Of course a person can only know one square kilometer of jungle in his lifetime; letting go, drifting, we could see that now. We felt we were in the center of a grand mechanism, a single functioning organism made of millions of organisms. Anything so complex and so exquisitely tuned had to be valuable. This jungle must indeed, as so many scientists had told us, offer solutions that would be foolish to throw away.

When we came back, we nosed the canoe into the bank a few yards down from the camp clearing. We could see, moving along the bank and across a mashed footpath, a steady line of leaf-cutter ants transporting what, for their size, was enough material to build the pyramids of Egypt. We sat and watched for an hour as they sliced up leaves with precision and organized thousands of workers to carry them across a charted course to a nest where they would ferment them for nourishment.

The next day we went back to the main camp and saw the American boys as they were getting ready to depart. One sat against a tree trunk wearing earphones connected to a cassette recorder on his belt. Eyes closed, he played an invisible guitar and whanged out chords to music only he could hear.

The youngest of the bunch, in full camouflage suit, had just come back from a trip to the neighboring Indian tribe. He was pleased with himself for swapping two pairs of pants and a shirt for a 6-foot blowgun. "They had sagging tits," he offered, as his opinion of the tribe's women.

From behind us came a hissing sound. Not a snake. The son of the Exxon executive from Bogota was dousing a trail of leaf-cutter ants with a can of extra-strength Raid.

LETICIA

At first, the approach to Leticia looked like the approach to all the other river towns, and especially the seedier Peruvian ones. The stilt houses along the shore got closer together; instead of solitary figures we began to see clusters of women beating clothes on the bank; the air began to smell ripe with the wastes of civilization. We saw a boat docked by a house, a small speedboat with a fiberglass body and a large outboard engine. Not common in this part of the world. Then we saw another, and a third with a bigger engine—a 200-horsepower Johnson. An Evinrude 175 passed us, tearing a wide wake in the river. As we got closer to the town we saw a tall boathouse with a seaplane inside, then a whole row of seaplanes—maybe 10, which was six more than we had seen during the whole trip. The shoreline began to look like a marina at some resort lake in Upstate New York. There were even a few high-powered racing boats with long slim hulls and room only for the driver and a passenger. All this we saw set incongruously amid the muddy decay of what would otherwise have been a typical river town.

Leticia is a city that exists for the purpose of smuggling. It sits on a thin strip of Colombia that snakes down to touch the Amazon River. To the east is the Brazilian garrison town of Tabatinga and to the west is the Peruvian frontier, making Leticia an ideal haven for anyone who is trying to move goods from one country to another.

The chief commodity that moves through today is cocaine, coming in paste form by river and air from the mountains of Peru and Bolivia and moving north to the laboratories around Bogota where it is turned into powder. As an agent for the United States Drug Enforcement Agency told us, the thousands of tributaries and inlets around Leticia make it impossible to control the traffic of seaplanes and small boats.

But Leticia has become an international port and other things move through there as well, including counterfeit money that finds its way throughout South America and the United States; stolen art and jewelry; guns; and rare animals—alive and skinned. Once illicit cargo gets to Leticia, it can be in any one of three countries in a few minutes or can be on its way down the Amazon to Manaus or international waters.

Even if we had not been forewarned, we would have known from the moment we stepped on shore that something was wrong with Leticia. As we walked up the beach, we got stares but no smiles. A first. We felt more conspicuously tall and white than we had anywhere else as we walked a gauntlet between a row of shops running up from the river. In addition to the usual gewgaws and cheap goods, we saw stores that sold jewelry and expensive leather bags. At several currency stores, men sat with large briefcases on their laps filled with paper money from different countries.

Not far from the landing we found the Anaconda Hotel, the most substantial building in town, though the competition was sparse. It was painted yellow and looked out over the Amazon, which is about two miles wide at this point. The woman at the desk, her stringy hair falling out of a bun and sticking to the sweat on her neck, did not want to be bothered with giving us a room.

"All out," she said in Spanish. We looked at her, amazed.

"But if you give me something to remember you by, something may open up," she cooed.

We were slow on the uptake. In all our months in supposedly bribe-hungry South America, we had not greased anyone's palm—nor been asked to. We shook our heads no.

An older woman emerged from the office in back and said brusquely that we could have a double room for $50 a night. We took it, and for our money got two narrow, short beds, a cracked linoleum floor, a single low-wattage overhead bulb, a toilet without a seat and a shower that only dripped cold rusty water. Maybe the price of the bribe was included in the $50, but there was no better room in town.

Each room in the Anaconda had a peephole drilled in it, the kind you find in apartments in crime-wary cities. The hotel was, we found out, the home away from home for smugglers and dealers. Deals were made behind closed doors in the Anaconda because just about any place else in town was too perilous.

The men, all well dressed in creased pants, silk shirts and straw Stetsons, kept leather shoulder bags clutched tightly to their sides. They sat in the Anaconda's outdoor cafe and talked while boys shined their boots. The men looked prosperous and healthy and so did the shine boys, an indication that there was some trickle-down of the illegally gotten wealth.

But we had not come for the atmosphere. Our interest was in getting a boat to take us back downriver to cover the wild portion we had longed to see, but had missed when we got stuck in Manaus. All the big boats, we were told, docked across the river on the Brazilian side of the border at a town called Benjamin Constant. A toothless riverman said he'd take us over in his wooden speedboat for $100. For a 20-minute ride.

"The ferry does not come for four hours," he said with a shrug. "Gasoline is expensive."

Two other passengers showed up to share the cost—one of the leather-shoulder-bag boys, who also carried a finely made leather attaché case, and his stocky companion, a swarthy man in designer jeans and a faded workshirt. They sat in front of us as the speedboat roared diagonally across the wide Amazon, jolted by swells and flinching at the spray. At this level, it was easy to feel the river's power. The rains were by now heavy in the mountains of Peru and Colombia so the streams that fed the Amazon were swollen and the great river itself was beginning its sharp rise. It seemed an unruly body of water, whipping into sudden whirlpools, sweeping along a collection of natural refuse: mostly trees and chunks of riverbank, much the same as we had seen on the Araguaia, only bigger. Halfway over, the sky turned dark and a thin rain stung us. The pale brown surface of the water deepened in color and seemed more ominous and impenetrable. We recalled a warning. "People disappear in Leticia," a U.S. drug agent had said. "Anything that is dropped in that river isn't going to be found. And in Leticia it's not going to be missed." He ended with the unrequested advice, "Don't ask too many questions there."

The two in front of us were in a suddenly intense but unintelligible conversation. The leather bag boy had told us they were going to Manaus on the *Torres de Araujo* leaving the following evening. We told him we'd try to get passage on it.

He shook his head. "I don't think so, but you can try."

Now he flipped open his attaché case a crack and handed an envelope to the other man. He had tried to shield the open case with his body, but we both got a glimpse of the contents: neatly wrapped bundles of some kind of currency and a steel-blue pistol.

We sped up a quiet tributary that broke into the south bank of the Amazon, swept around a wide curve and there in front of us was one of the most notorious river fronts in the world, though it looked very tenuous, clinging to the narrow bank between the river and the deep green of the forest. The town of Benjamin Constant looked to be a single street cut back into the trees; the river front was lined with boats.

At the center of the long line nosed into the mud was the *Torres de Araujo*, a clean, white three-decker. The captain of the boat spoke Spanish, but in a foreign accent that sounded Germanic. He was going to Manaus.

"But not for six days," he said.

"But they," we pointed to our recent shipmates, "said you were leaving tomorrow."

"No they didn't," he advised.

A team of men, some of them with blond hair, loaded a steady stream of cardboard cartons into the ship's hull. At one point a speedboat pulled up alongside and a new collection of cartons was passed from hand to hand into the hold.

"There's no room for you," the captain said, and as he wheeled away, added his final word on the subject. "Good evening."

We traipsed through the mud in the dock area to find out about other departures. Everyone said curtly that the *Torres de Araujo* was leaving the next day and nothing else would go for four days. We got the impression we were not wanted on anyone's boat and that there was not a lot of passenger traffic out of Benjamin Constant. The equivalent of our weight in cocaine base, skins or bogus money was worth more than any passage we could afford.

Confused and unsure of what was going on, we stood on the dock, the conspicuous center of attention for all the boat workers. It was as though we had stumbled on somebody's secret and didn't know what to do about it. We only wanted to get downriver. But there was no one to appeal to. Darkness would soon close in and we had no choice but to return to Leticia and work out a new departure plan.

The driver occupied us with a litany of complaints about the cost of gasoline and living in general in Leticia. When we arrived, he wanted more than we had agreed on. Kelly stuffed the original amount—in a variety of currencies—into his hand and we stalked up the river bank, leaving him howling in his boat. It was probably a foolish thing to do in such a town. We were wearing down.

Back at the Anaconda, we each had stiff scotches, just about finishing off the bottle bought in Lima. There was a balcony outside our room and we could see the sunset, perhaps the most spectacular of the trip. A hazy, iridescent orange globe hung on a purple mat streaked with yellow. The bottom edge of the canvas was a dark fringe made by the silhouettes of the trees on the far river bank. For a moment, the world seemed all right.

We had dinner in the hotel dining room, a dark, curtained chamber. The only thing on the menu was oily fried fish dumped on a plate mounded with rice, wilted lettuce and beets.

At the next table were four Italian tourists. Peruvian officials had told us that the Red Brigade in Italy financed its terrorist operations through Colombian drug trafficking and our paranoia had grown so acute that we winced when the four sat down. A suspicious-looking group, all in matching safari suits, but of varying sizes. A dwarf, whose feet did not touch the floor when he sat, spoke in a loud, trilling staccato to an enormous, effeminate companion who wore eye shadow. The other two were reed-thin lounge-lizard types. One of the lizards struck up a conversation with us in halting English, and it turned out the four were tourists who for an extra few dollars had added the Jungle Adventure onto their package tour of Colombia and Ecuador. They were trying to find out how they might actually see some of the jungle.

After dinner we finally agreed our apprehension was feeding on itself and went out to see the town. The first thing we heard was gunshots. Crack! Crack! Crack! but not all at once. They were spread out at intervals and they seemed to be coming from a warehouse up the street. We approached slowly and heard men yelling. Then laughter and cheers after the Crack!

"*Teju*," a man at the door explained. It was a teju parlor, a game, we discovered, that is a kind of violent man's horseshoes. The warehouse had four teju "alleys," each about 50 feet long with a banked dirt pit at either end. The men played the game with heavy metal pucks tossed into the pit. Orange blasting caps were placed on the pucks that had been thrown, causing an explosion if they were struck by an incoming puck. The air smelled of cordite. We went back to the Anaconda and the last of our scotch.

We woke in the hot early morning to someone weeping. Below the balcony on the street was a funeral procession of maybe a dozen people, mostly children. They carried a tiny white coffin. Across the street was a contingent of green-uniformed military police that hadn't been around the day before.

There was a pool parlor down the block from the teju hall and we resolved to spend the morning shooting pool. The tables were beautifully ornate antiques that could have come from Dodge City. So could the clientele. We had just racked the second game when a fight broke out at the next table, something over an unpaid wager. A few people were swinging cue sticks and slapping each other until finally the main combatants squared off: a small rodentlike man and a fat one. Both threw a flurry of limp-wristed punches, then the fat man, who outweighed the other by 100 pounds, began to kick, landing a couple of blows to the rodent's legs and chest. The rodent responded by pulling a closed knife from his boot and flicking the long blade open with a snap. Blocking with his left arm, he held it loosely in his right hand, jiggling it toward the fat man's belly. Twice he struck out with a fast motion and slashed the fat man across the middle. Suddenly the fat man had no friends and no desire to fight. He cursed the rodent and backed out the door bleeding. The rodent slipped the knife back in his boot and returned to his game. So did everyone else.

We had racked the sixth game when the cops came. About 20 of the green-suited constables charged through each of the hall's four doors, wielding submachine guns, automatic pistols and nightsticks. A drug raid? We didn't know. They had everyone up against the wall in seconds. While they were checking identification documents, they found two men to haul out.

Our passports were passed from sergeant to lieutenant. We stood with our hands raised, guns in our stomachs.

"Where is your visa?" the sergeant wanted to know. "You need a visa to be in Colombia. You are here illegally."

He was right. We did need a visa to enter Colombia. But in this part of the world, no one had a visa. There are no border points that anyone cares about. We hadn't thought to bother with visas, and no one had asked to see.

The sergeant's eyes narrowed. "You must leave the country."

"Fine, we're gone," London said as he reached for the passports. The soldier held on to them.

"You can't leave the country unless you have a visa," the sergeant said. He smiled, the absurdity not escaping him. His helmet was too big for his head. The teeth in his grin were stubs.

We asked for our passports again.

"No," said the squad leader. "It is the law."

London, feeling the frustration of 24 hours of everything gone wrong, tried a crazy threat. "Give us the passports or I promise I will call the American Ambassador who will call your President who will make you give us the passports."

It was a flimsy weapon for a man surrounded by 17 armed soldiers and who was 700 miles in distance and God only knew how far in legal recourse from the American Ambassador and the President in Bogota. Yet something worked. The sergeant frowned, conferred with the lieutenant, then walked back and handed the blue books to us saying, "Please get a stamp at the customs office right away." Then the sergeant gave a short nod of his head and concluded, "You may go back to your game." A soldier replaced a ball he had accidentally knocked aside with the barrel of his submachine gun.

We tried once more to find a way downriver. Mike Tsalickis, the most famous man in Leticia and probably the best-known American in the Amazon as well, was our only chance now. We had heard and read about him many times before, particularly in a few glowing *National Geographic* pieces over the years. Tsalickis went to Leticia in the 1950s to find specimens to stock zoos around the world. His rough life-style evoked for us those old adventure stories that were by now so far behind us, and so strange. "Mike Tsalickis," wrote one fan, "is an adventurer who boldly challenged the world's greatest jungle, fought it on its own terms and emerged the conqueror."

To inspire such elegies, Tsalickis wrestled enormous anacondas into submission. A photograph of him straining with one beast adorns many Amazon chronicles. He had built the Anaconda Hotel.

Some thought there was a darker side of the man too. The United States Drug Enforcement Agency suspected him to have been at one time a major drug trafficker. He has never been charged with any crimes, although one of his planes once crashed with a sizable load of cocaine, of which Tsalickis said he had no knowledge. Articles in the Brazilian press claimed he had been the dominant force in Leticia's counterfeiting industry and other stories bestowed upon him the title of the largest dealer in contraband animal skins. If these stories were true, such a man could find a boat for us.

We looked for him at the lodge from which people disembark for their trip to Mike Tsalickis' Monkey Island. There was a curio shop. A middle-aged man with thick glasses who looked like the bookkeeper shuffled out from the back room and eyed us sideways. We told him what we wanted.

"Senor Tsalickis is gone. He has not been here much since his brother died in the plane crash. Maybe's he's back in the United States."

We asked if he knew any way we might get downriver toward Manaus.

He said simply, "No," then turned and shuffled back where he had come from. We left with a few postcards of Mike wrestling an anaconda.

And then we left Leticia and the Amazon. There was a flight out the next afternoon, and we booked it. That last day we spent on the lam. Afraid of being hustled, accosted or frisked, we stayed behind closed shades in shabby Room 306 at the Anaconda with our airline tickets in our hands. We knew we were missing a big stretch of river and an unknown land that would remain unseen by us. Probably it was the real Amazon, the jungle we had never quite found, the mythical land that took the breath away. There pink dolphins played and wild pigs swam the brown waters. The palm plantations there were the successful ones, the ones that would show the world. Maybe we could have found the site of the mysterious oil strike whose rumor had followed us across a continent. And a wise caboclo, fishing with a hand line from the bank of the Amazon River, would explain to us what was happening to his forest, and why, and what would become of it. We would get at last the gold we had been searching for, the answer. Then we realized that this was what everyone who had ever searched for his dream in the jungle had said.

In the late afternoon, we strapped into the first row of seats on Avianca Airlines Flight 60, tired and feeling beaten. We thought of Miami. We would be eating pastrami at the Rascal House on Collins Avenue before midnight.

ACKNOWLEDGMENTS

We wish to express our thanks to the many people whose help and generous advice made this book possible. We start, of course, with the two hundred or so characters who gave life to this book and richness to our lives.

In addition, we are especially indebted to Jim Hoge and the editors of the Chicago *Sun Times*—Ralph Otwell, Gregory Favre, and Joe Reilly; our friend and fellow traveler, Kevin Horan, photographer extraordinaire; Stu Loory; Bernard, Frank, Michael and Merrie Gordon; Joe Tydings; Mitch Cutler; Bob Washington; Bob Condon; Mike Kris; Riordan Roett of The Johns Hopkins University's School of Advanced International Studies; Peter Raven and Alwyn Gentry of the Missouri Botanical Garden; Ghillean Prance and Douglas Daley of the New York Botanical

Garden; Robert Skillings and Dennis Mahar of the World Bank; Georges Landau of the Inter-American Development Bank; Tom Lovejoy and Richard Bierregaard of the World Wildlife Fund; Betty Meggars and the late Clifford Evans of the Smithsonian Institution; Garrison Wilkes of the University of Massachusetts; the university relations department of the University of Chicago; Charles Wagley and Marianna Schmink of the University of Florida; Bill Baldwin of the First National Bank of Chicago; William Fisher and Charles Stauffacher of the National Bulk Carriers; Jack Child of American University.

Ambassador Antonio Azeredo da Silveira of Brazil; Ambassador Fernando Schwalb of Peru; from the Embassy of Brazil—Luis Felipe Seixas Correa, Jose Alfredo Graca Lima, and Paulo Campos; from the Embassy of Peru—Domingo da Fieno.

Berta Ribeiro of the Federal University of Rio de Janeiro; General Carlos de Meira Mattos; the Jornal do Brasil; Joao Carlos Meirelles of the Association of Amazon Impresarios; Warren Hoge of the *New York Times*; Bishop Moacyr Grecchi; Ana Cabral of Itamarati; Ambassador Tony Motley, McKinney Russell, and Ed Elly of the U.S. Embassy in Brasilia; Peter Eisner of the Associated Press; Dr. Francisco Pinheiro of the Chagas Institute; Armando Mendes; Gerhard Jansen and David Martin of Occidental Petroleum; Dr. Charles Calisher of the Center for Disease Control who assured us that whatever we had probably wouldn't kill us. We also wish to thank a number of Brazilian government officials whose help was invaluable but who asked to remain anonymous.

Finally, there are those special people who believed in this project and its authors from the very start. Mary and Larry Ott; the inimitable Dania Fitzgerald; our agent, Rafe Sagalyn, who made sure this dream would not die; Pat Wingert, who contributed a thoughtful pencil and endless moral support; and our editor, Sara Stein, who made this a book.

INDEX